OTHER A TO Z GUIDES FROM
THE SCARECROW PRESS, INC.

The A to Z of the Lesbian Liberation Movement

Still the Rage

JoAnne Myers

The A to Z Guide Series, No. 73

The Scarecrow Press, Inc.
Lanham • Toronto • Plymouth, UK
2009

Published by Scarecrow Press, Inc.
A wholly owned subsidiary of
The Rowman & Littlefield Publishing Group, Inc.
4501 Forbes Boulevard, Suite 200, Lanham, Maryland 20706
http://www.scarecrowpress.com

Estover Road, Plymouth PL6 7PY, United Kingdom

British Library Cataloguing in Publication Information Available

Library of Congress Cataloging-in-Publication Data

The hardback version of this book was cataloged by the Library of Congress as
follows:

Myers, JoAnne, 1954–
  Historical dictionary of the lesbian liberation movement / JoAnne Myers.
    p. cm.—(Historical dictionaries of religions, philosophies, and movements ;
  no. 45)
  Includes bibliographical references (p.).
  1. Gay liberation movement—History—Encyclopedias. 2. Gay rights—
History—Encyclopedias. 3. Lesbians—Social conditions—Encyclopedias.
4. Gay liberation movement—United States—History—Encyclopedias. 5. Gay
rights—United States—History—Encyclopedias. 6. Lesbians—United States—
Social conditions—Encyclopedias. I. Title. II. Series.
HQ76.5.M94 2003
305.9'0664—dc21   2002156624

ISBN 978-0-8108-6811-3 (pbk. : alk. paper)
ISBN 978-0-8108-6327-9 (ebook)

♾™ The paper used in this publication meets the minimum requirements of
American National Standard for Information Sciences—Permanence of Paper
for Printed Library Materials, ANSI/NISO Z39.48-1992.

Printed in the United States of America

Dedicated to my family—blood and chosen—especially to my partner L. K. and Alexandrea Rose, and to the memory of all lesbians who have paved the way.

Contents

Acknowledgments

I want to thank my partner, L. K., and all my friends and family (chosen and blood) for putting up with my single-mindedness during the past couple of years. I want to thank Casimar Norkilunas for supporting my application for sabbatical, Marist College for granting the six-month sabbatical, the reference librarians at Marist's Cannavino Library, especially Charyl Pollard and Pepper (Ruth) Boetcker, who joined with me in some arcane searches, the Lesbian Herstory Archives, the Duke University and Smith College Sophia Smith Archives (and all the other repositories of lesbian history) for their work in preserving our history and voices, and the Center for Lesbian and Gay Studies (CLAGS) for their provocative and educational seminars. And, finally, I want to thank Joan Tronto for her recommendation and support.

Editor's Foreword

The Lesbian Liberation movement (LLM) is the youngest of the many movements in this series, younger even than feminism or the Gay Liberation movement. That is partly because lesbianism was repressed even more strongly and effectively, partly because the specific movement was long overshadowed by the two broader movements to the point where its own agenda was curtailed or concealed. Only over the past few decades has the LLM come into its own, albeit in a relatively small portion of the globe. Outside of North America and Western Europe, lesbians remain largely invisible and their voices unheard. One major advantage to this book is that they can be seen and heard in their own terms, and the formative movement can be identified. Another important advantage is that, while noting any successes, the problems and setbacks are not hidden. Nor are the differences and controversies within the movement itself denied. Young, and undoubtedly growing, the movement still has a long way to go.

The A to Z of the Lesbian Liberation Movement traces its progress thus far. This is done, first in the chronology, most of whose political items only reach back a few years or a few decades. The broader context is drawn in the introduction. The dictionary entries then present many significant leaders and organizations, not only from the core areas but, to the extent they exist, around the world. Less usual in these volumes, but certainly useful in this one, there are numerous entries on the terminology used within the LLM, including some terms that have become familiar and many more that are unknown to outsiders. The bibliography sheds light on the still small but rapidly expanding literature on the subject. It includes works that have since become classics and others which are more tentative and experimental. All of them, however, contribute to the reader's knowledge.

This volume was written by JoAnne Myers, who is both an academic and an activist as well as an out lesbian. She teaches political science at Marist College where she is the codirector (and cofounder) of the Women's Studies program. She has written and lectured widely on feminism and the politics of lesbianism. Dr. Myers puts theory into practice as a coordinator of feminist conferences on gender issues and through her service on the Board of Directors of Grace Smith House. She also serves on the board of the Hudson River Sloop *Clearwater* and is engaged in environmental education and activism. These various strands come together in this latest addition to the subseries on movements in a presentation in which, along with information, the rage noted in the opening lines of the classic lesbian-feminist tract "Woman-Identified Woman" is still evident.

Jon Woronoff
Series Editor

Preface

Almost thirty years ago, Sidney Abbott and Barbara Love wrote *Sappho Was a Right-On Woman* (1972) ("one of the least known members of our culture") exploring the relationship of lesbians to feminism and gay liberation. Their ambition, stated in their introduction, was "to be most ordinary people . . . to be able to go about our lives—as human beings, as women, as Lesbians—unselfconsciously." This is the goal of liberation movements: to educate others about oppression and to eradicate oppression so that members of that group will have the freedoms that other citizens in society enjoy so that that once-oppressed group will be ordinary citizens. Sexual liberation movements also push the envelope of socially acceptable practices, in this case, sexual freedom from both heterosexual norms and practices.

The Lesbian Liberation movement (LLM) is both a movement that encompasses liberating a sexual practice from stigmatization and a political movement challenging the dual oppression of women by the patriarchy's assumption of male supremacy and heterosexuality. The Lesbian Liberation movement is for all intents and purposes the practice of lesbian politics—from lesbian feminism to equal rights lesbianism to radical feminism, from sexual outlaws to antipornographers, from lesbian separatists to assimilationists—with the goal of social change that would lead to the full recognition of lesbians and their civil and human rights so that lesbians would not be oppressed nor stigmatized. It is also a more subtle political movement, one in which just the act of being an out lesbian is a political statement that challenges the patriarchal hegemony. The Lesbian Liberation movement is a movement that is still alive and active, from the assimilationalists' push for equal rights for lesbians (gay, bisexual, and transgendered persons) in order to make the individual sexual orientation a nondiscriminatory issue and, thus, tolerable in the public sphere to the radical acts of lesbian visibility to the more radical lesbian separatists. LLM has become a global movement.

Over the ensuing years, much has been written on homosexuality and on the Gay Liberation movement (GLM), yet much of the focus has been on male homosexuals, especially male homosexual activity and the politics that that activity raises: fights against entrapment and sodomy laws, for instance. Women who are homosexuals—lesbians—are backgrounded, since these issues do not reflect their sexual practices. They are a minority within a minority. The lesbian political conscience as well as issues that are both similar and different from gay liberation, and most recently the queer agenda, get discounted and overlooked by the males in the gay rights and queer movements and by society as a whole.

While lesbian liberation raises issues of sexual self-determination that are concurrent with those of the Gay Liberation movement and the queer agenda, the Lesbian Liberation movement raises issues that are unique to women in our society, specifically those issues concerning the patriarchal oppression of women (and others). Thus, LLM intersects with the Women's Liberation movement (WLM) on issues of equality and equity for women, since lesbians are women (however, not all lesbians are feminists just as all women are not feminists).

Lesbians have been on the front lines in both women's and gay liberation organizations and actions; they are the strong but silenced partners in these movements. Lesbians have been the backbone behind AIDS activism, women's reproductive health issues, domestic violence, welfare rights, and equal rights, but for the most part, the media's and the public's focus has been on the gay men and heterosexual women who have benefitted from lesbian activism. Lesbians are rarely credited.

Public policy issues that are unique to lesbians, such as child custody rights, lesbian battering, or lesbian health, are not visible since public policies support both the puritanical heritage that sanctions procreational rather than recreational sexual practices and the concept of universal citizen, which is read as male. The result is that lesbians and their issues are absent from the public agenda, or they are submerged by the focus on male homosexual issues, or they are silenced.

There has also been the attempted silencing or the submerging of the lesbians themselves in these movements. For instance, in the early years of the National Organization of Women (NOW), Betty Friedan, the founder and first president, called lesbians "the lavender herring" and tried to maneuver known lesbians out of positions of power.

The purpose of this book is to provide a foundation from which the Lesbian Liberation movement is brought into sharp focus with issues, conflicts, and similarities with concurrent liberation movements examined; the chronology is set forward; significant people, theories, organizations, and terms are explained; and a comprehensive bibliography for further research is laid out. The ultimate purpose is to give the movement its unique voice without judgment. Readers and researchers are encouraged to use this as a research source from which to proceed. Lesbian politics queries the proper role of government in a liberal democracy to protecting all human rights. The government must insist on tolerance of and for all citizens if it is to uphold the values of liberty, justice, and equality. Lesbian politics underscores the hypocrisy when a modern liberal state allows a group of citizens to be privileged over those other less-privileged citizens—women, lesbians, other sexual minorities, the poor, and the raced—and allows for the (legal) subjugation and restrictions of the less privileged so that the privileged may remain in power.

This dictionary attempts to focus on the more political lesbian liberation and rights movement and does not attempt to list all the lesbian artists and literary figures—unless they have made a contribution to the movement or were so referential that omitting them would be heretical. These artists and literary figures are documented in other lesbian and gay reference books.

ACRONYMS

ABA	American Bar Association
ACLU	American Civil Liberties Union
ACT-Up	Aids Coalition to Unleash Power
ADGQ	Association pour les droits de la communauté gaie du Québec
AHF	Working Group for Gay Liberation
AI	Amnesty International
AI	Artificial Insemination
AIDS	Acquired Immune Deficiency Syndrome
AKOE	Homosexual Liberation Movement of Greece
ALA	American Library Association
ALGWE	Association of Lesbian and Gay Writers in Europe
ALN	Asian Lesbian Network
AMA	American Medical Association
ANC	African National Congress
APA	American Psychiatric Association
API	Asia/Pacific Island
ASK	Association for Social Knowledge
B and D	Bondage and Discipline
BBC	British Broadcasting Corporation
B/F	Butch and/or Femme
BI	Bisexual
BiGALA	Bisexual Gay and Lesbian Association
CAMP	Campaign Against Moral Persecution
CDC	Centers for Disease Control
CEDAW	Convention to End Discrimination Against Women
CGRO	Coalition for Gay Rights in Ontario
CHE	Campaign (formerly Committee) for Homosexual Equality
CLAGS	Center for Lesbian and Gay Studies

CLIT	Collective Lesbian International Terrors
COC	Cultuur-en Ontspannings Centrum (Culture and Recreational Center)
CR	Consciousness Raising
CUARH	Comité d'Urgence Anti-Répression Homosexuelle (Emergency Committee Against the Repression of Homosexuals)
CWA	Concerned Women of America
D	Democrat
DOB	Daughters of Bilitis
DOMA	Defense of Marriage Act
DNF	Det Norske Forbundet av 1948
EC	European Community
ECHO	East Coast Homophile Organizations
ENDA	Employment Non-Discrimination Act
ERA	Equal Rights Amendment
ERCHO	Eastern Regional Conference of Homophile Organizations
EU	European Union
FBI	Federal Bureau of Investigation
FDA	Federal Drug Agency
FEMA	Federal Emergency Management Agency
FGM	Female Genital Mutilation
FHO	Fellesraadet for Homofile Organisasjoner I Norge
FTM	Female to Male
GAA	Gay Activists Alliance
GALZ	Gays and Lesbians of Zimbabwe
GASA	Gay Association of South Africa
GAU	Gay Academic Union
GDP	Gross Domestic Product
GLAAD	Gay and Lesbian Alliance Against Defamation
GLAC	Gay and Lesbian Association of Cuba
GLAS	Gay and Lesbian Arabic Society
GLF	Gay Liberation Front
GLM	Gay Liberation Movement
GLOE	Gay and Lesbian Organization of Elders
GLOW	Gay and Lesbian Organization of the Witwatersrand
GNP	Gross National Product
GSA	Gay Straight Alliance
HAW	Homosexual Aktion Westberlin

HIV	Human Immunodeficiency Virus
HLRS	Homosexual Law Reform Society
HR	House of Representatives
HRC	Human Rights Campaign
HUAC	House Un-American Activities Committee
IDM	Identificacà-Documentaçà-Mulheres
IGLHRC	International Gay and Lesbian Association–Human Rights Commission
IGLHRC	International Gay and Lesbian Human Rights Commission
ILGA	International Lesbian and Gay Association
ILGA-J	International Lesbian and Gay Association–Japan
ILGA-P	International Lesbian and Gay Association–Portugal
ILIS	International Lesbian Information Service
INGLO	International Network of Lesbian and Gay Officials
INS	Immigration and Naturalization Service
IRS	Internal Revenue Services
KKK	Ku Klux Klan
KKLGN	Kelompok Kerja Lesbian dan Gay Nusantara (Indonesia)
LAN	Lesbian Arab Network
LBGQTs	Lesbian, Bisexual, Gay, Queer, Transgendered/Transsexuals
LGBTs	Lesbian, Gay, Bisexual, Transgender, and Transsexuals
LF	lesbian-feminist
LF	Lesbian Front (Sweden)
LGIRTF	Lesbian and Gay Immigration Rights Task Force
LL	Lesbian Licit (Slovenia)
LLDEF	Lambda Legal Defense and Education Fund
LLEGO	Latino/Latina Lesbian and Gay Organization
LLM	Lesbian Liberation Movement
LN	Lesbian Nation (Sweden)
LP	Lambda Praha (Lambda Prague)
MCC	Metropolitan Community Church
MLF	Mouvement Libération Féministe
MR	*Mattachine Review*
MRG	Minorities Research Group
MS	Mattachine Society
MSNY	Mattachine Society–New York
MSW	Mattachine Society–Washington
MTF	Male to Female

MULH	Moscow Union of Lesbians and Homosexuals
NAACP	National Association for the Advancement of Colored People
NACHO	North American Conference of Homophile Organizations
NARTH	National Association for the Research and Therapy of Homosexuality
NATO	North Atlantic Treaty Organization
NCLR	National Center for Lesbian Rights
NEA	National Endowment for the Arts
NFHO	National Federation of Homophile Organizations
NGLTF	National Gay and Lesbian Task Force
NGTF	National Gay Task Force
NGO	Nongovernmental Organization
NOGL	Lansforeningen for Bøsser og Lesbiske (National Organization of Gays and Lesbians)
NOW	National Organization for Women
NYDOB	New York Daughters of Bilitis
NYNOW	New York National Organization for Women
OCA	Oregon Citizens Alliance
OLGA	Organization for Lesbian and Gay Activists
OLOC	Old Lesbians Organizing for Change
OPOTH	Homosexuals' Initiative of Thessaloniki
PAC	Political Action Committee
PAC	Pacte Civil de Solidarté (Civil Solidarity Pact)
PC	Politically Correct
PDA	Public Display(s) of Affection
P-FLAG	Parents and Friends of Lesbians and Gays
PWA	Person(s) with AIDS
R	Republican
RFSL	Riksförbundet för Homo-och Bisexuellas rättigheter (Swedish Federation for Gay and Lesbian Rights)
RR	Religious Right
S & M	Sadistic and Masochistic Practices
SAGE	Senior Action in a Gay Environment
S.C.U.M.	Society for Cutting Up Men
SETA	Seksuaalinen Tasavertaisuus (Finnish Federation for Sexual Equality)
SGA	Straight Gay Activist

SHE	Sisters for Homophile Equality
SHL	Student Homophile League
SIR	Society for Individual Rights
SLRS	Sexual Law Reform Society
SMG	Scottish Minorities Group
S/M	Sadomasochism
SS	Schutzstaffel (Elite Guard, Nazi)
TG	Transgendered
TLF	The Library Foundation (Philippines)
TS	Transsexual
TV	Transvestite
TWGR	Third World Gay Revolution
UCLA	University of California–Los Angeles
UDHR	Universal Declaration of Human Rights
ULOAH	United Lesbians of African Heritage
UN	United Nations
WAC	Women's Action Coalition
WAC	Women's Army Corps (United States)
WEDO	Women's Environment and Development Organization
WHO	World Health Organization
WITCH	Women's International Terrorist Conspiracy from Hell
WIW	Woman-Identified Woman
WLM	Women's Liberation Movement
WTO	World Trade Organization
WWW	World Wide Web

Chronology

580 BC   Sappho (b. 612) writes her poetry and presides over a circle of girls on the Isle of Lesbos, teaching them the arts, music, and poetry.

160   Poet Anacreon uses "a girl from Lesbos" to suggest same-sex yearnings.

60 AD   Boudicca, Chieftess of Iceni, East Anglia, leads Celtic rebellion against Romans.

160   Lucian uses the term *hetairistrai* (masculine-acting women) in *Dialogue of the Courtesans*.

200   Christian theologian Clement of Alexandria uses the term *hetairistrai*.

c. 374   St. Ambrose writes: "A woman would desire a woman for the use of foul lust."

380   Sappho's poetry burned by order of Gregory of Nazianzus.

914   A commentator on Clement's writings defines *hetairistrai* in marginal notes.

937   Judith, Queen of Falasha, captures Ethiopia and rules until her death in 977.

1073   Constantinople and Rome's ecclesiastical authorities order all remaining copies of Sappho's poems burned.

1260   Women found guilty of lesbianism receive sentences ranging from clitoractomies to burning at the stake, depending on the number of offenses, as per the Orleans Legal School.

1610   Virginia Colony's sodomy law excludes women.

1636   John Cotton proposes that Massachusetts's laws should include prohibitions against lesbianism since lesbianism is "unnatural filthiness." His proposal is not adopted.

1641   Massachusetts Bay Colony's sodomy law is non-discriminatory.

1642   The laws of Plymouth (Massachusetts) Plantation include that "unnatural lusts of men with men, or women with women . . . be punished with death." In Salem, Massachusetts, a female servant, Elizabeth Johnson, is whipped for her "unseemingly practices."

1649   Plymouth, Massachusetts, charges were lodged against servant Mary Hammon and goodwife Sara Norman for "lewd behavior upon a bed."

1654   Christina of Sweden abdicates her throne instead of marrying.

1655   New Haven Colony, Connecticut, expands its definition of *sodomy* to include sexual practices between women. The law is unique because it includes lesbianism.

1682   The French lesbian nun novel *Venus in the Cloister* is published causing scandal.

1732   First known modern usage of *lesbian* in William King's *The Toast*.

1782   Deborah Sampson is excommunicated from the First Baptist Church, Middleborough, Massachusetts, for dressing in men's clothing and for loose and unchristian behavior.

1788   Mary Wollstonecraft coins "romantic friendship" to describe devoted friendships between women.

1791   Law Code in France decriminalizes sodomy.

1793–98   Moreau de St. Mery, a French lawyer, writes the earliest observation of lesbianism in Philadelphia: "[women] . . . are not at all strangers to be willing to seek unnatural pleasures with persons of their own sex."

1811   Trial of two Scottish schoolmistresses (Miss Pirie and Miss Woods) results in the British legal establishment declaring that sex between women is impossible since they lack a penis. First report of a Ketenai (Montana and British Columbia) Berdache, Qunqon, dressing in men's clothes, having three wives, and acting as warrior, peace mediator, guide, and prophet.

1812   James Miranda Barry (1795–1865) earns the first medical degree granted to a woman in England from the University of Edinburgh. She lives as a man.

1813   Napoleonic Code decriminalizes all sex acts between consenting adults.

1820   Florence Nightingale is born. She wrote: " I have lived and slept in the same bed with English Countesses and Prussian farm women . . . no woman has excited more passions among women than I have."

1848   The first feminist political treatise calling for women's control over their own lives, *The Declarations of Sentiments*, was written, read, and signed at Seneca Falls, New York.

1864   Early homosexual rights movement began with the publication of Karl Heinrich Ulrichs's writings on same-sex love.

1868   Karoly Maria Kertbeny uses terms *heterosexuality* and *homosexuality* in letter to Ulrichs on **May 6**. He then used these terms in his 1869 pamphlets.

1871   Adoption of Paragraph 175 of German Imperial Code of Laws that criminalizes (male) same-sex relations.

1882   Dr. Henry N. Gurnsey warns young ladies of self-abuse and of play[ing] with one another in *Plain Talks on Avoided Subjects.*

1883   First use of *lesbian* to denote a woman-loving woman (used in the medical journal *Alienist and Neurologist*).

1885   The Labouchère Amendment introduced in England criminalizes all same-sex sexual relations. Lesbians were exempt.

1886   Ma Rainey, mother of the Blues, is born. Annie Hindle, wearing men's clothing and calling herself Charles E. Hindle, and Annie Ryan are married in Grand Rapids, Michigan.

1892 In September, Dr. Irving C. Rosse delivers a paper at the Medical Society of Virginia, which includes the first medical description of tribadism, a prostitute that services women, and an orgy of women.

1897 The first edition of Ellis and John Addington Symond's *Sexual Inversion* contains a short history of an American lesbian "Miss S." and her "gift of loving," which they describe as a stepping stone to high mental and spiritual attainments. Wissenchaftlich-Humanitäres Komitee (Scientific Humanitatrian Committee) founded in Berlin, is the first homosexual rights organization.

1901 Murray Hall, a New York City politician, dies. Murray was really Mary Anderson, a cross-dresser who married two women.

1904 Renée Vivien (née Pauline Tarn) is born in Philadelphia.

1907 In China, Jio Jin (Qinxiong), wearing men's clothing, fights for women's rights. The Manchu government beheads her for treason.

1910 Attempt to extend Paragraph 175 of German Imperial Code of Laws to women defeated.

1911 Holland passes law prohibiting same-sex activity with persons under the age of twenty-one.

1912 Heterodoxy, a feminist luncheon club for "unorthodox" women, convenes.

1920 *Pensées d'une Amazon* by Natalie Barney is published.

1921 Attempt to extend Labouchère Amendment ("Outrages on Public Decency") to lesbians defeated in United Kingdom.

1923 The FBI declares Emma Goldman "the most dangerous woman in America" for her views on equality, gay rights, and anarchy. F. W. Stella Browne's "Studies in Feminine Inversion" published in *Journal of Sexology and Psychology*.

1924 Society for Human Rights founded in Chicago.

1926   *The Captive*, a play by Edouard Bourdet about lesbian infatuation, debuts in New York City and results in the New York State Legislature passing a law in 1927 outlawing the depiction of "sex degeneracy or sex perversion" on the stage. The law remains in force until 1967.

1929   American reaction to Alfred Knopf's publishing of Radclyffe Hall's *Well of Loneliness* results in obscenity ruling.

1935   Gay rights groups banned in (Nazi) Germany.

1936   *Mona's,* a lesbian bar, opens in San Francisco.

1937   Blues singer and lover of women, Bessie Smith, dies. Nazis begin to use black triangles to identify women who are "socially unacceptable" and pink ones for gay men.

1939   **January 12.** State of Georgia Supreme Court hears *Ella Thompson v. J. C. Aldredge, Sheriff.* Thompson was accused of sodomy with females. The ruling on the case sets a legal precedent: "crime of sodomy as defined by statute cannot be accomplished between two women."

1939–45   Homosexuals are incarcerated in German concentration camps. Because they are "criminals," they are not released at the end of the war.

1944   Sweden repeals antigay laws.

1946   Veterans Benevolent Association formed in New York City.

1947   *Vice Versa,* the first lesbian newsletter, published by Lisa Ben.

1951   The Mattachine Society is founded by Harry Hay in Los Angeles, California.

1952   U.S. immigration law bans lesbians and gays from entering the country (repealed in 1990).

1953   Arcadie, the first French gay rights organization, is founded. President Dwight D. Eisenhower signs executive order 10450, which excludes persons with sexual perversions from federal employment.

1954 Daughters of Bilitis founded in San Francisco by Del Martin, Phyllis Lyons, and six other multiethnic women. First all-female issue of *One* published in February.

1957 Wolfenden Report published in United Kingdom. Daughters of Bilitis incorporated in California. Crittenden Report by Department of Defense concludes that homosexuals do not pose a security risk. The report is ignored by the Pentagon.

1958 Barbara Gittings founds New York City Daughters of Bilitis Chapter.

1959 Homosexual Law Reform Society (HLRS) formed in United Kingdom to advocate for reforms in Wolfenden Report. U.S. Supreme Court rules that the impoundment of *One* magazine by Los Angeles postmaster was a violation of the First Amendment freedom of the press.

1960 First National Lesbian Convention held in San Francisco.

1961 Illinois is the first state to rescind its sodomy statute. Czechoslovakia repeals antigay laws.

1964 The Association for Social Knowledge (ASK) is founded in Canada; the Society for Individual Rights (SIR) is founded in San Francisco; and the Dorian Society is founded in New Zealand. The first homosexual rights demonstration is held in New York City to protest U.S. Army discharges of gays and lesbians. Jane Rule's *Desert of the Heart* is published.

1965 First political protest by lesbians and gays in front of the White House. This protest of government discriminatory employment practices was covered by the national media.

1966 The National Organization for Women (NOW) is formed. SIR opens Gay Community Center in San Francisco.

1967 Alma Routsong, a.k.a. Isabel Miller, publishes *Patience and Sarah* (née *A Place for Us*), the first lesbian-feminist novel with a happy ending. Student Homophile League founded at Columbia and New York Universities, New York City, by Rita Mae Brown and Karla Jay, among others.

1968   The Homosexual Law Reform Fund, Johannesburg, South Africa, is founded. First Congress to Unite Women actively discriminates against lesbians. Ti-Grace Atkinson proclaims: "Feminism is the theory, Lesbianism is the action." NOW treasurer allows lesbian couples reduced "couples" membership rates. Metropolitan Community Church opens in Los Angeles.

1969   **June 27–29.** Stonewall riots in New York City considered to be the beginning of the contemporary Gay Rights movement. **July 2.** First gay pride march held in New York City. **July 31.** The Gay Liberation Front (GLF) is founded. The Gay Activists Alliance (GAA) is founded by dissidents of the GLF. First Congress to Unite Women held in New York City in **November**; concurrent conferences held in San Francisco, Los Angeles, and Chicago.

1970   Campaign Against Moral Persecution (CAMP) formed in Sydney, Australia. American Psychiatric Association (APA) convention asked to remove homosexuality from classification as mental illness. Karla Jay becomes first lesbian chair of GLF. **April.** GLF holds its first of many women-only dances in New York City. First Gay-In held in a Los Angeles city park. Betty Friedan defeats NOW lesbian rights resolution calling lesbians in NOW "the lavender herring." A group of lesbians leave NOW, GLF, and GAA; they write the first lesbian-feminist manifesto "Woman-Identified Woman." **May 1–3.** Second Congress to Unite Woman held in New York City, taken over by the "Lavender Menace" who distribute their manifesto "Woman-Identified Woman." The group becomes the Radicalesbians. **June 12.** In Los Angeles, Rev. Troy Perry performs "the first marriage in the nation designed to legally bind two persons of the same sex," marrying Neva Joy Heckman and Judith Anne Belew. **June 28.** First Gay Pride Parade is held to commemorate the first anniversary of Stonewall; ten thousand lesbians and gay men march up Sixth Avenue, New York City. First legislative hearings on Gay Rights held by three members of New York Assembly. Amazon Bookstore, the first American feminist (and lesbian) bookstore opens in Minneapolis, Minnesota. The State of New York is the first state to pass abortion legislation. French Mouvement Libération Féministe holds its first general organizing meeting at the Paris Beaux-Arts; Arcadie lesbians meet separately. **August 26.** Women's Strike, New York City. **October 13.** The first meeting of the London Gay Liberation Front held at the London School of Economics. **October 28.** Kate Millett outed at Columbia University meeting. **December 14.** Kate Millett outed as a bisexual on the cover of *Time* magazine. **December 17.** Feminists Gloria Steinem, Flo Kennedy, and others hold New York City press conference in solidarity with lesbian liberation and Kate Millett.

1971   NOW convention resolution that women have the right to their own sexuality. David Susskind show aired with lesbians, including Barbara Love. Lesbian Mothers Union formed in Los Angeles at the West Coast Gay Women's Conference. Former Los Angeles GLF members form the lesbian-feminists. *The Lesbian Tide* begins publishing. **April 1.** The French leftist newspaper *Tout* editorialized in favor of complete sexual liberation, including that of homosexuals. The paper was seized as "an outrage to public morals." The state of Connecticut abolishes its laws against homosexual practices between consenting adults, becoming the second state to do so, ten years after Illinois. New York City Department of Consumer Affairs recommends the repeal of the law that has prohibited lesbians and gays from working in or drinking in the city's bars and cabarets.

1972   The Furies (Washington, D.C.) are formed and invoke separatism as a means to remove women from male dominance. East Lansing, Michigan, is the first city to ban sexual orientation discrimination in city employment. Camille Mitchell is the first open lesbian to win custody of her children in a divorce case, though the judge prohibits Mitchell from cohabiting with her lover. Presidential candidates Eugene McCarthy and George McGovern both vow to work in support of gay and lesbian rights. The night McGovern is nominated, there are two nationally televised speeches in favor of gay and lesbian rights from the Democratic National Convention. Jill Johnston declares "all women are lesbians" at public talk in New York City. San Francisco lesbians call for separation from North American Conference of Homophile Organizations (NACHO). Del Martin calls for lesbians separating from gay men, and joining forces with other lesbians in order to pursue lesbian rights. The Equal Rights Amendment passes the U.S. Senate. *Sappho Was a Right-On Woman* is published.

1973　**January 22.** *Roe v. Wade* is decided by U.S. Supreme Court in favor of a woman's right to a first trimester abortion *without* consulting with anyone else and to a second and third trimester abortion with her doctor's consent. "Roe" was Norma McCovey, a lesbian. **March 4.** NOW passes resolution making "lesbian rights" a top priority; a few weeks later, Betty Freidan publicly announces that "man-hating" lesbians are trying to take over NOW. Naiad Press, a lesbian book publisher, is founded by Barbara Grier and Donna McBride. Olivia Records, a lesbian collective, releases its first single with Cris Williamson and Meg Christian. Gail Bates and Valerie Randolph, Army WACs, are married in San Francisco. They are discharged from the Army. **April.** West Coast Lesbian Conference held at University of California, Los Angeles. National Lesbian Kiss-In is held at the Los Angeles County Museum of Art by the lesbian-feminists. **August 8.** The American Bar Association passes a resolution urging states to repeal sodomy laws. **September 20.** "The Battle of the Sexes" tennis match between Billie Jean King and Bobby Riggs. King wins. **Fall.** First class taught by lesbian-feminists on lesbianism at San Francisco State University. **November 5.** The U.S. Supreme Court upholds Florida's sodomy laws. **November 23.** First Gay Academic Union conference is organized by Joan Nestle, Jonathan Ned Katz, and John D'Emilio in New York City. **December 15.** The American Psychiatric Association removes homosexuality from its classifications as a psychiatric disorder or mental illness.

1974　National Gay Task Force (NGTF), precursor of National Gay and Lesbian Task Force, founded and holds first Conference on Sexuality and Lesbians. U.S. Congressional Representatives Bella Abzug and Edward I. Koch introduce first federal civil rights legislation (HR 14752) to protect the rights of lesbians and gays. Homosexuelle Interessen-Gemeinshaft Berlin petitions without success the East German government for recognition. Kathy Kozachenko, an open lesbian, is elected to the Ann Arbor, Michigan, City Council. Haworth Press publishes the academic *Journal of Homosexuality*. **June 30.** First lesbian conference held in Toronto, Canada. **November 5.** Elaine Noble becomes the first open lesbian or gay person elected to state office—the Massachusetts legislature. **December 18.** First International Gay Rights Conference, which will lead to the formation of the International Lesbian and Gay Association in 1978.

1975   **March 11.** Madison, Wisconsin, extends civil rights protections to lesbians and gays. **June 19.** The American Medical Association (AMA) passes a resolution urging states to repeal laws prohibiting acts of same-sex sodomy between consenting adults. **July.** Lesbians begin organizing for the first United Nations Conference on Women, held in Mexico City. Their presence at the conference causes scandals. Lesbian activists in Los Angeles begin publishing *The Lesbian News*. **July 3.** The U.S. Civil Service Commission rules that homosexuality will not automatically disqualify a person from federal employment. **July 15.** Santa Cruz County, California, becomes the first county in the United States to prohibit employment discrimination based on sexual orientation. **December 1.** Jill Johnston's essay "Are Lesbians 'Gay'?" is published. This essay concludes that "lesbians are feminists, not homosexuals."

1976   Brussels Tribunal on Crimes Against Women declares that "compulsory heterosexuality" is also a crime against women. **January 15.** The Vatican calls homosexuality a "serious depravity" in the "Declaration on Certain Questions Concerning Sexual Ethics." **March 12.** Jimmy Carter, the Democratic presidential candidate, states that he is willing to ban discrimination of gays and lesbians in housing, employment, immigration, and military service by issuing an Executive Order if elected. **April 7.** U.S. Congresswoman Barbara Jordan (D-Texas) states she cannot equate gay rights with black civil rights and will not cosponsor a federal gay rights bill. **August 1.** University of California at Los Angeles (UCLA) study finds that lesbian mothers' sexual orientations do not influence the sexual orientations of their children. **October 9–11.** National Lesbian Conference hosted by Lesbian Organization of Ottawa. **October 30.** First gay civil rights group in Quebec, Association Pour les Droits de la Communauté Gaie du Québec, is formed. **November 10.** Lynn Ransom, a lesbian mother, is granted custody of her two young children by a California Superior Court judge.

1977   The State of Florida bans gay and lesbians from adopting. **January 10.** The New York Episcopal Church ordains Ellen Marie Barrett, an out lesbian, as a minister. **January 18.** Dade County, Florida, passes gay rights ordinance. Anita Bryant soon will be rallying the Religious Right to repeal it. **February 7.** The U.S. State Department lifts its ban on employing homosexuals. **February 8.** The first official meeting between a gay rights organization and the White House takes place when Midge Constanza, President Carter's White House aide, meets with officers of the National Gay Task Force. A second meeting is held a few weeks later with two dozen gay rights advocates. **March.** The International Women's Year Conference, Houston, Texas, passes lesbian rights resolution after it was seconded by Betty Friedan. **March 17.** The State of Arkansas repeals its two-year-old repeal of its sodomy laws, recriminating same-sex sexual acts. **May 25.** The San Francisco School Board votes to include materials on gays and lesbians in the sex education curriculum. **June 7.** The Dade County, Florida, gay rights ordinance is repealed. Gay rights marches are held the next day across the country. Anita Bryant is named "Woman of the Year" by *People* magazine; *Good Housekeeping*'s readers name her as one of the most admired women. **June 25.** First autonomous French gay/lesbian demonstration initiated by women of Mouvement Libération Féministe. **November 2.** Senior

Action in a Gay Environment (SAGE) is founded. **November 8.** Harvey Milk, first openly gay political candidate, is elected to the San Francisco Board of Supervisors. **December 15.** The first lesbian and gay civil rights bill is enacted in the province of Quebec, Canada.

1978   National lesbian-feminist Organization founded. Lesbians of Color, founded in Los Angeles, California. **January 9.** Twenty-nine international celebrities including Simone de Beauvoir and Jean-Paul Sartre take out a full page ad in *Time* magazine to protest the backlash against gays and lesbians by Anita Bryant's campaign, and call for the civil rights of homosexuals to be included in President Carter's human rights policy, if it is to be credible. **January 15.** The Briggs Initiative is introduced in California. **January 23.** Mayor Koch issues an executive order in the New York city prohibiting discrimination against lesbians and gay men in city government, and all agencies that do business with the city. The Roman Catholic Archdiocese of New York, the Salvation Army, and other organizations take the city to court and win the overturn of this executive order. **February 7.** The Oklahoma State House of Representatives introduces a "teacher fitness" statute which would allow teachers to be fired if they are lesbian or gay, advocate homosexuality, or join a gay rights organization. The National Gay Task Force challenges the constitutionality of this statute. **March 8.** Wages Due Lesbians founds the Lesbian Mothers' Defense Fund. **March 20.** The San Francisco Board of Supervisors passes the most stringent gay rights law in the country; only Supervisor Dan White votes against it. **April 25.** St. Paul, Minnesota, voters repeal their gay rights ordinance after fourteen years. **May.** Lorena Hickok's 3,360 letters from Eleanor Roosevelt unsealed at Hyde Park, New York. **May 9.** Wichita, Kansas, repeals its ordinance prohibiting housing and employment discrimination against gays and lesbians by 5 to 1. **June 1.** The Moral Majority is founded by Jerry Falwell in opposition to gay rights and feminism, among other liberal issues. **June 7.** The Briggs Initiative qualifies to be Proposition 6 on the California ballot that November. **June 25.** Gay Freedom Day Parade in San Francisco attracts 350,000 marchers. Gilbert Baker designs the Rainbow Flag flown for the first time in the parade. **July 1.** A poll of junior and senior high school students conducted by *The Ladies Home Journal* names Adolf Hitler and Anita Bryant as the two people who have "done the most damage in the world." **July 26.** Mexico City's first public demonstration for lesbian and gay rights. The International Gay Association (now the International Lesbian and Gay Association) is founded in Coventry, England. **August 20.** Ronald Reagan announces his opposition to California Proposition 6, thus ensuring its defeat. **November 27.** Dan White assassinates Harvey Milk and the San Francisco city mayor, George Moscone.

1979   **March 10.** Lesbian rights are raised for the first time at Toronto International Women's Day. **July 1.** The Susan B. Anthony dollar, the first U.S. coin commemorating a woman (and a lesbian) is issued. **July 7.** Martina Navratilova and Billie Jean King win the Wimbledon Women's Doubles championship. **September 1.** A Columbia University report concludes that homosexuality is the result of socialization not biological factors. **October 12.** The National Coalition of Black Gays sponsors the First Third World Lesbian and Gay Conference in Washington, D.C. **October 14.** The first national lesbian and gay pride March on Washington. There are over 100,000 participants. **October 21.** The *New York Times* reports Eleanor Roosevelt's (ER) affair with Lorena Hickok (Hick) as a book on the letters between the two is published. **November 13.** San Francisco swears in its first openly lesbian and gay police officers.

1980   *Questions Féministes* split over lesbianism issue. At the mid-decade United Nation's Conference on Women in Copenhagen, Denmark, lesbian rights are entered into the dialogue on women's rights. **January 22.** The National Gay Task Force protests the film *Windows* which has the lead character depicted as a deranged lesbian. **March 6.** Marguerite

Yourcenar elected to the Académie Française; she is the first woman ever elected in the Academy's 350 years. **June 24.** The Democratic Party adopts a gay rights plank for its party platform. **October 17.** Two hundred women attend the first Black Lesbian Conference in San Francisco. **December 1.** In a *Ladies Home Journal* article, now divorced Anita Byrant says she is not that adamant against gay rights: "I'm more inclined to say live and let live." **December 20.** Statistics show that one person a day is physically assaulted in New York City for being gay or lesbian.

1981   **February 10.** The Moral Majority launches a $3 million media campaign against gay rights and homosexuality. **March 31.** Nancy Reagan, the First Lady, claims that "Woman's Liberation and gay liberation . . . [are] weakening the moral standards of this nation." **April 28.** Marilyn Barnett files a "palimony" suit against Billie Jean King. **June 17.** Senator Roger Jepsen (R-Iowa) sponsors the "Family Protection Act" aimed to "strengthen the American family and to promote the virtues of family life." **June 18.** Congressman Larry McDonald (D-Georgia) sponsors the successful McDonald Amendment which prohibits legal services from assisting in any case, including lesbian custody, that would promote homosexuality. **June 24.** The People for the American Way, television producer Norman Lear's group to combat the Moral Majority, begin their media campaign to promote social diversity and political pluralism. **June 30.** Florida Governor Bob Graham signs the Trask Amendment prohibiting state funds to universities that recognized gay groups. The Florida Supreme Court rules that this amendment is unconstitutional. Norway becomes the first country to enact civil rights legislation that protects the rights of lesbians and gays. **July 3.** The first reports of gay men contracting Kaposi's Sarcoma published in *The New York Times.* **October 7.** Lesbians Against the Right hold first lesbian pride march: Dykes in the Street. **October 24.** The first National Conference on Lesbian and Gay Aging is held in California. Kinney's Report issued stating that sexual orientation is not influenced by parents or society. California

Governor Jerry Brown appoints Mary Morgan, the first openly lesbian judge, to San Francisco Municipal Court.

1982 Bryton High School in Philadelphia, Pennsylvania, is founded as the first gay and lesbian high school in the U.S. **January 4.** The Gay Men's Health Crisis, Inc. is founded to help people with Acquired Immune Deficiency Syndrome (AIDS). **January 17.** Voters in Austin, Texas, reject a proposal that would allow housing discrimination based on sexual orientation. **January 27.** At congressional subcommittee hearings on federal gay rights legislation, National Pro-Family Coalition member Connie Marshier equates homosexuality with child abuse even though the majority of pedophiles are heterosexual. **February 5.** The film, *Personal Best,* about lesbian athletes starring Mariel Hemingway opens. **February 25.** Wisconsin becomes the first state in the United States to enact a lesbian and gay civil rights bill. **March 25.** *Cagney and Lacey,* the first female "buddy" television series premieres. **May 11.** Lincoln, Nebraska, voters defeat a gay rights ordinance after being primed with misinformation by Family Research Institute founder Paul Cameron. **June 30.** The Equal Rights Amendment (ERA) is defeated; it received ratification from only 35 states (38 states are necessary). **July 16.** In a ruling based on free speech and freedom of association, a federal judge rules that the U.S. Immigration and Naturalization Service's (INS) policy of refusing gays and lesbians entry into the United States is unconstitutional. **August 28.** First Gay Olympics held in San Francisco (name later changed to Gay Games). Twelve countries are represented by 1,300 athletes. **October 13.** National Gay and Lesbian Task Force director Virginia Apuzzo and Moral Majority leader Jerry Falwell debate gay rights on *The Phil Donahue Show,* a popular talk show. **October 25.** Northern Ireland repeals its sodomy laws. **December 18.** Quebec Parliament approves domestic partnership rights for same-sex couples. France decriminalizes homosexuality.

1983 Parents think that Linda Conway, a West Virginia kindergarten teacher, looks like a lesbian, forcing her to resign.

She sues the school board. Lesbianas Unidas is formed in Los Angeles, California. **March.** First National Lesbians of Color Conference held in Malibu, California. **March 19.** The first lesbian and gay rights demonstration held in Dublin, Ireland, after a court gave suspended sentences to five youths who had acknowledged assaulting twenty gay men and killing one. **April 1.** The FBI acknowledges that it did surveillance on the Daughters of Bilitis, Gay Activist Alliance, Gay Liberation Front, and the National Gay Task Force, among other gay and lesbian rights organizations. **June 12.** *The Color Purple* by Alice Walker makes *The New York Times'* bestseller list. **June 16.** First front-page article on AIDS in *The New York Times.* **June 19.** Jerry Falwell says AIDS "is the judgement of God." **June 21.** President Ronald Reagan's White House finally agrees to meet with the gay community about the administration's (non)response to the AIDS crisis. **August 26.** After being reminded by Virginia Apuzzo that Martin Luther King Jr. wanted civil rights for all people, black leaders announce their support of gay civil rights. Karen Thompson begins her fight to become guardian of her paralyzed lover, Sharon Kowalski, so that she may continue to care for her. Yvette Roudy proposes "antisexist" bill to French Council of Ministers.

1984 **June 30.** Unitarian Church recognizes gay and lesbian unions. **November 6.** Newly incorporated municipality of West Hollywood, California, which is 40 percent gay and lesbian, becomes the first "gay city" when it elects a majority of gays and lesbians to the city council. **December 5.** Berkeley, California, adopts a domestic partnership policy for its city employees, becoming the first city in America to do so.

1985 **February.** *Ms.* magazine petition for freedom of sexual choice, which condemns the government for failing to protect the civil rights of gays and lesbians, is signed by prominent women artists, writers, and performers. **March 26.** A 4–4 vote of the U.S. Supreme Court (because one of the justices was absent) overturned Oklahoma's ban on homosexuals teaching in public schools. **April 1.** New York City's

Harvey Milk School holds its first classes for lesbian and gay high schoolers. **July 23.** A Minnesota judge awards custody of Sharon Kowalski to her father, not to her lover Karen Thompson. Thompson vows to fight for her. **September.** Lesbian workshops are held at the United Nations Conference on Women in Nairobi, Kenya. **November 13.** Margaret Roff makes British history as the first out lesbian to become Lord Mayor of Manchester.

1986 International Lesbian and Gay People of Color Conference is held in Los Angeles, California. **March 20.** After fourteen years, New York City Council finally passes a gay rights ordinance. **May 1.** The first woman to reach the North Pole by dogsled is lesbian Ann Bancroft. **June 30.** *Bowers v. Hardwick* upholds constitutionality of Georgia's sodomy laws. **July 9.** New Zealand decriminalizes homosexuality. **December 2.** The Province of Ontario, Canada, passes a gay rights ordinance.

1987 First Latina Lesbian Conference held in Mexico City, Mexico. **March 24.** ACT-Up's first political action held at the corner of Wall St. and Broadway, New York City, to push the Federal Drug Agency's (FDA) approval of AIDS drugs. **August 7.** A "Kiss-In" is staged at Piccadilly Circus, London, to protest British law that outlaws public displays of affection by same-sex couples. **August 20.** New York State Consumer Protection Board reveals that the pharmacies are making exorbitant profits (17 to 398 percent) on drugs used by persons with AIDS. **October 7.** U.S. Justice Department report concludes that lesbians and gays are the most frequent victims of bias and hate crimes. **October 10.** During the second March on Washington, about two thousand same-sex couples stage a mass wedding on the steps of the U.S. Internal Revenue Service (IRS) building to dramatize the lack of rights for same-sex couples. **October 11.** Celebration of the first National Coming Out Day.

1988 **March 23.** Homosexual acts between consenting adults are made legal in Israel. **May 20.** First Conference on Homophobia Education is held in Washington, D.C. **May 23.** Four lesbians protesting Great Britain's Clause 28, which prohibits local governments and schools from promoting homosexuality, try to take over a news broadcast of the BBC. **May 24.** Clause 28 is implemented. **June 16.** Southern Baptists pass a resolution condemning (the act of) homosexuality, though noting that God loves the person. **November 1.** U.S. Department of Health and Human Services estimates that 40 percent of all teen suicides are gay and lesbian youth. **December 28.** Karen Thompson and other lesbian friends of Sharon Kowalski are granted visitation rights. Mr. Kowalski is still Sharon's guardian. Sweden becomes the first country to legislate protections regarding inheritances, social services, and taxes for lesbians and gays. Lambda Delta Lambda, a lesbian sorority at UCLA, ratifies its goals "to promote awareness of women's, minorities' and gay issues."

1989   **February 6.** The American Bar Association (ABA) finally passes resolution supporting federal legislation to ban discrimination against lesbians and gays. **May 26.** Denmark's Registered Partnership Act legalizes gay and lesbian unions. U.S. Department of Defense studies conclude that there are no reasons to exclude homosexuals from military service. **June 2.** The first Lambda Literary Awards. **June 25.** The U.S. Postal Service commemorates the twentieth anniversary of Stonewall with a "Lesbian and Gay Pride" postmark. **July 6.** New York Court decision upholds Rent Control regulation ruling by the New York State Division of Housing and Community Renewal that a same-sex couple is considered a "family." **August 31.** Jerry Falwell dissolves the Moral Majority. His Liberty Foundation continues to battle homosexuality, feminism, abortion rights, and pornography. **September 15.** Maud's, the oldest lesbian bar, closes in San Francisco. **October 27.** Lambda, a gay rights organization, is founded in Poland.

1990   Sgt. Miriam ben-Shalom wins overturn of her discharge from U.S. Army because of her lesbianism. She reenlists becoming the first openly lesbian to do so. Her victory is short-lived; the army, on appeal to the U.S. Supreme Court, wins. **April 28.** Queer Nation holds its first public action against homophobia. **April 28.** Gay and Lesbian activists are invited to the White House to witness President George H. W. Bush signing the Hate Crimes Statistics Act into law, though the Justice Department refuses at first to track crimes against lesbians and gays. **June 22.** For three days, the Empire State Building is lit up in lavender for Gay Pride Week. **August.** United Lesbians of African Heritage is founded. **September 27.** In Strasbourg, France, the European Court of Human Rights rules that transsexuals have no right to change their birth certificate's sexual designation. **October 27.** The U.S. Congress repeals the thirty-eight-year-old federal law that prohibits lesbian and gay foreigners (because sexual deviation was considered a mental illness) from entering the United States. **November 8.** Mary Robinson is elected the first woman President of Ireland having run on a gay rights and pro-abortion platform.

1991   Patricia Ireland, President of NOW, comes out as a bisexual; not only is she married, but she has a female lover. Audre Lorde is named Poet Laureate of New York State. **February 7.** The president of the USSR Academy of Medicine declares that homosexuality is a disease and that it must be legally controlled. **February 16.** OutRage! holds a "Kiss-In" at Piccadilly Circus, London, to protest the Sexual Offenses Act. **June.** The first Black Gay and Lesbian Pride Parade and Celebration is held in Washington, D.C. **September.** In Yokohama, Japan, Amnesty International passes a resolution to aid those persecuted because of sexual orientation and imprisonment for consensual same-sex acts. **September 29.** Governor Pete Wilson of California sets off months of protests when he vetoes lesbian and gay employment rights bill. **October 19.** After at least nine lesbian and gay employees of Cracker Barrel restaurants are fired because of the company's heterosexist values, Queer Nation and other groups begin series of protests and boycotts. **December.** Minnesota Court of Appeals awards Karen Thompson guardianship of her disabled lover, Sharon Kowalski.

1992   Acclaimed the Year of the Lesbian, the media's infatuation with "lesbian chic" grows. Yet for most lesbians, they are either invisible, passing, or closeted. Canadian pop singer k.d. lang is the first major recording artist to come out as a lesbian. Col. Margarethe Cammermeyer is dishonorably discharged from the Washington National Guard because she says she is a lesbian. The first chapter of Lesbian Avengers is founded in New York City. In Florida, the first lesbian serial killer (Aileen Wuornos) is sentenced to death. Audre Lorde dies of cancer. French Parliament amends civil union contract to insure all domestic partners of persons who are covered by Sécurité Sociale.

1993   **January 1.** The World Health Organization officially deletes homosexuality from its list of diseases. **February 14.** On Valentine's Day, the Lesbian Avengers erect a sculpture of Alice B. Toklas next to the one of her lover, Gertrude Stein, in Byrant Park, New York City. Alfred Spria's survey of French sexuality is published: a gross estimate of gays and lesbians in France is between 1.5 and 2 million. **April 22.** First Dyke March in Washington, D.C. **April 24.** Lesbian Avengers hold largest ever lesbian march and demonstration ever at the White House, Washington, D.C. **April 25.** The third national March on Washington for gay, lesbian, and bi equal rights. **May 7.** Hawaii Supreme Court says that the state must prove they have a "compelling interest" for denying same-sex couples marriage licenses. **June 30.** Ireland decriminalizes consensual same-sex acts between adults and lowers age of consent to seventeen for everyone. **July.** UN grants International Lesbian and Gay Association (ILGA) observer status. U.S. "Don't Ask, Don't Tell, Don't Pursue" guidelines for gays in the military are issued. **July 28.** New Zealand outlaws discrimination based on sexual orientation. First National Lesbian Conference, billed as a strategy meeting for lesbian liberation, draws 2,500 women. Governor William Weld of Massachusetts signs executive order granting lesbians and gays state workers family leave and bereavement rights. Canada lifts ban on gays and lesbians in the military. Canadian immigration grants immigrant status to Canadian citizen's Irish lesbian lover. **October 13.** Lesbian Avengers protest New York City speech by Senator Sam Nunn (D-Georgia, chair, Senate Armed Services Committee) because of his stance on banning lesbians and gays in the military.

1994   **June.** Stonewall 25 celebrations and march draw over one million participants in New York City. **December.** The UN revokes ILGA's observer status. South African interim Constitution adopted. It includes protections for lesbians and gays. The first Latina Lesbian Leadership and Self Empowerment Conference is held in Tucson, Arizona. The American Medical Association finally removes references to "sexual orientation related disorders" from its official policy to treat homosexuality.

1995   **September 15.** The fourth United Nations World Conference on Women is held in Beijing, China. Lesbian rights are linked to women's rights. **November 13.** In Auckland, New Zealand, at meeting of heads of Commonwealth governments, lesbians protest Zimbabwe President Robert Mugabe because of his statements that homosexuals are trying to destroy society. Cherry Jones, out lesbian actor, wins the Leading Actress Tony for her role in *The Heiress.*

1996   *Romer v. Evans* and *Baehr v. Miike* rulings that the state of Hawaii ban on same-sex marriages does not have any compelling state interest. South Africa's Constitution is ratified, becoming the first Constitution in the world to include protections for lesbian and gay people. The U.S. Supreme Court declares Colorado's Amendment 2 unconstitutional. Employment Non-Discrimination Act (ENDA) is defeated in the Senate by a vote of 50–49. **September 21.** Without fanfare, President Bill Clinton signs the Defense of Marriage Act. **December.** The first national Lesbian Rights Conference is held in Manilla, Philippines.

1997   State of Tasmania, Australia, repeals its sodomy laws. A U.S. Federal Appeals Court strikes down Alabama law barring gay-student groups from campus. "Ellen" (Morgan) is the first prime-time-lead lesbian television character. The actress playing her (Ellen DeGeneres) also comes out.

Texas Appeals Court rules that a lesbian is entitled to sue for visitation rights to her ex-lover's child. Walt Whitman Community School, the first private school for lesbian and gay children, is opened in Dallas, Texas. Spanish Fork, Utah, Volleyball Coach Wendy Weaver is fired with a gag order when she moves in with her female lover. She files suit against the Nebo School District. **October.** Virginia Apuzzo is appointed as President Bill Clinton's Assistant for Administration and Management; she becomes the highest ranking out lesbian in the White House. **October 20.** Portugal's first Gay and Lesbian Community Center opens in Lisbon. **November.** New Hampshire and Maine pass Gay Rights Law. **December.** A New Jersey gay male couple is granted the right to adopt the foster child they have been caring for. Gay and lesbian couples can also jointly adopt under New Jersey state custody laws after class action court case is decided. A U.S. Federal Appeals Court upholds Cincinnati, Ohio, voter initiative that prohibits antidiscrimination rights for lesbians and gays. President Bill Clinton is the first president to address a lesbian and gay rights organization—the Human Rights Campaign.

1998   South Africa's High Court declares sodomy laws unconstitutional. Anchorage, Alaska, Superior Court judge rules against Alaska state ban on same-sex marriage. *Shahar v. Hardwick* upholds Georgia attorney general's denial of employment to Shahar because of her impending marriage to her partner. The state of Washington becomes the twenty-seventh state to ban same-sex marriages when the legislature overrides the governor's veto. *Patience and Sarah* is made into first lesbian opera. Pediatrics study shows that half the teens who identify as gay, lesbian, or bisexual and who grow up without support are more likely to attempt suicide, be abused or harassed, and take risks sexually and/or with drugs. A U.S. Superior Court judge rules "Don't Ask, Don't Tell" violates the rights of gays and lesbians. The California National Guard is ordered to open ranks. United Methodist Church adopts same-sex marriage ban as canon. Maine rescinds its Gay Rights Law. **October 7.** Hate-crime victim Matthew Shepard is found beaten and tied to fence outside of Laramie, Wyoming; he dies on **October 12.** National protests are held for hate-crimes legislation across the country. In New York City, protestors are harassed by police and many are arrested. **December 2.** Over two hundred right-wing protesters stormed theaters in Bombay, India, forcing the theaters to suspend showing Deepa Mehta's *Fire,* the first Indian film about a lesbian relationship. The Campaign for Lesbian Rights is founded soon after.

1999   **January 16.** Ninety ministers bless the union of two women in Sacramento, California, defying United Methodist law. Amélie Mauresmo, women's singles finalist at the French Open, comes out. **February 15.** New Zealand Prime Minister calls for Justice Ministry study on laws affecting lesbians and gays. **April.** President Bill Clinton issues executive order calling for nondiscrimination on all accounts in federal employment (excluding the military). **April 30.** Bomb kills two people in gay pub in Soho, London; White Wolves, a supremacist group, takes responsibility. **May 3.** New Hampshire governor repeals ban on gay/lesbian adoptions. **May 20.** Canadian Supreme Court rules that legal definition of spouse as someone of the opposite sex is unconstitutional. **June 19.** Brazilian court rules that lesbian and gay couples enjoy the same legal rights as heterosexual couples. **June 30.** Massachusetts Supreme Court rules that gay/lesbians are entitled to child visitation rights if they had participated in raising the child. **October 13.** The French National Assembly approves a law giving unwed same-sex and heterosexual couples the same rights as married couples. **October 23.** Jerry Falwell meets with Mel White at an antiviolence forum in Lynchburg, Virginia, to address church leaders' incitement of antigay violence. **October 27.** The Ontario provincial government changes sixty-seven statutes which allow same-sex couples equality with heterosexual couples. **December 21.** Vermont Supreme Court rules that lesbian and gay couples have same legal rights and privileges as married heterosexual couples.

2000   **March 30.** Central Conference of American Rabbis announce they will celebrate same-sex unions. **April 6.** New

Jersey Supreme Court grants lesbian the same parental rights the biological mother of her twins has, saying she has "psychological" parental rights. **April 16.** Vermont approves "civil unions" for lesbian and gay couples affording them the same 300+ rights and privileges enjoyed by married heterosexual couples. France expands domestic partnership to include gay and lesbian couples. **May 10.** Lorena Hickok's memorial dedicated in Rhinebeck, New York. **June.** First Pride Weekend held in Tokyo. **November.** Germany grants legal recognition to same-sex couples. The Vatican issues the seventy-six-page "Family, Marriage and 'De Facto' Unions," which calls same-sex unions "a deplorable distortion" and allowing same-sex adoptions puts children in "a great danger." Tokyo's human rights guidelines include antidiscrimination against lesbian, gay, bisexual, and transgendered people clause. Thai lesbians announce plan to campaign in schools to increase awareness of homosexuality. **December 1.** Lesbian Avengers take part in first anniversary of World Trade Organization protests in Seattle, Washington.

2001   **January.** The Netherlands Parliament approves same-sex marriage and adoption laws to take effect in April. **January 14.** In Toronto, Canada, the Metropolitan Community Church announces the banns three Sundays in a row, thus, according to Ontario Marriage Act, legally marrying two couples, one lesbian, the other gay men. The Ontario government refuses to register the marriages. **April.** The Chinese Psychiatric Association removes the designation "mentally unfit" from lesbians and gays. **April 1.** Four lesbian and gay couples marry shortly after midnight at the Amsterdam City Hall when the Netherlands' new law recognizing same-sex marriages takes effect. **April 24–25.** Tokyo's Pride Weekend draws four thousand attendees. **May 24.** Teacher Dawn Murray settles her seven-year sexual orientation discrimination suit with Oceanside (California) Unified School District after the school district failed to take sexual-orientation harassment seriously. **June 30.** The first Yugoslavian Pride March held in Belgrade is violently disrupted by Serbian Nationalists. **July 19.** Rhode Island bans discriminntion against transsexuals and others who face discrimination based on gender, identity, or expression for those seeking housing, employment, or credit. **July 28.** Sharon Smith is the first lesbian partner granted legal standing in the wrongful death suit against a could whose dogs killed her lover. **August 1.** Germany's partnership law takes effect. Angelika and Gudrun Pannier are the first homosexual couple to be legally married in Germany. **August 20.** Florida judge upholds ban on adoptions by homosexual couples. **August 22.** U.S. census reports that there are self-reporting same-sex couples in nearly every county in the United States. **August 27–September 4.** One hundred LGBT leaders from forty countries attend the twenty-first world conference of the International Lesbian and Gay Association in Oakland, California. **September 11.** Terrorist attacks on World Trade Center, New York City, the Pentagon, Washington, D.C., and crash of United Flight 93 in Pennsylvania kill many acknowledged lesbians and gays, along with heterosexuals. Jerry Falwell attempts to blame homosexuals for the terrorist attacks. **September 27.** Panama's first gay and lesbian organization—Asociación Hombres y Mujeres Nuevos de Panama—legally recognized. **September 29.** Finland and South Africa register same-sex couples. They may inherit property and have hospital visitations but may not take a common surname. In Finland they cannot adopt. **October 15.** New York State Governor George Pataki issues executive order extending equal benefits to surviving same-sex partners of those killed at the World Trade Center on 9/11. **November 2.** The state of Washington Supreme Court rules that state doctrine, which provides equitable property distribution to unmarried heterosexual partners, also protects lesbian and gay partners should they separate or if one partner dies. **November 26.** The Maryland Anti-Discrimination Act of 2001 goes into effect protecting lesbian and gays' jobs, housing, and accommodations.

2002   **January.** Cathy Woolard elected as Atlanta City Council President. She is the first openly gay or lesbian politician in Georgia. **January 1.** California's domestic partnership law takes affect. **January 12.** In Seoul, South Korea, homosexual rights advocates file a lawsuit against the government for blocking the first gay and lesbian website. **February 5.** The American Academy of Pediatrics issues a policy statement saying lesbian and gay second parent or coparent adoptions are in the best interests of the children. **February 21.** Massachusetts Supreme Judicial Court rules that the state's sodomy laws do not apply to private consensual acts. **March 21.** Talk show host, comedian, and adoptive mother Rosie O'Donnell discloses she is a lesbian to help fight the 1977 Floridian law that bans homosexuals from adopting children. **April 10.** Students protest antigay bias with a day of silence. **April 16.** The New York City Council votes to recognize same-sex marriages from other jurisdictions. **April 19.** Australian Prime Minister John Howard vows to overturn a court ruling granting lesbians access to fertility treatments. **June.** The National Gay and Lesbian Task Force begins the effort to defeat "Anita Bryant II," the Miami-Dade antigay ballot initative. **August.** *The New York Times* announces it will begin publishing same-sex commitment notices using the same criteria as for heterosexual couples' engagement and wedding announcements. **November 6.** "Anita Bryant II" and other antigay initiatives fail at the ballot box. **November 14.** Queensland, Australia, proposes gay and lesbian civil rights employment protection. **November 15.** Eugene, Oregon, begins registering domestic partners. The United States Holocaust Memorial Museum in Washington, D.C., opens an exhibit titled "Nazi Persecution of Homosexuals 1933–1945." **November 19.** The British government decriminalizes gay sex. **December 2.** The U.S. Supreme Court announces it will hear an equal-protection case challenging Texas's same-sex-only sodomy law. **December 17.** New York State Sexual Orientation Non-Discrimination Act passes and is signed into law by Governor George Pataki. Banning, California School District is sued for prohibiting a female middle school student from participating in gym class because she is a lesbian.

2003   **January 3.** Monique Wittig dies in Arizona.

Introduction

In 1969, the U.S. Gay and Lesbian Liberation movements burst into the public consciousness with the Stonewall uprising. They quickly coalesced into a politically diverse revolutionary movement similar to the other revolutionary movements of the 1960s—civil rights, antiwar, free speech, the New Left, and women's liberation. In Europe, the Gay and Lesbian Liberation movement mirrored what was happening in the United States. The Gay and Lesbian Liberation movements were also influenced by the counterculture, which stressed sexual liberation, pleasure, and self-exploration as well as individualism. Early feminist theory, such as Kate Millett's *Sexual Politics,* and other theoretical feminist manifestos, clearly left their mark on the Lesbian Liberation movement (LLM). Theoretical work by Michel Foucault—and later Monique Wittig—on power and sexuality would influence the Gay, Lesbian, and Queer movements. Using a combination of grassroots organizing and in-the-street activism along with confrontational "zaps," gays and lesbians demanded full equality for themselves; this differed from what the older Homophile movement had been working toward—tolerance and acceptance through education and the legal system. In the early Homophile movement, males dominated both in Europe and the United States, even as lesbians were making their mark socially. This may be explained partially by the fact that only male homosexuality was criminalized in most countries.

The contemporary Gay and Lesbian Liberation movements officially began in the United States with the Stonewall Rebellion of June 27–28, 1969, though gay/lesbian theory was simultaneously being developed in the United States and in post-1968 Europe after the student uprisings in Paris.[1] The movements took on global proportions during the last twenty years of the twentieth century as gay and lesbian citizens in other countries demanded recognition and their (human) rights. Lesbian issues were brought to the table at international women's conferences such as

1

the United Nations Conference of Women held in Nairobi in 1985 and Beijing in 1995, where women's rights as human rights were expanded to encompass the right of women to control their sexuality. Sexual orientation was discussed at these conferences, but the Vatican and the Islamic delegates blocked its inclusion in the resulting documents. Around the globe, lesbians (and gays) were making inroads in both traditionally heterosexist cultures and the more liberal ones, though Chinese officials tried to trivialize the women at the Beijing conference by a misinformation campaign, which included the statement to taxi drivers that they should carry sheets and disinfectant to protect themselves from contracting AIDS from naked lesbians.

Both in the United States and in Europe, lesbian liberation took shape initially within the Women's Liberation movement and the male dominated gay liberation groups, as well as forming their own organizations to fight oppression. The more radical women developed lesbian-feminism, lesbian separatism, and radical lesbian theory and practices.

The key tension that the Lesbian Liberation movement brought to light was that because of the label "lesbian" or "homosexual," coupled with being female, lesbians were not afforded at minimum the rights and protections afforded all other citizens in the modern nation-state based on their (sexual) conduct of lesbian and being a lesbian. A lesbian is at once a sexual outlaw in a heterosexual society and a woman who is independent of men in a patriarchy.

As the movement matured, like all sociopolitical movements, it has become less radical in seeking reform via traditional organized politics and lobbying. The focus evolved from seeking to radically change society to seeking inclusion in existing societal institutions as a fully valued member of that society. Some call this the assimilationist phase: the mainstream gay and lesbian rights fervor becoming more transformative rather than revolutionary. The model being used was that of the normalized lesbian and gay citizen contributing to society as part of the mainstream rather than as marginalized radicals. This liberal argument that would allow those who want to participate in the institutions of the modern state—marrying and serving in the military, for instance—did not address the homophobia faced daily by those not served by mainstream organizations, the lesbians (and gay men) who do not easily melt into the crowds of society.

Not all lesbians became assimilationists. There was a resurgence of street activism by gay and lesbian activists in the 1980s over the government's weak response to the AIDS crisis. AIDS activism gave rise to both the Queer movement and to the Lesbian Avengers (the Lesbian Avengers because issues concerning lesbians and women with AIDS were not being addressed by the AIDS activists such as ACT-Up). There are radical thinkers and practitioners who believe that lesbians and lesbian liberation disappeared because of the inclusionary tactics that have developed in the mainstream gay and lesbian rights movement and in the more politically radical Queer movement. The still active lesbian-feminist and lesbian separatist groups help to challenge the push for inclusion in the unquestioned and unreformed hetero-patriarchal institutions such as marriage and global capitalism.

Overview

The goals of all liberation movements are to educate the rest of the populace about the oppression that the group seeking liberation is facing, and then to eradicate oppression so that members of that group will have the rights, protections, and freedoms that other citizens in a modern nation-state society enjoy. The Lesbian Liberation movement or Lesbian Rights movement follows this basic agenda, but it is also faced with having to make lesbians visible even among the two minority groups that lesbians identify with—women and (male) homosexuals.

Lesbian liberation is not just a political rights movement. It is also a sexual liberation movement pushing the envelope of socially accepted sexual practices. In order to educate others about sexual oppression this has to be done in public fora, even though many people—lesbians and heterosexuals alike—feel that sexual practices are private acts. "Lesbian" encompasses both being and conduct—being non-male identified, and having a woman-identified sexual orientation and non-procreational sexual practices. Recognition of lesbian sexual identity and sexual practices, along with the removal of any social stigma that the word "lesbian" evokes, are part of the goals of the LLM. Lesbians seek liberation from the traditional socially acceptable heterosexual norms and practices. In short, they seek sexual self-determination not granted to women in a patriarchal society.

Lesbian liberation is a movement that operates on two liberatory levels: it strives to liberate a sexual practice from stigmatization, and it is a political movement which challenges the dual oppression of women by the patriarchy's assumption of male supremacy and heterosexuality. The Lesbian Liberation movement is the ongoing struggle for lesbian rights. It takes many forms—from lesbian-feminism to radical lesbians, from sexual outlaws to antipornographers, from lesbian separatists to assimilationists. What ties these varied groups of lesbians together is that while their methods of achieving their goals are different, they have basically the same final aim: social change that would lead to the full recognition of lesbians, and their civil and human rights so that lesbians would not be oppressed nor stigmatized. The LLM is still vital and active around the globe—from the more radical direct actions of the Lesbian Avengers, to the mainstream lesbians in various nongovernmental organizations working for lesbian and gay rights, to lesbians successfully running for political office.

Lesbian liberation intersects, and diverges from the Gay Liberation movement (GLM), the Queer movement, and the Women's Liberation movement (WLM).[2] Because lesbian liberation brings to the forefront issues of sexual self-determination and a sexuality, which is divergent from the normal sexual practices, lesbians benefit from, and belong to, the more male-identified Gay Liberation movement and the queer agenda. But lesbians diverge from these two groups because lesbians as women have issues and concerns which are unique to women in a patriarchal society: the oppression and subjugation of women (and others) by and to men. With the feminist Women's Liberation movement, lesbians join in on issues of equality and equity for women since lesbians are women (however, not all lesbians are feminists, just as not all women are feminists). Yet not all participants in WLM accept the issues of sexual self-determination and sexual liberation that lesbians bring to the table.

Nonetheless, lesbians have been active in both the Gay and Women's Liberation movements. Their presence attempts to make the male-dominated, gay-rights organizations more feminist, and feminist organizations more aware of issues of heterosexism, homophobia, and the promotion of sexual self-determination. There has also been the attempted silencing or submerging of the lesbians themselves in the women's movements because of the fear that society will label all the women, for instance, in the feminist movement as lesbians, thus marginalizing the WLM even more. Lesbians tried to persuade their feminist sisters of the weakness of this argument. In the GLM, women got silenced because of the assumption of male privilege that male homosexuals were not willing to relinquish. The dominant male model is still evident in the more radical Queer movement in which the lesbian/woman is negated. Lesbians have always been actively involved in public policy issues, from the early abolitionist, temperance, social reform, and suffrage movements of the nineteenth century to the twentieth century's Civil Rights, peace, and environmental movements. In the latter part of the twentieth century, lesbians were key in the work to reform single policy issues such as AIDS, women's reproductive health issues, battered women/domestic violence, welfare rights, and equal rights. But the focus has been on the gay men and heterosexual women who have benefitted from lesbian activism. Lesbians are rarely credited for their actions, and in some of the areas, great concern is taken to distance the heterosexual women who have benefitted from lesbian actions and those women who have subsequently institutionalized such issues (for instance, domestic violence programs) from the lesbian activists who laid the groundwork.

Issues that are unique to lesbians such as child custody rights, lesbian battering, or lesbian health do not receive reciprocal support nor are they visible issues. This is because most public policies support the traditional view that sanctions procreational rather than recreational sexual practices. Coupled with the patriarchal concept of universal citizen, which is read as male and privileges the male over the female, the result is that lesbians and their issues are absent from the public agenda. Lesbians are, likewise, silenced or overlooked by the public focus on male homosexual issues such as entrapment or AIDS.

In short, the Lesbian Liberation or the Lesbian Rights movement queries the hypocrisy inherent in modern liberal democracies when the government claims it is protecting all human rights and promoting equality. The inequality that exists when it allows groups of citizens—women, lesbians, gays, the poor, the disabled, the raced—to be subjugated by laws and policies that invade privacy or try to control the individual's sexual self-determination. Government must insist on tolerance of and for all citizens; therefore, it must prohibit social and political discrimination.

The Sexual and Political Construction "Lesbian"

The early focus on women who had affinities for other women was on the sexual preferences and practices, not on the political meaning of lesbian. This focus was maintained and reinforced by the medical and psychological work of sexologists. The American Psychiatric Association (APA) removed homosexuality from its list of psychiatric disorders on December 15, 1972. However, it should be noted that homosexuality is still considered a personality disorder in Russia, and classified as a mental disorder in China.

Same-sex sexual practices, specifically sodomy, have been curtailed by both social condemnation and public policies. These practices are viewed as being non-procreational, and thus, crimes against nature. As of 2002 in the United States, fourteen states still have laws prohibiting acts of sodomy between consenting adults, and five of these states— Arkansas, Kansas, Missouri, Oklahoma, and Texas—target same-sex couples only. Some lesbians feel that their sexual practices take Carol Hanisch's statement "the personal is political" at its most intimate meaning.[3] Still, it was not until the 1980s and both AIDS and the Sex Wars, that same-sex sexual practices were seen as overt political actions by public policy makers.

Lesbians have been defined by their sexual affinity for other women since the lyric poet Sappho wrote of love for other women over 2,500 years ago. Her poems, written on the Isle of Lesbos, gave us the term used for women who have sexual desires for members of their own sex—"lesbians" (the Greek word for oral sex is *lesbiazein*)—or they were known as Sapphists, in Sappho's image of women loving women.[4] In 520 BC, the poet Anacreon used "a girl from Lesbos" to suggest same-sex yearnings.

The ancient term for women attracted sexually to other women was "tribade." This term reflected their sexual practice of rubbing together. The Greek author Lucian circa 160 AD in *Dialogues of the Courtesans* wrote of tribades and *hetairistrai* (masculine-acting women) from the Isle of Lesbos. The second-century Christian theologian Clement of Alexandria mentioned *hetairistrai,* and in 914, a commentator defined the term in a marginal note.

The first known modern usage of the term "lesbian" was in 1732 by William King in *The Toast.* In 1788, Mary Wollstonecraft chronicled devoted friendships between women, which were often called "romantic friendships." Later, these were termed "Boston marriages," but sexual activity between the women involved is not assumed in our post-modern era since the term "lesbian," as we know it today, was not used. Lillian Faderman, in *To Believe in Women,* though, argues that her subtitle "What Lesbians Have Done for America—A History" would more aptly read:

Women of the late Nineteenth and Early Twentieth Centuries, Whose Chief Sexual and/or Affectional and Domestic Behaviors Would Have Been Called 'Lesbian' If they Had Been Observed in the Years after the 1920s" and they recognized each other, and each other's relationships.[5]

Focus on same-sex relationships at this point was on the criminalization of sodomy, which usually referred to male-male sexual relations since women were not seen as sexual beings. The first sodomy law in the Americas was passed by the Virginia Colony in 1610. This law, though, excluded women. The Massachusetts Bay Colony adopted its nondiscriminatory antisodomy law in 1641. A year later, in Salem, Massachusetts, a female servant was whipped for "unseemingly practices between her and another maid."[6] The 1811 trial of two Scottish schoolmistresses (Miss Pirie and Miss Woods) for "improper and criminal conduct" resulted in the British legal establishment concluding that sex between two women was impossible since a penis was missing and the sex act required one.

In 1791, the then new law code in France decriminalized sodomy. The Napoleonic Code decriminalized all sex acts between consenting adults in 1813. Male-to-male sexual activity in Germany was recriminalized in 1851 by Paragraph 175.[7] In 1852, the year following Germany's Paragraph 175, Austria made woman-to-woman sex illegal. But for the most part, women were not considered to have a sex drive, nor were they seen to be able to have sexual relations without a phallus. Most laws aimed at women's sexuality prohibited adultery, the use of false phalluses, and women who cross-dressed to pass as men.

The term "homosexual" is one of recent construction. Karoly Maria Kertbeny used it in 1868. *Homo* is Greek for "same," added to the Latin root *sexual*. Previously, people who had sexual attractions for members of their own sex were known as "variants" or "deviants" (since they varied or deviated from the normal sexual attraction) or "Uranians" (woman loving women were *Urningins*, the feminization of the Germanic male *Urnings*). This term was coined by Karl Heinrich Ulrichs in 1862 as part of his "Third Sex" theory for those who loved members of their own sex or were trapped in bodies of another.

"Homosexual" gained wide use in Germany during an espionage scandal in the Kaiser's court in 1907. Women were called "female homosexuals" well into the twentieth century. Another term widely used at the turn of the century was "invert" which was short for "sexual invert."

These terms for practitioners of same-sex love reflected their sexual and/or erotic nature. Except for Ulrichs's theories and his political actions such as attempting to convince German jurists that Uranian love should be tolerated rather than the criminalized, Uranian Love, same-sex love was apolitical.

The term "homophile" was popularized after World War II as a less blatantly sexual term. Based on the Greek root "phile" which means love, the term was used to promote tolerance of homosexuality. The term's vagueness enabled closeted homosexuals to join the Homophile movement. This term fell out of favor in the late 1960s as one that promoted assimilation rather than equality and pride.

Homophile was replaced with gay (originally encompassing both men and women), lesbian, or woman-identified woman, depending on one's sociopolitical perspective during the height of the Gay and Lesbian Liberation movements. Most recently in the 1980s, the terms "queer" and "dyke" have been reclaimed by activists and academics alike to describe persons whose sexuality does not conform to social norms.

The terms "lesbian"and "dyke" have taken on a political construction when used by members of the dominant culture to silence women and to divisively keep heterosexual women and lesbians from working together. This term, as the Radicalesbians point out in *Woman-Identified Woman*, is politicized by being defined by males. Males only see women in (sexual) relation to themselves and when women do not relate to males, when they are independent, they are lesbians.

The Early Political and Social Organizations

Male homosexuals had begun to organize in Germany at the turn of the twentieth century, though by 1935, they were outlawed. Such formal organizing was a few decades away for American homosexuals. Gays and lesbians, though, had begun to develop an active subculture of clubs, restaurants, and in the arts (*see* Harlem Renaissance, Greenwich Village). The first known U.S. organization of homosexuals was the short-lived 1924 Society for Human Rights, which published two issues of *Friendship and Freedom*, the first gay liberation magazine. In 1947, Lisa Ben wrote and published the first lesbian newsletter *Vice Versa*. It was not until Harry Hays, father of the modern gay and lesbian movement, founded the Mattachine Society in 1950 that the modern homosexual (rights) movement took hold in America. The movement, known as the Homophile movement, stressed mutual support, social tolerance, and understanding through education rather than confrontation.

At first, lesbians identified with and were subsumed by the very early gay or homophile movements. While members usually adopted code names because of the fear of harassment, these early organizations made the claim that homosexuals, male and female, were a sexual minority no different from other minorities, and thus, entitled to the same rights and benefits as other groups of citizens. The Homophile movement's goal was to legitimize homosexuals by portraying homosexuals as responsible participants in the public sphere as opposed to the previous psychomedical model, which considered homosexuals to be social deviants. Claiming political legitimacy for homosexuals, these early groups began the demand for civil rights by protesting police harassment, antigay employment discrimination, and fighting for their right to congregate.

The Mattachine Society/Foundation promoted gay and lesbian rights by taking on issues such as police entrapment and discriminatory employment practices. By 1953, the society became more moderate, fearing reprisals against "sexual deviants" in the repressive McCarthy era. *The Mattachine Review,* published from 1955 until the society was officially disbanded in 1961, discouraged an activist approach to change. The more militant local Mattachine organizations continued after the national society was disbanded. These groups in New York City, Philadelphia, Washington, D.C., and Chicago staged demonstrations in which demonstrators were urged to come dressed for business and women demonstrators were told to wear skirts and stockings. These demonstrations included the first lesbian and gay pickets of the White House and Pentagon in 1965, protesting the U.S. government's employment practices that discriminated against gays and lesbians since they were seen as threats to national security.

One, Inc. was founded in 1952 to specifically publish the first national and openly homosexual magazine *One* and to meet the educational needs of gays and lesbians. In February 1954, the first all-female written and focused issue of *One* was published and immediately sold out. The October 1954 issue was seized by postal authorities as "obscene," which led to a U.S. Supreme Court ruling in January 1958 that established the right of gay and lesbian groups to use the mails and to write about homosexuality in contexts other than medical, legal, or religious.

The initially non-political Daughters of Bilitis (DOB) was founded in 1955 by a group of eight women who were both racially and class diverse. The originator of the group was a Filipina lesbian; Del Martin and Phyllis Lyon were the two women who fronted for the group; and the names of the others remain confidential. DOB's original purpose was to provide support for lesbians, to offer a social alternative to the bar scene for lesbians, and to advance the understanding of lesbianism. DOB grew quickly after it was incorporated in the State of California in 1957, with chapters in most of the major cities in the United States and in Melbourne, Australia.

The early meetings of DOB consisted of "gab 'n' java" discussions, encounter sessions, and research projects. DOB began to publish *The Ladder* in 1956 and organized the first National Lesbian Convention held in San Francisco in 1960. Internal conflict arose between those who wanted DOB to remain a social support group and those who wanted DOB to become an advocate for social change. Women who wanted a more activist or sexual organization splintered off. However, local chapters of DOB were often more radical and political than the national chapter.

The Homophile movement was united in its efforts through the formation of ECHO (East Coast Homophile Organizations) and NACHO (North American Conference of Homophile Organizations) in 1963 and 1968, respectively. Along with the other civil rights movements in the 1960s, ECHO and NACHO took more of an activist approach to achieving political change.

The first political picket of the White House by members of the Mattachine Society, and supported by NACHO, took place in 1965. The men and women were protesting the federal government's discriminatory employment practices. Not only were homosexuals given dishonorable discharges from the military, but in 1953, President Dwight D. Eisenhower had signed executive order 10450 into being. The executive order made sexual perversion grounds to be excluded from federal employment. This remained in place until April 1999 when President Bill Clinton issued the executive order that called for nondiscrimination in federal employment practices.

While homosexual rights groups had been banned in Germany in 1935, after World War II, homosexual rights groups began to emerge in France, Canada, and the United Kingdom. Lesbian groups were slower on the uptake. The Minorities Research Group (MRG) was founded in London in 1963. This was the first organization for lesbians in the United Kingdom. MRG published *Arena 3,* a newsletter. Soon after MRG was founded, Kenric, a social group, was formed.

These early national groups, both globally and in the United States, promoted the assimilation of gays and lesbians into mainstream society by urging tolerance and civil rights for sexual minorities. The local groups were more confrontational and political than the national organizations and they paved the way for the activist gay liberation groups that emerged after the infamous Stonewall Rebellion of June 27–28, 1969. In the days following the uprising, the New York City Mattachine Action Committee issued a flier organizing a protest of the police raid on the Stonewall Inn. These early meetings and protests ushered in the contemporary Gay and Lesbian Rights movement. The first Gay Pride March was held on July 2, 1969, with 500 people marching down Christopher Street to the Stonewall Inn.

Gay and Lesbian Liberation

The contemporary gay and lesbian movements are traced to the Stonewall Rebellion—an uprising of cross-dressing gay men who were being harassed by a police raid of the Stonewall Inn on June 27, 1969. Although there were other protests prior, none had ignited into a movement. The movement took from its parent Homophile movement the civil rights claim that homosexuals and lesbians were just like other members of society, and thus, entitled to the same rights, and from its older sibling liberation movements—the Civil Rights movement, the Antiwar movement, the Free Speech movement, and the fledgling Women's Liberation movement—the politics of confrontational protest. The Women's Liberation movement influenced the Gay and Lesbian Liberation movement's theory that gender and sexual oppression is directly tied to sexism, and specific gender roles are reenforced by the patriarchy, both in society and in the family. Lesbians who have been active in both the first and second waves of feminism, since they are outside the gender norm and they are not sexually available to men, brought feminist theory to the GLM.

While many social, special-interest, and political groups emerged after Stonewall, the first political group in the United States was the Gay Liberation Front (GLF), which, modeled on Marxist cells, strove for consensus as it pushed its radical vision of a restructured society that eliminated all oppression of all minorities. The GLF was infamous for both its social-affirming dances and its politically motivated demonstrations. Its commitment to decision making by consensus, though, limited its effectiveness and scope. Other GLFs appeared in London, Paris, as well in cities across the United States. But most of the GLFs suffered from being gay male oriented.

Another political group among the first groups was the Campaign for Homosexual Equality founded in London in 1969. This group was considered to be more reformist than the revolutionary GLF, but it, too, suffered by focusing on male interests and promoting male leadership. Within six months, the Gay Activists Alliance (GAA) was formed in the United States to address the political issues of gay rights. Instead of working toward consensus, the GAA operated via majority rule, thus enabling it to be more active than the GLF.

Both the GLF and GAA were trying to bring together a diverse group of people whose only tie, initially, was their membership as a sexual minority. Both groups were dominated (by sheer numbers) by middle-class, white males, who, while fighting for equal rights, had divergent issues from other members. These male-dominated groups also reflected society's inherent sexism. This was also true in other liberation movements—women were seen as food preparers and bed mates, not policy makers. While the gay men were not interested in their female counterparts as sexual partners, they looked to the women to tend to housekeeping issues. During meetings, women's voices were drowned out by louder male ones or the women were overlooked by the males leading the meetings. While some of the gay organizations tried to counter this by rotating meeting chairs, it was not always successful.

Gay men, even though society may castigate them for betraying sexual stereotypes, are still males with all the privileges a male supremacist society entails. It is acceptable to be in male-only groups, and sexual promiscuity is the norm for all males.[8] Gay men are not likely to challenge their own source of power and privilege. When gay males feel the oppression of sexism when society derogatorily calls them "sissies" or their actions "effeminate," they challenge heterosexism rather than sexism for their oppression, for as males they are (if they pass) already equal to males. It is only if they are perceived to be gay or they announce it that their civil rights would be truncated: they could lose their employment, housing, etc. It is/was this issue of being able to pass or blend into society that differentiates the Gay and Lesbian Liberation movement and other civil rights movements.

While gay and lesbian movements allowed the exploration of previously repressed sexual identities, the way in which these identities were examined produced clashes between the men and women. Gay men flagrantly practiced their newly liberated sexuality at dances, discos, and at the baths, finding exhilaration in anonymous encounters. Women were more apt to want to talk with their potential partners before consummating the relationship. This made coed socializing difficult. Also, the different styles of sexual expression led to different agendas when it came to political actions. Men were still interested in combating police entrapment practices (still practiced today) while women were more interested in employment issues—pay equity as well as access to jobs regardless of gender, sexual autonomy, and child custody issues (again, still relevent).

Other intraconstituency issues arose within these organizations such as those between lesbians and the drag queens and transvestites. Lesbians felt that the drag queens' exaggerated parody of femininity glorified the clothes, accessories, and mannerisms that kept women objectified, subservient, and sexually available to men—from high heels to sashaying walks. The drag queens and transvestites saw their drag as their style of sexual expression, the expression being one of the primary purposes of sexual liberation. They thought of themselves as more woman than the lesbians since they had chosen to be women.[9]

Lesbians formed caucuses within the GLF and GAA to deal with their specific issues, including sexism, within the gay movement. Conflicts arose between lesbians who were gay-movement identified, and thus, referred to themselves as "gay women," and those who were identified strongly with the women's movement and called themselves "lesbian women." Furthermore, while some women felt that men and women needed to work together to achieve their political goals, other women felt that the males were not responsive to their needs and concerns, and were as sexist as the heterosexual population. This would be echoed in gay and lesbian groups, and in other male-dominated groups in other movements around the world. The lesbians/women would feel their issues and agenda would be ignored or submerged while the male/gay male agenda would be put forward.

These women left the GLF and GAA to form Radicalesbians and Lesbian-Feminist Liberation, respectively, each reflecting a radically feminist philosophy that would give birth to lesbian feminism and lesbian separatism. Members of these groups would again splinter over support for revolution versus change. Members either went back into the gay movement with the Gay Liberation Front Women manifesto or off into revolutionary New Left bastions such as the Black Panthers or supporting other groups that sent guns to Cuba.[10]

Women's Liberation

Not being sexually available to men, and thus not under men's control in a patriarchal society, lesbians had always been active in the feminist movement. They understood both the inequities of being a female in the labor market (the pay inequities, the unequal division of labor, the unpaid labor of housework, and child rearing) the low-paid labor of women's work, and the devaluation of being considered the surplus labor pool. Lesbians also rejected the idea of woman as male's property and the controls society impose on women through marriage, divorce, and child custody. Lesbians recognized and were at the forefront for fighting women's oppression, though some fought the oppression by passing as males.

Lesbians were active in the first wave of feminism in the United States, most notably Susan B. Anthony. With the resurgence of feminism in the 1960s, lesbians, again, were in the forefront. The National Organization for Women (NOW), the largest of the women's liberation organizations, included many lesbians (from 20 percent up to 70 percent by some accounts), but most of the lesbians were closeted. Other women's liberation groups—New York Radical Women, the Redstockings, and WITCH, for example—conducted consciousness raising, developed feminist theory, and were politically active with their primary focus on the oppression of women. As long as the lesbians were closeted and nonvocal about their needs, the women's movement welcomed and used their energy and focus. Lesbians worked on issues of battering (now referred to as domestic violence) and on abortion and reproductive rights.

Involvement with the Gay Liberation movement, though, taught lesbians about the importance of being publicly out, proud of their independence from men, and of their sexuality. Barbara Love reiterated in conversation in June 1999 what she and Sidney Abbott had written in 1972, that lesbians are the women who epitomized the independent liberated woman: "Lesbians have economic independence, sexual self-determination, that is, control over their own bodies and life styles."[11]

Ti-Grace Atkinson's statement, "Feminism is the theory, lesbianism is the action," set into motion the lesbian-straight controversy.[12] When some of the members of NOW came out as lesbians and demanded that NOW listen to their specific needs, the leadership of NOW faced a predicament: if they acknowledged the lesbians among them, all the women would be branded "lesbians/dykes," and the movement would be discredited. "The greatest threat to men is solidarity among women and 'lesbianism' epitomizes that solidarity. . . ."[13] Men use the term "dyke" to frighten women back into their societal roles, keeping them dominated by male culture.[14]

Betty Friedan, president of NOW, felt that the societal pressure that discredited lesbians would be used to discredit all women who belonged to NOW. She believed that the uncloseting of lesbians in NOW would label the women's movement and its issues as too radical for the majority of society. Friedan confronted the lesbians, calling them the "lavender herring" that threatened to derail and undermine the women's movement.[15] Some women, such as Ti-Grace Atkinson, left NOW at this point and organized or joined already existing, more radical women's groups such as the Feminists, New York Radical Feminists, New York Radical Women, and Cell 16 in Boston.

The first Congress to Unite Women in 1968 was organized by NOW and saw active discrimination by the women's movement leaders against lesbians. Press releases were edited to omit the lesbian groups, including the group Ti-Grace Atkinson founded, The Feminists. A report on the congress listed a motion proposing a pro-lesbian workshop as having been "tabled" even though that motion had successfully passed. In NOW and other women's organizations, issues relevant to lesbians were untouched. Lesbians were silenced on all issues save those the movement felt important: child care and reproductive rights.

Three women—Rita Mae Brown, among them— left NOW in 1970, publishing a statement that explicitly charged NOW with sexism and heterosexism. "Enormous prejudice is directed against the lesbian. . . . the prevailing attitude is 'Suppose they flock to us in droves, how horrible.' . . . this is a male-oriented image of lesbianism."[16] Rita Mae Brown organized a meeting to discuss the discrimination against lesbians, not only in the women's movement, but also in Gay Liberation and other counterculture and leftist movements. Proposing a position paper on lesbianism that would be distributed at the second Congress to Unite Women, a six-member group consisting of lead writer Artemis March (then Marge Hoffman), Ellen Shumsky, Cynthia Funk, Rita Mae Brown, Lois Hart, and Barbara Gladstone, worked for six weeks from mid-March to the end of April 1970 on the impassioned piece. These women and others coalesced into the Radicalesbians, produced the germinative lesbian-feminist manifesto that was titled by Linda Rhodes "Woman-Identified Woman."[17] Sidney Abbott, in editing the piece, came up with the now famous line: "What is a lesbian? A lesbian is the rage of all women condensed to the point of explosion."[18] This manifesto is the first analysis of heterosexism and its affect on women and lesbians.

The second Congress to Unite Women was organized by a coalition of radical-feminist groups. It was held in New York City from May 1–3, 1970. At the Friday evening session, the Radicalesbians wearing t-shirts and proclaiming they were the "Lavender Menace," took over the auditorium where the congress was being held. They circulated mimeographed copies of the first lesbian-feminist analysis "Woman-Identified Woman." The agenda of the second congress thus changed, giving way to a discussion on lesbian issues. This paved the way for lesbian issues and lesbian-feminist analyses in the women's movement.

Although a 1971 NOW convention resolved that women had the right to their own sexuality, tensions still existed between the lesbians and the straight women. The analysis of societal oppression was markedly different: women's liberation theorized that it was sexism that kept women second-class citizens; lesbians theorized that it was heterosexism that kept women subservient and oppressed. The argument played out in a competition: who were the more political, more liberated, true feminists—the straight feminists or the lesbians? Lesbians claimed that since they had claimed their autonomy in an hostile world, they successfully challenged male domination both sexually and politically. Straight (heterosexual) women were compromising their feminism each time they submitted to a male partner during sex, thus still defining themselves through men. Straight women were sleeping with the enemy and accepting heterosexual privileges for doing so— economic support, emotional security, and social acceptance. Straight women who accepted the lesbians' logic either became celibate or political lesbians. Other feminists viewed lesbianism as a personal choice, civil rights issue, or cultural issue.

Even as late as 1999, feminism was seen as primarily dealing with issues of sexism. Former Redstocking member Carol Hanisch claimed that doing away with sexism is the first order to achieving women's liberation.[19] Other issues and claims—race, class, and sexual orientation—are secondary and take away focus from the primary goal. The 1971 NOW resolution also did not go as far as including support of women's sexual freedom to express themselves. This issue would give way to the Sex Wars that pitted sex-positive feminists and lesbians against those who were antipornography. It was not until 1999 that a resolution was adopted that accepted all manners of sexual expression.

Lesbian-Feminist Theory and Practice

The lesbians who left the women's movement saw themselves as more than just expressing themselves differently, though sex—the most personal of acts—was also the most political if it rejected men. Lesbian-feminists bring together their feminist and gay activist roots. The lesbian-feminists believe that their lesbianism is political even when they are not sexual. The theory that they developed in lesbian-feminism was a critique/analysis of heterosexuality as both an institution and an ideology. The construction of sexuality is social rather than essentialist.

The manifesto "Woman-Identified Woman" (WIW) was the first feminist analysis that looked beyond sexism to heterosexism. This analytic lens, which became known as lesbian-feminism, was traced by Artemis March back to Ti-Grace Atkinson's having been discredited by NOW leadership by being called a "dyke." "'Dyke' must be a very political term," March said she remembered thinking back then.[20] The three part analysis of WIW explains the fundamentals of lesbian-feminist thought: heterosexism, femininity, and their antitheses, being a woman-identified woman. A woman-identified woman is one who values and validates women for being women, not for their relationship with and to males.

In a heterosexist society, everything is defined in its relationship to men. Men see women as sexual objects who are available to them. Women who are sexually available to men are privileged by his protection, power, and status; they are "real women." Women who are independent and challenge men's primacy are labeled "dykes" or "lesbians" to imply that "you are not playing your socially assigned sex role . . . you are not a 'real woman' or a 'real man.'"(WIW) Heterosexuality, thus, is the key to patriarchal oppression. Sexism is the result of putting men and their definitions of the norm first. Sexism causes women and lesbians/homosexuals to become subservient to men.

The antithesis of heterosexism and femininity—being not only dependent on men, but the property of men—is that of being a lesbian or a woman-identified woman. Women must validate their own identities to achieve autonomy.[21] The political significance of lesbians, of being woman-identified, was of crucial importance to the Women's Liberation movement. As long as feminists did not realize this and recognize lesbians, they would remain oppressed according to lesbian-feminist theory.

This was reiterated in the lesbian-feminist analyses and taken a step further with the work done by the Furies. "Women's Liberation lacks direction because it has failed to understand the importance of heterosexuality in maintaining male supremacy. . . ."[22] The Furies went on to discuss race, class, and national oppressions that serve white male interests.[23] In short, patriarchal male society has defined lesbianism and lesbians from their point of view as not women since they are not available to them sexually. Lesbianism, thus, is seen as a sexual act by (male) society. Lesbians challenge male domination both sexually and politically.

The valuing of women for some lesbian-feminists, such as the Furies, developed into lesbian separatism as a means to achieve a lesbian-feminist politics via building community. Living separately from men, relying on women, not only developed pride, identity, self-sufficiency, and power, it also led to the legitimizing of lesbians' culture and issues. Separatism was/is a means to get out from under male domination. Separatism of thought, culture, and politics led to the development of lesbian communes and lesbian land. While some may feel that lesbian-only space cuts the women off from half the human race, separatists feel that since lesbians are still denied their rights and are openly discriminated against by the heteropatriarchy, heterosexual feminists, and internalized homophobia, living in a separatist community will enable them to be strong enough to combat all oppressions—from racism to ageism— along with sexism and heterosexism. It also allows them to confront issues within the community such as partner abuse, sexual violence, and masochism, while asserting the rights of all women against misogyny and male violence.

The focus on lesbian thought developed into lesbian ethics or lesbian moral thought. This philosophical undertaking developed the concept of revaluing women's traits, decentering the male ethic of rationality, empowering women's moral agency, and applying these concepts to lesbian culture and relationships. The concept of focusing on and celebrating women's nurturing and pacifistic nature gave rise to the practice of cultural feminism. This, in turn, allowed for the radical environmentalism of ecofeminism to develop in the 1980s as well as identity politics in the 1990s.

The lesbian-feminist position that lesbianism was both political and necessary for feminists to understand and embrace, was put forward again in Adrienne Rich's "Compulsory Heterosexuality and Lesbian Existence" (1980). She makes the claim that lesbians are not equated with male homosexuality even though they share some commonalities. It is the lesbian's gender not (only) her sexuality that is her primary and political identity. Thus, Rich recreates the linkage to feminism. In 1986, Rich amends herself to discuss the "complex" identity lesbians share with gay men.

This issue of with which group lesbians would find solidarity best—feminist, lesbian-only, women, or gay men—and the gender identity of lesbians has been theoretically debated over the years. Marilyn Frye believes that economics put women in solidarity with each other, and gay men have overdeveloped the male hatred of women.[24] Monique Wittig places lesbians outside the construction of gender: woman has meaning only in terms of heterosexism. Lesbians are, therefore, not women economically, politically, or ideologically.[25] She also draws a parallel conclusion regarding gay men.[26] Sheila Jeffreys finds that the closest solidarity lies with feminist women since gay men are complicit in oppression since they have "an influential role in defining what the feminine is in male supremacist culture."[27] These arguments continue into queer theory with lesbian-feminist analysis of the masculine bias of gay liberation seen as a corrective,[28] but gender is not a natural basis for solidarity.[29]

In France, the Front Homosexual d'Action Révolutionaire was founded in 1971 by lesbian-feminists. They wanted to form an alliance with their homosexual brethren. It quickly became evident that the gay male and lesbian views differed. The gay males were concerned with *plus jouir* (more pleasure), and the organization became male dominated. The lesbians left and formed the Gouines Rouges (Red Dykes), linking their liberation with that of the feminists or women's movement.[30]

In other countries such as the Netherlands, the push for homosexual and lesbian integration into society predated the contemporary homosexual rights movement. The Cultuur-en-Ontspannings Centrum (COC), formed in 1946, believed in solidarity of gay men and lesbians, and therefore, did not look favorably on women organizing on their own. The lesbian-feminist analysis of enforced heterosexuality did allow some women to critique the COC's methodology. Some of these women formed their own groups in 1971, specifically the Lavender September and Group 7152. Other women remained in the COC.

Coalition Building

For some members of the Radicalesbians, and later some of the members of the Furies, the total immersion in lesbian thought, politics, and the development of lesbian culture separate from gay men and other women did not make sense as a means to change the world. Coupled with the stringent pressure to adhere to antiheterosexual practices which were translated to antimonogamy or nonmonogamous relationships; an antielitist stance which meant that money and education were frowned upon, leading to a lower-class tyranny in attitude; antiestablishment and antistatus quo attitudes that mistrusted the media and political institutions; the concept of democracy that required the entire group be involved and agree on all decisions; and an attitude which considered all men the enemy because of the "cancerous growth between their legs" pushed more moderate lesbian-feminists into reforming.

These women thought that those tenets and the totalitarian adherence to them were very restrictive. Their vision was different, less radical in practice, and larger in scope: they believed that there needed to be an alliance between the many groups since these groups had an overlap of goals. The GLF Women then re-formed and issued a statement of purpose which said that they would work with gay men and the women's movement to achieve change, and furthermore, they would work with the above ground press (previously radical groups used the underground press, specifically *Rat*).

The men of the GLF were supportive not only of the issues they had in common with the women, but with the issues specific to the women. In order for the women to have a voice, they developed and worked in caucuses. These caucuses cooperated with both the gay and the women's movements as the issues dictated.

The spirit of the statement that the GLF Women made would guide not only the GLF, but the formation of the first progressive national gay civil rights organization: the National Gay Task Force (later the National Gay and Lesbian Task Force) in 1973. Though gay men comprised 80 percent of the membership and contributed more money (since they benefited economically from being males), lesbians were given gender parity: 50 percent of the seats on the board were held by women and their issues were supported.

Lesbians who rejoined both the women's movement and gay liberation as well as those who remained active are considered to be equal rights lesbians. Their primary goal—to achieve equality—was to be accepted as women and lesbians. Their secondary goals were to fit into the mainstream, both politically and culturally, were compatible with those goals of gay men and heterosexual women. Some have called this group "assimilationists."

Feminist and Lesbian Splits

Although there was cross-movement sharing of ideas, theories, and methodologies, it was not all smooth. One such concept was that women should identify lesbian, that lesbian was a political choice, that it showed solidarity among women to be women-identified. Lesbian-feminists felt that sexism was enforced by heterosexism in the patriarchal society. This led to the call for heterosexual women to either become celibate or become lesbians because they were "sleeping with the enemy." Heterosexual or straight feminists felt that feminist credentials were called into question based on their sexuality. This schism, which took place during the early 1970s, has been called the "gay/straight split" in the women's movement.

The Sex Wars

The gay/straight split would sow the ground for the feminist/lesbian Sex Wars which began over debates of sexuality and sexual expression. Feminists who were antipornography and antipornographic expression felt that pornography was a power play that demeaned and subordinated women, and also promoted violence against women and should be eliminated. The antipornographers felt that as long as women could be subordinated, women would not be able to achieve equality, and (men's) freedom of expression could and should be limited to this goal. Antipornography ordinances were introduced to this end, though most of the American ordinances were challenged in court on their First Amendment freedom of speech constitutionality; only Canada's law still exists. Ironically, this law is applied to lesbian-content, written material imported into Canada (written material published in Canada has not been affected).

The Sex Wars pitted the equality politics of feminism against the liberatory nature of a sexual movement based on sexual self-determination and lesbian claims for equality. The crucial concept that these debates center around is the politics of power. The argument against pornography, and certain sexual practices such as sadomasochism, is that it is the dominant-male culture that directs and dictates the erotic gaze.[31] This male gaze not only objectifies women, but pornography in itself is a practice that dominates women (and others who may be the object, such as children), and such domination is a power position. Pornography also may involve sadomasochistic practices, which are another form of domination as well as pain-as-pleasure practices and fantasies (rape fantasy). The feminist politics of sexuality, woman having autonomy over her (reproductive) body, is seen within a heterosexist model: whether or not males have access to her body and controlling that access. This is Catherine MacKinnon's concept of coercive sexuality and its power construct.

The fact that lesbians have been using fertility technology since the 1980s to procreate, queers the concept of the procreative couple being heterosexual. Lesbian sexual practices is seen as nonreproductive, therefore, it is as practiced a means of giving and receiving pleasure and intimate bonding. Lesbians further advanced feminist politics of sexuality by allowing that sexual bodies can be pleasurable; they are erotic, and thus one may control one's erotic autonomy.[32]

These arguments were extended to include gendered dress, lesbian butch-femme relationships and expression, and lesbian sadistic/masochistic sexual expression and sexual play. These feminists and lesbians became known as "sex negative." Others, who were sexual liberationists or "sex positive" (radicals) believed that women's sexual desires, fantasies, and expression of sexuality could not be and should not be limited, and freedom of expression should not be censored. These women believe that part of the goal of a LLM was to allow for lesbian sexuality in all its manifestations to be visible, and that the sex-negative women were trying too hard to assimilate and had become asexual to be accepted by the mainstream population. While the Sex Wars took root in the 1970s and blossomed in the 1980s, it was not until the 1990s with the proliferation of lesbian erotica, identity politics, queer theory's fluid self-presentation of sexuality, and even the adoption of a prosexual expression plank into NOW's platform that people have declared that the pro-sex side had succeeded.

Feminist and Lesbian Coalitions on Key Issues

While lesbians and feminists and lesbian-feminists and other lesbians debated and split over issues of sexual expression, other lesbians and feminists were working together on other issues vital to the women's community and to women achieving equality. The lesbian understanding of the feminist concept that the "personal is political" is deeply and immediately felt as it is transformative. The primary issues were, and still are, abortion rights and the access to reproductive health care, battered women, employment issues such as job opportunities and equal pay, and inheritance and property rights.

Abortion and Reproductive Rights

Lesbians and feminists have long seen the relationship between abortion and reproductive rights and women's equality. Without personal autonomy or control over one's body and bodily functions and sexual practices, one is not truly a full political individual. Although abortion has been legal in New York State since 1970 and in the United States since the 1973 *Roe v. Wade* decision by the Supreme Court, access to abortion and reproductive health services have been increasingly limited by state and federal legislation promoted by conservatives and the Religious Right (RR). Lesbians have been on the front lines helping women gain access to abortion and health care services, including walking the women down the gauntlet of antiabortion activists that surround most clinics. Lesbians have also been active in promoting reproductive health care funding and legislation. The first executive order issued by President George W. Bush on January 21, 2001—the anniversary of the *Roe v. Wade* decision—reinstated the Reagan-era abortion gag rule on international health organizations which receive funding from the United States. Lesbians are actively working to overturn this order.

Battered Women's Movement

Again, lesbians and feminists have been at the forefront of what originally was called the "battered women's movement" and now is known as "domestic violence." The fight against wife abuse has its roots in the concept that women—wives or daughters—are the property of their husbands (or fathers) and may be physically controlled by them. Lesbians who believe that women should be independent have long fought this women-as-property concept. Lesbians helped organize the first battered women's shelters in England and the United States in the late 1960s. They used their feminist training to help the women become strong and assertive against the males (usually their husbands or lovers) who were physically and emotionally abusive. While there has been legislation that prohibits wife abuse and battery, the model that is put forward is that abuse of this type only occurs in the familial home, hence the concept of domestic violence. Violence in a noncohabiting relationship has the same legal standing as a stranger's assault and battery, though it has many more emotional repercussions.

Lesbians have been active in trying to expand the definition of domestic abuse and its name since it removes the batterer from the concept almost entirely. They have also been trying to change the model for dealing with abuse. Currently, it is the abused victim who has to leave her home, her job, and her support network of friends and family to escape from her batterer. Her batterer usually retains all his (male) privileges.

Lesbians have also been active in uncovering battery and abuse in lesbian (and gay) couples. Lesbian battery has been a dirty secret in the lesbian community, which has promoted lesbian couples as the epitome of equal, utopian relationships. Lesbian battery occurs for many of the same reasons as in the heterosexual population—feelings of inadequacy and the need to dominate and control—but may also be aggravated by internalized homophobia. A lesbian battered by her lesbian lover is not recognized by society's laws and social programs.

Employment Issues

It was the result of a group of lesbians and feminists that included Kate Millett and Barbara Love picketing *The New York Times* that help-wanted ads became integrated. Prior listings were sex segregated with professional job listings for males, and temporary, dead-end, and much lower-paying job listings for females. It was also the custom for employers to take a "female discount" of up to 25 percent off the salary for any job given to a female since that female was not trusted to stay on the job. This practice also ended.

Comparable pay for comparable worth is still an issue. In 2001, women in the United States earned 74 cents per dollar of what males earned. The gender wage gap is somewhat smaller in parts of Western Europe, and much larger in Asia, Latin America, and Africa. It remains unacceptably large despite some narrowing over the years; the wage difference in the United States was 61 cents per dollar in 1972. Males with a high-school education stand to earn more than women with college educations, and males earn more even in predominantly female job classifications. Thus, women and lesbians have less earning power than males. Earning power is also seen as economic political clout, with discretionary monies left over from paying living costs available to fund prolesbian, prowomen political candidates.

Other employment issues remain for lesbians (and gay men). These issues include employment and job discrimination, and discrimination in employee benefits. The oppressive McCarthy era of the early 1950s led to President Dwight D. Eisenhower issuing an executive order prohibiting the hiring of homosexuals in federal service. Gays and lesbians began to protest federal job discrimination and discrimination in the military service in the mid-1960s. In many jobs and careers, there are moral turpitude clauses which prohibit homosexual practices even in private. Teaching is one such profession. Thus, lesbians must remain closeted to hold these jobs. Women can be fired or not even hired if they appear to be lesbian. In the United States there are two restaurant chains that have refused to hire and have fired women whom they thought to be lesbian, even if such is not the case. Unless there are antidiscrimination ordinances based on sexual orientation for that municipality, the women have no legal recourse. The federal Employment Non-Discrimination Act, which would give legal recourse, has failed to be passed by Congress (the last time it failed by one vote). President Bill Clinton issued an executive order in April 1999 which prohibits discrimination based on sexual orientation in the federal government, but excludes the military from having to abide by this.

The other area in which being an out lesbian or being accused of being a lesbian is detrimental to one's employment or career is in the U.S.

military service. Homosexuals were prohibited from serving in the U.S. military, and though many did and did so meritoriously, there were systemic purges of lesbians (and gays). Sergeant Johnnie Phelps, when asked by General Eisenhower to put together a list of lesbians, told him her name would be on the top of the list. The "Don't Ask, Don't Tell, Don't Pursue" policy adopted in 1991 in the wake of President Clinton's failed attempt to integrate the military, has increased the number of discharges based on homosexuality, and more women are being discharged then men. This may be in part due to lesbian baiting of women if they decline a male's sexual advances. Most countries have lesbian (and gay male) tolerant military policies. Of the countries belonging to the North Atlantic Treaty Organization (NATO), for instance, only the United States and Turkey prohibit lesbians and gay men from (openly) serving in their military forces.

Inheritance and Property Rights

Lesbians have been active globally to change inheritance rights so that women may own property and inherit property. In many countries such as those in the Middle East, citizenship is tied to property ownership, and if women are not allowed to own property, they are not recognized as citizens with rights. The lack of the right to inherit property and titles is another issue that affects women. These issues have been raised at the United Nations Conferences on Women.

Inheritance rights for lesbians in North America and Western Europe means gaining legal recognition of their same-sex relationships, which will allow them to inherit their partner's property without challenges.

Antigay Politics

During the 1970s the push for gay and lesbian civil rights, modeled on the black Civil Rights movement, gained some purchase in American political life. Ordinances and legislation were being proposed and passed on the municipal, county, and state level that would prohibit discrimination based on sexual orientation. Gay and lesbian rights planks were being proposed for inclusion in the Democratic National Platform and Congresspersons Bella Abzug and Ed Koch (both D-NY) even proposed a federal Gay Civil Rights Bill to Congress in 1974.

In the mid- to late 1970s, a conservative backlash against gays and lesbians resulted in arson at known homosexual clubs and churches. The Religious Right was beginning to become active. In early 1977, Anita Byrant led the "Save Our Children" campaign against homosexual rights in Florida. These and other incidents of backlash helped to reactivate the movement among both men and women.

The antifeminist backlash can also be seen as antilesbian since the result is that heterosexual feminists and activists are erasing, submerging, or covering up (what some lesbians call "disappearing") the involvement of lesbians in abortion rights work, especially at abortion clinics, in the battered women's movement, rape crisis centers, and in other activist areas in homophobic fear that all will be labeled dykes.

The guise of protecting family values is a hypocritical one since many of the defenders of family values have broken their own marriage vows. The idea that heterosexual marriages and families need protection from homosexuals belies the evidence that points to heterosexual men being more destructive of family values. Many males do not maintain monogamous relationships, 50 to 70 percent of marriages end in divorce, heterosexual men are the majority of pedophiles, and most lesbians and gay men are the offspring of heterosexual parents. Another fact that is overlooked in the use of family values to form backlash public policies that are punitive to women is that the same percentage of single-parent households existed in 1999 as at the turn of the twentieth century. The Religious Right has used this guise to become vehemently antigay and antiwoman. They believe that by denying lesbians and gay men the right to marry or join in civil union with their partners (and thus have the same rights that heterosexual married couples enjoy), the heterosexual marriage will be strengthened. Their antigay agenda includes denying gays and lesbians their equal rights, or what the RR calls their "special rights." Many individuals and groups funded by the Religious Right have even openly attacked homosexuals physically, at the ballot box, and via legislative initiatives.

The conservative Religious Right began to organize and fight gay rights initiatives. Since the 1970s, the Religious Right has been proposing antigay referendum and ballot initiatives. These initiatives allow the general public to vote on whether lesbians and gays are to be permitted the civil rights that other Americans enjoy. The first antigay campaign was led by Anita Bryant to repeal Dade County, Florida's Gay Rights ordinance in 1977. This campaign was called "Save Our Children" and was a premonition of the family values campaigns that the Religious Right would use in future fights to limit the rights of lesbians and gays. The "Save Our Children" campaign used misinformation about pedophilia and the destruction of families by homosexuals to scare voters into repealing the law.

While initiatives in other states such as the Briggs Initiative in California were not as successful, others, such as Colorado's Amendment 2, were successful at the voting booth. It was successful because the Religious Right portrayed gay and lesbian rights as being special rights that would diminish other people's civil rights. Amendment 2 stated that there was "no protected status based on homosexual, lesbian or bisexual orientation" and the government and agencies of the state could not entitle any such person to "claim any minority status. . . . or claim of discrimination," thus repealing any existing gay/lesbian rights ordinances and prohibiting any new ones. This was brought before the U.S. Supreme Court in 1996 (*Romer, Governor of Colorado, et al. v. Evans, et al.* [94–1039] 517 U.S. 620 1996). In a landmark decision, the court found that Amendment 2 violated the constitutional rights of lesbians and gays as per the Fourteenth Amendment to the U.S. Constitution, which guarantees equal protection of the laws to all citizens.

While this has put a damper on antigay ballot initiatives, the Religious Right continues to propose such initiatives. For example, in 2002 there were many antigay initiatives were on local ballots, including one in Dade County, Florida, which was labeled "Anita Bryant II." The majority of these antigay referendums failed, including Anita Bryant II.

The Religious Right has also continued to fight lesbian and gay rights by promoting family values. The RR uses social differences (sexual orientation, race, etc.) as a source of division in communities that are struggling with the anxieties of economic downturns. By focusing on the other(s) as the cause of concern, as the cause of "moral decay," the RR can promote their view of community, thus carrying on the culture war against liberal, progressive ideas, and those groups of individuals that represent those ideas. Their strength is seen as a political one since their misinformation campaign focuses on issues such as school curricula, which has resulted in the removal of the multicultural Rainbow Curriculum in New York City's public schools. The Religious Right's fight to deny same-sex marriage rights to gays and lesbians has resulted in the federal Defense of Marriage Act and the promotion of the ex-gay movement.

The ex-gay movement is founded on the idea that homosexuality is a choice, and that through embracing Jesus, homosexuals can make the "correct" choice and become heterosexual. The ex-gay movement is directly tied to the Religious Right in both its theory, practice, and funding. There is a secular group of psychologists, the National Association for Research and Therapy on Homosexuality, which promotes secular reparative therapy to convert homosexuals into normative heterosexuals.

Antigay religious fundamentalism is not limited to the United States. There are religious fundamentalist groups rallying around homophobic "family values" campaigns in countries such as the United Kingdom. But antigay sentiment is not limited to the conservative religious fringe: in November 2000, the Vatican released a seventy-six-page response to countries the recognize same-sex unions and adoptions. "Family, Marriage and 'De Facto' Unions" states that recognition of lesbian and gay marriages and adoption, besides being a grave danger to children, is a "serious sign of the contemporary breakdown in the social and moral conscience" of society.

AIDS Activism and Lesbian Health

During the early 1980s, a health crisis developed in the gay male community with AIDS/HIV. The local and federal government were not responding to the number of persons contracting AIDS/HIV, except to pass legislation to legitimate a sex panic to close gay bath houses and bars, and to increase police surveillance at other facilities where sexual encounters might happen. Medical research was minimally funded.

This crisis had a profound effect on the gay and lesbian community, politics, and culture since as of 1996, over 250,000 gay men and 8,000 lesbians had been infected in the United States alone. Globally, over 5 million men and women were estimated to be infected. In Africa, 55 percent of all adult women are infected with the AIDS virus because the social imperative to procreate does not allow them to have the sexual self-determination necessary to either reject sexual advances by males or to use condoms. Lesbians and gay men set up health-related service centers across the country and began education campaigns to stem the antigay and lesbian fears and prejudices. Lesbians contributed greatly to the support of gay men with AIDS and joined direct groups such as ACT-Up in the political fight to gain funding for research and medicines, and to gain recognition of the antigay discrimination in all areas—housing, health care, and employment—because of irrational fears of AIDS.

Several lesbians active in ACT-Up asked that the group also pursue and challenge not only how the government and society deals with males with AIDS/HIV health issues, but also how women (and lesbians) with AIDS/HIV are treated—including challenging the Centers for Disease Control's (CDC) definition of lesbian with AIDS/HIV for purposes of study and treatment. Their requests were dismissed by the gay male leaders, so the lesbians became activists in their own right. The birth of Lesbian Avengers, one of the key lesbian activist groups of the 1990s and into the new century, can directly be tied to lesbian issues being silenced in the AIDS movement.

Lesbian activists also brought to light other lesbian health issues, such as breast and ovarian cancer, that are affecting the lesbian community in greater proportion than the heterosexual population. Because lesbians are an invisible population and part of the population of women, they have doubly been excluded from access to adequate health care, they are not represented in clinical studies, and they may also receive inadequate care because of their reluctance to come out to their medical or mental health care worker fearing discrimination or sexual abuse.

As shown by Karen Thompson's protracted fight to gain guardianship of her critically disabled partner, Sharon Kowalski, so that she may be actively involved with Sharon's medical treatment and recovery, lesbians also need to have their partners involved in their health care issues and decisions where appropriate. Lesbian (and gay male) couples need to have over two hundred legal documents to replicate the same legal rights and privileges that a heterosexual married couple enjoys. And, if the lesbian partner should die, the surviving partner needs to have clear inheritance rights that may not be challenged by homophobic family members of the deceased.

Assimilation into Liberal Politics

Currently, the two largest national organizations in the United States —the National Gay and Lesbian Task Force and the Human Rights

Campaign—are at the forefront of setting a more assimilationist agenda for the lesbian and gay populations. The moderate to progressive agenda focuses on gay marriage/domestic partnership, gay adoption and child custody issues, as well as ending gay and lesbian discrimination in employment, employment benefits, health care, and equal/civil rights. The lesbian and gay activism is taking place in the mainstream political world of public policy and legal reforms. In some cases, this assimilation is leading to the endorsement by major lesbian and gay organizations of incumbent political candidates with poor lesbian/gay voting records over their challengers who are more lesbian/gay supportive.

Gays and lesbians are currently working to educate the public and to pass legislation and initiatives to achieve equality. They are trying to prove that even though they have a different sexual orientation, they are still good citizens and deserve to participate in the institutions and the protections of the state. There is some dissension among these groups as equal employment and housing rights have been supplanted by gays in the military and same-sex marriage issues. But the work they have done has borne fruit in some cases, such as the presidential executive order ending sexual orientation discrimination in the federal civil service. In other instances, such as gays in the military, while there are no longer purges of homosexuals, the "Don't Ask, Don't Tell" policy is still resulting in a higher proportion of women being discharged from military service than men, not to mention that this policy is grossly unequal and squelches the civil rights of the homosexual in favor of the comfort of the heterosexual. Hate crimes still happen, and the Employment Non-Discrimination Act has yet to be passed.

The concern exists that the mainstream lesbian (and gay) movements are not just movements for (comparable) civil rights granted to the recognized normative citizen. There needs to be consistent and constant critiques of such political activities. For instance, there should have been a lesbian-feminist critique of the institution of marriage before the right to marry became one of the primary goals on the movement's agenda. There needs to be a thorough analysis of what equality means and if it means assimilation- or inclusion-tolerating differences. If equality means inclusion in the heteropatriarchy without transforming society, then equal terms would mimic the existing sexist society. With this unreflective goal, lesbians would still not be equal since women are not fully equal. Without such critiques, there is a tendency to make lesbians, their needs, and issues indistinguishable from those of gay men as if sexism did not exist. This has been the argument of lesbians such as Del Martin, Sheila Jeffreys, and Sara Schulman who feel that lesbians are subsumed by the older Gay Liberation movement, the contemporary Gay Rights movement, and the Queer movement.[33]

White gay men complain when lesbianism and issues related to people of color are supported by gay and lesbian rights organizations. This also reenforces the concern that lesbians (and persons of color) have had all along, that there may be no commonality between gay men and lesbians except that they both make same-sex sexual object choices. According to Urvashi Vaid, the white gay males' attitudes, coupled with the focus on sexual orientation, reenforces rather than transforms society.

There are also concerns that there is a materialist capitalist undertone to the assimilationalist movement, since lesbians (and gays) are being actively marketed in the American consumer culture.

Lesbian activism is taking place at the grassroots level as well as nationally. Lesbians are fighting for visibility and their rights around the world. Current issues include coparent adoptions, custody, and visitation rights. Lesbians are actively working against the feminization of poverty, racism, classism, and discrimination based on sexual identity. Lesbians have been on the forefront working on issues that concern women's autonomy.

Queer Theory and Lesbian Activism at the Turn of the New Century

The gender fluidity of queer theory and activism is at the same time controversial and accepted within lesbian politics. Controversial in so much as the identity "lesbian woman" is being submerged into other, more male-identified identities. Lesbian-feminist critics of queer theory raise concerns that it is based on a deviance model of sex and sexual practice. Accepted, because lesbian politics has been about sexual liberation and the questioning of the social construction of sexual identity and being has been part of lesbian culture, queer activists and lesbian activists are pushing for more inclusionary politics. The confrontational, transgressive, and transformative nature of queer politics is very familiar to lesbian activists.

There are also concerns that lesbians are being influenced by gay male sexuality to such an extent that young lesbians are assuming male names and calling themselves by terminology that identifies their sexual practice (boyz, andros, etc.). This supports sexism, if not heterosexuality, and a male gay agenda. Some of these lesbians are even transitioning to males. There is also a trend toward lesbians (and gay men) being sexually involved with and even marrying members of the opposite sex, yet still calling themselves "lesbian" (or in the case of "gay" men, gay).

While current Supreme Court decisions point to more political tolerance of lesbians and gays in the United States, some decisions also underscore that same-sex conduct is still unacceptable and may be criminal, for example, *Bowers v. Hardwick* (1985) which upheld the state of Georgia's sodomy laws as applied to homosexuals and heterosexuals. The 2002–2003 Supreme Court session will hear an equal protection case which challenges a Texas law which criminalizes same-sex sodomy only. According to *Romer v. Evans* (1996), just being lesbian or gay was not seen as a reason to disallow equal political participation and protection. This case overturned Colorado's Amendment 2, which had precluded any governmental agency in the state to decree that homosexuals were a minority, so that as a minority, gays and lesbians may not be discriminated against. The latest Supreme Court decision that affects gays and lesbians was made in June 2000. *Boy Scouts of America v. Dale* upheld the Boys Scouts' right to exclude known or found-out gay members. Although the Boy Scouts are considered to be a public accommodation, since they are open to all boys and receive government funding, the case was decided on the right of the Boy Scouts to express their values which deem homosexuality counter to the moral-value message of the Boy Scouts. Since that decision is in favor of discrimination against gays for just being gay, many organizations which fund or provide services and space to the Boy Scouts have rescinded such support because of this exclusionary practice.

These actions, coupled with surveys across the United States, have shown that the American people believe that lesbians and gays deserve the same rights and protections against discrimination in housing and employment. Alan Wolfe's sociological studies and surveys of middle-class Americans have indicated that while they disapprove of homosexuality, they believe that lesbians and gay men should have the same rights as all other citizens.[34] It is when implied sexual conduct is included, for example discussion of same-sex marriage, that the American public becomes less tolerant of their fellow citizens.

International Lesbian Movement

While it appears that the contemporary lesbian and gay movements is measured by American standards, lesbians and gays have made greater strides toward achieving their political and civil rights in other countries such as South Africa, Denmark, the Netherlands, and New Zealand. In the Netherlands, for example, the Dutch government has been responsive in funding lesbian research and projects, and included lesbian issues on the agenda it brought to the 1985 United Nations Women's Conference in Nairobi, Kenya. In 1994, the Equal Rights Act formalized the equality between heterosexuals and homosexuals, and as of April 2001, same-sex marriages and adoptions are recognized.

Yet in still other countries such as Spain, Sudan, Malaysia, Ecuador, Saudi Arabia, and other Middle Eastern countries, lesbians (and gay men) are still invisible or persecuted. There are some countries where male homosexuality is specifically prohibited, but since women either do not matter or are not seen as sexual beings, the law remains silent on their sexuality. These countries include Zimbabwe, Japan, Nigeria, Ireland, and India among others. Still other countries have no legal restrictions on homosexuality, but there may exist cultural ones such as in Mexico, Poland, Italy, Panama, South Korea, Taiwan, and others.

There is, thus, a wide range of acceptance or not of lesbianism from considering homosexual activity as a cultural taboo or illegal (from crimes against public moral charges to specific mention of homosexual acts) to the acceptance of the fluidity of gender and sexual activity. International gay and lesbian human rights organizations are working with local grassroots lesbian and gay organizations to transform all social and political attitudes about gender and sexuality into attitudes of acceptance.

The same issue of sexism and male-identified privilege exists within the dominant international groups such as the International Gay and Lesbian Association. A lesbian-only group was formed in the late 1970s to focus on lesbian issues. This group, International Lesbian Information Service (ILIS), provides a forum for communication and information on issues among lesbians and for lesbians, as well as providing a network for lesbian activists. The ILIS participated in international political conferences such as the 1995 United Nations Conference on Women in Beijing, China, and in more social events such as the Gay Games. There are also regional lesbian-specific international groups. The two biggest ones are the Asian Lesbian Network (ALN) and the Caribbean and Latin American Encuentros de Lesbianas Feministas. Both groups hold conferences and provide networking opportunities for lesbians living within their region and for those outside. There is also an Arab lesbian network that exists mainly on the Internet.

Some religiously affiliated international groups also exist such as the World Congress of Gay and Lesbian Jewish Organizations and the Universal Fellowship of Metropolitan Community Churches.

The International Lesbian and Gay Association (ILGA) is a federation of over 300 organizations. It holds annual world conferences of LGBT leaders. The 2002 conference, the twenty-first held in Oakland, California, had one hundred lesbian, bisexual, gay, and transgendered leaders from over forty countries in attendance. An unfunded Women's Secretariat exists within the ILGA which follows, advises, and takes action on lesbian, bisexual, and transgendered women's issues. There are also organizations that monitor human rights violations based on sexual orientation, gender identity, and HIV status such as the International Gay and Lesbian Human Rights Commission (IGLHRC). IGLHRC also provides assistance to grassroots lesbian groups in developing countries, as well as ensuring lesbian visibility and participation at global conferences. Amnesty International, a non-homosexual human rights organization, has also begun to monitor abuses based on sexual orientation.

The international lesbian and gay movement is greatly influenced, though, by the Catholic Church and Islamic law, and when it comes to funding of the United Nations, by the Religious Right in America. This influence makes a lot of the work harder and more incremental.

The effect of globalization is seen in the lesbian (and gay) rights movement as forcing the movement to be more inclusive, and to respect the diversity of its constituency and the diverse needs of such a constituency. For lesbians, this also means that the sociopatriarchy needs to be transformed so that sexism and heterosexism are erased, and racism and classism are eradicated. Education about alternatives to the binary homosexual/heterosexual model of sexuality are necessary, as is education about alternatives to a patriarchal sexist society.

Conclusion

In summation, the Lesbian Liberation movement, while it may not be so identified in the twenty-first century because of the datedness of the 1960s' term "liberation movement," is still an active movement working toward lesbian visibility, lesbian inclusion in the modern nation-state definition of citizen, as well as to challenge existing social and political institutions. The push for lesbians to be included in the category citizen in the modern state, and for them to be afforded the same rights, protections, and freedoms as other citizens, is being made on many fronts around the world:

- In academia, Lesbian Studies is the standard bearer making lesbian herstory and politics visible through research, archival work, philosophical reflection, publication, and education.[35]
- In popular culture, through the introduction of lesbian characters in television from soap operas to prime-time shows, in films, in literature as well as pulp fiction, making lesbians visible and tolerable in mainstream society. Now the lesbian character does not have to die.
- In mainstream politics, through the work of assimilation lesbian and gay-rights groups working to bring issues of equal treatment and protection of lesbians and gay citizens to the fore, and through the political careers of out lesbian elected and appointed officials.
- In lesbian communities, strengthening and reenforcing lesbian values, culture, resources, and economics, and challenging the underpinnings of accepted institutions such as marriage and military service from a lesbian-feminist perspective.
- In the streets, with pride at dyke marches and politics in dyke/lesbian actions.

The people working on these various fronts, along with the myriad of lesbian organizations—political and social—make lesbian liberation a movement. They are all working toward the same goals, but not in the same way. They are helping lesbians to become visible—politically and socially—and to claim their rightful space.

In 1970, Sidney Abbott edited the first lines of the Radicalesbian manifesto *Woman-Identified Woman* to be more striking, to catch the attention of all women, to ring true to all women, and to connect sexism and heterosexism: "What is a lesbian? A Lesbian is the rage of all women condensed to the point of explosion."[36] Lesbian liberation is still the rage.

Notes

1. Michel Foucault. *The History of Sexuality, vol. 1, An Introduction.* New York: Penguin, 1981 (Fr: 1976). Kate Millett. *Sexual Politics.* New York: Simon and Schuster, 1969, 1990.

2. Both women's liberation and gay liberation owe much to the Civil Rights movement and the New Left including the Antiwar (Vietnam) movement. These movements not only gave a language of civil rights to both the women's and gay movements, but also served as a training ground, since a majority of early participants in the newer movements had participated in the Civil Rights movements and/or the New Left.

3. Carol Hanisch. "The Personal Is Political." In *Redstockings: Feminist Revolution.* New York: Random House, 1978, pp. 204–205.

4. Sappho also had relationships with the opposite sex.

5. Lillian Faderman. *To Believe in Women: What Lesbians Have Done for America— A History.* Boston: Houghton Mifflin, 1999, p. 3.

6. *Lesbian Almanac.* New York: Berkeley Books, 1996, p. 7.

7. Because Paragraph 175 was still enforced, making male homosexuals criminals, male homosexuals held in Nazi concentration camps were not liberated when the Allies freed their fellow (noncriminal) inmates at the end of World War II in 1945.

8. Gay males curtailed their promiscuous sexual practices when the advent of HIV/AIDS was linked to unsafe sexual practices and multiple partnering.

9. Beginning in the late 1990s, there are drag kings, women who impersonate men—as opposed to cross-dressing women who pass as men to gain some of society's privileges.

10. Barbara Love. In conversations. Truro, Mass. June–July, 1999, Easthampton, N.Y. August 1, 1999, and via telephone August 15, 1999.

11. Sidney Abbott and Barbara Love. *Sappho Was a Right-On Woman.* New York: Stein and Day, 1972, p. 136.

12. T-Grace Atkinson. *Amazon Odyessy.* New York: Links, 1968.

13. Sidney Abbott and Barbara Love. "Is Women's Liberation a Lesbian Plot?" In Vivian Gornick and B. Moran. *Woman in Sexist Society.* New York: Basic Books, 1971, p. 601.

14. Radicalesbians. "Woman-Identified Woman." N. p. 1970. This article can be found at http://scriptorium.lib.duke.edu/wlm/womid.

15. "Lavender Herring" was a play on the concept of an argument's "red herring" that would tend to mislead or redirect an argument from its original point.

16. Love & Abbott, in Gornick & Moran, p. 614.

17. Artemis March. In conversation. August 15, 1999.

18. Artemis March and Sidney Abbott. In conversations. Truro, Mass. June 1999.

19. Carol Hanisch in remarks at the ninth Women & Society Conference, Marist College, Poughkeepsie, N.Y. June 8, 1999.

20. Artemis March. In conversation. Truro, Mass. June 1999.

21. Artemis March in remarks at the ninth Women & Society Conference, Marist College, Poughkeepsie, N.Y. June 12, 1999; and in conversations, Kingston, N.Y., and Truro, Mass. June 1999; on the telephone March, May, June, and August, 1999. She has said this is the part of the WIW that is the most misinterpreted: not all women have to be lesbians but they should be woman-identified, they should value women apart from women's value and relationship to men.

22. The Furies, 1972. In Charlotte Bunch. *Passionate Politics.* New York: St. Martin's Press, 1987, p.167.

23. Charlotte Bunch. *Passionate Politics.* New York: St. Martin's Press, 1987, p. 164.

24. Marilyn Fyre. *The Politics of Reality: Essays in Feminist Theory.* New York: The Crossing Press, 1983, p. 140.

25. Monique Wittig. *The Straight Mind and Other Essays.* Boston: Beacon, 1992, p. 20.

26. Ibid., p. 30.

27. Sheila Jeffreys. "The Queer Disappearance of Lesbians: Sexuality in the Academy." *Women's Studies International Forum* 17 (1994): p. 461.

28. Annamarie Jagose. *Queer Theory.* New York: New York University Press, 1996, p. 75.

29. Ibid., p. 84. Sidney Abbott. In conversation. Truro, Mass. July 1999.

30. The lesbian rights movement in France remained connected with the feminist movement, though the lesbians were marginalized and accused by heterosexual women seeking equality while maintaining relationships with males, of derailing the movement with their radical attacks on the patriarchy.

31. Andrea Dworkin and Catherine MacKinnon among others.

32. Joan Nestle, Pat Califia, and Amber Hollibaugh among others.

33. Sheila Jeffreys. *The Lesbian Heresy.* Australia: Spinifex Press, 1993; Del Martin. In conversation. National Women's Studies Conference, Boston, Mass. June 17, 2000, and in "Sexism of Gay Men" in *The Advocate,* 1970; and Sarah Schulman. *My American History.* New York: Routledge, 1994, and in conversation, August 2000, among others.

34. Alan Wolfe. *One Nation, After All.* New York: Viking, 1998.

35. Lesbian Studies may stand alone as an academic discipline, but usually it is subsumed in Women's Studies, Gender Studies, Gay Studies, or Gay and Lesbian Studies, or, more recently, Queer Studies.

36. Radicalesbians. "Woman-Identified Woman." N.p., 1970.

References

Apuzzo, Virginia. In private conversations. January 1996–December 1999; 2001–2003.

Birkby, Phyllis et. al., eds. *Amazon Expedition.* Washington, D.C.: Times Change Press, 1973.

Califia, Pat, and Robin Sweeney. *The Second Coming.* Los Angeles: Alyson, 1996.

Clendinen, Dudley, and Adam Nagourney. *Out for Good.* New York: Simon and Shuster, 1999.

Cruikshank, Margaret. *The Gay and Lesbian Liberation Movement.* New York: Routledge, 1992.

D'Emilio, John. *Sexual Politics, Sexual Communities.* 2nd edition. Chicago: University of Chicago Press, 1998.

Duggan, Lisa, and Nan Hunter. *Sex Wars.* New York: Routledge, 1995.

Dworkin, Andrea. At Women & Society Conference and in conversation, Poughkeepsie, N.Y. June 1997.

Freeman, Jo. *The Politics of Women's Liberation.* New York: David MacKay, 1975.

Goodman, George, et al. *No Turning Back: Lesbian and Gay Liberation for the '80s.* Philadelphia: New Society, 1983.

Grier, Barbara, and C. Reid, eds. *The Lavender Herring.* Baltimore: Diana Press, 1976.

Halperin, David. *Saint Foucault.* New York: Oxford University Press, 1995.

Hanisch, Carol. 9th Women & Society Conference. Poughkeepsie, N.Y. June 11, 1999.

Jay, Karla. *Tales of the Lavender Menace.* New York: Basic Books, 1999.

Jay, Karla, and Allen Young, eds. *Out of the Closet.* New York: New York University Press, 1992.

——. At the National Women's Studies Association Conference. Oswego, N.Y. June 1998.

Katz, Jonathan Ned. *Gay American History.* New York: Meridian, 1992.

Koedt, Anne, E. Levine, and A. Rapone, eds. *Radical Feminism.* New York: Quadrangle Books, 1973.

Leeds Revolutionary Feminists. *Love Your Enemy?* London: Onlywoman Press, 1981.

Linden, Robin Ruth, et al. *Against Sadomasochism: A Radical Feminist Analysis.* Palo Alto, Calif.: Frog in The Well, 1982.

Martin, Del, and Phyllis Lyon. *Lesbian/Woman.* Volcano, Calif.: Volcano Press, 1991.

Millett, Kate. In on-going private conversations. 1987–2003.

The National Museum and Archive of Lesbian and Gay History, comps. *The Lesbian Almanac*. New York: Berkely Books, 1996.

Pellegrini, Ann. 9th Women & Society Conference, June 12, 1999, in conversations, and Center for Lesbian and Gay Studies Seminars, New York, Fall 1998 and June 1999.

Radicalesbians. "Woman-Identified Woman." *Out of the Closets, 20th Anniversary Edition*. Karla Jay and Allen Young, eds. New York: New York University Press, 1997.

Rich, Adrienne. "Compulsory Heterosexuality and Lesbian Existence." *Signs*, 5,4 (1980): p. 648.

—— *Blood, Bread and Poetry*. New York: Norton, 1986.

Stein, Arlene. *Sisters, Sexperts, Queers: Beyond the Lesbian Nation*. New York: Plume Book, 1993.

—— *The Stranger Next Door*. Boston: Beacon Press, 2001.

Vaid, Urvashi. *Virtual Equality*. New York: Anchor/Doubleday, 1995.

Weed, Elizabeth, and Naomi Schor, eds. *Feminism Meets Queer Theory*. Bloomington: Indiana University Press, 1997.

Wittig, Monique. *The Straight Mind and Other Essays*. Boston: Beacon, 1992.

THE DICTIONARY

– A –

ABBOTT, BERENICE (1898–1991). Photographer. She is known for her photographs of writers and artists in 1920s Paris. Among those who sat for her portraits were members of the expatriate lesbian salons such as those of writer Djuna Barnes (q.v.) and her lover, the sculptor Thelma Wood. Her portraits are relaxed and revealing. Abbott is also known for her compelling architectural photographs of New York City prior to World War II.

ABBOTT, SIDNEY (1937–). Author with Barbara Love (q.v.) of *Sappho Was a Right-On Woman* (1972), the first book about lesbians by lesbians that relates lesbianism to feminism (q.v.), both the connections and the tensions therein. The other piece she wrote with Barbara Love is "Is Women's Liberation a Lesbian Plot?", which has been anthologized in many collections. This piece explains that lesbians have been in the feminist/women's movement all along, and that "the common enemy of feminists and lesbians is sexism (q.v.)." Abbott and Love were among the early feminists to join the Gay Liberation movement. They were both members of CR One (q.v.). Abbott was on the board of the National Gay Task Force (q.v.). She was also the first out (q.v.) lesbian to serve on a community board in New York City. Abbott is currently active in lesbian health, class, and aging issues (qq.v.).

ABORTION RIGHTS MOVEMENT. The movement initially to secure and then protect the right to abortion for women. In the United States (q.v.), women in New York State first gained the right to abortion by legislation passed in 1970. Nationally, the right to terminate a pregnancy through the second trimester was given to women by the Supreme Court decision *Roe v. Wade* (410 US 113 [1973]) as part of a woman's right to privacy. This right has been eroded by various court decisions and state and federal legislation depending on the woman's economic need and age. The Religious Right (q.v.), operating under various guises such as Operation Rescue (q.v.), has successfully lobbied for legislative changes that limit women's access to information about abortion as an alternative, as well as physically blocking access to health clinics and threatening (and in some cases murdering) health care providers.

Lesbians also have been active in securing the right to abortion in European countries. Lesbian-feminists have been active in the abortion rights movement because they realize the connection between bodily autonomy and sexual liberation.

ABZUG, BELLA SAVITSKY (1920–1998). Former Congresswoman from New York and activist. Abzug founded the Women's Strike for Peace (1961–1970) and the National Women's Political Caucus (1971). She also founded Women's Environment and Development Organization (WEDO), one of the prominent nongovernmental organizations (NGOs) at the United Nations Women's Conferences in Mexico City, Nairobi, and Beijing (qq.v.).

Abzug was elected in 1970 to the first of three terms in the United States House of Representatives. On May 21, 1970, as Democratic candidate for the nineteenth district (New York) congressional seat, Abzug became the first U.S. politician to openly court the gay and lesbian communities' votes when she met with the Gay Activists Alliance (q.v.). She and then Congressman Ed Koch proposed the first federal lesbian and gay civil rights legislation, H.R. 5452, the Civil Rights Amendment of 1975, which sought to end discrimination based on "affectional or sexual preference." Abzug supported Kate Millett when Betty Friedan (qq.v.) did not, which led to Friedan resigning from the Women's Strike for Peace.

ACHTENBERG, ROBERTA (1951–). Former San Francisco Board of Supervisor member, Achtenberg has worked as a civil rights attorney and teaching fellow at Stanford (California) Law School. She has also served as executive director of the National Center for Lesbian

Rights and dean of the New College of California School of Law. In 1993 Achtenberg became the first openly lesbian (or gay) person confirmed by the U.S. Senate. She served as Assistant Secretary for Housing and Urban Development from 1993 until she resigned in 1995 and returned to California.

ACQUIRED IMMUNE DEFICIENCY SYNDROME/HUMAN IMMUNODEFICIENCY VIRUS (AIDS/HIV). HIV is the virus that can develop into full-blown AIDS. Fully developed AIDS is that point in which an opportunistic disease may kill the person with AIDS (PWA). First called the "gay cancer" because it was found in the gay male population in the early 1980s, HIV/AIDS is nondiscriminatory and may be communicated among sexual partners, through blood transfusions, and with intravenous drug usage. Most of the research has centered around gay men. Women (and lesbians) who become HIV-positive and/or develop AIDS manifest different symptoms than men. Research on HIV/AIDS and women/lesbians is still minimal in part due to the fact that the Centers for Disease Control (CDC) in the United States defines lesbians as women who have had no sexual contact with a male since before 1976. Most lesbians do not fit the CDC's definition; because of compulsory heterosexuality and lesbian continuum (qq.v.), many lesbians come out (q.v.) after being in sexual relationships or marriages with males. Also, due to the primacy of gay males contracting AIDS, women with AIDS have been overlooked. The Lesbian Avengers (q.v.) was formed partly in response to the invisibility of lesbians and women in the fight for more AIDS research. This is especially true, as the statistics released on World Aids Day, December 1, 2002, reveal that women are currently contracting HIV/AIDS at the same rate as men.

AIDS is rampant in Africa among the adult population. Of the 5.4 million new AIDS patients in 1999, 4 million of them lived in Africa. These numbers, unfortunately, have remained relatively constant—in 2002 out of 5 million new cases, 3.5 million were in Sub-Saharan Africa. Sub-Saharan Africa has 12.1 million children orphaned by AIDS and 90 percent of all children in the world living with AIDS (of which 470,000 will die each year). Children contract AIDS through their mother at birth or through their own sexual activity. AIDS has reduced the life expectancy in Zimbabwe (q.v.), for instance, from 61 years of age to 33. In Asia, women who have been sold into prostitution are also contracting HIV/AIDS. In some countries, sexworkers are prohibited by their pimps from demanding that their johns use condoms.

The number of PWA worldwide is leading to a crisis. Political leaders with the support of NGOs have asked that the drugs used to mitigate AIDS/HIV be made available generically. But to date the United States (q.v.) has upheld the proprietary nature of drug formula so that drug companies may recoup their research costs. The high cost of proprietary drugs also affects their availability to those persons around the world with AIDS who do not have health insurance or are not able to pay.

ACTIVISM. Activism is broadly defined as participation in political or social movements. It is the practice of engaging politically, socially, and/or culturally to change society. Participation may assume a support role or a public one and range from taking a political stance on an issue to doing something publicly to make others aware of the issue. Actions range from being out (q.v.) lesbians to taking part in pride marches and direct actions (qq.v.) or protests.

Lesbians have been active in many of the political movements from the first wave of feminism (q.v.), also known as the suffrage movement, to social reform movements, labor movements, the Civil Rights movement, and the New Left, as well as the second wave of feminism (q.v.) and the issue movements that were spawned from that, such as abortion rights (q.v.) and battered women (a.k.a., domestic violence [q.v.]). Lesbians were also active in the modern Homophile movement taking part in public protests of governmental policies and practices such as the 1965 demonstration in front of the White House. The Gay and Lesbian Rights movement also had issue-related offshoots in which lesbians were quite active such as AIDS activism, the fight against homophobia, and the antigay and lesbian political initiatives (qq.v.).

Lesbians have also been very active in procuring and protecting their rights, from the more social activism of the Daughters of Bilitis, through the more political and radical lesbian-feminist and separatist movements, to the more contemporary Lesbian Avengers (qq.v.) among other groups. Lesbian Avengers have chapters in cities around the world. Grassroots lesbian activism is prevalent in many countries. This may take the form of providing social venues and alternatives to political activity. For some women, simply living as out lesbians is a political act—since lesbianism challenges the hegemonic patriarchal (q.v.) culture. Thus, being an out lesbian is an act of resistance (q.v.). Many lesbians live their lives practicing their feminist values as they create alternative women's cultures and communities (q.v.). While some of the contemporary radical lesbian activists have joined in the Queer (q.v.) movement engaging all gender identities and sexualities, still others are intent on not having the lesbian identity submerged, and thus, have remained lesbian separatist or dyke (qq.v.) activists. While many lesbian activists focus on lesbian-related issues or single issues such as domestic violence (q.v.), they have also formed coalitions with other groups such as environmentalists and civil rights organizations to affect change. Some lesbians have joined with the mainstream gay and lesbian rights groups such as the National Gay and Lesbian Task Force (NGLTF) and the Human Rights Campaign (HRC) (qq.v.) in the United States.

A good organizing tool is *The Lesbian Avenger Handbook: A Handy Guide to Homemade Revolution* self-published by Sarah Schulman (q.v.); it is available on the Internet. The Internet itself has become a great networking and organizing venue since word can spread quickly about issues and actions.

Lesbian activists who speak out for their rights, thus making themselves visible, run risks that range from social stigma and media censorship in the United States to jail or death in some countries. This has not stopped lesbians from organizing in countries as diverse as China (q.v.), which held its first lesbian conference in 2000; Sri Lanka, where lesbians held their first lesbian convention in 2001 (the first gay and lesbian convention was held there in 1999); and Zimbabwe, where members of Gay and Lesbians of Zimbabwe (GALZ) (q.v.) have received international funding for their human rights protests.

Organizing pride marches (q.v.) is another form of activism, especially in traditional cultures which are not gay-friendly. Such public visibility is a political act that may lead to changes. For instance, Israel's first major gay pride parade was held in 1998, and shortly thereafter, out lesbian Michal Eden was elected to Tel Aviv's city council. Lesbian activism has resulted in lesbians' rights being considered along with women's rights at global conferences such as the United Nations' Conference on Women held in Nairobi, Mexico City, and Beijing (qq.v.). *See also* Coalition Politics.

ADDAMS, JANE (1860–1935). Social worker. She founded Hull House in Chicago, Illinois, and was the cofounder of the American Civil Liberties Union (ACCU) (q.v.). She won the Nobel Peace Prize in 1931. Addams lived and worked with Ellen Starr at Hull House until the early 1890s. She then enjoyed what she called "married folk" life with Mary Rozat Smith until Smith's death in 1934.

ADOPTION. Adoption is the legal means for creating familial relationships. Adoption law varies from country to country, and in some countries from state to state. While many states and countries allow unmarried adults to adopt children, sexual orientation may preclude many lesbians and gay men from adopting children since homosexuals have been seen, erroneously, by some as unfit to parent. The National Center for Lesbian Rights (NCLR) and the American Civil Liberties Union (ACLU) (qq.v.) have been at the forefront working to change adoption laws in the United States to allow lesbians, gays, and same-sex (q.v.) couples to adopt. Lesbian and gay rights groups have also been involved in securing the right of adoption for gays and lesbians as they pursue related issues that recognize homosexual families. Currently in Florida, New Hampshire, and other countries such as Australia, Finland, and Germany (qq.v.), lesbians and gays are still prohibited from adopting children. In 2001, the Netherlands (q.v.) passed legislation allowing lesbians and gays to adopt children.

Lesbian couples who wish to jointly adopt children face different issues from single lesbians who wish to adopt. Many courts do not recognize a child potentially having two mothers. Couples may want to ensure custody rights of the other mother if the legally recognized mother should die, if the couple breaks up, or if the other mother dies because the child may not have the right to inherit with no legally recognized relationship between the other, or second mother, and the child.

Joint adoption and second parent adoptions are necessary to enable lesbian families the security afforded to heterosexual families. The NCLR has suggested that joint adoption be dealt with in the same way a stepparent may adopt a child: the child may end up with her biological mother as well as her stepmother. This mechanism, which does not sever the recognized familial and legal bond of the biological parent, is also the means used to secure the adoption of a child by the nonbiological mother in a lesbian couple where one of the women has birthed the child, or allow for both women to become the child's legal mothers. This adoption process is called "second-parent adoption" (q.v.). While some states' courts have ruled that second-parent or joint adoptions are permissible, others, such as Colorado and Wisconsin, have not permitted lesbian second-parent or joint adoptions. In February 2002, the American Academy of Pediatrics issued a policy statement supporting lesbian and gay second-parent or coparent adoptions as being in the best interest of the children.

Comedian, talk-show host, and adoptive mother Rosie O'Donnell came out (q.v.) publically in response to the state of Florida's denying lesbian and gay foster parents the right to adopt children. As a celebrity, she is bringing this issue to the mainstream agenda. *See also* Child Custody and Visitation.

AFRICA. Most of the countries in Sub-Saharan Africa have laws against same-sex relations, though same-sex relations exist. There have been "woman marriages" within trading/economic networks of women, usually between an older widowed woman and a younger woman, though there is some question as to whether these were sexual unions since marriage is compulsory in most traditions. Only South Africa (q.v.), under the leadership of Nelson Mandela, adopted in its Constitution (1996) a gay and lesbian civil rights amendment. South Africa and Zimbabwe (q.v.) have active gay and lesbian rights groups, namely Gays and Lesbians of Zimbabwe (GALZ) and Gay and Lesbian Organization of the Witwatersrand (GLOW) (qq.v.). Informal gay and lesbian groups exist in Botswana, Ghana, Nigeria, and Uganda.

Currently, while AIDS (q.v.) has reached crisis proportions in Sub-Saharan Africa, it is predominately spread through heterosexual intercourse. There are 3.5 million newly infected adults and children with HIV for the year 2002 alone.

AFRICAN AMERICAN LESBIANS. *See* **BLACK LESBIANS.**

AFRICAN ANCESTRAL LESBIANS UNITED FOR SOCIAL CHANGE. The oldest black lesbian (q.v.) social and political organization founded in 1974 as Third World Women. The founders, Rev. Dolores Jackson, Harriet Austin, Sonia Bailey, and Luvenia Pinson among others, came together, according to their newsletter, because no other groups were dealing with issues facing Third World gay women, and to provide an alternative to the lesbian bar scene. The group later changed its name to the Salsa Soul Sisters. Black lesbians (q.v.) were also early members of the homophile and gay rights organizations, but marginalization led many to form organizations of their own.

AGE OF CONSENT. The age at which legal (and penal) codes deem individuals capable of marrying or having sexual relations as consenting adults, usually at puberty or close to the age of majority (age eighteen). The age of consent has been higher for male homosexuals than for heterosexuals and lesbians in Great Britain (q.v.), for instance, until legislation in 2001. In the United States (q.v.), age of consent laws are in place for heterosexual sexual acts to protect minors under the age of sixteen.

AGEISM. Negative, prejudicial attitudes toward anyone older, but predominantly women and/or lesbians who do not fit the youth ideal anymore. Ageism is systemic and institutionalized oppression of older people by younger people.

Older women, especially in western society, become invisible and powerless since they are no longer seen as sexually attractive or sexually active. Lesbians, who do not have sexual relationships with men, tend to suffer less in the greater society partly because they have always been self-reliant. Yet, in the lesbian community (q.v.) ageism is prevalent, and older lesbians instead of being valued for their life experience and wisdom are often marginalized.

Older lesbians are becoming active in organizations that fight ageism and allow them to be visible and vocal about their rights and needs. Some of these organizations include Old Lesbians Organizing for Change (OLOC) and Senior Action in a Gay Environment (SAGE) (qq.v.). *See also* Body Image.

AIDS. *See* **ACQUIRED IMMUNE DEFICIENCY SYNDROME/ HUMAN IMMUNODEFICIENCY VIRUS (AIDS/HIV).**

AIDS COALITION TO UNLEASH POWER (ACT-Up). This direct-action (q.v.) group was founded in response to the AIDS (q.v.) crisis in the United States. It staged demonstrations to bring to light the government's inadequate research and funding of AIDS and the lack of humanistic policies by local governments and the Catholic Church. Many lesbians were involved in this group. There was a split when some lesbian activists realized that women and lesbians who are HIV positive or have AIDS were not readily included in the group of persons with AIDS (PWAs) that ACT-Up was fighting for, that lesbians were still invisible. These activists formed the Lesbian Avengers (q.v.).

ALEXANDER, DELORES (1935–). Activist Alexander was the first executive director of the National Organization for Women (NOW). She later owned the New York City feminist restaurant *Mother Courage* with her then partner. She is currently involved with the nonprofit North Fork (Long Island, New York) women's community helping to fund health (q.v.) care for needy older lesbians.

ALLEN, PAULA GUNN (1939–). Professor, writer, and activist. Gunn is a Native American feminist lesbian poet, author, and scholar. Her writings have provided a groundwork to understanding the concepts of gender and sexuality within a Native American context. The two primary goals of her texts are to gain respectability for lesbians and to explain that lesbians and gays have always been present in Native American cultures. According to her work, lesbians and gays have traditionally been ritually and socially valued in Native American culture; it is only since colonization that they have been devalued.

ALLISON, DOROTHY (1949–). Writer and activist. Allison founded the Lesbian Sex Mafia, the East Coast version of Samois (q.v.), the prosex, sadomasochism (S/M) (q.v.) group. She was one of the first writers to receive two Lambda Literary Awards (q.v.) in 1988 for *Trash*. She also received the American National Book Award for *Bastard Out of Carolina* (1992) which traces the life of an illegitimate daughter who experiences abuse and incest. Her work, which includes poetry, short stories, and novels, explores her identities as lesbian, feminist, femme, (qq.v.) working-class woman, as well as incest survivor.

ALTERNATIVE INSEMINATION (AI). A heterosexist term applied to all forms of introducing sperm into the uterus in hopes of pregnancy. With the Lesbian Baby Boom (q.v.), the term "Donor Insemination" is used to describe methods of insemination from the use of a turkey baster at home to the use of sperm banks and clinics. *See also* Artificial Insemination (AI).

AMAZONS. In classical Greek mythology, a legendary race of female warriors who lived without males near the Black Sea in the twelfth century BC. Men were used for procreative purposes only. More generally, the term "amazon" is used to describe a strong, independent, and aggressive woman, as well as woman-identified woman (q.v.). Natalie Barney (q.v.) first applied this term in the 1920s to describe lesbians. Lesbian-feminists (q.v.) have since adopted it.

AMENDMENT 2 (COLORADO)/*ROMER v. EVANS.* After a few cities in the state of Colorado passed gay and lesbian rights or nondiscrimination in housing and employment laws—a movement which some felt was promoting homosexuality and giving lesbians and gays special rights (q.v.)—the Religious Right (q.v.) and its allies put Amendment 2 to the state's Constitution on the 1992 ballot. Amendment 2, which was voted on and passed by the citizens of Colorado, stated that there was "no protected status based on homosexual, lesbian or bisexual orientation" and that the government and agencies of the state could not entitle any such person to "claim any minority status. . . . or claim of discrimination," thus repealing any existing gay/lesbian rights ordinances and prohibiting any new ones, in short prohibiting lesbians and gays from equal political participation or protections.

The case went before the U.S. Supreme Court in 1996 (*Romer, Governor of Colorado, et al. v. Evans, et al.* [94-1039] 517 U.S. 620 1996). In a landmark decision, the court found that Amendment 2 violated the constitutional rights of lesbians and gays as per the Fourteenth Amendment to the U.S. Constitution, which guarantees equal protection of the laws to all citizens. The majority opinion of the court found that Colorado's amendment put " . . . homosexuals . . . in a solitary class in transactions and relations in both the private and governmental spheres . . . " thus precluding them from governmental protections. This amendment was "inexplicable by anything but animus toward the class it affects; it lacks a rational relationship to legitimate state interests." The Supreme Court found that being homosexual did not preclude one from full citizenship. *See also Bowers v. Hardwick; Boy Scouts of America v. Dale*; Oregon Citizens Alliance.

AMERICAN CIVIL LIBERTIES UNION (ACLU). This organization is the United States' leading advocate for all individual rights, thus, it supports and advocates lesbian and gay rights. The ACLU's Lesbian and Gay Rights Project's goals are to help gays and lesbians attain equal treatment and facilities from government, in employment, in public places, and for lesbian and gay couples. The project has targeted discrimination based on sexual orientation including antigay initiatives, parenting, custody and adoption issues, domestic partnerships and marriage (qq.v.) relationships, gay and lesbian teens and education, laws which criminalize sexual intimacy, and limits placed on the freedoms of expression and association used by lesbians and gays to politically organize, such as limits on lesbian and gay marches (q.v.) and demonstrations. The project handles court cases, promotes policies, educates the public and politicians, and drafts legislation to help ensure equal treatment regardless of sexual orientation.

AMERICAN FAMILY ASSOCIATION. This Christian political organization of over 600,000 members in 640 chapters across the United States targets homosexuality, pornography, and the liberal media in its campaigns to control public school curricula and National Endowment for the Arts (q.v.) funding. *See also* Religious Right.

AMERICAN LIBRARY ASSOCIATION (ALA). This was the first professional organization to have a Lesbian and Gay Task Force (1970). The task force was coordinated by Barbara Gittings (q.v.) from its inception until 1986. The task force and the ALA were influential in shaping all libraries' holdings, presenting critiques of reference and other books with regard to their stance on homosexuality, and promoting the terms "gay" and "lesbian," which help young lesbians and gays especially when they first look for information about their sexuality. The task force also supported employment and benefits for gay and lesbian librarians. The task force is now known as the Gay Lesbian BiSexual Transgendered Roundtable.

AMERICAN PSYCHIATRIC ASSOCIATION (APA). This professional organization had considered homosexuality "a sociopathic personality disturbance" since gays and lesbians were "ill primarily in terms of society and of conformity with the prevailing cultural milieu" according to the 1952 *Diagnostic and Statistical Manual, Mental Disorders (DSM-1)*. In the 1968 edition, homosexuality was listed as a "non-psychotic mental disorder." These classifications had major impacts on the treatment of homosexuals (for example, homosexuals could be committed to mental institutions and subjected to drug and other therapies such as lobotomies and electric shock treatments) and policies such as immigration and criminal statutes.

Thus, the APA was targeted for education and demonstrations to get the designations changed. There was a secret group of gay and lesbian APA members that supported the proposed changes; they were called GAY-PA. Barbara Love and Barbara Gittings (qq.v.) were among the gays and lesbians who made presentations to the APA in 1971 that led to the APA's December 15, 1973 decision to remove homosexuality from the *DSM*. However, homosexuals could still be treated as having a "sexual disturbance disorder" or "ego-dystonic homosexuality."

In 1975, GAY-PA came out (q.v.) and changed its name to Association of Lesbian and Gay Psychiatrists. There is also a Committee on Gay and Lesbian Concerns with APA. Today, the APA is gay and lesbian friendly, and most recently in response to the Religious Right's homophobia (qq.v.), reasserted that homosexuality is not a mental disorder, and therefore, treatment is not necessary.

Nonetheless, there is a group of psychologists who founded the National Association for the Research and Therapy of Homosexuality which promotes secular reparative therapy as a way to convert homosexuals into heterosexuals. *See also* Ex-gay.

AMNESTY INTERNATIONAL (AI). Organized in 1961 to prevent and fight governmental abuse of human rights. While Amnesty International confirmed in 1979 that individuals imprisoned for advocating lesbian/gay rights were, indeed, prisoners of conscience, it was not until 1991 that the organization included a mandate to actively fight for the human rights of persons imprisoned for their sexual orientation.

ANARCHIST-FEMINISM. This feminist theory is based on anarchist Emma Goldman's argument that the state and its laws are coercive and are responsible for gender inequality. As with all anarchistic thinking, domination by the state or any hierarchical institution is unnatural, and since people are naturally good and sharing, the individual should be respected and will make her own cooperative relations. Anarchist-feminists share this utopian vision; they also feel that women cannot achieve legal equality in the current male-dominated state.

ANDERSON, MARGARET (1886–1973). Publisher, editor, and memoirist. She belonged to the expatriate group of lesbians living in Paris in the 1920s. With her lover Jane Heap, she edited *The Little Review* which first published James Joyce's *Ulysses*.

ANDROGENOUS. Having the gender characteristics and mannerisms of both male and female. From the Greek words for man and woman: *andros* and *gyne*. During the height of the women's liberation and lesbian-feminist movement of the 1970s and 1980s, the androgenous look in clothing (jeans and flannel, work shirt or tee shirts), hair styles (short hair), no cosmetics, and behavior was preferred. Today, young queers (q.v.) who wish to blur their sexual identity will refer to themselves as "Andros." *See also* Androgyny; Butch; Femme.

ANDROGYNY. Constructed from the Greek words for man and woman, it is used to describe someone with both female and male features and/or self-presentation. During the 1970s and 1980s when butch-femme (q.v.) behavior fell out of favor, lesbians and feminists adopted an androgynous (q.v.) ideal and presentation.

ANTHONY, SUSAN B. (1820–1906). Suffragist. She was the co-organizer of the 1848 Seneca Falls, New York Convention at which the *Declarations of Sentiments,* the first public call for the civil rights and autonomy of women, was delivered. She is thought to have been a lesbian, having been in relationships with women. Her surviving letters include emotional and erotic ones to Anna Dickinson, and ones Anthony wrote to friends about her love for Emily Gross.

Anthony was more radical than most of her contemporaries. She publicly spoke out against heterosexual marriages and arrangements, and when called "manly," redefined the term to mean a woman who was simply fully human, and suggested that men should develop their "womanly" qualities to become, likewise, more fully human. She believed that women had a right to develop their talents and to be self-reliant. The Nineteenth Amendment to the U.S. Constitution, which gives women the right to vote, is named after her posthumously. Her image on the silver dollar was the first female image to ever appear on U.S. money.

ANTIBIAS LAWS. These are laws that prohibit employment, housing, and civil rights (qq.v.) discrimination based on biases such as race, ethnicity, religion, sex, sexual orientation, and gender presentation. *See also* Special Rights.

ANTIGAY INITIATIVES. In the United States, these are referenda put to the voting public to repeal existing legislation/laws that extend civil rights antidiscrimination coverage to include sexual orientation (and/or gender presentation), such as in Dade County, Florida, Oregon's Proposition 6, and Colorado's Amendment 2 (qq.v.). The campaigns to repeal civil rights extended to lesbians, gays, and transgendered people are usually based on the claim that these rights are "special rights" (q.v.). Other antigay initiatives decree that marriage is only for heterosexuals, such as California's Knight Amendment (q.v.). *See also* Family Values; Oregon Citizens Alliance; Religious Right.

ANTI-SEMITISM. Anti-Semitism is the oppression and/or hatred of Jewish people. In lesbian and feminist politics, where Jewish lesbians were quite visible (due in part to the Jewish tradition of fighting for social justice), anti-Semitism is ignored or overlooked as a form of racism (q.v.). Some of lesbian anti-Semitism is by Jewish lesbians themselves—internalized anti-Semitism similar to internalized homophobia (q.v.). As Jewish people try to assimilate into the mainstream culture, they seek to erase any differences between themselves and the "other." For other lesbians, anti-Semitism ranges from unspoken, covert silences about Jewish lesbians and their achievements to overt derogatory remarks and exclusion. Anti-Semitism needs to be named in order that all lesbians may be free of oppression.

ANZALDÚA, GLORIA (1942–). Mexicana lesbian-feminist, writer, editor, and educator. She is "patlache," which is Nahuatl Indian for lesbian. Her works, such as *Borderlands*, deconstruct historical sources of oppression, white supremacy, and Nahuatl myths and traditions. She believes that sexuality is just one component in a person's identity and that politics, class, culture, ethnicity, and gender are some of the other components. She is also the coeditor of one of the most important lesbian-feminist books by women of color, *This Bridge Called My Back*.

APUZZO, VIRGINIA (1941–). Activist and public official. She is a former nun who joined a (teaching) order to enable her to understand her sexual orientation in light of her faith. She was the executive director of the National Gay Task Force when it became the National Gay and Lesbian Task Force (NGLTF) (q.v). She coauthored the first lesbian and gay civil rights plank adopted by a national political party, the Democrats. In 1983, after she reminded Martin Luther King Jr,'s widow, Coretta Scott King and other black leaders that King preached civil rights for all people, Coretta Scott King stated: "We believe that the rights of all people must be protected and guaranteed. We believe that the gay and lesbian community must be supported in their civil rights as well as their own sexual preference." As executive director, Apuzzo also negotiated with the Reagan administration social security commissioner to secure social security disability benefits for persons with AIDS (q.v.).

Apuzzo was the first open lesbian (or gay person) to be confirmed by the New York State Senate as Commissioner of the New York State Civil Service. Prior to that, she had served as Commissioner of Consumer Affairs, then as Executive Commissioner of the Division of Housing and Community Development. When she was Commissioner of Consumer Affairs, she commissioned a pricing survey of AIDS drugs which revealed that persons with AIDS were being overcharged. Because of this study, drug prices were substantially lowered. As Commissioner of Civil Service, she secured domestic partnership (q.v.) rights for New York State employees. She resigned her civil service commission to become Associate Deputy Secretary of the U.S. Department of Labor in the Clinton administration. From there, she became the highest ranking out lesbian (or gay person) when she joined President Bill Clinton's White House as Assistant to the President for Management and Administration. After retiring from the White House staff, she held the Apuzzo Chair in the National Gay and Lesbian Policy Institute of the National Gay and Lesbian Task Force, working on labor issues and election issues in key swing states. Apuzzo recently retired to her home in upstate New York to travel, write, play racquetball, and canasta. She also volunteers, helping with lesbian and gay youth programs under the auspices of Planned Parenthood.

ARCADIE. The oldest French gay and lesbian rights organization and publication founded in 1953. Arcadie ceased operation in 1982 when the Pétain-de Gaulle law (q.v.) was repealed. It was considered politically to be a reformist organization, similar to the American Mattachine Society (MS) and Daughters of Bilitis (DOB), advocating assimilation of lesbians and gays into French society as it promoted their civil rights. As with the movement in the United States, the more radical and short-lived Gay Liberation Front (GLF) and Front Homosexuel d'Action Révolutionnaire came to the fore. Arcadie joined the coalition of sixteen gay and lesbian organizations in the late 1970s—the Comité d'Urgence Anti-Répression Homosexuelle—supporting François Mitterand's pro-gay candidacy in 1981.

ARGENTINA. Twentieth-century lesbian social culture in Argentina maintained strict gender codes, feminine if upper class and butch-femme (q.v.) if working class. The first lesbian political group, Safo, was formed in 1972 and became the only lesbian member of the Homosexual Liberation Front. In 1976 with the military coup d'etat, most of the members either went into exile or formed study groups. When democracy returned to Argentinia, the Argentine or Argentinian Homosexual Community was formed in 1984 and Lugar de Mujer, the feminist group, sponsored lesbian workshops. *Cuadernos de Existencia Lesbiana*, both a lesbian group and magazine, was formed in 1987 on International Women's Day (q.v.). Other social and political lesbian groups have joined in in making lesbians visible. Since 1996, lesbians have taken an active role in the pride marches (q.v.) held in Buenos Aires. Even though the cities of Buenos Aires and Rosario include sexual orientation in their antidiscrimination statutes, lesbians are still harassed, lose custody of their children, and are fired from their jobs.

ARNOLD, JUNE (DAVIS) (1926–1982). Lesbian-feminist activist. Arnold was a writer and cofounding feminist publisher of Daughters, Inc. She was a militant feminist and became a public advocate of lesbian separatism (q.v.). She organized the separatist Women in Print Conference, believing that what was needed was a strong women's communication network. Arnold advocated against lesbians publishing with patriarchal publishing houses. Her own writings include the lesbian classic novels *Applesauce* (1967) and *The Cook and the Carpenter* (1973).

ARTIFICIAL INSEMINATION (AI). Artificial insemination is the term used to cover methods of conceiving a child other than female and male sexual intercourse. Heterosexual and lesbian women who have reproductive difficulties and wish to give birth may seek the assistance of medical reproductive clinics. The methods used include the medical process of harvesting of donor eggs, inseminating them in a petri dish, and implanting the fertilized eggs back in a woman's womb. This is very expensive, averaging $10,000 per try, and is not covered by most health insurance. It is, also, a medically challenging process since the woman has to undergo hormonal treatment to produce the required number of eggs. A relatively simple method of AI involve using donated sperm, a male friend's or from a sperm bank, and having that sperm introduced into a woman's body. This method is called the "turkey-baster method" and many lesbians who have access to sperm use this method as it is very cheap. *See also* Alternative Insemination (AI).

ASIA. While lesbians and gays rarely live independently of their families, they are beginning to organize politically with Beijing's Chinese Rainbow (q.v.), Hong Kong's Ten Percent Club, Japan's (q.v.) predominately male International Lesbian and Gay Association-Japan, India's (q.v.) Bombay Dost, the Philippines's (q.v.) The Library Foundation (TLF), Indonesia's Kelompok Kerja Lesbian dan Gay Nusantara (KKLGN), Sri Lanka's informal Companions on a Journey, and Malaysia's Pink Triangle. An annual conference of these groups has been established.

The Japanese lesbian-feminist group Re-Gumi Studio Tokyo was founded in 1987. This group works at reclaiming "lesbian" in Japanese culture from its pornographic use. There is a slowly growing recognition of lesbians and gays and their rights in Japanese culture, though most lesbians (and gays) remain closeted (q.v.). Some four thousand gays and lesbians attended Tokyo's 2001 Pride weekend which included concerts and a march.

The Campaign for Lesbian Rights in India was organized to combat the violence that erupted after the December 1998 screening of Deepa Mehta's film *Fire*. This group's mission is to make lesbians visible, create an awareness about lesbian issues, and develop cultural and political recognition of lesbian rights.

In 1990, the Asian Lesbian Network (ALN) was formed to bridge language, ethnicity, color, religion, and regional and class distinctions between and among Asian lesbians as they work for lesbian rights. The ALN has held conferences that have attracted lesbian participation from over thirteen countries giving Asian lesbians of diverse backgrounds, cultures, needs, and politics a place to share and dialogue. There are concerns about the definition of Asians, as well as ideological issues that challenge this growing and dynamic organization.

Many lesbian social and political networking organizations exist on the internet such as Korea's Virtual City for Lesbians and Pu-San/Kyung Nam (Women's Human Rights Group for Sexual Minority), Taiwan's Between Us, and Thailand's Lesla. *See also* Australia; China; New Zealand; Pride March.

ASIAN AMERICAN/PACIFIC ISLAND (API) LESBIANS. Lesbian (and gay) members of Asian and Pacific Island ancestry are more visible and activist, though homosexuality is taboo among many API cultures. The first U.S. group, the Lesbian and Gay Asian Collective, was organized in 1979, and a Filipina was a founding member of the Daughters of Bilitis (DOB) (q.v.) in the 1950s. Other API groups include the Asian/Pacific Lesbian Network, the Gay Asian Pacific Alliance, and the Asian Lesbian Network. Prominent API activists and writers include Melinda Paras, Urvashi Vaid (q.v.), Barbara Noda, Kitty Tsui, (q.v.) and Merle Woo.

ASIAN LESBIAN NETWORK. *See* **ASIA.**

ASSIMILATIONISTS. People and political organizations working for social acceptance that want to become part of the norm. Also called "participationists," these lesbians seek full inclusion in the patriarchal institutions, such as the military or marriage. The issue is whether they can "assimilate" to the societal norm of white, heterosexual, male, property owner with all the attendant privileges thereof. The Human Rights Campaign (HRC) and the National Gay and Lesbian Task Force (NGLTF) (qq.v.) are accused of promoting an assimilationist agenda with issues such as same-sex marriage (q.v.).

Some feel that pushing for assimilation removes sex from the lesbian and gay identity; lesbian and gay liberation was for both sexual liberation as well as for civil rights for lesbians and gays. *See also* Lesbian Separatism; Male Privilege; Patriarchy.

ASSOCIATION FOR SOCIAL KNOWLEDGE (ASK). ASK was founded in 1964 and modeled on the Mattachine Society (MS) and Daughters of Bilitis (DOB) (qq.v.). It was the prominent lesbian and gay rights organization in Canada during the 1960s. It helped to mobilize lesbians and gays to support decriminalization of consensual sexual acts between adults. It disappeared after the reform of the Canadian Criminal Code in 1969. Other gay and lesbian rights groups emerged in its place such as the Front de Libération Homosexuelle in Montreal and Vancouver's Gay Liberation Front (GLF).

ASTRAEA NATIONAL LESBIAN FOUNDATION. This organization is a funding source founded in 1977 to address the inequality of resources directed to women, especially lesbians and women of color who are working for social change and economic justice in the United States. Astraea gives competitive grants and awards to community organizations and individuals to support activism and creativity in the lesbian community.

ASYLUM. Meaning safe harbor or protection from arrest or extradition, political asylum is a form of diplomatic immunity given to refugees fleeing harmful practices and persecution of their home country. Ten countries—Australia, Belgium, Canada, Finland, Germany, Ireland, the Netherlands, New Zealand, the United Kingdom, and the United States—grant asylum from persecution based on sexual orientation. This is in part a direct result of the international Gay and Lesbian Rights movement (q.v.).

ATKINSON, TI-GRACE (1939–). Writer and lesbian-feminist activist. Atkinson was a founding member of the New York chapter of the National Organization for Women (NOW) (q.v.), which she left in protest of its hierarchical structure in 1968. She was a member of the Feminists (q.v.) until she was prohibited from contacting the press in 1970. Atkinson said, "lesbianism is to feminism what the Communist

Party was to the trade-union movement" (1973). Her writings on lesbian-feminism are collected in *Amazon Odyssey* (1974). She currently teaches biomedical ethics at Columbia University.

AUDRE LORDE PROJECT. This New York City social and political center was founded to help educate, organize, and mobilize lesbian, gay, bisexual, two-spirited, and queer (qq.v.) persons. Its goals are for community wellness (health issues) and progressive social and economic justice. The project provides space and aid for individuals and groups to work together across their differences. It also participates in other local, regional, and national coalitions. *See also* Lorde, Audre.

AUSTRALIA. This island nation has had an active lesbian and gay rights movement since 1964 when Campaign Against Moral Persecution (CAMP) was founded. In 1977, New South Wales became the first Australian state to pass gay and lesbian rights legislation; South Australia adopted its gay and lesbian civil rights protections in 1984.

Australia's lesbian and gay rights movement became revitalized after countrywide protests of police arrests of lesbian and gay Mardi Gras revelers in Sydney in July 1978. Some have called this "Australia's Stonewall" (q.v.).

A nation of immigrants, immigration and residency rights for members of same-sex couples have been the focus of the Gay and Lesbian Immigration Task Force in Australia since 1984. The group's efforts met with success in 1991 with the Non Familial Relations of Emotional Interdependency (a euphemism for same-sex unions) regulation that allows for same-sex partners to become residents. Gays and lesbians were allowed in the military in 1992. There is still discrimination against lesbians and gays in the area of adoption (q.v.) and family rights. The prohibition of lesbians being artificially inseminated (q.v.) was overturned by court order. Australia has an active lesbian culture.

AUTONOMY (SEXUAL). The concept of control over one's sexuality, and one's body. For women, and especially lesbians, this is extremely important. It disrupts the current patriarchal concept where men have access to and control over women's bodies (physically and legally). In the United States (q.v.), a male has complete control over his body (unless he is poor and a minority), yet all women's bodies are controlled by legislation and court decisions. For instance, in the United States, women cannot decide on their own if they want to terminate a pregnancy after the start of the second trimester, and women receiving welfare are urged to be either celibate or married to a male (the Personal Responsibility Act).

In the United States and other countries, women may also be controlled by religious laws and practices ranging from the prohibition against abortion (q.v.) (even in the case of rape or incest in Ireland) to the "honor killings" in many Muslim countries. Honor killings supposedly reclaim the honor of the families of women who have been raped or are sexually active; this reclamation happens when the woman is murdered by a male member of her own family.

Women are further controlled by the threat of male sexual violence against them including rape. Men may feel that raping a lesbian will help "straighten" her out. Lesbians have also been driven to take their own lives, especially in cultures that reject their sexual orientation. Suicides because of sexual orientation are prevalent not only in traditional societies such as Sri Lanka, but in western countries as well. At the 1976 International Tribunal on Crimes Against Women held in Belgium, women held the first Take Back the Night (q.v.) candlelight protest to help educate the world that violence against women robs them of their autonomy.

– B –

BABY BUTCH. A young (teens to mid-twenties) lesbian who presents herself as masculine and tough, but who is relatively inexperienced.

BACKLASH. This term originated with the concept of feminist backlash, that the current feminist movement has harmed society, and thus, there needs to be a rollback of feminist gains ranging from child custody (q.v.) to employment rights. The concept of backlash has been extended to include lesbians' rights and issues.

***BAEHR v. LEWIN* (1993)/*BAEHR v. MIIKE*.** The Hawaii Supreme Court decision that the refusal to issue marriage licenses to lesbian and gay couples violates the state's constitutional right to equal protection. The case was brought by Nina Baehr and Genora Dancel, a gay male couple and another lesbian couple who all sought the right to marry. This court decision had national political repercussions such as the Defense of Marriage Act (q.v.). The court ordered the state to show compelling interest to continue denying same-sex marriage (q.v.) licenses. The state legislature voted, however, to change the state constitution so that marriage is only between heterosexuals.

BANNON, ANN (1932–). Writer. Bannon's first novels were among the most influential depictions of lesbian life, from repressive society to the bar culture (q.v.) in Greenwich Village, New York City, during the late 1950s to before Stonewall (q.v.) in the late 1960s. These novels form the formulaic base of lesbian pulp fiction. Her butch (q.v.) character, Beebo, meeting femme (q.v.), Laura, is classic in its butch-femme dance of tensions.

BAR CULTURE. Bars played a large role during the 1930s, 1940s, and 1950s in lesbian (and gay) social cohesion and culture in the United States (q.v.). They were a public setting where lesbians gained acceptance and recognition. Bar communities were the center of most lesbian life. The earliest bars were in New York City—Harlem and Greenwich Village. Other towns and cities, such as Buffalo, New York, developed an active working-class lesbian bar culture during World War II. Bars outside of New York City tended to be homogeneous partly due to racism and the fact that black lesbian (q.v.) culture centered around house parties.

Bar culture led to lesbian resistance and the formation of lesbian and gay politics. There were strict laws that prohibited disorderly conduct, which the State Liquor Authority interpreted as having any homosexual or lesbian patrons drinking at the bar or same-sex couples dancing together. Women made sure to wear at least three pieces of female clothing in case the police raided the bar. Bar owners frequently paid off police or the mafia for protection from, or at least, tipoffs of police raids. Lesbian bars still play a role today especially for young lesbians' first social outings. Bars also support softball teams.

In European countries, bars also attracted the lesbian subculture and the lesbian patrons became social and political forces during the twentieth century. For instance, in Amsterdam, Netherlands (q.v.), during the period between the world wars, there was an emerging lesbian subculture at the cafés and bars. During World War II, when many Dutch lesbians joined the Resistance, the bars in the red light district such as Bet van Baran's He Mandje, were used for meetings and arms depots. After the war, working-class and middle-class lesbians who enjoyed a butch-femme (q.v.) lifestyle, also visited bars and were known as "bar dancers."

During the women's movement, women's cafés began to be the meeting place of lesbian-feminists. *See also* Bar Dyke; Rikki Streicher.

BAR DYKE. A lesbian who frequents lesbian/women's bars. *See also* Bar Culture.

BARNES, DJUNA (1892–1981). Writer. Barnes's novel *Nightwood* is considered to be the first modern lesbian novel. She wrote *Ladies Almanack*, which was a satire on Natalie Barney's (q.v.) lesbian circle of friends in Paris. The characters in the *Almanack* included Barney as Dame Evangeline Musset, Janet Flanner (q.v.) as Nip, and Radclyffe Hall (q.v.) as Lady Tilly-Tweed-in-Blood.

BARNEY, NATALIE (1876–1972). Art patron and writer. This expatriate American hosted one of the most famous—next to that of Gertrude Stein (q.v.)—Parisian lesbian and literary salons in the early twentieth century. Barney was an outspoken promoter of lesbianism and the arts. Attendees at her salons at 20 rue Jaçon included Colette, Djuna Barnes, Renée Vivien (qq.v.) as well as well-known gay male writers and artists. Her primary lover was the artist Romaine Brooks, but Barney was nonmonogamous and had many passionate and dramatic affairs. She believed in lesbian adventure and conquest as well as sexual abandon. She was generous with her inherited monies. Influenced by Ezra Pound, Barney was an admirer of Mussolini's fascism and an outspoken anti-Semite. She spent World War II in Italy. She proclaimed herself the "Amazon (q.v.) of letters" having written two dozen novels, memoirs, and plays, and being the role model for characters in the works of many other lesbian writers of the times.

BARS. *See* BAR CULTURE.

BATTERING. *See* **DOMESTIC VIOLENCE.**

BATTS, DEBORAH (1947–). Judge. The first openly lesbian, African American federal judge. She was appointed a Manhattan Federal District Judge by President Bill Clinton in June 1994. She also teaches at Fordham University School of Law.

BEACH, SYLVIA (NANCY) (1887–1962). American expatriate bookseller. She ran the bookstore, Shakespeare and Company, in Paris. The bookstore was a meeting place and reading room for expatriate avant-garde writers from James Joyce to John Dos Passos. Beach was part of the Paris Exiles or Lost Generation and the lesbian colony between the world wars. She shared her life with Adrienne Monnier (1892–1956).

BEARD. A person of the opposite sex who knowingly dates and/or marries a lesbian or homosexual, allowing his/her partner to pass as heterosexual. Such a marriage is called a "front marriage" or a "marriage of convenience."

BEAUVOIR, SIMONE de (1908–1986). Beauvoir is the French existentialist philosopher best known for writing *The Second Sex* (1953), which seeks to understand how women are "othered." This work is considered to be a key to the rebirth of feminism (q.v.) known as the second wave of feminism (q.v.). Though Beauvoir did not like to be called "the mother of second wave feminism," she was nonetheless.

She thought of lesbianism as a freely chosen choice, and that between women through reciprocity one becomes simultaneously the subject and the object. Though her main lover was Jean-Paul Sartre, in her later years she took female lovers; Sylvie le Bon was at her side when she died.

BECHDEL, ALISON (1960–). Cartoonist. She is the creator of the syndicated cartoon strip (and books) *Dykes to Watch Out For.* The characters in this cartoon strip track popular lesbian culture, trends, and politics.

BED DEATH (LESBIAN BED DEATH). The experience of lessening or ceasing sexual activity among lesbian partners after a number of years of cohabitation. This also feeds into the stereotype (q.v.) of the sexless lesbian.

**BEIJING CONFERENCE, 1995 UNITED NATIONS CONFER-
ENCE ON WOMEN.** At this global conference, lesbians were well represented by nongovernmental organizations (NGOs) and were active in organizing their campaign for inclusion of lesbian rights in the agenda. The Chinese authorities tried to marginalize all the women and their work by promoting disinformation campaigns, which included statements to taxi drivers to carry sheets to cover the naked lesbians and disinfectant spray to protect them from the AIDS (q.v.) that lesbians may carry. While lesbian rights were discussed and workshops held, the Vatican and Muslim countries vetoed the inclusion of the word "lesbian" in the adopted plan of action, though women's right to control their sexuality was included. *See also* Human Rights; Mexico City Conference; Nairobi Conference; United Nations.

BELGIUM. In Belgium, a small Catholic country, the lesbian (only) movement is only a decade old, even though there were lesbian study groups such as Sappho in Ghent as of 1974. Suzan Daniel Fonds (a pseudonym) was the first known lesbian activist. In 1996, the gay and lesbian archive was named after her. The Lesbies Doe Front holds a national lesbian day, and since 1997 there is a monthly meeting of all Flemish political lesbian groups, the Lesbian Table.

Politically, women in Belgium have only had the right to vote since 1948. While lesbianism is not illegal, lesbians can be discriminated against in issues involving marriage, family, and children. Lesbian activists are building the lesbian community and participating in politics. Some lesbians have also joined a coalition with gay men on partnership/family legal issues.

BEN, LISA (EDITH EYDE) (1921–). Activist and writer. Using a pseudonym, which is a play on "lesbian," she began to write and self-publish the first known publication for lesbians, *Vice Versa* (q.v.), in 1945. The nine-issue magazine, distributed from friend to friend, became the prototype for gay and lesbian magazines that followed, establishing a positive forum for lesbians through book and film reviews, fiction, letters, and editorials. Ben joined the Daughters of Bilitis (DOB) (q.v.). A musician by training, the Los Angeles chapter of DOB released her recording of lesbian renditions of popular folk songs in 1960. She was billed as "the first gay folk singer." She remains a supporter of the lesbian political struggle.

BENEDICT, RUTH (1887–1948). Academic and cultural anthropologist. Benedict was Margaret Mead's (q.v.) professor, mentor, and lover. She was the first woman to hold the rank of full professor of Political Science at Columbia University. Benedict and Mead wrote about deviancy in culture, trying to change how society conceived of abnormal behavior and traits. Benedict also worked for and wrote about racial equality. Her works include *Patterns of Culture* (1993) and *The Races of Mankind* 1943). Benedict also wrote poetry under the pseudonym Anne Singleton.

BENTLEY, GLADYS (1907–1960). Singer. Part of the Harlem Renaissance (q.v.), Bentley came out as a bulldagger (q.v.) singing at rent parties, buffet flats (qq.v.), and nightclubs. Wearing a white tuxedo and squiring glamorous women, she parodied show tunes and blues standards. She also sang at lesbian clubs. During the 1940s, she was harassed by police for wearing men's drag (q.v.). In the 1950s, she married a man and was to be ordained in an evangelical church when she died of influenza.

BERDACHE. A colonist term used by French explorers who observed in Native American culture a woman or man who lived as either the opposite sex/gender or somewhere in-between. Usually, these people were thought of as shamans and healers. Female berdache took wives and were recognized as guides and warriors as well as shamans.

BIAS CRIME. *See* **HATE CRIMES.**

BIREN, JOAN E. (JEB) (1944–). Photographer, filmmaker, and activist. JEB worked in the Civil Rights and Antiwar movements before joining the women's movement. She is a founding member of the Furies (q.v.). Her films, *For Love and For Life* and *A Simple Matter of Justice,* document the 1978 and 1993 Marches on Washington (q.v.), respectively.

BIRKBY, (NOEL) PHYLLIS (c. 1930–1994). Activist and architect. Birkby was the first woman to graduate from the Yale School of Architecture (New Haven, Connecticut). She founded the Women's School of Architecture and Planning, and with Leslie Kanes Weisman, included lesbian issues and goals in envisioning women's space and culture. A member of CR One (q.v.), Birkby documented via photographs the women's and lesbian rights movement; these photographs and other memorabilia are housed at the Sophia Smith Collection, Smith College (Northampton, Massachusetts).

BISEXUAL GAY AND LESBIAN ASSOCIATION (BiGALA). This is the name of some student groups. Others are known as Lesbian Bisexual Gay Queer Transgendered and Transsexuals (LBGQTs). The conservative and Religious Right (q.v.) has attempted to get public schools and universities to not recognize or fund these groups; and at some religious universities, these groups are banned. There are also Gay Straight Alliances, which are currently coming under scrutiny by the conservative and Religious Right since these alliances receive public monies and resources in schools and universities.

BISEXUALITY/BISEXUAL (BI). A person who has sexual relations with both women and men. Bisexuality was in vogue during the Harlem Renaissance (q.v.) and has been revived during the late 1990s. Some bisexual people are now calling themselves "omnisexual."

Bisexual women are considered by some lesbians as not fully committed to lesbianism. For some lesbians, bisexual women are seen as heartbreakers since they may revert to having sexual relations with men and/or can be untrustworthy, as they may reclaim their heterosexual privilege (q.v.).

The first bisexual organization, the National Bisexual Liberation Organization, was founded in 1972. A major focus of the current bisexual movement is for inclusion in the Gay and Lesbian Rights movement and queer (q.v.) groups. Some lesbian and gay groups have amended their names to include "bisexual" such as Bisexual Gay and Lesbian Association (BiGALA) (q.v.) student groups. There have been international conferences on bisexuality, and political groups such as BiPol and BiNet have been organized to focus solely on bisexual rights.

BISHOP, ELIZABETH (1911–1979). Poet. A traditional and free-structure poet, Bishop did not reveal her politics or her sexual inclinations readily in her award-wining poetry. Known to her friends as a lesbian, she believed in "closets (q.v.), closets, and more closets" because she did not feel that society would accept same-sex partnerships (q.v.).

BITCH MANIFESTO. Written by Jo Freeman of the Chicago Women's Liberation Union and reprinted in *Notes from the Second Year* (1970), this manifesto redefined an "unfeminine" woman to be the feminist ideal of a woman—assertive, ambitious, and self-determined.

BLACK LESBIAN FEMINISTS. These women were the first to critique racism and ethnocentrism in lesbian politics and theory as well as to promote a black lesbian politics demonstrating how culture and background shape lesbian experience. They embraced their Latina sisters. Prominent black lesbian-feminist theorists include Audre Lorde, Cherríe Moraga, Barbara Smith, and Gloria Anzaldúa (qq.v.) as well as Eva Johnson and Kitty Tsui. Lorde and Smith founded Kitchen Table: Women of Color Press in 1980 (which closed operations in 2000). Some of the other black lesbian groups include the African American Lesbian and Gay Alliance (1986), the Black Gay and Lesbian Leadership Forum (1989), the National Coalition of Black Lesbians and Gays (1978), and the African Ancestral Lesbians United for Social Change (q.v.), later the Salsa Soul Sisters (founded as Third World Women in 1974). *See also* Combahee River Collective; Women of Color.

BLACK LESBIANS. In the United States (q.v.), black lesbian lives and communities have been documented since the middle of the nineteenth century. However, this documentation is limited due to the lack of written records, the perspective of white northerners' observations, racism, and classism besides neglect or avoidance on the part of scholars. The Harlem Renaissance (q.v.) in the 1920s allowed women performers, artists, writers, and entrepreneurs their economic autonomy, which led to their social autonomy from the heterosexist norms. During the twentieth century, the continued migration to urban areas increased the opportunities for black lesbians to form social groups and communities. While usually centered around house parties, some black lesbians began expanding their public presence with softball leagues and by going to bars (q.v.) as well as participating in the (straight) black community.

Black lesbians joined the Civil Rights movement, but for the most part, they were invisible as lesbians as they fought against the oppression of racism. Some black lesbians joined the Homophile movement (q.v.) including Lorraine Hansberry and Ernestine Eckstein (qq.v.). With the advent of the contemporary Gay and Lesbian Rights movement (q.v.), some black lesbians came out (q.v.). "The Black Lesbian," written by Elandra Henderson in 1971 for Chicago's *Lavender Woman,* clearly states the position and feeling of most black lesbians toward what they perceived to be the white lesbian movement. They, therefore, formed their own groups, not joining the white women because of perceived racism. Other black lesbians joined the feminist movement, forming their own groups such as the National Black Feminist Organization and Combahee River Collective (q.v) (1974) to challenge the pervasive racist attitudes in many of the white women's groups. Although these groups were feminist first, they did raise issues of lesbianism. The black lesbian-feminists (q.v.) raised issues of race, class, gender, and homophobia (qq.v.).

The first really lesbian-feminist group formed by women of color (q.v.) was founded by Rev. Delores Jackson in 1976 in New York City. This group, initially called the African Ancestral Lesbians United for Social Change (q.v.) and later the Salsa Soul Sisters, included black and Latina lesbians. In the 1980s and 1990s, coalitions of black lesbians and gay men began to emerge as black lesbians became more visible. Black lesbians also joined mixed-race gay and lesbian political groups to help in the fight against antigay politics as well as joining with Third World lesbians.

BLACK TRIANGLE. The inverted black triangle was used by the German Nazis from 1933 to 1945 to distinguish what they regarded as antisocial women—prostitutes, misfits, and lesbians. The pink triangle was used to distinguish homosexual men. Lesbians have adopted the black triangle to remember lesbians killed by the Nazis during World War II. Both lesbians and gay men also use the pink triangle as both a unifying symbol and a means to remember gays who perished at the hands of the Nazis.

BODY IMAGE. Feminists and lesbians have located women's concept of and their attitudes toward their bodies in the male gaze of the patriarchy (q.v.). This male gaze not only prescribes the norms for the female body—youth, beauty, and thinness—but controls females' behavior by focusing their attention and energies on their bodies. Too much attention to attaining the societal norms has resulted in body-image problems. Some of the means to attain this body lead to severe health risks. The means range from voluntary surgery to achieve the perfect breasts to vaginal surgery to make the sex act more pleasurable for men, which includes female genital mutilation (FGM) (q.v.) to plastic surgery to achieve perfect youthful facial features or the surgical removal of fat. Other less invasive practices to control one's body image are no less potentially harmful, such as dietary practices that may lead to bulimia or anorexia.

Lesbians have been involved in the fight against fatism (also known as "fat liberation"). Because of this movement and the lesbian-feminist analysis of the effects of the patriarchally constructed body image, the lesbian community (q.v.) tends to be more accepting of diverse lesbian body sizes and images. Nonetheless, internalized homophobia (q.v.) may manifest itself in a lesbian's self-loathing of her body.

Lesbians may reject the male-directed standards of body image and beauty while imposing their own standards. These standards, or markers, that identify lesbians to each other and to the heterosexual population include hair length, dress, appearance, and behavior. For instance, long-haired lesbians are considered unidentifiable or invisible to other lesbians. Their ability to pass (q.v.) as heterosexual women is considered not to be political enough according to the lesbians who prescribe short hair. Long-haired lesbians are seen as not only able to pass in heterosexual society, but to assume some of the privileges (q.v.) of being heterosexual that are not available to those who are readily identifiable as lesbian. *See also* Ageism; Heterosexism; Lesbian Symbols; Racism.

THE BODY POLITIC. The leading lesbian and gay newspaper in Canada for the fifteen years it was published (1971–1987). The *Body Politic* collective (q.v.) included lesbians Chris Bearchell (the first lesbian member) and Gillian Rodgerson; other lesbians were contributing writers, Jane Rule (q.v.), for instance. The Toronto-based newspaper's purpose was to chronicle as well as analyze gay liberation.

The Canadian government continually harassed this newspaper. In 1977 the Toronto police charged the newspaper with "using the mails to distribute immoral, indecent, and scurrilous material," and again in 1982 for publishing an obscene article. These legal battles, for which the newspaper was acquitted, helped to mobilize gay activists. The newspaper ceased publication in 1987 due to rising publication costs and a declining subscription base.

BODY POLITICS. An elaboration of Michel Foucault's (q.v.) theories that the human body is perceived, interpreted, and represented differently in different historical and political contexts. This "discourse of the body" allows for different social, political, and cultural meanings to be ascribed to female (and male) bodies. Thus, the body is seen as a social and ideological construct based on current normative attitudes.

BOND, PAT (1935–1990). Activist, playwright, and actor. She is best known for her one-woman plays *Gerty Gerty Gerty Stein Is Back Back Back* and *Lorena and Eleanor: A Love Story.* In 1945, she was discharged from the U.S. Army medical corps in Tokyo as one of 500 servicewomen caught as lesbians during a witchhunt. She returned to the United States (q.v.) and began her career as a lesbian comic while managing a club. She is the founder of the New York Eulenspiegel Society, which she called "the only aboveground S/M [sado-masochism] (q.v.) group in the world."

BONDAGE AND DISCIPLINE (B and D). This is a form of sadomasochistic (q.v.) sexual activity in which the submissive partner is bound and punished by the other partner(s) for sexual pleasure. This activity is considered by some lesbian-feminists as replicating the heterosexual sexual power structure, and by other lesbians as empowering. *See also* Pornography; Sex Wars.

BONHEUR, ROSA (1822–1899). A French androgynous (q.v.) painter who adopted the male role and partnered Anna Elizabeth Klumpke, an American artist she called her "wife."

BONNET, MARIE-JO (1949–). French militant activist and scholar. In 1971, she was a member of the Mouvement de Libération des Femmes. Bonnet was also a cofounder of both the Front Homosexual d'Action Révolutionaire and the Gouines Rouges. Receiving her doctorate in history from the University of Paris-VII, she is currently researching the history of women's artistic creations. She is still politically active, defending women's equality with men, and homosexuals' equality with heterosexuals. *See also* France.

BORN WOMAN. Refers to women/lesbians who were female at birth. This is to distinguish them from Male to Female (MTF) transgendered or transsexuals (qq.v.) who are usually excluded from lesbian-separatist or women-only space. A born woman has never experienced male privilege that a MTF has when they were male. *See also* Michigan Womyn's Music Festival.

BOSTON MARRIAGE. A late-nineteenth-century New England term to refer to a long-term monogamous relationship between two women who set up house together. These women were financially independent and usually at least one of the women had a professional career that would not have been possible if they had partnered men. The sexual nature of these relationships have been described as ranging from platonic to lesbian. *See also* Romantic Friendship.

BOTTINI, IVY (19??–). Activist. Bottini was a founding member of the New York chapter of the National Organization of Women (NOW) (q.v.). She was forced from office during the lesbian purges of 1970. Bottini is credited with creating the technique of consciousness-raising (q.v.). She was active fighting the antigay initiative "No on Briggs (Initiative)" (qq.v.). She has been an AIDS (q.v.) activist as well as working on hate crimes (q.v.). She calls herself a "feminist lesbian liberationist."

BOTTOM. The passive sexual recipient, opposite of top (q.v.).

BOWERS v. HARDWICK (1986). The U.S. Supreme Court ruled in a 5–4 decision that the U.S. Constitution does not prohibit a state from enacting sodomy (q.v.) laws and, by implication, that gays and lesbians do not have a constitutional right to privacy for consensual sexual acts. It is then permissible to make homosexual sexual conduct illegal. That the Georgia statute also criminalized heterosexual acts of sodomy was, and has been, overlooked in this and subsequent opinions. *See also Boy Scouts of America v. Dale; Amendment 2* (Colorado)/*Romer v. Evans*.

BOY SCOUTS OF AMERICA v. DALE. This June 2000 Supreme Court decision upheld the right of the Boy Scouts of America (and by extension any group or organization) to exclude known homosexuals or those found to be homosexuals from their organization on the basis that homosexuality is counter to the message of moral values that the Boy Scouts express. This decision is based on freedom of expression rather than the fact that the Boy Scouts are a public accommodation since they are open to all boys (except gay ones) and accept government funding. The argument is similar to that of the New York City St. Patrick's Day Parade organizers, which also exclude Irish gay and lesbian groups from marching in their public parades because the gay and lesbian groups' message is counter to that of the organizers.

Subsequent to this decision, private groups that fund the Boy Scouts (e.g., The United Way) and both public and private groups that provide services and space to the Boy Scouts (e.g., public schools and some religious organizations) have decided to end their support, primarily since the Boys Scouts discriminate against persons for just being homosexual. *See also* Amendment 2 (Colorado)/*Romer v. Evans*; *Bowers v. Hardwick*.

BOYCHICK/BOYZ. The current self-nomenclature used by young butch queer (qq.v.) lesbians who are pushing the ideas of gender (q.v.).

BRADLEY, MARION ZIMMER (1930–). Writer. Bradley wrote over fifty books covering many genres including lesbian pulp fiction. In the 1950s, when Barbara Grier (q.v.) introduced her to the Daughters of Bilitis (DOB) (q.v.), she became involved in the Homophile movement (q.v.), writing for *The Ladder* (q.v.) and *The Mattachine Review*. Her science-fiction writing during the 1970s included the Darkover series, which had polymorphously gendered characters. Her writings continued to explore gender (q.v.) and themes of lesbian and gay issues; her female characters were all strong and independent women. Bradley became estranged from lesbian politics when it became separatist, excluding males. An ordained Eastern Orthodox priest, she provides pastoral counseling at the Gay Pacific Center.

BRANT, BETH (1941–). Canadian American writer. Brant, a Bay of Quinte Mohawk, explores themes of identity—lesbian and gay, Native American—class, as well as themes of alcohol abuse, relationship abuse, and recovery. According to her, writing is a conscious political act, making connections between oppressed people and challenging the power of homophobia and racism (qq.v.).

BRAZIL. Lesbians have fought the rightist government's repression from 1964 until the early 1990s. Since then, many lesbian groups have become active working for lesbian visibility and rights. For instance, the Grupo Lesbico-Feminista was a group of lesbian-feminists (q.v.) that formed to deal with sexism (q.v.) in the Gay and Lesbian Rights movement (q.v.) and heterosexism (q.v.) in the women's movement. The lesbians won representation in the feminist movement, and now play a major and equal role in the gay rights movement in Brazil. By the Second Gathering of Organized Homosexuals in 1984, there were only seven groups. These groups have been successful in having professional organizations endorse the Federal Council of Health's abolishment of homosexuality as a form of deviance, and during the 1987–1988 constitutional revisions, included a provision to outlaw discrimination based on sexual orientation (which already existed in some Brazilian states' constitutions). The International Lesbian and Gay Association (ILGA) (q.v.) held its 1995 meeting in Rio de Janeiro where lesbian activists organized the Exposition of Lesbian Visibility. Since then, lesbians have held conferences and seminars in major cities in Brazil. Currently, a domestic partnership (q.v.) bill is under consideration by the Brazilian legislature.

BREAST CANCER. One of the prevalent cancers, next to ovarian cancer, that lesbians are susceptible to because they may not have birthed children. Lesbians have become active in the campaign to find a cure for breast cancer and to provide public education about breast cancer. *See also* Health/Lesbian Health Issues.

BREEDER. A derogatory term for heterosexuals who "glorified" child-bearing/rearing and overpopulated the world. This term fell out of fashion with the lesbian baby boom (q.v.) of the 1980s and 1990s.

BRIGGS AMENDMENT/BRIGGS INITIATIVE. A California public referendum (1977–1978) named after California State Senator John V. Briggs who proposed it. This referendum was directed against homosexuality and homosexual rights. It specifically targeted gay and lesbian teachers by finding them unfit to teach. This citizen-initiated referendum was based on the successful Dade County, Florida (q.v.), campaign spearheaded by fundamentalist Anita Byrant (q.v.) to repeal Dade County's homosexual rights ordinance. The anti-Briggs campaign, "No on 6," was better organized than the Floridians', Briggs did not have the same clout as Bryant, and Californians not only respected public-school teachers, but realized the implications for their own privacy should the initiative be successful. It was with the issue of government involvement in the individual's privacy that the "No on 6" group recruited the future presidential candidate Ronald Reagan to come out in opposition to Briggs. The initiative was defeated by a 58 to 42 percent margin on November 7, 1978.

BRIGHT, SUSIE (1958–). Sex-positive activist and writer. Bright was one of the sex-positive radicals during the lesbian Sex Wars (q.v.). She cofounded and is a former editor of *On Our Backs* (q.v.), the erotic lesbian magazine. Her pseudonym is Susie Sexpert, a sexual advisor on issues of sexual orientation and practices.

BRING OUT. To assist in the coming-out process. "She brought her out" refers to a lesbian who has a sexual relationship with a woman who had never had sex with a woman before and is now only in lesbian sexual relationships.

BROOKS, (BEATRICE) ROMAINE GODDARD (1874–1970). Painter. Brooks was the longtime lover of Natalie Barney (q.v.). Her best known portrait is of Lady Una Troubridge, Radclyffe Hall's (q.v.) lover. Her portraits were among the first that viewed women as sexual objects from a female perspective, and she presented the lesbian body openly. She challenged the cultural markings of both sexuality and women.

BROUMAS, OLGA (1949–). Greek American poet, translator, and educator. Broumas's first book of poetry, *Caritas* (1976), contained five lesbian songs of praise. Her work, direct and imaginative, is extremely lyrical and sensual, leading to her work being compared to Sappho's (q.v.).

BROWN, RITA MAE (1944–). Writer and activist. Brown was one of the founders of the Student Homophile League of New York University and Columbia University. She joined New York National Organization for Women (NOW) (q.v.) in 1968, but her insistence on open inclusion of lesbians and lesbian issues helped to spur NOW's purge of lesbians, or the "lavender herring" or "Lavender Menace" (q.v.) as Betty Friedan (q.v.) called them.

Brown invited lesbian members of the Gay Liberation Front (GLF), Redstockings (qq.v.), NY Radicalwomen, and NOW to meet to discuss forming a lesbian organization. Out of that meeting what would become the Lavender Menace and then the Radicalesbians (q.v.) was born, and the writing of "Woman-Identified Woman" would begin. This theoretical manifesto provides some of the more astute analyses of heterosexism as well as sexism. Brown left the Radicalesbians and went to Washington, D.C., where she founded the Furies (q.v.), a seminal lesbian-feminist collective (qq.v.), with theorist Charlotte Bunch (q.v.). With the Furies, Brown focused on issues of classism and economics. *Class and Feminism,* the first critique of class in the feminist movement, contains Brown's essay "The Last Straw."

Her first novel, *Rubyfruit Jungle* (1973), explores coming out into lesbianism and is now a classic among lesbian novels. Her current books are mysteries. *See also* Come Out.

BRYANT, ANITA (1940–). Singer and spokeswoman for the Florida Citrus (Orange Juice) Commission, and fundamentalist. Anita Bryant led the 1977 Dade County, Florida (q.v.), movement to "Save Our Children" from homosexuals that resulted in the repeal of the Dade County gay rights ordinance. She prayed and quoted scripture, and put forth a picture of gays as being a threat to the very safety of children (based on the 1972 Democratic gay rights plank that included the abolition of age of consent (q.v.) laws) plus she raised money to win. She was also helped by the fact that local gay and lesbian groups were fragmented: the Dade County Coalition for the Humanistic Rights of Gays could not decide to join in the national boycott of orange juice; and some of the gay rights groups were talking about sexual liberation rather than human rights issues. The repeal of the gay rights ordinance won by an overwhelming 69 percent of the voters.

In 2002, another antigay rights initative, nicknamed after Byrant—Anita Byrant II—failed. *See also* Religious Right.

BUFFALO ORAL HISTORY PROJECT. One of the best-known lesbian oral history projects (q.v.). This project documents the butch-femme (q.v.) working-class subculture of the Buffalo, New York, bar culture (q.v.) of the 1950s.

BUFFET FLAT. A term used in Harlem in the 1920s to describe an after-hours party at an apartment where African American lesbians and gays had a smorgasbord of sexual party possibilities. *See also* Harlem Renaissance.

BULKIN, ELLY (1944–). The editor of *Conditions* and *Amazon Poetry*. Bulkin has written on racism and homophobia (qq.v.). With Minnie Pratt, and Bruce and Barbara Smith, she coauthored *Yours in Struggle*.

BULLDYKE/BULLDAGGER. A term used in the twentieth century to refer to a tough butch (q.v) lesbian. According to Judith Grahn, the term may have come from Boudica, the first-century AD Celtic warrior queen. The term has been reclaimed by lesbians to refer to lesbians' proud Amazonian roots and is used as a term of lesbian resistance to polite, heterosexual society. It has been shortened to "dyke" (q.v.). It is a derogatory term when used by a heterosexual.

Bulldagger is a race-specific term used by black women. Bulldyke is nonrace specific. The earliest usage of bulldyke can be traced to the turn of the twentieth century. The term "bulldyker" was used in Philadelphia's prostitution district to refer to lesbian lovers. *See also* Amazon.

BUNCH, CHARLOTTE (1944–). Feminist writer and activist. Bunch was a cofounder of the lesbian-feminist collective, the Furies (q.v.). Prior to that, she was the first woman to receive tenure at the Institute of Policy Studies in Washington, D.C. Bunch is currently the director of the Center for Global Issues and Women's Leadership at Rutgers University (New Brunswick, New Jersey). In the 1970s, she was a confirmed lesbian separatist (q.v.) since she felt that the Women's Liberation Movement (q.v.) analysis of sexism (q.v.) was an incomplete one by which to fight male supremacy. She saw lesbianism as a political choice.

Bunch later disavowed separatism in favor of coexistence and active cooperation. She served on the National Gay Task Force (q.v.) in the mid-1970s and has since focused on feminist global issues. She founded the Center for Women's Global Leadership at Rutgers University in 1989. The United Nations Conference(s) on Women in Nairobi (1985) and Beijing (1995) (qq.v.) included lesbian issues because of her insistence and work on behalf of women's and lesbian human rights (q.v.).

BURSTEIN, KAREN (1942–). American politician and judge. She was elected to the New York State Senate in 1973 and served until 1978. She was president of the New York State Civil Service Commission from 1983 to 1987. She was elected to a New York State Family Court judgeship from 1990 to 1994, from which she ran an unsuccessful campaign for New York State Attorney General.

BUTCH. A lesbian who adopts masculine dress and self-expression. Butch women, because of their dress and self-presentation, are seen by the heterosexual population, making them the more visible lesbians. Butches are sometimes referred to as "masculine lesbians." *See also* Butch-Femme; Cross-Dressing (Drag); Femme; Passing.

BUTCH-FEMME. The common lesbian code of behavior during the 1940s–1960s, which some lesbian-feminists decried as mimicking heterosexual sexuality. Considered to be an erotic form of communication and partnership between two women, one butch and the other femme (qq.v.). *See also* Butch; Femme; Kiki.

BUTLER, JUDITH (1956–). Philosopher. Her theoretical writing on gender and identity, specifically her 1990 book *Gender Trouble:*

Feminism and the Subversion of Identity, along with Michel Foucault's (q.v.) work, informs queer theory (q.v.). Butler writes that gender is socially constructed and privileges heterosexuality. She also writes about how the deconstruction (q.v.) of gender and sexuality leads to gendered beings. These gendered beings, she states, are performing gender based on cultural and regulatory constructs. She, thus, legitimates the lesbian and gay subject.

– C –

CALFIA, PAT (PATRICK) (1954–). Writer and sadomasochism (S/M) (q.v.) activist. Calfia is currently transitioning from female to male (FTM) (q.v.). A sex-positive (q.v.) radical, Calfia claims that since sexual practices have a mixed reception among lesbian-feminists (q.v), "derivations of heteronormative sexual practices can constitute acts of resistance and liberation." While some theorists agree, others argue that she depends on male theories and practices that do not address adequately lesbian issues, and as a pornographer (q.v.), she advocates subordination of women.

CAMMERMEYER, MARGARETHE (1943–). Activist and former U.S. Army National Guard Colonel. Cammermeyer was discharged from the Army National Guard after proclaiming her lesbianism, even though at that point in time she had not acted on it (she was a Mormon wife and mother). Subsequently, a television movie—*Serving in Silence* based on the book of the same name—has been made about her. She has run unsuccessfully for public office.

CAMP. Stylized, dramatic, humorous, and distinctive characteristically gay male behavior prior to 1969. Camp style transforms the serious into the frivolous and is a conscious act of deviance. Esther Newton believes that gay men use(d) theatrical camp behavior to cope with their perilous social positions. Campy behavior includes the chorus line kick routine that the drag queens performed the first night of the Stonewall (q.v.) rebellion or the comment to police officers that their gloves did not match their shoes.

Many feminists found gay male camp to be misogynic. Lesbian camp did not exist prior to Stonewall. Subsequently, it did begin to develop in the butch-femme (q.v.) community and is manifest in drag king (q.v) performances. Lesbian vampire movies and the revival of lesbian pulp fiction are other forms of lesbian camp. The theatrical performance value of camp is also evident in some of the protests and direct actions of the Lesbian Avengers, ACT-Up, Queer Nation, and OutRage! (qq.v.).

CAMPAIGN AGAINST MORAL PERSECUTION (CAMP). CAMP was the first lesbian and gay rights organization in Australia (q.v.), founded in 1970 as a result of the Stonewall rebellion in the United States (qq.v.). CAMP was an educational and support network valuing lesbians' and gays' coming out (q.v.).

CANADA. The Canadian lesbian movement was inspired in part by the fledgling Gay and Lesbian Rights and Women's Liberation movements in its neighbor to the south, the United States (q.v.). In 1969, the University of Toronto Homophile Association was formed and was followed by other organizations across the country such as the Vancouver Gay Liberation Front (GLF) (1970). The Vancouver GLF was replaced by the moderate Gay Alliance toward Equality. The first lesbian and gay rights march on Ottawa was held in 1971. This resulted in the gay rights agenda, which focused on human rights (q.v.) protections, equal rights for same-sex couples, civil rights/antidiscrimination protections, the right to serve in the Canadian military and in the Royal Canadian Mounted Police, the gay male agenda of penal code reform, age of consent (q.v.) reform, and the destruction of police records. As in the United States and elsewhere, lesbians felt that their needs and issues were being subordinated by the gay male agenda, and some women left to join the feminist movement.

Lesbians and gays were also active in the nationalist Parti Québec movement, which added sexual orientation to its provincial human rights charter in 1977. Ontario added "sexual orientation" to its human rights code in 1986, and the provincial governments of Manitoba and the Yukon Territory followed suit in 1987. Nova Scotia and British Columbia then followed. The Canadian Human Rights Act was finally amended to include protections based on sexual orientation. In 1987, a National Lesbian Forum was founded within the National Action Committee for the Status of Women. The National Lesbian Forum provided a base for a national lobby along with the group Equality for Gays and Lesbians Everywhere.

A key issue for lesbians (and gays) was domestic partnership (q.v.) benefits, especially after the 1988 Toronto Library worker Karen Andrews had her application for health benefits for her lover and child turned down in the courts. An antifeminist group R.E.A.L. Women joined the religious groups to protest same-sex couples receiving recognition or benefits. In 1999, same-sex couples were finally granted the recognition and benefits given to heterosexual couples.

CARD, CLAUDIA (1940–). Lesbian philosopher and academic. Card's work develops lesbian ethics and culture. *Lesbian Choices* (1995) explores the complexity of lesbian identity and sexual agency. She states that in a (hostile) patriarchal society, lesbians are actively engaged in choosing their sexuality while heterosexual women are less conscious of their choice of sexuality. Card currently teaches philosophy at the University of Wisconsin-Madison.

CARTER, MANDY (19??–). Activist. Carter focuses on countering the Religious Right's (q.v.) work in communities of color. She works to form coalitions between communities of color and lesbian and gay communities. Carter is the field director of the National Black Lesbian and Gay Leadership Forum. She formerly worked with the Human Rights Campaign (q.v.) and on the Stonewall (q.v.) 25 Celebration. She has also been active in organizing the Gay Games (q.v.) and other sports activities to reach the lesbians who would not go to the bars (q.v.).

CELIBACY. To allow women to discover themselves, some feminists and lesbians advocated celibacy to conserve sexual energy that would be spent on men and/or in relationships that should be better used for the movement.

CELL 16. Formed in 1968, Cell 16 was a group of radical feminists in Boston, Massachusetts. The group advocated celibacy and separatism (qq.v.) as well as promoting women's self-defense through karate. It published the journal *No More Fun and Games*. The group folded in 1973 after an attempted takeover by the Socialist Workers.

CENSORSHIP. The act of removing or silencing writings, speech, or art because it does not meet society's standards. During the Sex Wars, (q.v.) sex-positive (q.v.) radicals—lesbians and feminists—accused other lesbians and feminists who were part of the antipornography movement of trying to silence them, thus abridging their freedom of speech.

CENTER FOR LESBIAN AND GAY STUDIES (CLAGS). CLAGS is located at the City University of New York Graduate Center. Established in 1991, this is the first American university-affiliated research center devoted to the study of lesbian and gay subjects exclusively. CLAGS sponsors public programs, symposia, and conferences and serves as a national clearinghouse for scholarly research on lesbian and gay issues.

CENTRAL AMERICA. *See* **LATIN AMERICA.**

CHAMBERS, (CAROLYN) JANE (1937–1983). Playwright and novelist. Chambers's lesbian-positive play *A Late Show* was the first such play to reach a wide audience when it was produced in 1974. In 1980 *Last Summer at Bluefish Cove* was presented, sealing Chambers's reputation as the most popular lesbian playwright. In 1981, she was diagnosed with brain cancer, ironically the same as her lead character in *Bluefish Cove*. She received many awards for her sixteen plays. Chambers helped found the New Jersey Political Caucus in 1971. To help other women in the theater, she was instrumental in establishing the Woman's Interart Theater in 1972. Chambers was active in the Long Island (New York) East End Gay Organization.

CHEMICAL-FREE SPACES. In feminist and separatist parlance, this is the area in which the use of alcohol, nicotine, caffeine, and drugs is banned. Recently, this ban has been extended to the use of perfumes, cosmetics, and deodorants that are scented.

CHERRY GROVE. Since the 1930s, a predominantly middle- and upper-class lesbian summer community on Fire Island, New York.

CHILD CUSTODY AND VISITATION. Lesbians have been fighting for custody of their children as one of their top political agenda items.

Lesbians who have children are seen as unfit mothers and are denied custody of their children in cases of divorce or in a court challenge by other members of their family. In the United States (q.v.), over the course of the 1990s, the most publicized custody case was in Virginia where Sharon Bottoms, a lesbian, lost custody rights to her mother because she cohabited with another woman. Her son is not allowed to visit her at her home nor meet her lover. Lesbians are also prohibited from having home-visitation rights of their children if they live with their lovers.

Visitation rights of children for the nonbiological, nonadoptive mother in cases of lesbian couples splitting is another issue that is being decided on a case-by-case basis in the courts. In 2000, the New Jersey Supreme Court ruled in one case that there may be "psychological parenthood" which ties the nonbiological/nonadoptive parent to the child. *See also* Adoption.

CHINA. Beijing's Chinese Rainbow (q.v.) is the political lesbian and gay rights group. The second Nutongzhi (lesbian and bisexual women) Conference was organized by the underground group Beijing Sisters in Beijing from June 25–28, 2000. Attended by fifty women, this conference illustrated the lack of commonality among the lesbians as well as an urban/rural or modern/traditional cultural attitudinal split. Chinese history and politics range from considering homosexuality a filthy habit to a bourgeois behavior and a mental disorder, and is censored by the government as well as considered a "hooligan" crime. The current lesbian community is predominately made up of educated, middle-class, urban women who self-identify. Beijing Sisters coordinates meetings and discussions, and by utilizing mailing lists and the Internet, maintains a forum for educated lesbians to share information safe from government censorship. One of the newest groups is Lavender Phoenix, an Internet social group of mainland (and those from the mainland) lesbians and bisexuals. Lesbians tend to be invisible in China, meeting on-line in chat rooms or in private salons.

In 2001, the Chinese Psychiatric Association withdrew its previous diagnosis of lesbians and gays as officially mentally unfit. That same year the first feature-length lesbian film *Fish and Elephant* was released, which explores the Chinese attitudes toward lesbians. Directed by Li Yu, its was shot in Beijing, and won a prize at the Berlin Film Festival.

CHINESE RAINBOW. A group of Chinese bisexuals, lesbians, and gay men founded in 1995 in the People's Republic of China (q.v.) who are fighting for their rights.

CHORUSES AND BANDS. Since the 1970s, there has been a lesbian and gay chorus and band movement in both the United States and Canada (qq.v.). Of the 128 choruses, 25 are women only, and 41 are mixed gender. Many of the original women's bands and choruses were lesbian-feminist (q.v.) ones. The choruses and bands perform at fund-raisers and are fixtures at gay pride (q.v.) events. The Gay and Lesbian Chorus Association and Gay Bands of America help the 6,500 members organize and reach their audiences.

CHRISTIAN COALITION. *See* **RELIGIOUS RIGHT.**

CHRISTIAN RIGHT. *See* **RELIGIOUS RIGHT.**

CHRISTINA, QUEEN OF SWEDEN (1626–1689). She assumed rule of Sweden on December 17, 1644, and abdicated the throne in 1654. Christina adopted a masculine quality about her dress and voice; to others, she appeared as an Amazon (q.v.). Her only known partner was Countess Ebba Sparre whom she met in 1654. The film *Queen Christina* (1932), based on her life, starred Greta Garbo.

CHRYSTOS (1946–). Native American poet, writer, and "two-spirited" (q.v.) activist. A part of the lesbian bar culture (q.v.). Since she was nineteen, Chrystos, through her poetry, expressed anger at the predominately white gay and lesbian movement and its condescension to Native Americans. She has worked to help forge a deeper understanding of how colonialism, class, and gender oppressions (qq.v.) of Native Americans manifest themselves in substance abuse, hunger, governmental policies of forced sterilization, and land theft among other manifestations.

CITIZENSHIP. In the modern nation-state, people who are born in that state or have naturalized, enjoy certain rights, privileges, protections, and freedoms afforded by that state. Lesbians and gay men by virtue of their sexual orientation, sexual conduct, or just being have been excluded from being able to be full citizens participating in civil and public life—from serving in the military in the United States (q.v.), for instance. With the presumptions of male and heterosexuality as the normative for citizens, lesbians are not able to meet the criteria implicit for full political, social, and economic citizenship since they are neither male nor heterosexual.

Political scientist Shane Phelan claims that economic earning power is used to measure one's status as full citizen—those who earn more have more political power, and thus, rights as citizens—since a citizen's earning power affects a nation's Gross Domestic Product (GDP). Women who are part of the unpaid labor force as housewives and mothers, the underpaid labor force in Malaysian sweatshops, minimum wage earners in a child-care center, or those not being paid wages comparable to men in similar jobs do not have the same access to goods and services, and their voices are not heard in the political arena. Single women and lesbians most often fall into this category.

Phelan also claims that lesbians and gays are strangers in relation to the social and political state. Even if they possess full legal rights, this is not sufficient to be considered equal or full citizens since lesbians and gays are still recognizable as lesbian or gay, and are figures of ambiguity or ambivalence. Thus, lesbians and gays have to manage their identities since they may be called into strangeness at anytime by passerbys or may have their rights legally repealed. She likens lesbians and gays to German Jews in the 1930s: they were full citizens, but recognizable as Jews.

CIVIL UNION. Civil union is the concept that extends legal and social rights to homosexual couples in lieu of marriage. In the United States (q.v.), the state of Vermont in 2000 passed legislation that grants civil unions to same-sex couples. Same-sex couples have the same rights as married heterosexual couples, yet without the appellation "marriage." To dissolve their unions, same-sex couples will have to live in Vermont for one year and apply for divorce. Civil unions apply to only Vermont, but might be challenged under the "Full Faith and Credit" clause (q.v.) of the U.S. Constitution.

In some countries in Europe (q.v.), homosexual couples enjoy recognized domestic partnerships (q.v.) that provide the same social and legal benefits that heterosexual couples enjoy in marriage. This recognition ranges from the Partnership Act in Denmark to the Pacte Civil de Solidarité in France (qq.v.). *See also* Commitment Ceremony; Same-Sex Marriage.

CLARK, KAREN (1945–). Public health nurse turned lesbian activist. Active in the peace, economic, and social justice movements, Clark ran as an out (q.v.) lesbian for the Minnesota State Legislature in 1980 and won her seat. As of 2001, she is the longest-serving out public official in the United States.

CLARKE, CHERYL (1947–). Poet and activist. She helped cofound Kitchen Table: Women of Color Press. She authored "Lesbianism as an Act of Resistance," which is included in the anthology *This Bridge Called My Back*. Her poetry collection *Narratives: Poems in the Tradition of Black Women* (1982) is a form of resistance (q.v.) especially of negative stereotypes (q.v.) of black women who are lesbians. Her poetry embraces the sexual politics of lesbianism.

CLASSISM. The concept of economic class where, according to Audre Lorde (q.v.), there exists "the belief in the inherent superiority of one class over the other and thereby the right to dominance." The critique of both feminism and the Gay and Lesbian Rights movement is that they are dominated by middle-class white women (and men), and thus issues of class are made invisible unless acknowledged.

CLAUSE 28 (1988). The section of the British Local Government Act that prohibits the promotion or teaching of the acceptability of homosexuality and homosexual families that was enacted during the conservative government of the Margaret Thatcher years. This clause has been a rallying point for the gay and lesbian movement in the United Kingdom over the past two decades.

CLINTON, KATE (1945–). Lesbian-feminist comedian and writer. Clinton, a former English teacher, uses her quick wit to drive home her feminist and pro-lesbian humor. She calls lesbian comedy "humor activism."

CLIT-TEASE. A female who flirts with another female with no intention of consummating the sexual relationship. Also used to describe straight feminists who toy with the erotic possibility of sex with a lesbian but do not carry it out.

CLOD, BENTE (1946–). Danish writer and activist. A cofounder of the Kvindetryk (Women's Press) with her first lover and other women in 1978. Clod was also a member of the editorial group of the magazine *Sexual Politics,* which "confronted political parties with sexual reality." Her 1977 novel, based on her own relationship, *Brud (Break-Up or Bride)* is considered one of Scandinavia's most influential books for lesbians.

Clod was active in the lesbian movement. She supported the founding of Women's Centre and cofounded the Women's Cultural Foundation and the Women's Group of the Danish Writers' Association. She continued to write novels, short stories, and screen/stage plays. A member of the Association of Lesbian and Gay Writers in Europe (ALGWE), Clod teaches creative-writing workshops popular with younger lesbians.

CLOSET/CLOSETED (IN THE CLOSET). A term used to describe the state of secrecy around a person's sexuality. To conceal one's true sexual attraction to members of the same sex from the rest of society, one is said to have constructed a closet for that aspect of one's life, thus, to be in the closet. When one openly acknowledges one's lesbianism (or homosexuality), she is considered to be "out of the closet." It is possible to be out of the closet in certain instances such as socially, but in the closet when it comes to employment or family. Someone who has not acknowledged her lesbian or his gay sexuality is considered to be "closeted" or a "closet case." Closeted persons who wield power, especially political power, over other lesbians (and gays) have been "outed" by other lesbians and gays. *See also* Outing.

COALITION FOR GAY RIGHTS IN ONTARIO (CGRO). A coalition of gay and lesbian organizations in the Province of Ontario, Canada (q.v.). It was founded in 1975 to help amend the Ontario Human Rights Code and to advance lesbian and gay rights. CGRO, working in coalition with other lesbian and gay rights groups, succeeded in having the Ontario Human Rights Code amended. Known as Bill 7, the revision included sexual orientation.

Adopted in 1986, Ontario became the second province, after Quebec, to protect the rights of gays and lesbians in employment, housing, and association.

COALITION POLITICS. Political action (and analysis) that makes connections across diverse political groups to achieve social and political change via strength in numbers and working toward common goals. In some cases, this might be the bridging of all groups working on a particular issue such as gay and lesbian rights. For instance, Sexuaalinen Tasavertaisuus (SETA) (q.v.) is the Finnish national umbrella organization of sixteen local and national groups working for sexual equality. In the case of lesbian politics, this involves primarily connections with other groups dealing with issues of race, class, and gender such as gay men's groups, women's groups, human rights groups, and other social justice groups that embrace the ideal of doing away with oppression(s) such as in civil rights movements. For instance, Virginia Apuzzo (q.v.), as the executive director of the National Gay and Lesbian Task Force (NGLTF) (q.v.), enjoined black American civil rights leaders to fight for the rights of all people.

Coalition politics have been effective in organizing sweeping political change such as the French Comité d'Urgence Anti-Répression Homosexuelle. This group cultivated the political left leading to François Mitterand's successful pro-gay candidacy in 1981. Coalitions have also been effective in legitimizing political claims of formerly invisible groups, such as when human rights organizations join and support lesbian groups in their actions and conferences.

COLLECTIVE (LESBIAN-FEMINIST COLLECTIVE, WOMEN'S COLLECTIVE). A nonhierarchical group where each member has an equal vote in decisions that affect the whole. Decision making may be by consensus, where all have to agree, or by majority. Collectives flourished during the 1960s and 1970s and were reflective of the politics of that time—feminist, leftist, lesbian, lesbian and gay. The most famous lesbian-feminist (q.v.) collective was the Furies (q.v.). There were political action collectives as well as labor-specific collectives such as press/media collectives (Toronto's *The Body Politic* [q.v.]). Some collectives existed on woman-owned land such as the one founded by Barbara Deming (q.v.) at Sugar Loaf Key, Florida. Some collectives tried to be self-supporting, removing themselves from the capitalist economy, others were formed to empower their members. There are still some lesbian-feminist collectives in existence. *See also* Combahee River Collective; The Furies; Lesbian Separatism.

COLONIALISM/POSTCOLONIALISM. Colonialism is the process by which one country's people and politics appropriates another country's traditions, politics, people, and resources. This is usually done by either acts of imperialism or aggression. Western European countries colonized Africa, Asia, North America, and South America. Thus, Western European norms have been applied to other cultures, regardless of whether they are consistent with the indigenous cultures.

The norm of heterosexuality and the concept of sexual deviance is the Western European norm. The concept of lesbianism as it is understood by the Western European norm is not the only definition of same-sex sexuality and practice, gender differences, or even kinship in many cultures.

Postcolonialism is the analysis of social culture, politics, and economics in countries that have been colonies of the West. Post-colonialism looks at traditional, indigenous culture, the colonial (period) culture, and culture as it is presented today. For Third World/Southern Hemisphere lesbians, this analysis is very important as applied to issues of lesbianism, acceptance, and solidarity.

Postcolonial analysis has begun to recover the indigenous cultures' concepts. One such is the idea of Native Americans that persons may be "two-spirited" (q.v.), meaning their identity is spiritual and communally orientated, not based on their sexual affinity. In other cultures, such as among some African groups, kinship and economics are the defining terms, not acts, of same-sex intimacy. The modern western-lesbian identity is then a social construction (q.v.) at odds with the indigenous culture's concerns. This is an issue that complicates both contemporary lesbian identity in postcolonial countries as well as lesbian politics in those countries.

COLORADO'S AMENDMENT 2. *See* **AMENDMENT 2 (COL-ORADO)/ROMER v. EVANS.**

COMADRES. A southwestern American term for two unmarried Chicana women who live together, as in a modern Boston marriage (q.v.).

COMBAHEE RIVER COLLECTIVE. A Boston (Roxbury, Massachusetts) black feminist (q.v.) organization founded in 1974. It was named after the South Carolina site where Harriet Tubman freed 750 slaves in 1863. This socialist-feminist group developed black feminist thought. The collective's (q.v.) members examined and wrote about the intersection of race, class, and gender in their daily lives, and used the lens of economics, sexual politics, race, class, and gender to further their analysis of feminism (q.v.). The group opposed separatism (q.v.), stressing the necessity for an inclusive lesbian position. In 1977, Barbara Smith (q.v.), Beverly Smith, and Demita Frazier wrote the "Combahee River Collective Statement," which has been widely circulated over the years as a declaration that black women's sexual orientation was not to be hidden so that the women could participate in political struggle. The group brought together Third World women and feminists in a political coalition.

COME OUT. To come out of the closet (q.v.), to publicly acknowledge being lesbian/homosexual. Coming out is referred to as being a process, since one might need to come out to different people or groups of people at different times over the course of one's life.

COMING-OUT STORY. A person's story or stories about realizing their lesbianism/gayness, their first sexual experiences, and/or "public" announcement of their sexuality. *See also* Come Out.

COMITÉ D'URGENCE ANTI-RÉPRESSION HOMOSEX-UELLE /EMERGENCY COMMITTEE AGAINST THE REPRESSION OF HOMOSEXUALS. The French coalition of gay and lesbian rights organizations that superseded Arcadie (q.v.). This group opposed antigay hostilities and promoted gay and lesbian rights. It successfully supported François Mitterand's 1981 election which led to the elimination of many discriminatory laws. The political success of the group led to its slow dissolution in the early 1980s. However, it continued to published the journal *Homophonies* (1977–1986) and the newspaper *Gay Pied* (1979–1992).

COMMITMENT CEREMONY. The same-sex ritual that honors the union of a lesbian (or gay) couple. This ceremony may be either secular or religious, public or private.

Since same-sex marriages (q.v.) are not recognized in the United States (q.v.) or most other countries, the commitment ceremony is a ritual that publicly recognizes and honors the lesbian or gay union.

COMMUNITY FOR HOMOSEXUAL EQUALITY (CHE). This group came into being after the United Kingdom's North-Western Committee of the Homosexual Law Reform Society helped pass the 1976 Sexual Offenses Act, which decriminalized male homosexual relations. This new group promoted gay and lesbian cultural and social needs as well as legislation. It published the magazine *Launch* and the newspaper *Out*. Like most gay and lesbian rights organizations, its focus was primarily male and it tried to foster communication between males and females. But many lesbians left to join the women's movement.

COMMUNITY CENTERS. In the lesbian and gay community, these are places where lesbian and gay social, health, and other services are provided. They are also places where various groups and members of the community can meet, hold dances, provide programs or classes, and share ideas. Lesbian and gay community centers exist in most major cities.

COMPULSORY HETEROSEXUALITY. Coined by Adrienne Rich (q.v.) in the 1970s to explain the social, political, and economic conditioning of women in a patriarchy (q.v.) to think that marriage (to a male) and motherhood are inevitable. *See also* Lesbian Continuum.

CONCERNED WOMEN OF AMERICA (CWA). A politically active group of religious conservative women founded in 1979 by Beverly La-

Haye. LaHaye has continued to chair the group which claims to be the largest United States' (q.v.) women's organization. It has over 2,500 local chapters. CWA advocates women resuming their traditional roles. It promotes antigay, antiabortion, and pro-family values. This group of women is high powered and visible. CWA members have access to the media including the *New York Times'* editorial pages. CWA is extremely vocal in its antifeminist and antilesbian stances and pressures elected officials. There are 600,000 members in 800 U.S. chapters of CWA.

CONFRONTATIONALISTS. These are people who work for social change and are involved in direct actions (q.v.).

CONGRESS TO UNITE WOMEN. These were regional meetings of all women's liberation and feminist (qq.v,) organizations first held in New York City. The first congress was held from November 21–23, 1969, with over 500 women in attendance. The second Congress to Unite Women was held in May 1970 in New York City. At this conference, when the lights went down, lesbians who had infiltrated the conference wearing "Lavender Menace" tee shirts and who had left the National Organization for Women (NOW) (q.v.) and other organizations, took over the podium, presenting their "Woman-Identified Woman" (q.v.) treatise, making their case as to why lesbianism is a viable political choice for feminists in a patriarchy (q.v.). These lesbians became known as the Radicalesbians (q.v.). Subsequent congresses were held in other cities regionally across the United States (q.v.).

CONSCIOUSNESS RAISING (CR). Created by second-wave feminists, CR groups were small groups of women who trusted each other and who met formally to discuss their personal experiences, thus educating and politicizing themselves. This process was brought to the early contemporary gay rights movement, specifically the Gay Liberation Front (q.v.), to help its members deal with oppression. *See also* CR One.

CONSTRUCTIONALISM v. ESSENTIALISM. The debate over whether sexuality is environmentally and socially constructed or a natural phenomenon. Essentialists believe that one's sexuality or gender (q.v.) is biologically determined and immutable. Social constructionists believe that sexuality is fluid and is a learned response to social and environmental stimuli. *See also* Essentialism; Social Construction of Gender.

COOK, BLANCHE WIESEN (1941–). Academic historian, activist, and author. Cook is best known for her controversial multivolume biographical work on Eleanor Roosevelt (q.v.). She is considered to be one person who outed Roosevelt and Lorena Hickok (q.v.). She has written on the historic denial of lesbianism and the impact of such exclusion and denial.

CORRINE, TEE A. (1943–). Writer, photographer, activist, and educator. Corrine's advocacy of homoerotic art predated the lesbian Sex Wars (q.v.) with her pro-sex and prolesbian erotic and romantic art, writings, and lectures in the 1970s. She is considered to be one of the most influential lesbians of the 1980s as well as a leading lesbian photographer. In 1997, she received the Women's Caucus for Art's President's Award for her service to women in the arts. She cofounded the Gay and Lesbian Caucus of the College Art Society as well as the Women's Caucus for Art Lesbian and Bisexual Caucus.

COUNCIL ON RELIGION AND THE HOMOSEXUAL. Founded in San Francisco in December 1964, this was an interfaith group to promote communication between lesbians, gay men, and heterosexuals, and to foster gay and lesbian civil rights. Del Martin and Phyllis Lyon (qq.v.) were part of the original group. The United Church of Christ and the Universal Fellowship of Metropolitan Community Churches continue the council's work.

CR ONE. Considered to be the first lesbian-feminist (q.v.) consciousness-raising group. Members of CR One included Kate Millett, Barbara Love, Sidney Abbott, Phyllis Birkby, Artemis March, and Alma Routsong (qq.v.) among others. The documentation of CR One is in the Sophia Smith Collection at Smith College (Northampton, Massachusetts).

CRIME AGAINST NATURE. Term "found" in the Bible and used by religious fundamentalists to describe lesbian/homosexual sexual activity. Homosexual sexual practices are seen as against nature since this type of sexual activity does not lead to procreation. *See also* Religious Right; Sodomy.

CRONE (OR HAG). Derogatory terms used to describe old women who are not dependent on men and are no longer sexually attractive to men because they are no longer able to reproduce. Sometimes these women are thought to be witches and in the past have been burned at the stake or drowned. The terms "crone" and "hag" were reclaimed in the 1970s and are used proudly by, and for, older and wiser women. *See also* Ageism.

CROSS-CULTURAL PERSPECTIVES. Taking into consideration that the Western Hemisphere and culture is not the only culture nor even the only referent culture, this concept is extremely valuable to the radical lesbian, black feminism, third-wave feminism (q.v.), and queer politics as they challenge hegemonic white patriarchal society. They are embodied in theories, which bring to the table issues of race, class, gender (q.v.), and culture that are given equal import. These theories balance cultural differences and illustrate that these cultural differences are just that, culturally defined. These perspectives allow for the enlarging of current perspectives on issues such as sexual orientation. For instance, the concept of "two-spirited" (q.v.) taken from Native American culture helps to enrich a definition of gender. *See also* Colonialism/Postcolonialism.

CROSS-DRESSING (DRAG). Dressing in clothes traditionally worn by members of the opposite sex. In past centuries, cross-dressing allowed women to pass as men and gain employment in professions closed to females, such as the military and even pirateering. In other times, it allowed women economic and physical freedom not granted to women. In the late twentieth and early twenty-first centuries, wearing male drag is seen by some as lesbian camp (q.v.), satire, or as a sexual or political statement. *See also* Drag King; Passing; Transvestism.

CRUIKSHANK, MARGARET (1940–). Educator and writer. Cruikshank's work has been essential in establishing a lesbian presence in Women's Studies and in the development of Lesbian Studies (q.v.). Her 1992 book *The Gay and Lesbian Liberation Movement* provides a crucial look at the roles lesbians played in the politicized gay communities and the affects of lesbian feminism and lesbian separatism (qq.v.). *Lesbian Studies* (1982, 1996) articulates the experiences lesbians have had in academia as well as a crucial argument for pursuing Lesbian Studies. Cruikshank was the founding director of Women's Studies at Mankato State University in Minnesota and taught at City College of San Francisco (1981–1997).

CULTURAL FEMINISM. Cultural feminism is a later form of radical feminism (q.v.). It promotes and celebrates female characteristics and differences as women and reclaims women's value(s). Cultural feminism's other major tenet is to promote women's potential by advocating separatism (q.v.) so that women can fully develop their skills and values in order to transform society. It promotes women's culture. Kate Millett's (q.v.) Women's Art Colony and Christmas Tree Farm was a manifestation of cultural feminism, since the women artists in residence learned construction and farming skills in a feminist (q.v.) separatist environment. Major cultural feminist theorists include Mary Daly and Adrienne Rich (qq.v.).

CULTUUR-EN-ONTSPANNINGS CENTRUM (COC). This group has provided a social and cultural outlet for lesbians and gays throughout the Netherlands (q.v.) since 1946. It has promoted and supported lesbian and gay rights organizations and legislation, and has received government subsidies to carry out its mission (since 1973). Some of its legislative initiatives included the revision of the Dutch Penal Code to prohibit discrimination based on sexual orientation (1992), the General Equal Treatment Act (1993), which prohibits the private sector from discriminating against lesbians and gays, and the 1998 Gay and Lesbian Partners Registration Act.

CURES. As late as the 1970s when the American Psychiatric Association (q.v.) removed homosexuality from its list of illnesses, lesbianism was treated as a disease or mental illness. It was thought that lesbianism could be cured by electroshock, hysterectomy, or lobotomy. Many women found themselves placed in insane asylums by their families.

CUSTODY. *See* **CHILD CUSTODY.**

– D –

DADE COUNTY, FLORIDA. The first major antigay initiative (q.v.), which repealed the Dade County, Florida, gay rights ordinance, occurred in 1977. This antigay initiative brought national attention to the role and the power of the Religious Right (q.v.). Boulder, Colorado, had seen a similar repeal in May 1974. The local gay community was not politically sophisticated, though the Dade County Coalition for the Humanistic Rights of Gays, a political coalition (q.v.) of Gay Catholics, a gay motorcycle group, and the lesbian caucus of the local National Organization for Women (NOW) (q.v.) chapter had come together to form a coalition in support of candidates who supported gay rights in the previous election. When they were elected, the coalition asked a member of the metro council to propose the gay rights ordinance, which passed that December.

The gay rights ordinance was rejected by many conservatives, and ultimately repealed in a special referendum in which almost 70 percent of the voters voted to repeal the gay rights ordinance. This successful campaign was spearheaded by Anita Byrant (q.v.) after she was alerted by her pastor that the ordinance would force parochial schools to hire homosexuals. The campaign to "Save Our Children" was the first step in using the emerging fundamentalist conservatives, the Religious Right (q.v.), as a fund-raising mechanism and political force, a tactic which would be replicated across the country. Using a combination of faith, scripture, and patriotic songs, along with her wholesomeness, Byrant appealed to other parents as a mother, soon gathering over six times the needed ten thousand signatures on a petition to call for a special referendum repealing the gay rights ordinance.

The National Gay Rights Task Force (NGTF) (q.v.) was not too concerned, since it felt that Bryant and the campaign demonstrated why gay rights ordinances were needed. Besides, some felt that this was just a publicity stunt to boost Byrant's career. A national boycott was launched against Florida orange juice since Byrant was the Florida Citrus Commission's spokeswoman. The local gay coalition, though, did not join the boycott. Both the local gay coalition and the NGTF underestimated the coalition of religious leaders that joined in the antigay campaign along with the power of the Religious Right to mobilize the local electorate.

In November 2001, two gay and lesbian initiatives were on the Dade County ballot for the first time since 1977. This time, the two measures passed with over 65 percent of the vote. Measure 102 extends domestic partnership (q.v.) benefits to both homosexual and unmarried heterosexual employees of the city of Miami. Measure 115 extends pension benefits to the domestic partners of fire and police personnel. An antigay rights initiative nicknamed "Anita Bryant II" was defeated in the November 2002 elections.

DALY, MARY (1928–). Radical feminist activist and academic theologian. Daly's first book of feminist theology was *The Church and the Second Sex* (1968) in which she attempted to persuade the church to reject sexism (q.v.). Her second book, *Beyond God the Father* (1973), stated that it was the church that was sexist and feminists needed to leave the church and create their own means of spirituality. In this book, she outlines the interconnectedness between the oppression of sexism and homophobia (q.v.) because of the church's sexual ethic which promotes heterosexuality. According to Daly, patriarchy (q.v.) is itself the religion of the entire planet (1978). She thus supports the necessity of separate feminist space where women's powers can grow. Her theories apply what she calls "the labyrs (q.v.) the double edged ax of critical feminist consciousness to cut through misogyny and the labyrinth of patriarchy."

Currently, Daly has been forcibly retired from her teaching position at Boston College since she did not allow a male student into her class. Her position was that she would teach male students on an independent basis, but her feminist classrooms have been all women. This male student was unprepared academically, though she still offered to teach him as an independent study. He went to a religious conservative rights organization which applied pressure on the Jesuit college to fire this radical feminist thinker. Daly was involved in a suit against the college to regain her position; a confidential settlement was reached and Daly retired.

DANISH REGISTERED PARTNERSHIP ACT (1989). Enacted on May 26, 1989, this statute was the first of its kind and is the model for the recognition of the civil rights of lesbian and gay couples. Similar legislation exists in Canada (q.v.), Greenland, Hungary, Iceland, the

Netherlands, New Zealand, Norway, Sweden, and the state of Vermont in the United States (qq.v.). *See also* Civil Union; Domestic Partnership.

DAUGHTERS OF BILITIS (DOB). Founded in San Francisco, California, in 1955, this was the first lesbian organization. It was founded by a Filipina who gathered a multiethnic group of eight women, including Phyllis Lyon and Del Martin (qq.v.), who were open enough to give their names (this was during the McCarthy era [q.v.]). The Daughters of Bilitis (pronounced Bil-E-tis) was only opened to women whereas the two other homophile groups, the Mattachine Society (MS) and One, Inc. (qq.v.), had both male and female members. At the 1959 Mattachine Conference, DOB had to defend its women-only status by explaining that the generic "he" did not fit them, and "lesbians were not satisfied to be auxiliary members or second class homosexuals." While the predominantly male organizations focused on criminal law and police entrapment, DOB focused on family and civil law and issues. While it was taboo to discuss sex until the late 1960s, DOB did in a moderate way demand the rights of lesbians to be acknowledged via education at public fora. Public lectures and interviews were held jointly with other political, social, and religious groups.

Since it had only fifteen members, it initially met in "gab 'n' java" sessions. It also started to publish *The Ladder* (q.v.) in 1956 to reach more women. This publication existed until 1972. DOB organized and held the first lesbian conference (San Francisco, 1960). One of the points of the conference was to begin a dialogue with the church, another was a survey to study lesbians to help dispel myths about themselves. Conferences were held biennially through 1970 and garnered favorable press. When the national DOB disbanded in the early 1970s, local chapters continued to exist. In some communities, DOB was seeing a rebirth in the late 1990s.

DAVIS, ANGELA (1944–). Black, Marxist feminist and lesbian activist. Formerly on the FBI's most-wanted list for her revolutionary work in the Black Power movement and her support of the Soledad Brothers in the 1970s, Davis realized that there was sexism (q.v.) in that movement. Davis remained a member of the Communist Party-USA until 1991 when she went back to academia. She came out at the National Black Gay and Lesbian Leadership Forum in 1993, crediting younger activists for their insights into how sexuality is the focus of struggle. She currently teaches philosophy at University of California, Santa Cruz, and lectures on coalition building while constructing a new concept of democracy that includes economic, racial, gender, and sexual-orientation equally. Her current work looks at the implications and economics of the prison industrial complex.

DAVIS, MADELINE D. (1940–). Playwright, singer, lecturer, historian, and activist. Davis founded the Mattachine Society of Niagara Frontier (Buffalo, New York) and Lesbians Uniting. She was responsible for getting the George McGovern 1972 presidential campaign to include a gay liberation plank. In 1972, Davis taught the first course on lesbianism in the United States. Davis helped found the Buffalo Lesbian Community Oral History Project in 1978 with Elizabeth Kennedy (q.v.) and others. This project is considered to be the most comprehensive history of a lesbian community ever undertaken. Kennedy and Davis wrote *Boots of Leather, Slippers of Gold: The History of a Lesbian Community* (1993) as a result. In 1995, Davis and her partner Wendy Smiley were the first lesbian couple to be married by a rabbi at a reform temple.

DAY WITHOUT ART. December 1 is the day that AIDS (q.v.) activists have chosen to black out art to commemorate the impact of gay men (and lesbians) artists who have died because of AIDS.

DECONSTRUCTION. The academic postmodern term used to describe the unpacking of social and cultural phenomena. It explores and questions the underlying assumptions at the root of "self-evident" claims on which intellectual arguments are based. Feminist analysis deconstructed patriarchy (q.v.) and uncovered the socially constructed subordinate role patriarchy expects women to play. Lesbian, gay, and queer (qq.v.) analysis deconstructs gender (q.v.) so that the social construction of gender can be seen for what it is—roles. *See also* Butler, Judith.

DEFENSE COMMITTEES. Groups that are organized to fund and support persons and issues that are either being contested in court or in the media. In the lesbian and gay communities, these groups support lesbian and gay rights.

A current example is the Mary Daly (q.v.) Defense Fund that is organized to help defray her legal costs in her suit against Boston College for "retiring" her against her will.

DEFENSE OF MARRIAGE ACT (DOMA). In order to reserve marriage as a heterosexual privilege and right in case some states might legalize gay/lesbian marriages, the U.S. Congress passed the Defense of Marriage Act. It was signed into law by President Bill Clinton in 1996. DOMA states that the federal government and other states do not recognize same-sex marriages (q.v.). This runs counter to the "Full Faith and Credit" clause (q.v.) of the U.S. Constitution.

DEGENERES, ELLEN (1958–). Lesbian comedian and actor. De Generes brought out (q.v.) her lesbian lead character on a prime-time television show the same time she outed herself.

DELARVERIE, STORMÉ (1922–). Performer. A recipient of the Senior Action in a Gay Environment (SAGE) (q.v.) Lifetime Achievement Award, DeLarverie has been transgressing gender and race (qq.v.) since the 1950s. During the 1950s and 1960s, she was the mistress of ceremonies in black theater. She also was the sole male impersonator in early drag (q.v.) shows. She has served as vice president of the Stonewall (q.v.) Veterans Association.

DEMING, BARBARA (1917–1984). Writer and peace and social justice activist. Deming felt that the lesbian spirit that motivated women in the peace movement shaped the movement by promoting a feminist critique of the war system and provided alternatives of shared power based on lesbian/women's community and values. She was the founder of a women's collective community on Sugar Loaf Key, Florida.

DEMONSTRATIONS. See **DIRECT ACTION.**

DENMARK. This Scandinavian country was the first to recognize homosexual relationships (in 1989), bar discrimination based on sexual orientation, and grant equal rights to homosexual and heterosexual citizens.

Homosexual and lesbian organizing began discreetly after World War II with the first organization, the Association of 1948. The association promotes both tolerance and equality for homosexuals and lesbians. Since 1978, the group has been known as the National Organization of Gay Men and Lesbians, evidence that the organization was achieving its goal of tolerance. But like most gay and lesbian organizations, it was dominated by gay men.

The advent of the women's movement empowered the lesbians and the radical feminist (q.v.) group Lesbian Movement, founded in 1974. The Lesbian Movement members broke from the Redstocking movement. This group offered critiques not only of the heterosexual patriarchy (q.v.), but of capitalism, too. In the 1970s, the movement created its own culture and space. It turned squatters' houses into women's centers. By the mid-1980s, most of the focus was on single issues such as rape (q.v.) and battered women. The Lesbian Movement, like the Bøssernes Befrielses Front (Gay Liberation Front [q.v.]) were founded as alternatives to the more conservative Homophile (q.v.) Association.

The National Organization of Gay Men and Lesbians again took the forefront working on political issues to improve the legal status of gays and lesbians. This group's successes began in 1980 with the removal of homosexuality from consideration as a psychological disturbance. In 1986, gay and lesbian couples were allowed to inherit from their surviving partner (similar to married couples). In 1987, sexual orientation was added to the list of categories under the antidiscrimination law. And finally in 1989, the Law on Registered Partnership Between Two Persons of the Same Sex was passed, though without religious ceremony or the right to artificial insemination. Feminist and radical lesbians questioned the unanalyzed assumptions of the Partnership Law, and make up only 25 percent of same-sex couples recognized by it.

DENTAL DAM. A thin square piece of latex that is used to ensure that no bodily fluids are exchanged in the practice of lesbian safe (oral) sex. This is to protect the partners from the possible transmission of HIV in vaginal fluids, though there is a debate about this form of transmission of the virus. AIDS (q.v.) activists recommend the use of dental dams for the first six-plus months of sexual activity until partners test negative for HIV, if one (or both) of the partners are HIV positive, or there are multiple partners. Dental dams are also known as Venus Veils and Rubyfruit Suit among other nicknames.

DET NORSKE FORBUNDET. The primary Norwegian federation of lesbian and gay rights groups founded in 1948. The group has promoted domestic partnership and hate crimes (qq.v.) codes in Norway (q.v.).

DETECTIVE FICTION. A genre of lesbian (and gay) fiction writing that allows the authors to explore social and political issues from the lesbian baby boom to pornography (qq.v.), from homophobia (q.v.) to environmental issues, as the protagonist not only solves the mystery before her, but lives her life as an out lesbian. Some lesbian detective series writers are Ellen Hart, Val McDermid, Claire McNab, Jaye Maiman, Sandra Scoppetone, and Eve Zaremba (q.v.).

DEVIANCE. Lesbianism (and homosexuality) are seen as sexual practices that are not normal, i.e., not heterosexual and do not lead to reproduction of the species. Lesbianism in a patriarchal (q.v.) society is also seen as going against societal norms because a lesbian does not make herself sexually available to men and does not "need" men.

DIGITAL QUEERS. One of many lesbian and gay Internet/on-line groups (some others are GayNet Digest, QueerNet, Gay.com, Planet Out, Lesbian.com, and Lesbianation.com). Digital Queers promotes lesbian and gay workplace rights by developing a lesbian and gay computer infrastructure. The Internet is seen as a political organizing tool as well as a way to make social connections.

DIGNITY. A Catholic lesbian and gay organization that helps lesbians and gays who are Catholic bridge the chasm between their faith and their sexuality. This is especially important when the Vatican insists on labeling homosexuality a "serious depravity" as it has in the 1976 "Declaration on Certain Questions Concerning Sexual Ethics" and more recent edicts such as "Some Considerations Concerning the Catholic Response to Legislative Proposals on the Non-Discrimination of Homosexual Persons," the four-page letter to U.S. bishops that urged them to actively oppose gay and lesbian civil rights laws.

DIRECT ACTION (ZAP). A protest or political action taken by a group in order to disrupt, inform, and/or change the social political order. Direct actions were, and continue to be, used by second-wave feminists and lesbian and gay activists such as Radicalesbians, Lesbian Avengers, Queer Nation, and ACT Up (qq.v.). Some direct actions used humor to get across their point, others were very serious. For instance, a 1968 protest against Colgate-Palmolive's exploitation of female workers included the dumping of Colgate-Palmolive products down a toilet borrowed from one of Kate Millett's (q.v.) sculptures. Another direct action taken in New York City on Valentine's Day 1993 was the erection of a statue of Alice B. Toklas by the Lesbian Avengers (q.v.) next to the one of Gertrude Stein (q.v) in Central Park. The first series of public zaps by gay activists in New York City started on April 13, 1970 to get Mayor John Lindsay to support a ban on lesbian and gay housing and job discrimination. These zaps resulted in a meeting with the mayor's office to discuss the gay and lesbian community's political concerns.

DISABLED LESBIANS. The Disabled Lesbian Alliance was formed in New York City in 1978 by Connie Panzarino (q.v.) and others to promote disabled lesbians' visibility and rights in a sociopolitical culture of able-bodied privilege. Members of this group have also (re)sexualized disabled lesbians since there is a mind-set that tends to desexualize or asexualize disabled people. Disabled lesbians were among the first to call able-bodied people the "temporarily able-bodied," emphasizing the fleeting nature of abilities and reversing the oppressive nature of assuming only able-bodied persons are whole.

Lesbian performers were the earliest to recognize disabled lesbians among their audiences. Sign language interpreters have shared the stage with performers since the early 1970s.

Other resource groups for disabled lesbians and gays include the Lambda Resource Center in Chicago, Illinois, that provides books for the blind.

DITSIE, PALESA BEVERLEY (1972–). South African activist. In 1989, Ditsie helped found the Gay and Lesbian Organisation of the Witwatersrand (GLOW) (q.v.). A journalist and documentary filmmaker, she was the first out lesbian to addressed lesbian issues at the 1995 United Nations Conference on Women in Beijing (q.v.). She asked that discrimination against lesbians be acknowledged in the Platform for Action. She also addressed the 1998 United Nations Global Women's Tribunal held in New York City.

DOBKIN, ALIX (1941–). Folksinger, writer, commentator, lecturer, and lesbian-feminist activist. Dobkin (also known as "Her Dykeness" or "Head Lesbian") injects humor into her progressive politics combining feminist politics and lesbian culture into award-winning columns ("The Scum Also Rises") and songs (*Lesbian Alphabet Song*). A strong advocate for women and a community builder, she has taken stances to protect and promote woman-born woman (q.v.) space, but she appears before all audiences.

DOMESTIC PARTNERSHIP. Official recognition by employers or political entities of cohabiting couples who are not, or cannot be, legally married. Domestic partnership allows the employee bene-fits—health, family leave— to be extended to their partner, although the employee is taxed as the economic cost of the benefit is consid-ered to be part of the employee's income.

In November of 2001, the Washington State Supreme Court in *Vasquez v. Hawthorne* found that lesbian and gay partnerships have the same protections as long-term heterosexual unmarried partners. Washington's equitable doctrine protects all unmarried partners; in case of separation or if one partner dies, there will be a fair distribu-tion of the couple's property.

Some countries, such as Denmark and France (qq.v.), recognize domestic partnerships. Germany (q.v.) began recognizing domestic partnerships officially on August 1, 2001; a lesbian couple were the first to register their partnership. In the United States (q.v.), only the state of Vermont recognizes same-sex unions. Other countries are also perusing domestic partnership regulation, but have run into strong opposition from religious and conservative groups, which feel that same-sex unions diminish heterosexual marriage. *See also* Civil Union; Defense of Marriage Act; Religious Right.

DOMESTIC VIOLENCE/BATTERED WOMEN'S MOVE-MENT/BATTERING. The use of violence, physical and emotional, by the husband/male to dominate and control his wife/female (95 per-cent of all reported battery cases are males battering females). In most cultures, especially patriarchies (q.v.), husbands feel that they have the right to control their women (and children) in whatever manner necessary. Even when there are laws against physical abuse in marital relationships, judges in the United States (q.v.) are known to be lenient toward batterers. Women who leave a battering situation are more likely to be killed by their estranged husbands/lovers.

Lesbians have been at the forefront of the battered women's movement, bringing a feminist perspective to help women who are battered and abused, physically and emotionally, by their husbands/lovers to regain their lives. As the battered women's movement matured, it was professionalized, and lesbians who helped found the movement in the late 1960s and 1970s were not so discreetly replaced by social workers. The term "domestic violence" takes the focus off the batterer as it places this phenomenon in a heterosexual family setting.

A secret in the lesbian community (q.v.) is that there are lesbians who batter their lovers in cases of "lesbian battering." This is a dirty secret because lesbian couples are seen as the epitome of relationship equality, and lesbian battery is the physical and emotional domination of one partner over another. Moreover, battered lesbians hide the problem. It is also difficult to get the police, social services, and court system to recognize lesbian battery since lesbian couples do not fit the heterosexual cohabiting couple model of domestic violence.

The causes of lesbian battery, like that of heterosexual battery, are unique to that relationship, though alcohol, drugs, unequal economic situations, and for lesbians, internalized homophobia (q.v.), may be contributing factors.

Lesbian activists continue to be active in working in the now traditional domestic violence shelters helping heterosexual women, and within the lesbian community, helping to identify and deal with lesbian battery.

DON'T ASK, DON'T TELL. This is the lesbian separatist/women's-only space version of the U.S. military's compromise policy (Don't Ask, Don't Tell, Don't Pursue [q.v.]), in which women are not asked if they are women-born women. If they choose to self-identify as other than lesbian or woman, then they are either not invited in or evicted. Supposedly, this is to keep women's-only space free from male privilege (q.v.) and male testosterone.

This policy and separatism (q.v.) have become a volatile issue among lesbians in the transgendered (q.v.) community who may be anywhere along the transgendering process, from just feeling like the opposite gender in a body of the wrong sex to having had some or all of the sexual reassignment surgery. To lesbians in the Queer (q.v.)

movement whose gender identification may be very fluid, these policies are also problematic since they may not identify themselves as women or lesbians, but as boyz, andros, or queers. *See also* Michigan Womyn's Music Festival; Woman-Born Woman.

DON'T ASK, DON'T TELL, DON'T PURSUE. More commonly known as "Don't Ask, Don't Tell" this is the compromise policy that the U.S. military adopted after President Bill Clinton failed to open military service to gays and lesbians in the first months after his election. This policy requires gay and lesbian service personnel not to disclose their sexual orientation, which some find an abridgement of their First Amendment rights to free speech and freedom of association. Officers are not to question personnel who serve under them about their sexuality or to investigate alleged homosexuals.

This policy was enacted to make heterosexual males comfortable since they did not want homosexuals openly serving in the military; some people felt so because then they would have to admit the homoerotic nature of the military. It should be noted that gays and lesbians have served in the U.S. military and have been decorated, and gays and lesbians serve openly in the military of other nations. While all sexual activity is discouraged in uniform, it is still a macho heterosexual culture.

Since the enactment of this policy the number of military personnel discharged for their sexual orientation has increased. The number of women discharged for their alleged lesbianism far outnumber males who are alleged homosexuals. *See also* Cammermeyer, Margarethe; Phelps, Johnnie.

DR. LAURA (SCHLESSINGER) (1947–). A popular radio talk-show and television host in the style of Rush Limbaugh (a right-wing radio personality and call-in show host who called feminists "feminazis" for being stridently politically correct). Dr. Laura, though not a psychologist, acts like one telling people how they ought to live their lives. On the air in 2000, she called "same-sex marriage (q.v.) a slippery slope that will lead to pederasty, incest, and bestiality." Lesbians and gays have been politically active to persuade advertisers not to support her views and shows with their advertising dollars.

DRAG. Dressing and acting like a member of the opposite gender. Drag may be used for theatrical effect. Drag may also be used to pass in society as a member of the opposite sex. For lesbians in drag, this would allow them to reap the benefits of male privilege (q.v.) including being with another woman. In the butch-femme (q.v.) culture as well as in heterosexual culture, the ability for a lesbian to pass as male may be seen as a survival tactic, both economically and socially, since a passing (q.v.) couple is less prone to homophobic (q.v.) attacks, and males are better rewarded economically in a capitalist economy. Drag may also be used to emphasize the arbitrariness of gender (q.v.). *See also* Cross-Dressing; Drag King.

DRAG KING. The lesbian variation of the gay male drag queen who adopts the dress of the opposite sex sometimes in parody or caricature, passing (q.v.) as male. Drag kings assume full male dress including, in some instances, packing (stuffing their trousers to simulate the bulge of male genitalia). There are drag king contests held at lesbian bars (q.v.) and social functions to find the female who best passes as male, and performs masculinely.

A drag king culture exists which goes beyond the occasional wearing of drag (q.v.). This culture supports magazines, books (i.e., Judith Halberstein's *Female Masculinities*), drag king troupes, and an annual Drag King Conference held in Columbus, Ohio, in the fall. This conference attracts drag kings from across the United States and Canada (qq.v.).

Some drag kings refer to themselves as "gender illusionists," which refers to the concept that gender is socially constructed (q.v.) performance. Many drag kings see their performance of masculinity as a political act in which they parody masculinity as well as assume male privilege (q.v.). *See also* Butler, Judith.

DWORKIN, ANDREA (1946–). Writer and radical feminist activist. Dworkin is best known for her writings about sexual roles and power and her antipornography work. Dworkin and Catherine MacKinnon helped draft the Minneapolis Pornography Ordinance, which defines pornography (q.v.) as "sexually explicit subordination of women, graphically depicted in words or pictures." Although Minneapolis' ordinance was never signed into being, it was used as the model for one adopted by Indianapolis. It was overturned by the courts as abridging free speech. This also led to the feminist and lesbian Sex

Wars (q.v.) between the antipornography camp and the free speech, artistic, and political value camp.

Canada's (q.v.) antipornography law is also based on Dworkin's work. Ironically, Canada's antipornography law has been used to stop lesbian and gay fiction and nonfiction from being imported into Canada including Dworkin's work.

DYKE. If used by heterosexuals the term is a derogatory term for a butch (q.v.) lesbian. But the term has been reclaimed by lesbians. *See also* Bulldyke; Gangster Woman.

DYKE MARCHES. These are marches that are organized for and by lesbians. The first International Dyke March in Washington, D.C., was organized by the Lesbian Avengers (q.v.) and took place in 1993. *See also* Dyke.

DYKEWOMON, ELANA (NACHMAN) (1949–). Writer, activist, and cultural worker. Her lesbian novel *River Finger* (1974) was one of the first lesbian novels published by a women's press in North America. She has written other books and is the editor of *Sinister Wisdom*.

– E –

EAGLE FORUM. Founded by Phyllis Schafly, this 80,000 member women's group is extremely influential in Republican national politics. It opposes sex education, day care, family leave, abortion, (q.v.) and AIDS (q.v.) education among other issues. *See also* Religious Right.

EAST COAST HOMOPHILE ORGANIZATIONS/EASTERN REGIONAL CONFERENCE OF HOMOPHILE ORGANIZATIONS (ECHO/ERCHO). Founded by the Daughters of Bilitis (DOB) (q.v.) and other gay rights groups in 1963, ECHO was the first regional federation of lesbian and gay rights organizations. In 1966, it founded the North American Conference of Homophile Organizations (NACHO) (q.v.), the first national federation of homosexual rights groups in the United States (q.v.). While some of its members believed in pursuing homosexual rights through the court system, others were more confrontational. ERCHO helped organize the first lesbian and gay rights demonstration on federal job discrimination held in Washington, D.C. The more politically active and radical post-Stonewall (q.v.) movement, especially the Gay Liberation Front (GLF) (q.v.), led to the dissolution of ECHO and NACHO.

EASTERN EUROPE. The gay and lesbian rights movement in the former Soviet-bloc countries is still in fledgling stages, though the Hungarian lesbian and gay rights group Homeros Lambda (q.v.), which was replaced by Szivarvany, helped Hungary become the first Eastern European country to allow lesbian and gay marriages.

In the former Yugoslavia, there is the group Arkadija and the Serbian lesbian group Labrys. Arkadija's Lesbian Working group conducted a street survey in 1994 to ascertain the status of lesbians, since they are invisible in law. The results were homophobic, with men wanting to "sexually cure" lesbians. Labrys works to end discrimination against lesbians as "single women" in areas of employment and housing, street harassment, social isolation, adequate health care, and child custody (q.v.) issues. Slovenia's lesbian groups are LL (Lesbian Licit) and Lezbiska Sekcija.

The first Yugoslavian Pride March held in Belgrade on June 30, 2001, was violently disrupted by homophobic (q.v.) Serbian Nationalists.

ECKSTEIN, ERNESTINE (Pseud.). Lesbian of color and activist. She was active in the Daughters of Bilitis (DOB) (q.v.) New York chapter, assuming a leadership position. Already active in the National Association for the Advancement of Colored People (NAACP), Eckstein tried to make DOB more politically militant; she advocated changing DOB's policies to include direct actions (q.v.) rather than just education. She helped organize the East Coast Homophile Organizations' (q.v.) political actions, including the picketing of the White House in 1965.

ECOFEMINISM. This is the philosophical theory and practice that equates the domination and abuse of the earth with the patriarchal domination (and abuse) of women, minorities, and animals. Ecofeminists believe that all life is interconnected and they explore and expose the relationship of environmental issues and global capitalism through environmental racism and economics, and women's issues.

EIKVAM, TURID (1948–). Norwegian journalist and activist. Eikvam joined and became a leader of the radical Working Group for Gay Liberation in 1978. She was part of the editorial board of the groups journal *Løvetann*. Most recently, Eikvam has written a historical series on women and lesbians for the journal. She helped organize the first Norwegian gay film festival which has been held annually since 1986. Since 1987, Eikvam has been very active on issues concerning AIDS (q.v.) including coauthoring the book *AIDS and Society* (1987). She is also active in the Network for Gay Research which presents research seminars on homosexuality. *See also* Norway.

ELECTIVE LESBIAN. A woman who feels that she has chosen to be a lesbian rather than being innately lesbian. During the 1970s, many feminists felt that having sexual relations with men was sleeping with the enemy and that to be truly feminist they would have to forswear men. They also felt that to show their solidarity with other women, they needed to fully love them, thus they became political lesbians (q.v.).

ELITISM. The use of economic status, race, sexual identity, education, and social class to dominate others. In the feminist and lesbian communities, there have been charges that women's and lesbian movements are dominated by white, educated, middle-class women. This also applies to white gay men because they have male privilege (q.v.) in a patriarchy (q.v.) that enables them to earn more, thus they tend to set the agenda in the gay and lesbian rights movement. These charges led to lesbians leaving the Gay Liberation Front (GLF) (q.v.) in the early years of the gay and lesbian movement. Charges of elitism and elitist goals of assimilation (q.v.) are still leveled at the major lesbian and gay rights organizations. *See also* Human Rights Campaign; National Gay and Lesbian Task Force.

EMPLOYMENT NONDISCRIMINATION ACT (ENDA). Legislation proposed, but not yet passed by the U.S. Congress that would prohibit workplace discrimination based on sexual orientation. It was defeated by one vote (50-49) in the Senate in 1996. ENDA is on the agenda for both the top mainstream gay and lesbian rights organizations, namely the National Gay and Lesbian Task Force and the Human Rights Campaign (qq.v.).

ENCUENTROS DE LESBIANAS FEMINISTAS. These are a series of encounters between lesbian-feminists (q.v.) of Latin America and the Caribbean (qq.v.). The first meeting took place in 1987 in Cuernavaca, Mexico. These meetings bring lesbian-feminists together in a coalition of support as they advocate for visibility, identities, and rights. The group enables recognition of individual culture differences as it allows for regionalization of the lesbian rights movement.

EQUAL RIGHTS. The Religious Right (q.v.) has transmuted the lesbian and gay claim for civil rights or equal rights—the right not to be discriminated against in employment, housing, health care, etc.—into a claim that lesbians and gays are trying to get more rights than the average citizen already has. It, therefore, complains that homosexuals are seeking "special rights." The Religious Right has used this slogan to fund raise and orchestrate ballot initiatives against gay and lesbian rights. In particular, the Religious Right has produced a series of films such as *The Gay Agenda* and *Gay Rights, Special Rights*, both of which distort and vilify lesbians and gay men. The *Gay Rights, Special Rights'* audience is primarily conservative people of color in an effort to convince them that the lesbian and gay rights movement is trying to co-opt their civil rights, as if there were only a finite quantity of civil rights to go around. *See also* Special Rights.

EQUAL RIGHTS AMENDMENT (ERA). This amendment to the U.S. Constitution would ban discrimination based on sex. While it was first introduced in 1923, it did not pass the Senate until March 22, 1972, and needed to be ratified by thirty-eight states by 1982. It failed ratification by three states. The movement against ratification claimed that the ERA would destroy the nuclear family, give gays and lesbians civil rights, and mandate unisex public bathrooms among other erroneous claims.

Some states, such as Iowa, have amended their state constitutions to include ERAs. The Religious Right (q.v.) attempted to stop such amendments by campaigns, as in Pat Robertson's letter which was sent to households in Iowa claiming that passage of the ERA would make women leave their families and become "feminists, witches, and lesbians."

EROTICA. The literary and/or artistic representation of sexual activities, though what some might consider erotic, others consider pornographic. Lesbian erotica—films, artworks, and literary pieces—by and for lesbians may still fall under the rubric pornography (q.v.) depending on who is viewing the work. *See also* Dworkin, Andrea; Sex Wars.

EROTOPHOBIA. Coined during the 1980s Sex Wars (q.v.), this term was used to describe a fear of erotic sexual play by lesbians and feminists who tried to censor lesbian (and heterosexual) sexual expression such as sadomasochism (S/M) and butch-femme (qq.v.).

ESSENTIALISM. The theory that one's gender (q.v.) or sexuality is biologically determined and immutable as opposed to being socially constructed. Essentialists believe that it is a woman's biology that defines her as maternal, and feminine values such as caring and nurturing are unique to women's maternal nature.

Some essentialists believe that heterosexuality is natural and normal. And if homosexuality is biologically determined, it must be because of a defective gene or a dysfunctional organ. Other essentialists believe that homosexuality is as "normal" as heterosexuality and are searching for the "gay gene" or the determining factor. The danger herein is that such a gay gene or other determining factor could lead to fetuses with such markers being aborted. *See also* Constructionalism v. Essentialism.

ETHERIDGE, MELISSA (1961–). Mainstream rock guitarist and singer. She came out (q.v.) after she had a mainstream record contract and following. Her lesbianism did not diminish her audience, though her lyrics and videos depict lesbian images. Her former partner, Julie Cypher, was artificially inseminated (q.v.). Their children helped articulate the lesbian baby boom (q.v.) to heterosexual America.

EUROPE. The original birthplace of the modern concept of homosexual and homosexual rights starting in the 1860s. Karl Heinrich Ulrichs and Karoly Maria Kertbeny protested Paragraph 175 of the German Imperial Legal Code that criminalized sodomy (q.v.). The writings of Ulrichs, Havelock Ellis, and Edward Carpenter among others helped to develop an understanding of homosexuality, as did the early rights organizations, though the focus was mainly on male homosexuality. While gay men and lesbians lived more freely in the urban centers such as Berlin, London, and Paris between World War I and World War II, the Nazi extermination of gays set back the early homosexual rights movement.

After the end of World War II, the first homosexual rights and social groups emerged in 1946 in the Netherlands, namely Cultuuren-Ontspannings Centrum (q.v). The Danish group Lansforeningen for Bøsser og Lesbiske was founded in 1948, the French group Arcadie (q.v.) in 1953, and the British Homosexual Law Reform Society in 1958. The American Stonewall (q.v.) riots in 1969 echoed in Europe, changing gay and lesbian rights movements into a politicized mass movement.

Gay and lesbian civil rights are recognized in Denmark, France, the Netherlands, Norway, and Sweden (qq.v.), as are lesbian/gay unions. The European Union (EU), aided by the International Lesbian and Gay Association (q.v.) and the Stonewall Group, have included lesbian and gay civil rights as part of the EU's stipulations. In 1997, the EU revised its governing Treaty of Amsterdam to allow the European Commission to act against member states, which discriminated based on sexual orientation. Most recently, the United Kingdom (q.v.), as part of its EU membership, had to allow gays and lesbians to serve openly in the military. *See also* Belgium; Eastern Europe; Finland; Greece; Italy; Portugal; Spain; Soviet Union (Former).

EX-GAY/EX-GAY MINISTRY MOVEMENT. This is an international movement founded in 1978 that is predominantly made up of members of the Protestant Christian Right who believe that homosexuality and the gay rights movement have led to the secular society's demise and that lesbians and gay men can be converted to heterosexuality through reparative therapy and/or submission to Jesus Christ. The primary religious ex-gay group is the Seattle, Washington-based

Exodus International. The leading secular group is the National Association for the Research and Therapy of Homosexuality (NARTH) founded by members of the American Psychology Association (APA) (q.v.) who value social conformity and disagree with the APA's position on homosexuality.

The ex-gay movement has been called fraudulent by two of its founders who fell in love with each other, and by members of the lesbian and gay movements. In 1998, the ex-gay movement in conjunction with the Religious Right (q.v.) promoted a media campaign based on homophobia (q.v.) to raise money for its work against lesbian and gay rights.

– F –

FADERMAN, LILLIAN (1940–). Writer, historian, and educator. Faderman has explored and recorded the history of women's relationships and lesbian subculture(s). Her book *Surpassing the Love of Men: Romantic Friendships and Love between Women from the Renaissance to the Present* (1981) explored women's relationships before the modern usage of lesbian to denote sexual identity. *Odd Girls and Twilight Lovers: A History of Lesbian Life in Twentieth-Century America* looks at the lesbian community (q.v.) and the subculture. Her book *To Believe in Women: What Lesbians Have Done for America: A History* (1999) develops further her belief that lesbian is a social construction of gender (q.v.) rather than a biological nature, as she focuses on women suffragists and social reformers.

FAMILIES AND LESBIANS. Lesbians are frequently disowned from their birth families if they come out (q.v.) to their families. Many teenage suicides are by lesbians (and gays) who do not know how to deal with the homophobia (q.v.). Lesbians who are accepted by their families may find that as their parents age, they are the ones who are called upon to care for their elderly and sometimes infirmed parents over their heterosexual siblings. This may be because the parents do not recognize the lesbian adult child's relationship as being equal to that of a heterosexual adult child's responsibilities in marriage.

Lesbians have also developed their friendships in such a way as to give them the support and nurturance that biological families should. They, therefore, refer to their network of friends as their families of choice.

As lesbians seek to have their relationships publicly acknowledged with commitment ceremonies and civil unions (qq.v.), they are forming publicly and legally recognizable families. The lesbian baby boom (q.v.) allows lesbians to move beyond just forming affectional families. In some cases, via artificial insemination and/or adoption (qq.v.), lesbians are forming biological families. These lesbian families parallel the composition of heterosexual families.

FAMILY RESEARCH COUNCIL. This public policy group split from Focus on the Family (q.v.) and opposes lesbian and gay rights, women's rights, reproductive freedom, government-sponsored health care, and child care. Its founder and former president, Gary Bauer, has run unsuccessfully in Republican primaries for the presidential nomination. With the Christian Coalition, Family Research Council is one of the leading antigay groups. It publishes a weekly newsletter, *Culture Watch,* which has entirely antigay content. *See also* Religious Right.

FAMILY VALUES. This is the term used to validate laws and policies that discriminate against so-called liberal values that threaten the traditional family, especially nonheterosexual, nonmarital relations. Family values is code for the white patriarchal tradition of male-headed households where the woman stays at home raising the children. Lesbian and gay civil rights, marriage, and hate crime (q.v.) laws are seen as contrary to the traditional family as is multicultural school curricula.

The first legislative initiative to protect family values was the 1981 "Family Protection Act" aimed to "strengthen the American family and to promote the virtues of family life" sponsored by Senator Roger Jepsen (R-Iowa). This bill stated that no homosexual or anyone who intimates that homosexuality is acceptable shall receive any federal funds such as social security, student assistance, veteran's benefits, or welfare. The bill also mandated that school curricula reinforce the traditional roles of men and women. This bill did not pass, though variations of it resurfaced over the years. Ironically, Jepsen lost his seat after his membership in a health spa was revealed to be membership in a house of prostitution.

Later that same year, Congressman Larry P. McDonald (D-Georgia) sponsored the successful McDonald Amendment which prohibits legal services from assisting in any case that would promote homosexuality. Thus, legal services could not take on lesbian mothers' custody (q.v.) battles or any other gay discrimination cases.

Family values is also used to promote welfare policies such as the Personal Responsibility Act of 1996, which encourages poor women to be either married or celibate, and pushes poor mothers into the minimum wage (unlivable wage) workforce without a child care or health care safety net in order to receive government funds.

A slogan that the lesbian and gay community came up with to underscore the hypocrisy of "Family Values" is that "Hate Is not a Family Value." *See also* Religious Right.

FEDERAL BUREAU OF INVESTIGATION (FBI) HARASS-MENT. Surveillance and threats of disclosure of one's sexual identity by the FBI kept many gays and lesbians in the closet (q.v.) during the McCarthy era (q.v.) and well into the contemporary gay and lesbian movement. The FBI also harassed members of other movements which threaten the status quo, such as the women's movement and the peace and environmental movements.

FEINBERG, LESLIE (1949–). Author and activist. She wrote the first book about being transgendered *Stone Butch Blues.* Feinberg is a transgender (q.v.) activist.

FEMALE CHAUVINISM. Members of the radical lesbian group, the Furies (q.v.), were accused of favoring and believing in the superiority of women and women's ways, and thus depicting men and men's ways as inferior. Cultural feminists (q.v.) and other radical feminists and lesbians also stand accused of being female chauvinists. This is the opposite of "male chauvinism," which second-wave feminists (q.v.) used to denote a male who believed in the superiority and the naturalness of a patriarchal (q.v.) society.

FEMALE GENITAL MUTILATION (FGM). The cultural practice of clitorectomy and/or infibulation of a female's genitals in order to make the female marriageable. This act is done either as a coming of age ritual or premarital ritual and is performed without anesthetics or sometimes sterilized tools. The purpose is that the male will receive more sexual pleasure and the female's sexual activity will be curtailed. This practice, which affects more than 80 million women and girls in thirty different countries, is practiced primarily in Africa and the Middle East among Muslims. Originally, the practice was the culmination of many years of teachings and religious training, now all that remains is the ritual cutting, and in some cases, this is being done to girls as young as three years old. Some countries are allowing the practice only to be conducted in sterile hospitals; other countries, such as France (q.v), now outlaw this cultural practice altogether. Girls and women fleeing from FGM have been granted political asylum in Canada, and most recently, in the United States (qq.v.).

FEMALE TO MALE (FTM). This refers to the transgendered woman-born woman (qq.v.) who is either transitioning or has transitioned to the male gender (q.v.) by living as a man and/or hormonally and surgically reconstructing her body to be male. FTMs are referred to using masculine pronouns See also Sex Reassignment.

FEMINISM. The belief that women should be treated as social and political equals to men. In theoretical analysis, feminism looks at patriarchal (q.v.) society and institutions that make women racial and economic minorities, and lesbians second-class persons, and the need, therefore, for societal change to make women (lesbians and minorities) equal. There are different types of feminism that apply different foci and analyses, and have different societal and political repercussions such as liberal feminism, lesbian feminism, radical feminism, black feminism, and Marxist feminism (qq.v.).

FEMINIST. A person who believes that women are, at minimum, equal to men and thus deserve equal social and political rights. There are as many types of feminists as there are feminisms (q.v.), each reflecting different perspectives and analyses.

FEMINIST ANTICENSORSHIP TASK FORCE. This free speech advocacy group developed as a response to the antipornography movement during the so-called Sex Wars (q.v.). It filed an amicus curiae brief with publishers opposed to the Indianapolis, Indiana, Antipornography Ordinance in 1985. The group believes that anti-censorship ordinances will be used against lesbians' and feminists' ideas and ideals, and will stop information that is beneficial to women and that challenges sexism (q.v.). This was shown to be true in the case of Canada's (q.v.) stringent censorship law, which has been used to stopped lesbian and feminist books from being imported into Canada. The group of feminists has come together since to sign petitions against other acts of perceived censorship. The group has spawned other feminist anticensorship groups such as the Feminists Against Censorship. *See also* Dworkin, Andrea; Pornography; *Regina v. Butler.*

FEMINIST BOOKSTORES. These are women's bookstores that focus on books and paraphernalia related to the women's movement, feminism, and lesbian communities (qq.v.). These independent bookstores are women-owned and are major outlets for the small feminist and lesbian presses which feature nonracist, nonsexist, and nonclassist works for children and adults. The oldest lesbian/feminist bookstore in the United States (q.v.), Amazon Bookstore Cooperative, founded in 1970 and located in Minneapolis, had its name (and website) challenged by the comparatively new on-line bookseller Amazon.com. Amazon.com felt it might be losing business to Amazon, the feminist bookstore. This resulted in a dirty court fight in which the (lesbian) sexuality of the members of the women's collective (q.v.) that owns and operates Amazon Bookstore was used to intimidate and discredit the women and the bookstore. The 1999 court decision did allow Amazon Bookstore to keep its name.

FEMINISTES REVOLUTIONAIRES. *See* **WITTIG, MONIQUE.**

THE FEMINISTS. A radical feminist group founded first as the October 17th Movement in 1968. The Feminists had a commitment to non-hierarchical organization. To this end, the Feminists rotated all jobs and positions among its members even though some of the members were not as capable as others, or in the case of Ti-Grace Atkinson (q.v.), were pursued by the media to make statements. Atkinson, though one of the founders of the group, left after clashes on this issue in 1970. The group also had stringent and compulsory attendance requirements, restricted the percentage of members who could be in relationships with men (so as to not privilege the heterosexual norm), and limited the amount of time that each member was allotted to speak in group. The group disbanded in 1973 in part due to the stringent rules.

FEMME (FEM OR FLUFF). Femme comes from the French word for woman and refers to a lesbian who is feminine in dress, actions, and identity. A femme is considered more invisible to the heterosexual eye unless she is on the arm of her butch (q.v.). During the mid-twentieth century, feminine lesbians were called "femmes": in the late twentieth century, they may also be referred to as "lipstick lesbians." Young feminine queer (q.v.) lesbians also refer to themselves as "girlz." *See also* Androgenous; Gender.

FILMS, EARLY PROTESTS AGAINST. Lesbian and gay characters have been cast as evil or deranged in many mainstream films. In many of these productions, the homosexual characters are punished for their "perversity" by death. In 1979, gays and lesbians began protesting against this negative stereotyping in the film *Cruising*. In 1980, the National Gay Task Force (q.v.) protested the characterization of Elizabeth Ashley as a deranged lesbian who would do anything for the affections of her divorced female neighbor in the film *Windows. See also* Media Coverage.

FINLAND. In 1889, this Scandinavian country modified its penal codes, changing "man" to "person," and thus, criminalizing female same-sex acts. Lesbians, therefore, fearing legal action, were almost invisible until the first gay organization formed in 1969, Psyke, began to hold dances for both men and women. Sexuaalinen Tasavertaisuus (Sexual Equality) (SETA) (q.v.) split off from Psyke and worked on gay politics and rights. Homosexual behavior was decriminalized in 1971, and in 1981 was no longer considered to be a medical disorder. In the late 1990s, Finland made civil union (q.v.) possible through the Act on the Recognized Partnership between Two

Persons of the Same Sex, a separate but comparable act to that of heterosexual marriage.

During the 1980s, lesbian-feminist groups, such as Akanat, were formed as was the sadomasochistic (q.v.) group Ekstaasi. Lesbian activism in Finland includes the Lesbian Studies Network and the formation of a lesbian publishing company Meikänainen. Lesbians have joined in coalition with SETA, winning political victories such as making discrimination based on sexual orientation illegal. They are continuing to work on other issues including partnership and family issues.

FIRST WAVE OF FEMINISM. During the mid 1800s and early 1900s, women strove for the rights of married women to retain their property, the right to be educated, and the right to vote. *See also* Anthony, Susan B.; Seneca Falls.

FLANNER, JANET (GENET) (1892–1978). *New Yorker* correspondent/columnist. Flanner sent missives from Paris under the nongendered name "Genet." She was part of Natalie Barney's (q.v.) lesbian salons as were other expatriates.

FOCUS ON THE FAMILY. This organization played a major role in the passage of Colorado's Amendment 2 (q.v.) and provides national training seminars to teach its members how to be effective in the political process so that they may promote their antigay agenda. Focus on the Family also owns more than 1,550 radio stations, which deliver its Christian message to listeners worldwide. *See also* Religious Right.

FOUCAULT, (JEAN-) MICHEL (1926–1984). French philosopher. Foucault, a gay male who died of AIDS (q.v.), is considered to be the father of queer theory (q.v.) with his books on sexuality, culture, and power; his two volume *History of Sexuality* (1976) is considered to provide and theory for AIDS activists and a voice for queer activists. An orthodox social constructionalist (q.v.), he writes that sexuality is an invention and that it is the discourse on sex and sexuality (specifically laws against sodomy [q.v.]) that has been mutated into the homosexual as a personal identity. Thus, the homosexual identity is an artificial construct. Because his writing is from a white male's point of view, many feminists and lesbian-feminists (qq.v.) feel his work continues to promote sexism (q.v.). *See also* Butler, Judith; Constructionalism v. Essentialism.

FRANCE. In France, the feminists incorporated gay and lesbian rights into their protests. As in the United States (q.v.), lesbians left the French Gay Liberation Front (GLF) (q.v.) and the Front Homosexuel d'Action Révolutionnaire (q.v.) when it became clear that the males were more interested in sexual liberation and pleasure than in political rights, especially feminist and lesbian issues. The lesbians formed the Gouines Rouges (Red Dykes) to fight for their rights. This group worked closely with other feminist groups. Lesbian issues and rights were incorporated into the French women's movement, even though some feminists tried to exclude radical lesbianism. Lesbian theorists such as Monique Wittig (q.v.) continued to develop radical lesbian thought as part of the French intellectual culture. There is still a strong lesbian movement, which publishes *Lesbia* monthly and holds a lesbian film festival. There are twenty active lesbian organizations still existing in France as witnessed by La Fierté Lesbienne Parisienne of June 24, 2000, which included a forum and march. *See also* Pastre, Geneviève.

FREE CONGRESS FOUNDATION. An educational and research organization that focuses on mobilizing the Religious Right (q.v.). It also produces television programming. This politically and cultural think tank is located in Washington, D.C.

FREEDOM RINGS. A group of rainbow-colored rings usually strung as a necklace, created in 1991 by David Spada, to signify gay pride (q.v.). *See also* Rainbow Flag.

FRENTE DE LIBERACIÓN HOMOSEXUAL DE MEXICO. This was the first gay and lesbian rights organization founded in Mexico in the early 1970s. It was superseded in the late 1970s by the Frente Homosexual de Acción Revoluncionaria, the Grupo Lambda de Liberación Homosexual, and Oikabeth. El Closet de Sor Juana is Mexico's lesbian group.

FREUD, SIGMUND (1856–1939). Austrian founder of psycho-analysis. Freud, on the basis of his practice in prewar Vienna, claimed that women suffer from "penis envy" and that lesbians (and all homosexuals) suffer from a retention of infantile sexual behavior. Normal sexuality for females is feminine, maternal heterosexuality.

FRIEDAN, BETTY (1921–). Founder and early president of the National Organization of Women (NOW) (q.v.). She feared that all feminists would get branded as lesbians (feminists equal lesbians), thereby lessening their political clout, legitimacy, and ability to achieve equality. She called the lesbians who were trying to include lesbian rights and issues, and the lesbians in NOW, the "lavender herring." The lesbians who left NOW adopted "Lavender Menace" (q.v.) when they took over the second Congress to Unite Women (q.v.) in New York City in May 1970. In 1977, at the International Women's Year Conference held in Houston, Texas, Friedan seconded the resolution affirming lesbian rights, which passed.

FRONT HOMOSEXUEL D'ACTION RÉVOLUTIONNAIRE. Founded in Paris on March 10, 1971, after a group of lesbians and gays disrupted a psychoanalytic meeting on the problem of homosexuality. This group had a coalition membership of feminists, gay rights activists, antibourgeois, and racial-justice activists. It dissolved in 1973, but not before seeding the idea that individual identities should be liberated from ideologies that were oppressive and destructive.

FRYE, MARILYN (194?–). Activist, philosopher, writer, and educator. Frye is the author of essays and books on feminist theory. Her 1977 essay on separatism (q.v.) and power is a radical rethinking on separatism since she claims all women, regardless of their sexuality, form the basis of all feminism (q.v.) because separatism exists to some extent in all feminist actions and practices. She also states that separatism moves beyond mere removal of men from women's actions, but actually seizes power from men by denying them access to women, and thus, women's bodies.

FUCK BUDDY. A casual sexual partner.

FULL FAITH AND CREDIT CLAUSE. The U.S. Constitution's Fifth Amendment "Full Faith and Credit" clause, which calls for reciprocity between states on such civil matters as driver's licenses, marriage licenses, divorces, etc. The Defense of Marriage Act (q.v.) is an attempt by the federal government to circumvent "Full Faith and Credit" in the case of any state granting marriage or civil union (q.v.) rights to same-sex couples. *See also* Same-Sex Marriage.

THE FURIES. Founded 1971 in Washington, D.C., by Rita Mae Brown, Joan E. Biren (JEB), and Charlotte Bunch (qq.v.) among others. The Furies is probably the most prominent lesbian-feminist separatist collective (qq.v.). The collective lived together in two houses, sharing all resources and convening confrontational consciousness-raising (q.v.) sessions. It provided political and cultural analyses with a strong lesbian focus.

The Furies' analyses of political lesbianism, lesbian-feminist separatism, and heterosexism (qq.v.) built on the foundations of the manifesto "Woman-Identified Woman" (q.v.). It believed that every woman must "come out as a woman-identified woman or be subjected to male supremacy in all of its economic, personal, and political implications." It called for universal separatism.

It published a widely read radical newspaper also called *The Furies* after the Furies of Greek mythology since they were angry about their oppression by male supremacy. The Furies disbanded in 1972, although their newspaper continued publication for another year. The causes for their disbanding were internal clashes on issues of class privilege, race, age, and children.

The legacy of the Furies is that lesbians found their voice in America. The legacy continues in global politics and culture.

FUSION/MERGING. An intense intimacy between lesbian partners so that they seem to be undifferentiated as individuals.

– G –

GANGSTER WOMAN/GANGSTER DYKE. Used by African Americans to describe a young, street-smart butch (q.v.), African American lesbian.

GAY. A term that refers to both male and female homosexuals, though many women feel the term erases the female homosexual and prefer to call themselves "lesbians." This is noted in the addition of "lesbian" to the name of the National Gay Task Force in the 1980s, thus becoming the National Gay and Lesbian Task Force (NGLTF) (q.v.). An equal number of women prefer "gay" since lesbian is a loaded term that has been used to silence women in the late twentieth-century patriarchy (q.v.). Gay was used for female heterosexual prostitutes during the nineteenth century.

Gay did not catch on until after Stonewall (q.v.), and thus could be used in coded references such as those used by Lisa Ben (q.v.) in her publication *Vice Versa*, "America's gayest magazine" and using "gay gals."

"Gay" it means "pleasurable." It politically connects both male and female homosexuals and has been used as the generic term to refer to things associated with the homosexual subculture (i.e., gay books and gay music).

GAY ACADEMIC UNION (GAU). An association of gay and lesbian college and university students and faculty founded in 1973. The GAU held meetings and conferences about gay and lesbian issues. Founding members include Joan Nestle (q.v), and it is out of the GAU's history group that the Lesbian Herstory Archives (q.v.) was born.

GAY AND LESBIAN AMERICANS. This coalition of grassroots leaders was founded in the mide-1990s with the commitment to gain civil rights for lesbians and gays. The formation of this coalition illustrates the rift between the grassroots volunteer groups and the gay and lesbian movement professionals. The Gay and Lesbian Americans criticized the Human Rights Campaign (HRC) (q.v.) for ignoring grassroots activists' demands for partnerships and dialoques.

GAY ACTIVIST ALLIANCE (GAA). Founded in New York City by disillusioned members of the Gay Liberation Front (GLF) (q.v.), the constitution of the GAA was approved on December 21, 1969. The GAA focused solely on gay and lesbian liberation and civil rights. The GAA had a more structured organization than the GLF and followed Roberts Rules of Order. It did not affiliate with other left-wing groups since it was felt that these groups were antigay and diffused their energy. The GAA was political, undertaking both legal actions and focusing on electoral politics. The GAA used its clout by questioning politicians and elected officials directly on issues that affected the gay and lesbian community. If the public officials were not forthcoming, the GAA sometimes engaged in zaps or direct actions (q.v.). The GAA also took part in other political demonstrations such as pickets and protests and helped organize, along with other gay groups, the first pride march (q.v.) to mark the anniversary of the Stonewall Riots (q.v.).

The GAA political demands included the end of police entrapment and police harassment of gay bars (q.v.), the repeal of sodomy (q.v.) and solicitation laws, protection against employment discrimination, and the end of media (q.v.) defamation of gays and lesbians. The GAA founded the Firehouse, one of the first gay and lesbian community centers.

Criticism by feminists and black membership accused the GAA of being controlled by white gay males. The feminist lesbians formed the Lesbian Feminist Liberation (q.v.) group as a result. The GAA disbanded in 1974, but leaders/activists founded the National Gay Task Force, now the National Gay and Lesbian Task Force (NGLTF) (q.v.) in 1973.

GAY AND LESBIAN ALLIANCE AGAINST DEFAMATION (GLAAD). Founded in 1985, this advocacy group fights gay and lesbian stereotypes (q.v.) in popular culture and media (q.v.), and "the defamation of lesbians and gays and their enforced invisibility in the popular culture." GLAAD has had a major impact on the media—news coverage, programming, and advertising.

GAY AND LESBIAN ARABIC SOCIETY (GLAS). Founded in the United States (q.v.) in 1988, this international organization has chapters worldwide that work on promoting gay and lesbian rights in Arab countries and Arab communities.

Arab lesbians feeling that GLAS was male-dominated formed the Lesbian Arab Network (LAN) in 1990. LAN lasted only until 1991 since by then, Arab lesbians had formed an informal, yet strong, international network. They maintain contact through e-mail listservs such as the one run by Katherine Sherif, and through conferences such as the Marin, California, 1997 National Queer Arab Women's Gathering.

GAY AND LESBIAN ASSOCIATION OF CUBA. Founded in 1994, this was the first gay and lesbian rights organization in Fidel Castro's Cuba. The Grupo de Acción por la Libertad de Expresión de la Elección Sexual has taken its place and is committed to gaining official recognition from the Communist party and government.

GAY AND LESBIAN ORGANIZATION OF ELDERS (GLOE). One of the many gay and lesbian organizations which were inspired by the New York City group Senior Action in a Gay Environment (SAGE) (q.v.). It aims at protecting elder gay and lesbian rights in the community and providing social and educational services as well as outreach programs to the homebound. The Gay and Lesbian Organization of Elders is located in San Francisco, California. Other similar groups exist across the country such as Metropolitan Retirees in Washington, D.C. *See also* Ageism; Lesbian Health.

GAY AND LESBIAN ORGANIZATION OF THE WITWATERSRAND (GLOW). Founded by Linda Ngcobo, Palesa Ditsie (q.v.), and others in 1989, this group joined with the Organization of Lesbian and Gay Activists to promote gay and lesbian rights in the antiapartheid movement of South Africa. In 1990, GLOW organized the first gay and lesbian pride march (q.v.) in Johannesburg. This was the first pride march ever on the continent of Africa.

GAY AND LESBIAN RIGHTS MOVEMENT. This is the contemporary movement that began in the United States (q.v.) after the Stonewall Riots (q.v.) in 1969 and has become an international movement with lesbians and gays calling for their human and civil rights. The modern gay and lesbian movement, also known as the Homophile movement (q.v.), started in the United States in the middle of the twentieth century. The Homophile movement strove for mutual support and educated society to gain acceptance and tolerance for gays or lesbians. It was not as politically active as the post-Stonewall movement in part due to the oppressive McCarthy era (q.v.).

The post-Stonewall era brought political activism to the fore as gay and lesbian liberation and rights organizations modeled themselves on the Civil Rights movement, the Antiwar movement, and the Women's Liberation movement (q.v.). The split here was between a movement for sexual liberation or for civil rights for people who are discriminated against because of their sexual orientation. The issues that were on the agenda ranged from stopping police entrapment and (better) media (q.v.) representation of gays and lesbians, to nondiscrimination in employment, housing, and health care. Lesbians were also concerned with issues such as child custody (q.v.), wage equity, and sexism (q.v.).

Lesbians seeking more visibility left the women's movement and the gay rights movement in the late 1960s and early 1970s and formed organizations such as Radicalesbians and the Furies (qq.v.). They developed political theories such as lesbian-feminism (q.v.) and practices such as lesbian separatism and cultural feminism (qq.v.). While many lesbians saw the value of strength in numbers and rejoined the Gay Rights and Women's Liberation movements in the late 1970s, others remained separate. Still others, including the next generation of lesbians who had joined the Gay Rights movement and/or became AIDS (q.v.) activists, became frustrated at the invisibility of lesbian issues (still) and formed lesbian activist groups such as the Lesbian Avengers (q.v.).

The development in academia of Women's Studies has allowed lesbian history and theory to be developed. In turn, this led to Gay (and Lesbian) Studies, and Queer Studies (qq.v.). Feminists and lesbians critique Gay and Queer Studies, stating that lesbians disappear in the more male-identified studies.

A backlash (q.v.) led by the Religious Right (q.v.) against gay and lesbian rights began in the late 1970s with the Dade County, Florida, "Save Our Children" campaign of Anita Bryant (qq.v.), and continues today with the Religious Right's and ex-gay ministries' homophobia (qq.v.).

The current gay and lesbian movement is diverse, made up of the more assimilationist (q.v.) groups such as the Human Rights Campaign (HRC) (q.v.), which seek normative and nonsexual rights for lesbians and gays such as the right to marry, to serve in the military, and to have a political voice, but also includes radical lesbian separatists and queer activists who put sexual differences on the table. *See also* Equal Rights; Gay Civil Rights; Special Rights.

GAY AND LESBIAN VICTORY FUND. This is a network based in Washington, D.C., of U.S. donors who pledge donations (of at least $100) to support a minimum of two gay and lesbian political candidates. It has recently begun a partnership with the International Network of Gay and Lesbian Officials (q.v.).

GAY CIVIL RIGHTS. These are political and civil rights that lesbians and gays have been fighting for in the United States (q.v.) and around the world. These rights include nondiscrimination in housing, employment and status, the equal protection of the U.S. Constitution, and the protection granted by the Declaration of Human Rights worldwide.

GAY GAMES. Originally named the "Gay Olympics" until the U.S. Olympic Committee claimed proprietary rights to the name "Olympic," the Gay Games are an international athletic event modeled on the Olympics and held every four years featuring gay and lesbian athletes. The initial purpose of the Gay Games, according to founder Thomas Waddell, was to fight the homophobia (q.v.) in sports, and to provide lesbians, gays, bisexuals, transgendered persons, (qq.v.) and their supporters, at all skill and age levels, a venue to compete in a safe and friendly atmosphere.

The first Gay Games were held in San Francisco from August 28 to September 5, 1982. In 1998, the Gay Games V were held in Amsterdam, the Netherlands, and attracted 14,715 athletes from eighty-eight countries.

The Gay Games allow lesbian and gay athletes to compete and to act as role models for others. For instance, Barbara Love (q.v.), a collegiate swimmer who had made the Olympic swimming trials forty years earlier, realized her dream of swimming in the Gay Games in Amsterdam and brought home numerous gold medals for competitions in the senior women's age group.

GAY GHETTO. The neighborhood(s) in which gays and lesbians tend to congregate and to live. These areas are usually in marginal urban areas where the lesbians and gays can feel comfortable and accepted. In these gay ghettos, gay and lesbian communities and cultures can develop and flourish. In many cases, lesbian and gay residents gentrify industrial areas into chic neighborhoods. Some people feel that the existence of gay ghettos stymies the acceptance of gays and lesbians into mainstream culture. Examples of these neighborhoods include the West Village, Chelsea, and Park Slope in New York City; Cherry Grove and Fire Island in New York; Provincetown (qq.v.) in Massachusetts; and the Castro in San Francisco, California.

GAY LIBERATION FRONT (GLF). Immediately following the Stonewall (q.v.) riots, the GLF was formed in New York City (after a series of meetings in July 1969) as a political and militant front or inclusive movement that all gays and lesbians could belong to, superseding the pre-Stonewall Homophile movement (q.v.) and organizations. Based on the North Vietnamese guerrilla group, the National Liberation Front, Martha Shelley (q.v.) proposed the name Gay Liberation Front. This was the first time that a homosexual organization had proudly and prominently stated the sexual orientation of its membership in its name. The GLF's statement of purpose was printed in *Rat,* the underground leftist community newspaper, on August 12, 1969:

> We are a revolutionary group of men and women, formed with the realization that complete sexual liberation for all people cannot come about unless existing social institutions are abolished. We reject society's attempt to impose sexual roles and definitions of our nature . . . the Gay Liberation Front [declares its allegiance to] all the oppressed, the Vietnamese struggle, the third world, the blacks, the workers.

The GLF marked the split between pre-Stonewall politics of the Homophile movement and the confrontational politics of the new gay and lesbian movement. The GLF, besides taking part in political actions, also sponsored a variety of alternatives to the bar culture (q.v.), social activities, and dances. The radical concept of the GLF was emulated on college campuses and in communities across the United States, Canada, and Europe (qq.v.).

Subgroups or cells emerged within the GLF. One such group, formed in early 1970 by Martha Shelley (q.v.) and Lois Hart, was the women's caucus. Called the GLF Women, this caucus was to deal specifically with lesbian issues since these issues were being overlooked as the gay men of the GLF retained their male privilege (q.v.). The GLF Women combined their allegiance to both the women's and gay liberation movements. Quite a few women left this group, feeling it wasn't feminist (q.v.) enough, when Rita Mae Brown (q.v.) proposed a meeting of lesbians from both the GLF and the National Organization for Women (NOW) (q.v.) which resulted in the formation of the Radicalesbians (q.v.). Some members of the Radicalesbians later rejoined the GLF, feeling that they could best pursue lesbian liberation in coalition with the gay men.

The GLF members had ideological conflicts over the purpose of the organization—whether the group should primarily be a sexual liberatory organization or a political gay and lesbian rights organization—and what its allegiance to other liberatory movements should be. These conflicts, along with the GLF's lack of structure and the heterogeneity of its membership, diffused the GLF's effectiveness on gay and lesbian issues and gender issues (cross-dressing and butch-femme [q.v.] presentation were discouraged). The GLF disbanded in late 1970.

GAY LIBERATION MOVEMENT. *See* **GAY AND LESBIAN RIGHTS MOVEMENT.**

GAY RIGHTS. *See* **GAY CIVIL RIGHTS.**

GAY/STRAIGHT SPLIT. This was a conflict between lesbians and heterosexual women in the women's movement in the United States (q.v.) during the early 1970s. This conflict arose over heterosexual feminists feeling that the role of lesbians and lesbian issues on the feminist agenda would undermine the feminist agenda, while the lesbians felt that the agenda should also include heterosexism as well as sexism (qq.v.). Some women saw feminists as traitors if they slept with the enemy, i.e., had male sexual partners. Some women became political lesbians (q.v.) to show their solidarity with all women. A number of lesbians left the mainstream women's organizations such as the National Organization for Women (NOW) and The Feminists (qq.v.) and formed more radical feminist (lesbian-feminist) groups such as the Radicalesbians and the Furies (qq.v.). The key manifesto was "Woman-Identified Woman" (q.v.) which outlined heterosexism.

Similar splits occurred in other countries, such as the Netherlands (q.v.), when lesbians declared that the only real feminists were lesbians, based on the idea that the personal is political. *See also* Europe.

GAY VOTE (GAY VOTING BLOC). The tendency of lesbians and gays to have certain political needs and issues such as achieving equal rights, the ability to serve openly in the military, child custody, and same-sex marriage (qq.v.) and to vote as a group reflecting their political needs. Most lesbians and gays tend to vote Democrat in the United States (q.v.), but there are some, usually male, who vote Republican. Politicians may court this minority's vote or may use their stance against gay civil rights as a means to garner votes from politically conservative groups. *See also* Equal Rights; Gay Civil Rights; Log Cabin Republicans; Religious Right; Special Rights.

GAYDAR. Gaydar, a word constructed from the words gay and radar, refers to the ability lesbians and gays have to recognize other homosexuals. Detecting other homosexuals is done by reading sociocultural cues that might not be understood or noticed by heterosexuals. For lesbians, these clues may be the wearing of culturally coded jewelry such as a labrys or triangle (qq.v.) or may be encoded in language references or length of eye contact. Many lesbians and gays consider the ability to spot fellow homosexuals to be innate and some claim to be able to recognize persons with lesbian/gay tendencies even before that person has come out (q.v.) to herself/himself. *See also* Lesbian Culture; Symbols.

GAYS AND LESBIANS OF ZIMBABWE (GALZ). This predominantly white Zimbabwe organization was founded in September 1990. The lesbians have been the most accepting of black gay participation, but racism and the traditional Shona and Ndebele law do not recognize homosexuality, thus rendering same-sex relations in the black population invisible. *See also* Africa.

GEARHART, SALLY MILLER (1931–). Lesbian-feminist activist, writer, and professor. She has written widely on the relationship of gays and the church. Gearhart codirected the Organization to Defeat (the) Briggs Initiative (q.v.) that would have deemed gay and lesbian teachers unfit to teach based solely on their sexual orientation.

GENDER. In normative society, sex and gender may be used interchangeably. The socially and culturally constructed presentation of sexual identity is coded so that it is read as either male or female based on clothing, actions, and characteristics; race, ethnicity, and class also play a role in gender depiction. In Gay and Lesbian Studies and queer theory (qq.v.), gender is considered also to be the psychological counterpart to biological sex. Gender and sexual identity is also thought to be fluid. To this end, there are lesbians (and gay men) in (sexual) relationships with either members of the opposite sex or persons who have transitioned to the opposite sex such as Female to Male (FTM) transgendered (qq.v.) persons. Some women—those in relationships with men or those who have transitioned to male—still identify themselves as lesbians. Likewise, men who are transitioning to female and who are in relationships with females (either born-women [q.v.] or transgendered women) also consider themselves to be lesbians even if they still retain male genitalia. *See also* Lesbian Continuum; Sex Reassignment.

GENDER BENDER. A blurring of gender specificity such as wearing the dress of the opposite sex. *See also* Cross-Dressing; Gender Fuck.

GENDER FUCK. Gender bending (q.v.) with attitude, to play with one's gender presentation so as to confuse those who are reading (viewing) one's presentation.

GENDER NEUTRAL. Supposedly not favoring one gender over another, but in reality, feminist and lesbian political analysis of "gender neutral" terms and policies has shown that the "neutral" stance either is, or favors, that of the white, heterosexual (and married), male property owner over the age of majority.

GENDER ROLE. *See* **GENDER.**

GERMANY. Lesbians have not received the same amount of recognition as male homosexuals in Germany, though Berlin had a prominent lesbian and women's subculture at the beginning of the twentieth century. During the Nazi (q.v.) era when homosexual and feminist organizations were outlawed, lesbians became invisible. It was not until the women's movement of the 1970s that lesbians became visible again. The student movement in 1971 gave birth to the first lesbian political group. In 1972, lesbians founded the women's section of the gay and lesbian activist Homosexual Aktion Westberlin (HAW). They held the first lesbian protest, a leafleting campaign against a negative lesbian stereotype (q.v.) in a newspaper series in February 1973. The following year, Berlin lesbians founded the first lesbian community center and published the first lesbian journal since the end of the Weimar Republic, *Unsere kleine Zeitung*. During the 1980s, lesbians became visible in the feminist community and the lesbian community began to acknowledge its diversity—lesbians of color, disabled lesbians (qq.v.), and Jewish lesbians.

The reunification of Germany has resulted in many lesbian-led political and social initiatives. During the 1990s, lesbians and gays became more visible, holding pride marches (q.v.) and forging alliances between gays and lesbians. While feminist politics remain important to lesbians, they have begun to move past gender (q.v.), focusing on issues of sexuality.

A law allowing homosexual couples the same rights as married heterosexual couples was enacted in 2001. Two lesbians, the first homosexual couple to officially register their domestic partnership (q.v.), did so on August 1, 2001, when the law took effect in Berlin. The enactment of antidiscrimination legislation remains on Germany's lesbian community's political agenda.

GILDROW, ELSA (1889–1986). British-born, Canadian American philosopher and poet. Gildrow's poetry and writings were explicitly lesbian from the early 1920s publication of her book of lesbian love poems, *On a Grey Thread* (1923), to her autobiography *Elsa, I Come with My Songs* (1986). Gildrow founded Druid Heights, a women's publishing house and center in the San Francisco area as well as the Society for Comparative Philosophy in 1962. She joined the Daughters of Bilitis (DOB) (q.v.) in the 1960s. In 1975, she wrote the essay "Ask No Man Pardon: The Philosophical Significance of Being a Lesbian."

GITTINGS, BARBARA (1932–). Gay rights activist. Gittings considers herself a gay woman. She founded New York Daughters of Bilitis (DOB) (q.v.), and was president from 1958 to 1961. She edited *The*

Ladder (q.v.) from 1963 to 1966. Gittings joined the Mattachine Society's (q.v.) protest of the federal government's discriminatory hiring practices in Washington, D.C. Her work with the American Library Association (q.v.) was critical to having lesbian and gay books and issues become part of the resources of all public libraries.

GLAMOUR DYKE. A lesbian for whom being fashionable and glamourous are extremely important. *See also* Femme; Lipstick Lesbian.

GLOBAL CAPITALISM. Global capitalism involves the growth of multinational corporations, which use their economic clout to ensure favorable labor and environmental laws. Since the early 1990s, global capitalism has become a multicultural issue that includes labor, environment, race, and sexism (q.v) as multinational corporations are seen by some activists, of which lesbians are a part, as raping natural resources and the environment of Southern Hemisphere countries and exploiting the labor pool in those countries in order to reap bigger profits with little governmental regulation to impede them. In many cases, lesbians are part of the exploited labor pool in these countries since they are single women who have to work either to support their birth families or themselves.

In the United States and Europe (qq.v.), this has resulted in the loss of manufacturing jobs to the cheap labor markets in Southern Hemisphere countries and the growth of megastores, that with cheaply manufactured goods and the use of minimum wage labor, put local independent stores out of business. This leads to the collapse of neighborhoods as countless people lose their jobs and the available jobs in the megastores and remaining industries do not pay living wages. In some cases, the Religious Right (q.v.) has used lesbian and gay rights and moral panic as the scapegoats for declining communities. Arlene Stein documents this in her book *The Stranger Next Door: The Story of a Small Community's Battle over Sex, Faith, and Civil Rights.*

Lesbians and gays also feel the affects of global capitalism with the loss of jobs due to the merging of megacorporations, and then, if they do not lose their jobs, in repeals of benefits to lesbian and gay employees. The merger of Exxon and Mobil Oil companies, for instance, resulted in former Mobil Oil employees losing their domestic partnership (q.v.) benefits. Health care is also affected with the high cost of medical and pharmaceutical care especially in respect to the cost of patented drugs to combat AIDS (q.v.) and inadequate health care services. The material commodification of gay and lesbian culture results in spot marketing to gays and lesbians, since they are portrayed as having more discretionary cash to spend on material goods.

Gays and lesbians, including the Lesbian Avengers (q.v.), have protested against the World Trade Organization (WTO) at the WTO's meeting in Seattle, Washington, in December 1999 and at the anniversary of the Seattle protests in 2000. The WTO is seen as the largest intergovernmental organization that promotes globalization by enforcing the reduction of sovereign state environmental, employment, and trade regulations that might hinder corporations from their continued expansion and exploitation.

GOMEZ, JEWELLE (1949–). Poet, writer, editor, and black lesbian and feminist activist. This award-winning writer served on the founding boards of the Gay and Lesbian Alliance Against Defamation (GLAAD) and the Astraea National Lesbian Foundation (qq.v.). She currently is on the board of the National Center for Lesbian Rights among other groups. Gomez's writing encompasses fiction, erotica (q.v.), fantasy, biography, poetry, television, and performance. *Bone and Ash: A Gilda Story* creates a new American myth: a powerful black lesbian. Her writings confront racism, sexism, and homophobia (qq.v.) among both the black and white communities.

(UNE) GOUINE/ETRE AUX FEMMES. French-Canadian for lesbian.

GRAHN, JUDY (1940–). Activist, poet, and writer. Grahn's focus is on working-class lesbians, butch-femme, and the construction of gender (qq.v.). Grahn took part in the 1963 White House protest against employment practices organized by the Mattachine Society (q.v.). She is also the author of *Another Mother Tongue: Gay Words, Gay Worlds* (1990), which puts forward her argument that gay culture is ancient, and though underground, has not perished.

GRANOLA/CRUNCHY LESBIAN. A health-conscious lesbian. Depicted in lesbian culture as wearing Birkenstocks and jeans, and eating vegetarian.

GREAT BRITAIN. *See* **UNITED KINGDOM.**

GREECE. Lesbians were invisible in Greece due to Greek Orthodox traditions and male dominancy until the late 1970s, even though the Greek Isle of Lesbos was home to Sappho (q.v.). The Homosexual Liberation Movement of Greece (AKOE) was formed a year before any women joined it in 1978. These women formed the Autonomous Group of Homosexual Women, and in 1980, left AKOE to join with feminist women in the House of Women in Romanou. They published *Lavris* from 1982 until the late 1990s. The lesbian magazine, *Madame Gou,* is now published in Athens by another group of lesbians. In Thessaloniki, the lesbian group shared space with local feminist groups until the Homosexuals' Initiative of Thessaloniki (OPOTH) was founded in 1988. Former members of OPOTH formed the group Cooperation to Combat Homophobia in 1995. This group publishes *Vitamin O,* a monthly pamphlet. The lesbians in Greece have been gradually rejecting their invisibility.

GRIER, BARBARA G. (1933–). Activist and publisher. Grier believes that "the closet is our sin and shame." She was active in the Homophile movement and Daughters of Bilitis (DOB) (qq.v.). Grier helped organize the first National Conference of Homophile Organizations (NACHO) (q.v.) in 1966. She was the editor of *The Ladder* (q.v.) from 1967 until it ceased publication in 1972. She was also known by her pseudonym Gene Daman. According to Del Martin (q.v.), Grier and Rita La Porte stole the mailing list and in effect *The Ladder,* which led to the closing of the national DOB.

In 1974, Grier cofounded Naiad Press, the largest publisher of lesbian works, with her partner Donna McBride.

– H –

HACKER, MARILYN (1942–). Poet, writer, editor, and activist. Hacker has received the National Book Award (1975) and the Lambda Literary Award (1995) among others. She is a lesbian activist (q.v.) and breast cancer (q.v.) survivor. There is a close relationship between her writing and her convictions. Hacker teaches creative writing at colleges in the greater New York area. She is considered to be a literary formalist as well as an outspoken queer (q.v.) writer. A native New Yorker, she divides her time between New York and Paris.

HALL, MURRAY (1830–1901). Hall was a passing (q.v.) politician in New York City's Tammany Hall political machine in the late 1800s. Her "true" sexual identity was only discovered at her death.

HALL, RADCYLFFE (1880–1943). English poet and novelist. Hall is best known for the novel *The Well of Loneliness.* This book was first banned as obscene in the United States (q.v.) because it dealt with lesbianism as a natural occurrence—lesbians did not choose to be lesbians, they were born with this sexual inversion. Hall used Havelock Ellis's theories on sexual inversion in order to portray lesbians to the rest of the public. The author portrayed herself in the novel as the invert (q.v.) (a man in a woman's body) John, and recounted her loves. The book was first published in England in 1928 and in the United States in 1929. For many lesbians, this tragic depiction of the mannish lesbian is one of the first books they read and one of the first books in the lesbian canon. Hall's most famous lover was Una, Lady Troubridge.

HAMMER, BARBARA (1939–). Lesbian filmmaker. In 1974, Hammer made the first explicit short film on lesbian sexuality, *Dyketactics.* She believes that "radical content deserves radical form" (1993), thus lesbians must invent their own art forms and not use those of the male heterosexual culture. She has produced seventy documentaries. Her most recent film, *History Lessons,* is part of a trilogy on gay and lesbian history she began in 1990. In 2000, Hammer was awarded the Frameline Award for outstanding contributions to lesbian and gay cinema. She is currently a fellow at the Radcliffe Institute in Cambridge, Massachusetts.

HAMTON, MABEL (1902–1989). An entertainer during the Harlem Renaissance (q.v.), she became a cleaning woman when entertainment jobs became scarce. She developed a passion for African American history and lesbian culture that led to her activism and her involvement with the Lesbian Herstory Archives (q.v.). Hamton is featured in films and books about the pre-Stonewall (q.v.) lesbian world. She was a role model to many younger lesbians, black and white, and in 1984 addressed the New York City Gay and Lesbian Pride Rally.

HANSBERRY, LORRAINE (1930–1965). Black playwright, feminist, and lesbian. Hansberry was an award-winning playwright. She won the Drama Desk Award for *A Raisin in the Sun*. She also wrote *To Be Young Gifted and Black*. A member of Daughters of Bilitis (DOB) (q.v.), she wrote articles for *The Ladder* (q.v.) on various issues such as the plight of being a married lesbian.

HARLEM RENAISSANCE. The 1920s cultural movement of black Americans that was centered in Harlem, New York City (but spread to other cities). Black musicians, writers, painters, photographers, artists of all types, business owners, and nightclubs were in their heyday. The atmosphere was open. There were nightclubs frequented by white patrons with black entertainers; there were black nightclubs and parties where blacks and whites mixed, as did gays, lesbians, and straights. *See also* Buffet Flat; Rent Parties.

HARRIS, BERTHA (1937–). American writer. Harris is known best for her work *Lover* (1976, 1993) and *The Joy of Lesbian Sex* (1977). She protested the disappearance of lesbians from literary history and she noted the impact of lesbianism as a major form of identity (before identity politics [q.v.]) of the Parisian literary crowd in the 1920s in an essay in *Amazon Expedition*. She was also a member of CR One (q.v.).

HARRIS, SHERRY (19??–). Politician and activist. Harris was the first openly lesbian African American elected official in the United States (q.v.). She was elected to the Seattle, Washington, City Council.

HART, PEARL M. (19??–1975). Activist. Hart was a Chicago, Illinois, lawyer who specialized in lesbian and gay rights cases in the 1950s. She was very active in the Mattachine Society (q.v.) and headed the Chicago chapter. In 1953, she was part of the conservative faction which made Mattachine more accomodationalist. The Gerber Hart Gay and Lesbian Library in Chicago was named, partially, in her memory.

HARVEY MILK SCHOOL. Named after slain, out (q.v.) gay, and San Francisco Board of Supervisor member, this New York City school is the first public school for lesbian, gay, bisexual, and transgendered (qq.v.) youth. It opened in 1985 after staff of the Hetrick-Martin Institute, a social service agency for lesbian, gay, bisexual, queer, and transgendered/transsexual (LGBQTs) youth, realized that students often met with violence and intolerance in schools, were under pressure at home and in school, and therefore were likely to drop out of school and/or run away from home. The Hetrick-Martin staff worked with the New York City Public Schools in developing individualized education programs and to provide counseling to the youth so that they might grow up to be responsible members of society.

HASBIAN. This is the term given to lesbians who fall in love with or sleep with males. A majority of these women still identify with the lesbian community and identify themselves as lesbian. Joann Loulan (q.v.) so identifies herself, for example. Other lesbians who sleep with men consider themselves as queering lesbian sexuality by not limiting their choice of sexual partners. Some members of the lesbian community feel that lesbians who sleep with men are suspect politically since they are benefiting from heterosexual privilege (q.v.) and are no longer lesbians, but "has been [lesbian]" or "hasbians" (pronounced has-be-in).

HATE CRIMES. These are acts of violence against persons because of their gender, sexual orientation, or another bias or prejudice. While hate crimes, also known as bias crimes, are hard to distinguish easily against lesbians as lesbians rather than as just crimes against women (rape/murder), sometimes the perpetrator makes statements or takes actions that are undeniably antilesbian. *See also* Hate Crimes Statistics Act.

HATE CRIMES STATISTICS ACT. The 1990 act signed into law by President George H. Bush that tracks the number of hate crimes (q.v.) committed against lesbians and gays. The April 23 signing of the bill into law was the first time that gay and lesbian activists were invited to the Bush (41) White House. The Justice Department, charged to collect the statistics on crimes motivated by race, religion, ethnic orientation, or sexual orientation bias, was at first reluctant to do so.

That women or crimes based on sex were excluded ultimately led to the Violence against Women Act.

HEALTH/LESBIAN HEALTH ISSUES. Because lesbians are an invisible population and part of the population of women, they have doubly been excluded from access to adequate medical and mental health care. Lesbians are not represented in clinical studies since most clinical trials use the male body as the norm. Lesbians may also receive inadequate care because of their reluctance to come out (q.v.) to their medical health or mental health care worker fearing discrimination or sexual abuse.

Besides access to appropriate health care, lesbians face the following health care issues: pregnancy, sexually transmitted diseases, substance and alcohol abuse, battery, aging, and breast and ovarian cancer. Lesbians also need to have their partners involved in their health care issues and decisions where appropriate. *See also* Breast Cancer.

HEATHER HAS TWO MOMMIES. Written by Leslea Newman (q.v.), this book triggered the Queens, New York, Board of Education to object to the multicultural Rainbow Curriculum (q.v.) because it promoted lesbian families and did not support the Religious Rights' family values (qq.v.). The book was only one of many suggested to be included in school libraries.

HENSONS, BRENDA and WANDA (1945– , 1954–). Activists and founders of Camp Sister Spirit, Ovett, Mississippi. Camp Sister Spirit is women's land that has come under physical attack by neighbors who do not want lesbians there. Camp Sister Spirit provides social services for the poor in and around Ovett. *See also* Lesbian Lands.

HERMAPHRODITE/INTERSEXED. A person born with both female and male sexual organs or genes. One baby in a thousand births is born intersexed. Usually a baby is sexually reassigned surgically (and with hormones) based on the prominence of the visible sexual organs; assigning a child "female" is the easiest and most common. *See also* Transgender; Transsexual.

HERSTORY. The history of lesbians and women, which is commonly missing from the male (his)story of wars and kings. This term was coined by early lesbian-feminists (q.v.) to recover the history of lesbians and to name their own history as opposed to the patriarchy's (q.v.) history. Many feminist and lesbian archives which reclaim lesbian/women's past are herstory archives. One of the first such archives was the Lesbian Herstory Archive (q.v.) located in New York City.

The International Gay and Lesbian Archive in Los Angeles, while begun in 1943 by Jim Kepner, was not open to the public until 1976. The first academic archivist of lesbian material was Brenda Marston at Cornell University (Ithaca, New York).

HE-SHE. The term used before 1969 to describe a woman who others read as male based on her appearance and actions.

HETERODOXY. A New York City club founded in 1912 for "free-willed women." This influential club had both lesbian and heterosexual members. The women were active in the suffrage, peace, and labor movement. This group no longer exists.

HETEROSEXISM. The bias towards male-female sexual activity; the consideration of procreative male-female heterosexual relationships as the only "real" relationships. *See also* Heterosexual Assumption; Heterosexual Privilege; Homophobia.

HETEROSEXUAL ASSUMPTION. The belief that everyone is heterosexual and that heterosexuality is the normative, moral, and correct sexuality. This assumption results in many children, teenagers, and adults who are ashamed and silenced if their sexuality does not meet the norm of heterosexuality. This shame is so severe that teens are more likely to commit suicide over their homosexuality than any other reason.

HETEROSEXUAL PRIVILEGE. The act of privileging or preferring male-female relationships and sexuality over that of lesbians and gays.

HICKOK, (ALICE) LORENA "HICK" (1893–1968). Journalist. Hickok was one of the first woman Associated Press (AP) reporters. She covered the Lindbergh kidnapping trial. Later, she was sent to cover the New York State gubernatorial race in which she met

Eleanor Roosevelt (q.v.), soon to become her intimate friend and lover as well as First Lady of the United States. Hick lived in the White House with Roosevelt. After giving up her position as reporter, since she could no longer be objective, she traveled Depression era America sending back reports to Harry Hopkins of the Federal Relief Agency and letters to Roosevelt. Her reports and letters were translated into many of Franklin D. Roosevelt's policies and programs. Hick traveled with Eleanor Roosevelt on official business besides vacationing together.

Although their relationship faltered, their friendship did not, and Hick moved to Hyde Park, New York, to be near Roosevelt at ValKill in their later years. Hick left eighteen boxes of letters (over 3,360 letters) from Roosevelt to her to be opened ten years after her death. They were opened in 1978 and formed the basis of Doris Faber's 1979 biography of Hick, Pat Bond's (q.v.) play about Hick and Roosevelt, and Blanche W. Cook's (q.v.) biography of Eleanor Roosevelt. These letters are quite intimate and may be read at the Franklin Delano Roosevelt Library in Hyde Park, New York.

On her death in 1968, Hick was cremated, her ashes remaining unclaimed at the funeral home until they were buried in an unmarked grave in the late 1980s. After a production of Pat Bond's play about Hick and ER, a memorial fund was set up by Linda Boyd Kavars (q.v.) to mark Hick's grave in the Rhinebeck, New York, cemetery and to start a scholarship fund in her memory. Her grave was marked on May 10, 2000, with a memorial remembering her as an activist, reporter, and intimate friend of Eleanor Roosevelt.

HIV. See ACQUIRED IMMUNE DEFICIENCY SYNDROME/HUMAN IMMUNODEFICIENCY VIRUS (AIDS/HIV).

HOLLIBAUGH, AMBER (1947–). Sex radical, feminist, lesbian-feminist activist, and filmmaker. She came out (q.v.) in the women's movement at McGill University, Montreal, Quebec. As a political organizer, she worked on the "No on 6" anti-Briggs Initiative (q.v.) campaign. As a former sex worker and a femme (qq.v.), she found herself at the heart of the lesbian Sex Wars (q.v.) when she delivered a talk at the 1981 Barnard Conference on Sexuality, which is considered as ground zero of the Sex Wars. Hollibaugh founded and became the director of the Lesbian AIDS Project of Gay Men's Health Crisis. Her writings articulate issues of class as well as butch-femme (q.v.) desire.

HOMEROS LAMBDA. The first sanctioned gay and lesbian rights group in Hungary. It was founded in 1988. It helped to promote the rights of same-sex couples to marry. Homeros Lambda dissolved because of internal conflict in 1995, shortly after a court decision that found the law prohibiting gay and lesbian marriage unconstitutional. It was replaced by Szivarvany and other gay and lesbian political rights groups.

HOMOEROTIC. Suggestive sexually erotic (q.v.) expression in print, film, or advertising of two women (or two men).

HOMOPHILE. Term used in the twentieth century (until 1969) to mean homosexual. *See also* Homophile Movement.

HOMOPHILE MOVEMENT. This was the name of the modern homosexual rights movement from 1945 (post–World War II) until 1969 (the Stonewall Riots [q.v.]) in the United States (q.v.). This movement promoted tolerance and understanding of homosexuality. The key homophile groups were the Veterans Benevolent Association, the Mattachine Society (MS), and the Daughters of Bilitis (DOB) (qq.v.).

HOMOPHOBIA. The fear of homosexuals and homosexuality. Homophobia may be practiced by society as a whole, or individually. Homophobia can also be internalized (internal homophobia) by gays and lesbians as self-loathing, since they are not like the norm, i.e., heterosexual. *See also* Internalized Homophobia.

HOMOSEXUAL LAW REFORM SOCIETY (HLRS). This group came into being in 1958 after the publication of the Wolfenden Report (q.v.). The focus of this group was to foster the repeal of existing British laws against homosexuality and sex reforms in general. The group published various journals including *At Work* and *Man and Society*, and conducted educational, research, and counseling activities. With the Sexual Offenses Act of 1967, the group's support declined, and in the early 1970s, more people joined the Gay Liberation Front (GLF) (q.v.). The group changed its name in 1970 to the Sexual Law Reform Society (SLRS). As SLRS, the group continued to work for the liberaliztion of obscenity laws, the abolition of consent laws, and the elimination of sexual offenses as a separate and distinct category in British law.

HOMOSEXUAL PANIC. Fear of one's own possible homosexuality. A woman to prove herself not a lesbian may deny she is a lesbian and may date men and marry. Homosexual panic has been used as a defense in hate crimes (q.v.), as in, "It was homosexual panic that made me kill the homosexual." It has also been one of the reasons gays and lesbians have been barred from serving in the military.

HOMOSEXUELLE INTERESSEN-GEMEINSCHAFT BERLIN. The first gay and lesbian rights group to emerge in the German Democratic Republic. Although never officially recognized, it was banned in 1978. The Lutheran/Evangelical church helped gay and lesbian groups and formed the base of the 1990 secular and religious federation of gay and lesbian groups. *See also* Germany.

hooks, bell (GLORIA WATSON) (1952–). Writer, theorist, and radical academic. Watson is an academic who writes under the pen name of bell hooks. She believes that homophobia (q.v.) is a logical extension of sexism (q.v.), thus it privileges gender (q.v.) over sexuality. Michele Wallace, Barbara Smith, and Adrienne Rich (qq.v.) all have critiqued Watson, since she omits a thorough discussion of lesbianism.

HOUSING. An area in which gays and lesbians may be discriminated against. Landlords do not have to rent to homosexuals and banks can deny mortgages to homosexuals. The lesbian or gay person has no legal recourse unless there is a specific law or statute that prohibits housing discrimination based on gender and sexual orientation. Discrimination from landlords can range from refusing to rent to homosexuals because of their sexual orientation to homosexual partners not being considered in line of succession to inherit a lease if their partner moves or dies.

HR-14752. "A Bill to Prohibit AntiGay Discrimination across United States." This is the first (1974) federal gay and lesbian civil rights bill proposed by New York Representatives Bella Abzug (q.v.) and Ed Koch. While this bill (also known as the Civil Rights Amendment of 1975) was not passed, it laid the groundwork for future bills and for politicians to take the lesbian and gay voters as serious constituents.

HUGHES, HOLLY (c. 1955–). Openly lesbian and feminist performance artist. She was one of NEA 4—the artists who were defunded by the National Endowment for the Arts in 1990 because of the sexually explicit nature of their work. A court order refunded them. The Religious Right (q.v.) began this controversy since it felt that the federal government should not fund art at all, much less art that is lesbian or sexual in nature.

Hughes was part of the experimental lesbian theater movement that originated on the lower east side of New York City in the early 1980s. She cofounded the National Fund for Lesbian and Gay Artists in 1991. She uses her art to promote lesbian visibility as well as critique lesbian and orthodox feminism (q.v.) conventions as she challenges assumptions about identity and gender (qq.v.).

HUMAN RIGHTS. These rights are sometimes referred to as "natural" rights as they are rights that should be held by everyone and not given or taken away by any governmental entity. These rights include the right to life, liberty, and security; freedom from torture and cruel and unusual punishment; freedom of expression, association, and conscience (or religion); and human dignity.

The Universal Declaration of Human Rights (UDHR), initiated by Eleanor Roosevelt (q.v.), was adopted by the United Nations (UN) in 1948. This is the primary document which sets out the rights all people should enjoy, including the right to adequate housing and standard of living, education, and equal protection of the law. This document, though, is aimed at government to public citizen relations and does not fully address private and cultural issues. To this end, the United Nations has proposed the Convention to End Discrimination Against Women (CEDAW), which has been signed by 162 countries, but not the United States (q.v.). CEDAW covers such issues as violence against women, including female genital mutilation (FGM) and sexual autonomy (qq.v.) of women.

These treaties do not mention sexual orientation or lesbian rights. The human rights of all women have been the subject of the UN Conferences on Women in Mexico City, Nairobi, and Beijing (qq.v.). Lesbian rights and issues have been discussed at these conferences, but have not yet been incorporated in the official platforms.

Lesbian human rights include the right to sexual self-determiation including the right against state-sponsored persecution because of one's sexuality, the right not to be discriminated against based on sexual orientation, and the right not to be persecuted because of sexual orientation by families and individuals (cultural persecution) along with all the other human rights.

The European Court of Human Rights has begun to include sexual orientation and lesbian rights in its interpretations of treaties. Other nongovernmental agencies which monitor human rights such as Amnesty International (q.v.) and Human Rights Watch and feminist groups such as the Center for Women's Global Leadership and the Feminist Majority, have begun to include sexual orientation and lesbian (and gay) rights in their definitions of human rights. The International Gay and Lesbian Human Rights Commission (q.v.) has been monitoring human-rights violations against lesbians as well as advancing lesbian rights.

HUMAN RIGHTS CAMPAIGN (HRC). Formerly the Human Rights Fund, this is one of the largest gay and lesbian political rights organizations in the United States (q.v.). It was founded in 1976 as the Gay Rights National Organization. A political action committee (PAC), the HRC can and does give money to politicians who support gay and lesbian rights, and the HRC lobbies the federal and state governments for lesbian and gay rights.

The HRC is seen as a centrist, assimilationist (q.v.) organization. It drew the wrath of many lesbians (and gay men) when it decided to support the 1998 reelection campaign of then New York Republican Senator Alphonse D'Amato because the HRC thought he might have more power to push through the Employment Non-Discrimination Act (ENDA) (q.v.) as an incumbent than his opponent, Democratic Congressman Charles Schumer. D'Amato had a bad track record when it came to legislation that he had supported in the Senate concerning women and minorities, and his political power over New

York State politics had kept a hate crimes (q.v.) bill from reaching the floor of the New York State Legislature.

The HRC's involvement in the Millennium March and its support of same-sex marriage (q.v.) to the detriment of other issues brought further criticisms. The HRC does support National Coming Out Day (October 11) and provides public education programs and assistance in fighting antigay ballot initiatives.

HWAME. The Native American Pima word for lesbian shaman.

– I –

IDENTITY POLITICS. The political and social alliance of minority groups based on one dominant feature such as race, gender, sexual orientation, religion, or ethnicity. For some people, the identity is self-proclaimed, for others it is "read" on to them. For example, Cracker Barrel restaurant was refusing to hire gays and lesbians and firing employees it perceived to be gay or lesbian regardless of whether the person so self-identified.

IMMIGRATION. Immigration reform is one of the key areas on the lesbian agenda. While lesbians and gay men are no longer excluded from or deportable from immigration into the United States (q.v.), they are harassed and limited to immigrating only by being sponsored by their professional employer or claiming asylum from persecution based on their sexual orientation in their home country. Former Attorney General Janet Reno advocated for the Immigration and Naturalization Service (INS) to adopt a policy to grant asylum from sexual orientation persecution policy. Immigration judges still require documentable evidence of persecution based on sexual orientation. This is especially true for lesbians (in re Pitcherskaia) and women in general because violence and harassment against women is not state sponsored but a cultural phenomenon.

The other, more common method for immigration is to be sponsored by one's spouse or family member. In the United States it is not possible to sponsor one's same-sex lover, even if one has legally "married" the foreign lover in one of the countries that recognize same-sex unions.

This discriminates against lesbians (and gays) because heterosexual married couples can sponsor the immigration of their spouse. The Lesbian and Gay Immigration Rights Task Force (LGIRTF) is advocating for INS to change its policies. *See also* Female Genital Mutilation; Human Rights; Same-Sex Marriage.

IN THE LIFE. A term coined in the 1920s by the African American lesbian and gay community to distinguish other lesbians and gays, as in, "Mabel is in the life." Many gay and lesbian magazines use this in their title, as does one of the longest running gay and lesbian television shows in the United States (*In the Life*) (q.v.).

INDIA. India's cultural history is repleat with lesbian desire and imagery, with myths of independent goddesses and Jami, the feminine twins. Lesbianism was made taboo c. 2 BC as per the Laws of Mamu—girls who committed lesbian acts were fined and received ten lashes, adult women had their heads shaved or two fingers amputated, and rode through town on a donkey. British colonial rule reinforced the repression of homosexual desire, and in 1861, the Penal Code criminalized homosexual acts.

Postcolonial India has winessed lesbian marriages and suicides. Most lesbians remain closeted (q.v.) and isolated. The Indian culture practice of arranged compulsory (heterosexual) marriages further isolates lesbians.

Sakhi (Female Friend) was founded in New Delhi in 1990 and was the first lesbian networking and political organization. Sakhi also maintains archives.The Mumbai group Stree Sangam (Fusion Between Women) works to make lesbians visible. The Campaign for Lesbian Rights (Caleri) came into being after the screening of Deepa Mehta's film *Fire*. This group also works for lesbian visibility and political recognition of lesbian rights. Other lesbian support, social, and political groups are forming in major cities as well as using the anonymity of the Internet.

INSTITUTIONALIZED MISOGYNY. The insidious way political, social, and corporate organizations promote the male norm, thus maintaining the status quo to the detriment of women. An example of this may be seen as young men and women with the same educational backgrounds enter the workforce and only the young women are given typing tests.

INTERNALIZED HOMOPHOBIA. Self-hatred because one's sexual orientation is not acceptable to the society and culture at large. This internalized homophobia (q.v.) may manifest itself in many ways: suicide (30 percent of all youth suicides are due to questions of sexuality); alcohol and substance abuse to reduce or numb the feelings of being abnormal; battering (q.v.) a partner because that partner represents what the batterer does not like about her/himself; or remaining closeted (q.v.).

INTERNATIONAL GAY AND LESBIAN HUMAN RIGHTS COMMISSION (IGLHRC). This is part of the International Lesbian and Gay Association, founded in 1991 to monitor and advance international human rights (q.v.) for lesbians, gays, bisexuals, transgendered (qq.v.) people, and persons with AIDS (q.v.). Its report to the 1995 United Nations Conference on Women in Beijing (q.v.) detailed thirty-one countries that had abused the human rights of lesbians.

INTERNATIONAL LESBIAN AND GAY ASSOCIATION (ILGA). This federation of over four hundred gay and lesbian groups represents fifty countries. Founded in 1978, ILGA publishes a newsletter, issues reports on the state of international gay and lesbian rights (*The Pink Books*), and facilitates contacts and information on the legal, social, and political status of lesbians and gays worldwide. It also supports the basic civil rights of lesbians and gays. ILGA succeeded in getting Amnesty International (q.v.) to recognize the persecution of gays and lesbians as an infringement of their human rights (q.v.).

Because some of the member organizations support lowering (or repealing) age of consent (q.v.) laws, U.S. Senator Jesse Helms, with support from the Religious Right (q.v.), proposed and passed legislation that stated the United States (q.v.) would not fund United Nations (UN) bodies that support or fund any organization that promotes pedophilia. The UN, under this pressure, rescinded ILGA's status as a nongovernmental organization, thus severely limiting ILGA's effectiveness in lobbying the United Nations and other international bodies. ILGA has held regular world conferences for lesbian, gay, bisexual, and transgendered (qq.v.) leaders. Some criticize the ILGA for being Eurocentric (the 2001 conference had representation from over forty countries with as many non-European attendees as European ones), and it still needs to reach out to leaders in developing nations.

INTERNATIONAL NETWORK OF LESBIAN AND GAY OFFICIALS (INLGO). Founded in 1985, this organization's goals are to repeal laws that discriminate against lesbians and gays and to encourage lesbians and gays in public activities. The mission of the group is to support and educate openly lesbian, gay, bisexual, and transgendered (LGBT) (qq.v.) public officials and leaders regardless of ethnicity or religion so that they may serve their communities. The group advocates equality, AIDS research, domestic partnership (qq.v.), and legal recognition of LGBT families and children. INGLO holds annual conferences, regional gatherings, and provides mentoring opportunities.

INTERNATIONAL WOMEN'S DAY. In socialist countries, International Women's Day is celebrated on March 8. The celebration began in 1910 as a way the Socialist Women's International could recruit women into the socialist and suffrage movements. Other countries joined in celebrating women with the advent of the second wave of feminism (q.v.).

INVERT. Term used by psychologists and physicians from 1860 until the 1940s to refer to a lesbian or gay man, as homosexuality was thought to be the reversal (or inversion) of the "normal" heterosexual instinct. Some masculine lesbians, such as Radclyffe Hall (q.v.), thought of themselves as inverts because they felt they were men living in women's bodies.

INVISIBILITY. *See* **LESBIAN INVISIBILITY.**

IRELAND, PATRICIA (1945–). Feminist activist and former President of the National Organization for Women (NOW) (qq.v.). A self-identified bisexual, Ireland is a former airline stewardess and corporate lawyer.

ITALY. Lesbians in Italy have been staging "Lesbian Weeks" since 1991. Alhough the first week was one that promoted lesbian separatism (q.v.), the later ones have been coalitions of lesbians whose aim is to better articulate the lesbian movement in Italy. To that end they have organized The Lesbian Forum.

– J –

JAPAN. Most Japanese lesbians remain closeted (q.v.). The first lesbian-feminist (q.v.) group Re-Guimi Studio Tokyo was founded in 1987 to reclaim lesbians from pornographic use. Lesbians and gays remain closeted, though there is a movement for lesbian and gay recognition and rights in Japan. The first Tokyo Pride (q.v.) Weekend (2001) had over 4,000 attendees—lesbian and gay—and the first lesbian and gay day at Tokyo Disneyland in August of that year was attended by a crowd of 3,000 lesbians and gays. Tokyo became the first Asian city to include antidiscrimination against lesbian, gay, bisexual, and transgendered (LGBT) (qq.v) people in their human rights guidelines.

JAY, KARLA (1946–). Writer, academic, and activist. Jay was a member of the Radicalesbians (q.v.). She has coedited and written many texts on lesbian and gay history and studies including *Out of the Closets: Voices of Gay Liberation* (1972) and most recently *Tales of the Lavender Menace: A Memoir of Liberation* (1999). She is a leading commentator and lecturer on lesbian and gay history and issues. She directs the Women's and Gender Studies program at Pace University in New York City.

JEAN, LORRI L. (1957–). Activist, lawyer, former deputy regional director of the Federal Emergency Management Agency (FEMA). Jean was the highest-ranking, out lesbian (or gay) person in the Ronald Reagan administration. She served as the executive director of the Los Angeles Gay and Lesbian Community Center before becoming the executive director of the National Gay and Lesbian Task Force (NGLTF) (q.v.) from 2001 to 2003.

JEFFREYS, SHEILA (1948–). Lesbian-feminist activist in the United Kingdom and Australia (qq.v.). Jeffreys has been an activist since her involvement in the antiviolence and antipornography women's movement in 1973. She cofounded the London Women Against Violence Against Women (1980), the Lesbian History Group, and the London Lesbian Archive. She currently writes and teaches Lesbian Studies and Political Science in Australia. She is adamant about the damage queer theory (q.v.) does to lesbians by submerging them in what she feels is a predominantly male-oriented theory.

JIMENEZ, PATRIA (19??–). Mexican lesbian-feminist activist and politician. She was elected to Mexico's Congress in July 1997. A member of Okiabeth, this feminist and lesbian activist is also an activist in the Zapatista movement. Her aim is to fight the "serious climate of intolerance" that exists in Mexico that is perpetuated by the police and judiciary, the culture, and the media (q.v.).

JOB DISCRIMINATION. Lesbians (and gay men) are discriminated against by employers. In some cases, if a woman "looks" like a lesbian she may be denied a job or fired without any recourse. In the United States (q.v.), two restaurant chains are known for discriminating against lesbians—Denny's and Cracker Barrel. Many teachers remain in the closet (q.v.) for fear that they will be fired under the moral turpitude clause in their contract.

JOHNSTON, JILL (1929–). Journalist. In the *Village Voice* (New York City), Johnston was the dance and social critic. Her columns became part of the development of her consciousness as a lesbian. Johnston coined the term "Lesbian Nation" which became the title of her collection of columns and essays. This lesbian-feminist (q.v.) envisioned a lesbian nation of women successfully living independently of men, yet she was not a lesbian separatist (q.v.).

JORDAN, JUNE (1931–2002). Jamaican American poet, academic, and activist. Jordan equated sexual oppression with racial and ethnic oppression. The Ku Klux Klan (KKK) (q.v.) tried to stop the performance of her 1986 drama that urges women and men of different ethnicities, sexual orientations, and races to unite against their enemy, the KKK. The show continued for five weeks.

– K –

KAVARS, LINDA BOYD (LK) (1941–). American producer and activist. Kavars managed and signed the first all-woman rock band, Fanny, to a major label (Warner Brothers) in 1969. From 1989 to 1991, she managed Kate Millett's (q.v.) Women's Art Colony and Christmas Tree Farm where she also organized the first Feminist Day conference. She has documented via videotape many notable feminists and lesbian-feminists including Alma Routsong, Barbara Love, Kate Millett, and Alix Dobkin (qq.v.). In the mid-1990s, while producing an east coast tour of Pat Bond's (q.v.) play about Eleanor Roosevelt and Lorena Hickok (qq.v.), Kavars learned that Hickok's ashes were buried in an unmarked grave. Kavars began the Lorena Hickok Memorial and Scholarship Fund that resulted in a memorial marker being placed at the site of Hickok's grave on May 10, 2000. Kavars produces women singer-songwriter concerts and plays. She publishes a quarterly community newsletter, *The Scene*, and is founding a nonprofit organization to help mentor young girls and women artists, musicians, and writers. She also continues to document the lesbian and feminist community.

KENNEDY, ELIZABETH LAPOVSKY (1939–). With Madeline Davis (q.v.), Kennedy founded the Buffalo Women's Oral History Project in 1978.

KENRIC. This is a British lesbian group that was founded in 1963 to provide social and educational opportunities for lesbians. It has its origins in the Minorities Research Group (MRG) founded by Esme Langley. MRG was very closeted (q.v.), although lesbianism was not outlawed in the United Kingdom (q.v.) as male homosexuality was at the time. The goal of the eight-hundred-member MRG was to change public attitudes and perceptions of homosexuals. Kenric was founded after internal divisions and named for the two areas in London—Kensington and Richmond—the members came from. It is the longest-running social and support organization for lesbians in the United Kingdom. It publishes a monthly magazine and holds regional social events and conferences as well as taking part in pride (q.v.) events. Kenric is decidedly nonpolitical, unlike its predecessor MRG and Arena 3.

KIKI. Term used in the mid-twentieth century for a lesbian who did not identify as either butch or femme (qq.v.). The term was also used for butch-butch couples or femme-femme couples, since members of these couples did not fit into the highly structured butch-femme coded social world of lesbians in the 1940s and 1950s.

KING, BILLIE JEAN (1943–). This tennis champion won the Wimbledon Doubles championship with Martina Navratilova (q.v.). She also won the "Battle of the Sexes" tennis match against Bobby Riggs in 1973.

In 1976, she was sued for palimony (q.v.) by Marilyn Barnett, her lover of four years. Barnett claimed that they had a lesbian affair and she was entitled to half the tennis star's earnings and their Malibu, California, beach house. At the time, King denied her lesbianism and the relationship (she was married then), but later she rescinded her denial of the relationship. Barnett lost her suit in 1982, but not before King lost many endorsements due to her lesbianism.

KINSEY 6. Based on the 1948 Kinsey Report, someone who identifies as completely homosexual.

KLEPFISZ, IRENA (1941–). Activist, educator, poet, and essayist. Klepfisz is one of the cofounders of *Conditions* (1986), the magazine of a feminist and lesbian collective (q.v.). She continued to edit the journal until 1981. Born in Nazi-occupied Poland, she has been profoundly aware of her Jewish lesbian identity. Bringing a feminist perspective to Yiddish culture and traditions, she actively engages homophobia (q.v.), Judaism, and gay and lesbian anti-Semitism by teaching about oppression and resistance (qq.v.).

KNIGHT INITIATIVE/CALIFORNIA PROPOSITION 22. This initiative on the California ballot stated that marriage is only between a man and a woman. It was adopted on March 7, 2000. This successful initiative is the latest in a series banning same-sex marriages (q.v.). *See also* Antigay Initiatives; Civil Union; Defense of Marriage Act.

KOSKALAKA. Meaning "young man or woman who does not want to marry," this is the Lakota Sioux term for lesbian shaman.

KOWALSKI, SHARON and KAREN THOMPSON (1955– , 194?–). These two women were lovers when in 1983 Sharon Kowalski was critically injured in an automobile accident which left her a quadriplegic, brain damaged, and unable to communicate. Kowalski's family did not know about her lesbianism, and since Kowalski and Thompson were not related, Thompson was legally excluded from her lover's hospital room and decisions about her medical treatment. The Kowalski family did not allow Thompson into the hospital even though Kowalski markedly improved whenever Thompson was allowed to visit or care for her. Thompson fought for guardianship of Kowalski, which after many court battles she finally won in 1991. This battle makes real the lack of lesbian (and gay) couples' rights and the necessity for health care proxies if there cannot be same-sex marriages (q.v.).

KU KLUX KLAN (KKK). The Klan is an American white supremist group that has violently protested, under the cover of white robes and hoods that mask their identity, black civil rights, lesbian and gay rights, Catholics, and Jewish people.

KUDA, MARIE (1939–). Lesbian writer and literary activist. Kuda founded the Womanpress, a lesbian small press publishing company, in Chicago, Illinois, in 1974. One of the first members of Mattachine-Midwest, she also has become an avid chronicler of lesbian and gay history, especially of those lesbians and gays living in the Midwest. She has produced over twenty slide shows documenting the rich history of midwestern gays and lesbians. Kuda was one of the first visible lesbians in the Chicago Democratic Party. She has served as liaison for the police and the gay and lesbian community. Kuda was also the first out (q.v.) lesbian book reviewer for *Booklist*. She writes for other publications and has published *Women Loving Women: A Select and Annotated Bibliography of Women Loving Women in Literature* (1975).

KUEHL, SHEILA JAMES (1941–). Actor, lawyer, and politician. She played Zelda in the *Many Loves of Dobie Gillis*. She was elected in 1994 to the California State Assembly where she was the first openly lesbian or gay member.

– L –

LABOR ISSUES. Lesbians in the labor pool, especially in global markets in traditional societies, are treated as single women who have no familial obligations. Thus, among other things, they will be assigned to the night shifts, longer hours, and more dangerous working conditions. They may also be fired first over women (and men) and be paid less because they are seen as having no families to support.

Since lesbians are an invisible minority, they have little to no protection from job discrimination and repressive labor practices. Lesbians also have less access to domestic partnership (q.v.) benefits than gay men who tend to be professional. Studies have also shown that lesbians tend to earn 5 to 14 percent less than their heterosexual counterparts and tend to be in lower-paid jobs than either other women or gay males. *See also* Global Capitalism.

LABRYS. Double-sided axe used as a weapon and harvesting tool in matriarchal societies and considered to be the Amazons' (q.v.) chief weapon. The labrys has been adopted by modern lesbians as a symbol of power and self-sufficiency and is prevalent in lesbian jewelry.

THE LADDER. The monthly publication of the Daughters of Bilitis (DOB) (q.v.). It was published from 1956 until it became an independent publication that ended in 1972. *The Ladder* aimed to educate lesbians about social, legal, political, and literary issues. The publication carried book reviews, news items, research, letters, and political commentary. Phyllis Lyon (q.v.) edited the publication under the pseudonym Ann Ferguson, until in a daring move Ann "died" in the fourth issue and Lyon revealed her own name in an article "Your Name Is Safe!"

LAMBDA. The eleventh letter of the Greek alphabet. This symbol was first used by the Gay Activists Alliance (GAA) (q.v.) since it is also the symbol in physics for kinetic energy. The lambda has since become the internationally recognized symbol for gay.

LAMBDA DELTA LAMBDA. The first lesbian sorority to be chartered. The Alpha chapter was founded at the University of California-

Los Angeles in February 1988, followed in May by the Beta chapter at San Francisco State University. The goal of the sorority is to network with women of similar ideas, to create a safe, alternative social environment, and promote lesbian and gay awareness on campus and in the community.

LAMBDA GROUPS ASSOCIATION OF POLAND. While homosexuality has not been criminalized in Poland, this federation of lesbian and gay groups including ETAP, Fil, Warzawski Ruch Homoseksualny, and others is primarily focused on making homosexuality socially acceptable. *See also* Europe.

LAMBDA LEGAL DEFENSE AND EDUCATION FUND (ORIGINALLY LAMBDA LEGAL DEFENSE FUND). Founded in 1972 and incorporated after a court battle in 1973, this national legal organization's purpose is to promote gay rights and educate the public in order to stop discrimination against lesbians and gays. The group takes on legal test cases (sometimes with other organizations such as the American Civil Liberties Union [q.v.]), researches legal issues, and provides education on a number of gay and lesbian civil rights (q.v.) issues. The defense fund has helped overturn sodomy laws, advocated for persons with AIDS/HIV, and assisted in overturning Colorado's Amendment 2 (qq.v.). It also helps gay and lesbian military personnel who have been discharged.

LAMBDA LITERARY AWARDS. Cosponsored by Lambda Rising Bookstore (Washington, D.C.) and Publishing Triangle, these annual literary awards, the "Lammy," recognize gay and lesbian writing in many categories and lesbian and gay small press publishers. The awards are held at the American Bookseller Association's annual convention.

LAMBDA PRAHA/LAMBDA PRAGUE. The first public lesbian and gay rights organization in the former Czechoslovakia. As one of the more gay-tolerant Eastern European (q.v.) countries, Czechoslovakia had decriminalized lesbian and gay sexual relations in 1961, but the age of consent (q.v.) laws still were higher for homosexuals than heterosexuals. It was not until 1990 that Lambda Praha was successful.

With the dissolution of Czechoslovakia, Lambda Praha continues to work to enact domestic partnership (q.v.) laws and political asylum (q.v.) in both the Czech Republic and Slovakia. Other gay and lesbian groups are emerging such as Sdruzeni organizaci homosexuálníchobcanú (SOHO), a Czech national federation of gay and lesbian organizations, and Lambda, providing national and international gay and lesbian news. L-klub Lambda, which publishes the magazine *ALIA*, provides lesbians community, sports, and cultural events. In Slovakia, Ganymedes (1992) has hosted conferences for the International Lesbian and Gay Association (ILGA) (q.v.) youth group. *See also* Europe.

LANE, ALYCEE (1976–). Editor. Lane was the editor of the first erotic (q.v.) magazine for black lesbians, *Black Lace.*

LAPINSKY, SHEILA (1944–). South African activist. A human rights (q.v.) activist, Lapinsky became involved in gay and lesbian rights in the early 1990s. She was part of the group that influenced the African National Congress (ANC) to adopt a gay rights platform plank. A founder of the group Lesbians and Gays against Oppression in 1985, she has also served as executive director of the National Coalition for Gay and Lesbian Equality (1994–1997). Currently, Lapinsky is an official in both the African National Congress and the South African Communist Party. *See also* South Africa.

LATIN AMERICA. There are strong cultural taboos against homosexuality in Central and South American countries, and lesbians who reject traditional feminine roles are marginalized. Gay and lesbian groups began to emerge in the 1970s in Mexico (q.v.) (Frente de Liberación Homosexual de Mexico) and Brazil (q.v.) (Somos). The first lesbian and gay magazine, *Lampiao,* began publication in Brazil during this period. While lesbians and gays still are discriminated against, Patria Jimenez (q.v.), a member of Oikabeth and a lesbian-feminist, was elected to Mexico's Congress in July 1997 on a platform that included freedom of sexual orientation. Lesbian activists in Mexico continue to be marginalized even by feminist groups, but they continue to work for their political rights and visibility.

A national congress of gay and lesbian groups—the First Gathering of Organized Homosexuals—was held in Brazil in 1980.

While Somos dissolved when working-class issues and leftist issues came into conflict, there were almost twenty other groups in existence.

Slowly following the lead of Brazil and Mexico, though they have not been able to achieve gay civil rights legislation yet, gay and lesbian rights issues are being discussed and gay rights political groups now exist in Peru, Costa Rica, and Chile, where gay and lesbian groups are illegal. There is the collective (q.v.) Ayuquelmin In Santi-ago, Chile. In Cuba, the Gay and Lesbian Association (q.v.) was formed in 1994. *See also* Argentina.

LATINA LESBIANS. Lesbians of Hispanic or Latin origin. These lesbians are ethnically, racially, and economically diverse, but share a rich cultural heritage that, even though it is influenced by the Roman Catholic Church, is also influenced by Native American and African American cultures and gender (q.v.) identities. Latina lesbians have sought greater visibility and an end to racism not only in society as a whole, but also within the lesbian and gay community. They have been organizing as a distinctive political group since the 1970s with Latino gays. The first Latina lesbian organization was Lesbianas Unidas (q.v.) founded in Los Angeles, California, in the early 1980s. The national Latino/Latina Lesbian and Gay Organization (LLEGO) (q.v.) was founded in 1987. In 1994, the first Latina Lesbian Leadership and Self-Empowerment Conference was held in Tucson, Arizona. Latina lesbians continue to develop their diverse culture and identity and have organized their own Latina History Project located in New York City.

LATINO/LATINA LESBIAN AND GAY ORGANIZATION (LLEGO). This is the only national Latino lesbian and gay association devoted to organizing the lesbian, gay, bisexual, and transgendered (LGBT) (qq.v.) communities on local to international levels. It was founded in 1987 at the March on Washington (q.v.). LLEGO works with the mainstream Latino/a communities to combat homophobia and sexism (qq.v.). Its goals include improving the status of LGBT Latinas/os in the areas of education, health care, and public policy. There are 172 network *afilidos* (allies). LLEGO hosts national symposia and annual gatherings.

LAVENDER HERRING. *See* **FRIEDAN, BETTY; LAVENDER MENACE.**

LAVENDER MENACE. Betty Friedan (q.v.) called the lesbians in the National Organization of Women (NOW) (q.v.) the "lavender herring," which got transmuted to "Lavender Menace." She felt that the lesbians' demand that issues relevant to lesbians be included in NOW's platform were diverting NOW from its true goal of equality for women. In addition, she thought all feminists would be branded as lesbians by the male power structure, thus jeopardizing any chances that women would become equal.

LAVENDER UNIVERSITY. Founded in 1974 by a group of gay men and women, this San Francisco "university for gay women and gay men" is considered the gay university. Classes were taught that are precursors of gay and lesbian studies. It has since disbanded, but Team San Francisco, which supports athletes going to the Gay Games (q.v.), is an offshoot of its athletic program.

LEATHER DYKE. A lesbian whose personal style includes the wearing of leather and sadomasochistic (S/M) (q.v.) accessories, thus implying she is into S/M practices.

LEATHER MENACE. Gayle Rubin (q.v.) coined this term modeled on "Lavender Menace" to reflect what she felt was an unreasonable fear of the lesbian and gay sadomasochistic (S/M) (q.v.) subcultures. Rubin feels, as do others, that sex-negative (q.v.) attitudes as manifested by anti-S/M politics gives the Religious Right (q.v.) and other homophobic groups too much leverage.

LESBERADO. This is a play on the words "lesbian" and "desperado," to indicate that lesbians are sexual outlaws (q.v.).

LESBIAN. Originally meaning "from the Greek island of Lesbos" where the poet Sappho (q.v.) wrote about love between women, it has come to mean a female homosexual or a woman-identified woman (q.v.).

LESBIAN AVENGERS. Founded in New York City in 1992 by Sarah Schulman (q.v.), Marie Honan, Ann Maguire (q.v.), Ann-Christine d'Adesky, Ana Maria Simo, and Maxine Wolfe (q.v.) "to fight for lesbian survival and visibility." The Lesbian Avengers strove to make lesbians and their issues visible by conducting direct actions (q.v.) and education. Their first action was at the June 1992 gay pride (q.v.) celebration. By the next April, the Lesbian Avengers rallied 20,000 lesbians at the White House for a nighttime march. Their trademark in all their actions is a sense of humor. Soon, Lesbian Avenger chapters existed in thirty-five cities across the United States, Canada, and Europe (qq.v.).

The Lesbian Avengers published the *Lesbian Avengers Handbook*, telling chapters how to fight the Religious Right (q.v.) and put together the Lesbian Avengers Civil Rights Organizing Project. The most recent actions of the Lesbian Avengers was the protest in August 2000 at the Michigan Womyn's Music Festival (q.v.) over the festival's "don't ask, don't tell" (q.v.) sexual identity policy and at the anniversary of the Seattle, Washington, World Trade Organization demonstrations on December 1, 2000.

LESBIAN BABY BOOM. Since the late 1980s, the occurrence of lesbians conceiving via artificial insemination (q.v.) and bearing children or adopting children regardless of whether they are in a committed relationship or not. For some, lesbian mothering is an indication of the essentialist (q.v.) nature of women to nurture; for others, it is part of the process to connect to others, to form families (q.v.). Gay men have also joined in the baby boom trend. It should be noted that children raised by lesbians (or gay men, for that matter) do not necessarily become homosexuals themselves. Studies also show that children raised by homosexuals tend to be more tolerant of others. *See also* Adoption; Child Custody.

LESBIAN BAITING. Calling a woman, especially a feminist, a lesbian in order to get her to stop her behavior. These are usually verbal attacks by heterosexuals on lesbians, feminists, or independent women by calling them dykes (q.v.), lesbians, lesbos, or queer (q.v) in order to disenfranchise them or to get them to cease their behavior. In certain situations, it is used to try and coerce women into sexual relations with a male, since the only way the woman may think she could prove her heterosexuality is by having relations with a male.

Betty Friedan (q.v.) was concerned that the Women's Liberation movement (q.v.) would be undermined by the patriarchy (q.v.), dismissing feminists as lesbians. The Radicalesbians (q.v.) realized the power of naming as set forth in their manifesto "Woman-Identified Woman" (q.v.).

LESBIAN BATTERING. Domestic violence (q.v.) or battering that occurs between same-sex couples. Lesbian battering has been called one of the lesbian community's dirty little secrets, since lesbian couples are thought of as being the utopian partnership with equal partners.

LESBIAN CHIC. The interest in lesbians by the mainstream media—journalism, television, and film (q.v.). Prior to 1992, lesbians were usually depicted derogatorily as old maids, suffering and dying in most films, plays, and books. In fact, it was so derogatory to call a woman a lesbian that when Kate Millett (q.v.) appeared on the cover of *Time* magazine in 1970, she was just called a bisexual. In 1992, lesbians became "hot," being featured in cover stories, on television, in advertisements, their fashions copied, and so forth. Although the media (q.v.) was infatuated with "lesbian chic," most lesbians are either invisible, passing, or closeted (qq.v).

Lesbian chic, though, has allowed lesbians in some more regressive countries such as Portugal, to begin to become more visible and to network and lobby for their political rights. *See also* Europe.

LESBIAN COMMUNITY. The women who make up a group of friends from the smallest to the largest, including that of a geographic or social organization that helps to dictate culture and mores. Jill Johnston (q.v.) had envisioned a total "Lesbian Nation." Others such as Sarah Lucia Hoagland "think of lesbian community as a ground of lesbian being, a ground of possibility. . . . that involves the area of ethics" (1990).

LESBIAN CONTINUUM. The spectrum of experience between heterosexual and lesbian including desired (fantasized), actual sexual experience. This is the "range—within each woman's life and throughout history—of woman-identified experience" coined by Adrienne Rich (q.v.) in 1979. Rich contrasted lesbian continuum with lesbian existence, in so much as lesbian existence is primarily about erotic and emotional choices made by women, and lesbian continuum includes the full range of woman-identified activity such as African women's trading networks. *See also* Compulsory Heterosexuality.

LESBIAN CULTURE. Practices that are distinctly recognizable at least to members of the lesbian community (q.v.) who are in the know, who can identify with these practices. Lesbian culture may be transmitted through cultural activities and separate institutions such as the Michigan Womyn's Music Festival (q.v.) or through lesbian writings, art, and politics. While some people would like to think there is a common lesbian culture that exists among all lesbians living in a patriarchal (q.v.) society, this presumes that all lesbians are political or feminists, which is not the case. Lesbian culture is diverse and may vary from community to community based on that area's mores and needs, and they may not be shared or even recognized as valuable by other lesbians from other communities.

LESBIAN ETHICS. The shared values that are rooted in being lesbian. This also includes the conduct of lesbianism as a sexual orientation—desires, sensuality, and sexual behavior. These values help lesbians understand the politics of being oppressed and to fight that oppression in a heterosexual patriarchy (q.v.). Lesbian ethics, also known as "lesbian moral theory," are based on the concept that patriarchal ethics diminishes women's moral agency while a woman-centered ethics empowers women. There is, thus, a valorization of the female and woman-identified identity, agency, and integrity.

Sarah Lucia Hoagland and Claudia Card (q.v.) among others, have written extensively on lesbian ethics. Hoagland's work focuses on the lesbian self that is both separate and connected. She coined the term "autokeonomy" from the Greek words for both "self" and "community" or "group" who have something in common, a connection. Card's work is based on the lesbian's knowledge of being oppressed, the politics of dominance, and subordination that promote lesbians connectiveness.

LESBIAN-FEMINISM. Lesbian-feminism is both a philosophy and political movement, which links women's oppression to the institution of both patriarchy and heterosexuality (qq.v.). It has its roots in the gender politics of radical feminism of the early 1970s, when "feminism was the theory, and lesbianism was the practice." Lesbian-feminism is the analysis of the norm of heterosexuality that maintains male supremacy.

The politics of lesbian-feminism are based on being woman-identified woman (q.v.)—women who are committed to other women for political and economic support as well as physical and emotional support. Being woman-identified or lesbian is seen as a political choice; it is the profound rejection of the power of patriarchy and heterosexuality. In an heterosexist society, as long as women put men first, women and lesbians will remain oppressed since the interests of self-determination and freedom are subjugated by and for men. Any women who adopt the male classification of people oppress their lesbian sisters and themselves by not being able to form primary attachments with other women.

There are many ways that lesbian-feminism beliefs are manifested from cultural feminism and separatism (qq.v.) to multicultural inclusion of issues of race, class, and culture. There is no correct political belief or behavior beyond being feminist and woman-identified; lesbian-feminism is diverse.

Lesbian-feminism has challenged gay liberation as a purely sexual liberatory movement. Lesbian-feminists feel that sexual freedom needs to be examined along with the concepts of "consent" and "power," especially in relation to issues such as sadomasochism (q.v.) and public sex. Lesbians also have different issues than those addressed by the predominantly male gay movement. The male supremacy of the Gay Rights (q.v.) movement is another challenge facing lesbians. Lesbians see sexism in how, and what, issues are addressed and the means by which political progress is made. For instance, lesbian-feminists feel that accepting same-sex marriage (q.v.) without interrogating the sexism (q.v.) inherent in that institution is not transformative politics but assimilationist (q.v.) politics, as well as showing contempt for women. Some early lesbian-feminist groups include the New York City-based Lesbian Feminist Liberation (q.v.) and CLIT Collective (Collective International Terrors), as well as the Gutter Dykes Collective in Berkeley, California.

Lesbian-feminism is also at odds with queer theory (q.v.) since queer theory tends to submerge lesbians and lacks the radical politics and the motivation to change society. Critics of lesbian-feminism such as Shane Phelan (q.v.) point to the exclusion of race as a point of oppression within lesbian-feminist theory and practice, thus making the goals of lesbian-feminism not inclusive. Other critics of lesbian-feminism point to the sex-negative (q.v.) aspects of the theory and practice. The Sex Wars (q.v.) illustrated the rejection of butch-femme (q.v.) roles and sadomasochism (q.v.) by lesbian-feminists. Lesbian-feminism has also been accused of silencing all who are not orthodox lesbian-feminists or shaming others into thinking and acting as prescribed in lesbian-feminist theory's practice, for instance, being visible lesbians who are constantly resisting the patriarchy.

Lesbian-feminism thrives as lesbian-feminists continue to organize politically and socially, challenging the heteropatriarchy's institutions from the sexism of marriage to the sexism and heterosexism of global capitalism (q.v.).

LESBIAN-FEMINIST. A woman who identifies politically as both a lesbian and as a feminist and feels that she cannot be a lesbian without being a feminist or vice versa. Her analysis critiques both the oppression of sexism and the oppression of heterosexism (q.v.). Lesbian-feminists are committed to changing society so that women can achieve political, economic, and social equality. Lesbian-feminists are anticlassist, antiracist and antisexist. Lesbian-feminists and their analyses have impacted every aspect of the women's movement, political culture, academic culture, and public policy from battered women (q.v.) to linguistics. *See also* Lesbian-feminism.

LESBIAN-FEMINIST LIBERATION. Formed in the 1970s in New York City as a separate group after feminists in the Gay Activists Alliance (GAA) (q.v.) felt that the GAA was dominated by (white) gay males and was not paying enough attention to lesbian and feminist issues. *See also* Lesbian-feminism.

LESBIAN HERSTORY ARCHIVES. Located in New York City, these archives were founded by Joan Nestle, Karla Jay, and Julia

Penelope (qq.v.) among others in 1974–1975 to preserve lesbian culture "in remembrance of the voices we have lost." The archive is the oldest lesbian collection and encompasses documentation, books, film/videotapes, pictures, and files on lesbians, lesbian cultural and political organizations, and lesbian herstory.

The archive was incorporated as the Lesbian Herstory Educational Foundation in 1980. The archives, now located in their own brownstone in Brooklyn, are open to the public, funded, and staffed by lesbian volunteer coordinators. The archives accept materials from famous and unknown lesbians.

LESBIAN INVISIBILITY. The omission of lesbians from popular culture, political discourse, and history, made worse when the media and politicians conflate homosexuality/gay to mean male. In patriarchal (q.v.) culture, the lesbian woman who does not need men is the most reviled and obscured.

LESBIAN LAND. Part of the 1960s' "back to the land" counterculture. It was spurred on by the lesbian-feminist separatists (q.v.) and the lesbian land movement of trusts, not-for-profits, and cooperative ownership of rural lands by and for lesbians. Most of these lands are used for self-sufficient lesbian communities and are political, feminist, pacificist, spiritual, and/or environmentalist in nature. There are lesbian lands that provide alternatives for disabled lesbians and lesbians of color (qq.v.). One of the most famous lesbian lands is "the Land" where the Michigan Womyn's Music Festival (q.v.) takes place each August. With separatist lands also comes controversy about allowing male children, transgendered women, and non-lesbians on the land.

Some lesbian separatists see the creation of lesbian-only space as creating a safe haven for women in a patriarchal (q.v.) capitalist system. Other more radical lesbians see the establishment of lesbian separatist lands and the social and economic alternatives developed by the lesbians as acts of resistance that will weaken the existing oppressive system by removing valuable resources from its control.

Some lesbian lands are not well received by their neighbors. For instance, the Hensons' (q.v.) Camp Sister Spirit has experienced harassment and violence as locals try to drive the women from their 120 acres in Ovett, Mississippi, where they run a food bank and educational services for the rural poor community.

LESBIAN LEGAL THEORY. Critiques of and theorizing about the relationship of lesbians and the law. Lesbian legal theory is much more than law reform with a lesbian focus. Based in part on Patricia Cain's 1989 work that highlighted the invisibility (q.v.) of lesbians in feminist legal theory and Ruthann Robson's *Lesbian (Out) Law: Survival under the Rule of Law* (1992), lesbian legal theory is a growing and evolving theory of law. It not only makes lesbians visible in legal theory, but notes how legal traditions make lesbians invisible and thereby hurt lesbians. It therefore begins to develop a legal theory based on both the elimination of sexism and heterosexism (qq.v.) to address the needs of lesbians without diminishing them.

LESBIAN LIBERATION. The radical and revolutionary social-political goal that would allow the free expression of lesbian love without social stigmas or political oppression. Lesbian liberation as a movement is composed of many social and political organizations, academics, individuals, and groups that while differing in their politics and ideas on how to achieve lesbian liberation, are all working toward that goal in their own manner from the mainstream assimilationist gay rights organizations to the radical lesbian separatists to the lesbian-feminists (qq.v.). Being a lesbian is an act of political resistance against the patriarchy (qq.v.) and its institutions.

LESBIAN NATION. Taken from the title of Jill Johnston's (q.v.) 1973 collection of articles and essays that looked at lesbians' distinct way of thinking about women, language, and patriarchy (q.v.). It made connections globally through the alternative lesbian community (q.v.).

LESBIAN PHILOSOPHY. Lesbian philosophy, like the traditional categories of philosophy, reflects on life, politics, and existence. By trying to answer the fundamental questions of existence, ethics, and what can be known about lesbian existence, lesbian values (and the value of lesbian life) and what lesbians know, lesbian philosophy observes what is and what ought to be. Lesbian philosophy is seen as feminist (q.v.). Some issues in lesbian philosophy include examining the hostilities in lesbian relationships and communities; the definition of lesbian sexual interaction and intimate relationships; the relationship of the lesbian individual to the state; the multiple definitions of lesbian identity; and the contexts of oppression.

LESBIAN POLITICAL THEORY. Political theory that frames how lesbians analyze existing political communities and envision what they ought to be. Most lesbian political theory is based on feminism (q.v.) and Marxism or socialist thought. Lesbian political theory, just like feminism, is grounded in liberalism. Liberalism gives both feminism and lesbian political thought the ideas of political and social equality and the concept of individual liberty. Marxism lends its economic analysis of capitalism and the concept of economic equality. Feminist political thought puts forward the idea that women are individuals, and thus, entitled to the same equality as male citizens. It, therefore, critiques sexism and the patriarchy (qq.v.). Lesbian political thought moves this forward in several ways. Lesbian-feminists add the analysis of heterosexism; black lesbians add the analysis of race. The concept of freedom of sexual self-determination and identity as well as the liberation from reproductive heterosexism, have different moral imperatives.

Lesbian political thought examines the multiple identities and positions that a lesbian assumes in the political arena. It also looks at the dynamics lesbians have as both a political group and a political force and posit how lesbians ought to best operate in politics dealing with the interlocking oppressions (q.v.) and to empower lesbians. Lesbian legal theory (q.v.) is also a part of lesbian political thought.

LESBIAN PRESSES. Small independent publishers that promote works by lesbians. These include Naiad Press, Firebrand Books, and Spinsters Ink. Some lesbian presses like Kitchen Table Women of Color Press have folded recently. Some are imprints of larger presses such as the Women's Press, Ltd.

LESBIAN RESISTANCE. By being lesbian and publicly announcing such, lesbians challenge the heterosexist patriarchy (q.v.). Lesbians are not sexually available to men and by forming lesbian relationships and lesbian communities with their own values and structures, they challenge the ones in existing society. They remove themselves as resources and resource producers to the existing community. Thus, being a lesbian is considered a political act. See also Resistance.

LESBIAN SEPARATISM. The radical feminist and lesbian theory and practice of living an utopian Amazonian (q.v.) life that physically, economically, politically, socially, emotionally, and psychologically removes men, male supremacy, male privilege (q.v.), and patriarchal institutions from the lives of lesbians. In some cases, this involves moving to lesbian lands (q.v.) where lesbians can develop economic self-sufficiency communally. This separation from male-dominated society allows lesbians to achieve self-determination and to value, strengthen, and affirm themselves by being removed from oppressors and oppressions.

The political theory behind lesbian separatism can be found in works by Julia Penelope, Sarah Lucia Hoagland, Mary Daly, Jill Johnston, Monique Wittig, Marilyn Frye, Charlotte Bunch, and The Furies (qq.v.) who practiced and theorized lesbian separatism. Hoagland highlights lesbian separatism's strong anarchist tendencies. Lesbian utopias appear also in fictional works such as the writings of Elana Dykewomon and Sally Gearhart (qq.v.) among others.

Critiques of lesbian separatism range from those of some black feminist theorists such as Audre Lorde and Barbara Smith (qq.v.), who say that separatism cannot affect political change or be an effective analytical tool because it promotes the ideas of biological determinism and race and class privileges. Other concerns with lesbian separatism are over exclusivity—does lesbian separatist theory and practices include women who are not lesbians or not woman-born woman (q.v.)?—and issues of procreation and of male children living in lesbian separatist space.

Lesbian separatism as a cultural movement worldwide thrives through venues such bookstores (q.v.), political writings, journals, music festivals such as the Michigan Womyn's Music Festival (q.v.), and lesbian lands. Cultural feminism (q.v.) is considered an outgrowth of lesbian separatism.

Lesbian separatists and radical lesbian-feminists are still active. Most recently, *Rain and Thunder*, a radical feminist journal, began publication in Northampton, Massachusetts. *Raging Dykes* is a quarterly publication of lesbian separatism and radical feminism that is published in Lancaster, England. In November 2000, there was a lesbian-feminist and separatist conference in Pennsylvania. The Internet also allows lesbian separatist and radical lesbian-feminists to be visible and to network.

The opposite of lesbian separatists are assimilationists (q.v.) or what some call "participationists." These are lesbians who are seeking for the full inclusion of lesbians in patriarchal institutions.

LESBIAN STUDIES. Lesbian Studies is the academic field of producing and conveying knowledge about lesbians primarily by lesbians. It began as an outgrowth of the gay and lesbian and women's movements (qq.v.) when grassroots groups of women began to study lesbian history, publish lesbian research, and develop lesbian theory and philosophies as well as study lesbian politics and the interrelationship of culture and lesbianism. Some of this work found its way into archives, resource centers, and with the advent of Women's Studies at universities, into academia.

Some Women's Studies programs, marginalized by the traditional academy, feared further stigmatization by lesbian visibility—both lesbian scholars and lesbian subject matter. This tension paralleled the lesbian-straight tensions in the women's movement. By the mid-1980s, lesbian scholarship and inquiry was a force on campuses, although tenure and promotion of lesbians in the professorate, whether they engaged in lesbian scholarship, was greatly hindered by overt and covert lesbiphobia (q.v.). Nonetheless, professional discipline caucuses and lesbian scholarship were gaining a strong foothold. Margaret Cruikshank's (q.v.) naming of the field "Lesbian Studies" further codified this academic field.

Lesbian Studies, by being challenged by lesbians of color (q.v.), working-class lesbians, and disabled lesbians (q.v.), has expanded to become more inclusive than the original elitist discipline. Lesbian Studies deals with issues of difference and identity politics, lesbian-feminism, postcolonialism, queer theory (qq.v.) as well as issues of race, class, and culture. *See also* Lesbian Philosophy.

LESBIAN THOUGHT POLICE. A play on the idea of the Thought Police in George Orwell's *1984.* The Lesbian Thought Police—a form of peer pressure in the lesbian community (q.v.)—impose a correct way for a lesbian to think, look, and act. The cultural mores tend to be local community specific—what is considered appropriate lesbian clothes and make-up in Los Angeles is not appropriate (or recognized) in Cleveland, for instance. Other lesbian symbols (q.v.) are more universal. For example, the androgenous (q.v.) look—jeans, work shirts, and boots—was considered appropriate lesbian wear in the 1970s and 1980s, along with short, cropped hair. These cultural cues help lesbians identify who belongs and who does not. *See also* Gaydar; Style Wars.

LESBIANAS UNIDAS. This group is an offshoot of the Gay and Lesbians Latinos Unidas (1981) and was founded in 1984 in Los Angeles, California. It provides grassroots support to Latina lesbians (q.v.). It runs the Latina Lesbian Oral History Project (q.v.) as well as other Latina lesbian herstory (q.v.), pride, and education services. It also advocates for Latina lesbians and equality.

LESBIANS OF COLOR. The term is an inclusive one, referring to all non-Caucasian lesbians: black or African American lesbians (q.v.) and Third World or Southern Hemisphere Lesbians (Asian, Arab, and Latina lesbians [q.v]). This group of lesbians has felt "triply bound" by racism, sexism, and homophobia (qq.v.).

Lesbian-feminists (q.v.) and lesbian women of color have critiqued the white lesbian-feminist movement and white lesbian culture for excluding, ignoring, or alienating women of color. Audre Lorde, Barbara Smith, and Cherríe Moraga (qq.v.) are three key theorists. The Combahee River Collective (q.v.) position paper provides a strong analysis on the intersectionality of racism, sexism, heterosexism, and classism.

LESBIPHOBIA. Antilesbian hatred that culturally, socially, economically, and/or politically discriminates, harasses, abuses, silences, or forces lesbians into the closet (q.v.). Lesbiphobia is considered analogous to homophobia (q.v.), combined with misogynistic sexism (qq.v.) aimed specifically at lesbians, women thought to be lesbians, or lesbian ideas.

LEVITICUS. The section of the Bible's Old Testament that the Religious Right (q.v) uses to justify antigay and antilesbian hatred and discrimination. Fundamentalists call homosexual sex a "crime against nature" since it does not lead to procreation. The most common reference is Leviticus 18:22, "Thou shall not lie with mankind, as with womankind: it is an abomination." Most references do not mention lesbians. The only place in the Bible which mentions lesbian sexuality is Romans I:26–27: " . . . for even their women did change the natural use into that which is against nature . . . "

One response to this religious homophobia (q.v.) is to point out that there are also other prohibitions in Leviticus that are ignored such as combining fabrics, cutting one's beard, and eating shellfish. Why choose one prohibition over another?

LIBERAL FEMINISM. Liberal feminism is based on modern liberal political theory and its basic tenets, the basis of traditional democracy—the liberties and freedoms such as equality and ideals of individual rights, justice, and liberty are the most highly valued. Liberal feminism puts its emphasis on equality and individual rights. Liberal feminists believe that gender (q.v.) equality will allow individual autonomy (q.v.) and maximize equality of opportunity. This is considered to be mainstream feminism. Organizations such as the National Organization for Women (NOW) (q.v.) and the National Women's Political Caucus, which promote gaining equality through working within the existing political system, are considered mainstream feminist organizations.

LIFESTYLE. The term used by heterosexuals to describe and deprecate lesbian and gay life as if only heterosexuals had real lives.

LINDSTAD, GRO (1960–). Norwegian activist. Since 1983, Lindstad has been a lesbian activist in the two Norwegian gay rights groups—the oldest group Det Norske Forbundet (DNF-48), and the more radical Fellesraadet for Homofile Organisasjoner I Norge (FHO). She advocates cooperation among the different lesbian and gay rights groups, and served as a member and leader on the women's committees of both groups. She also works with the International Lesbian Information Service. She has represented DNF-48 at numerous conferences of the International Lesbian and Gay Association (q.v.). She helped to establish and served as elected leader (1992–1998) of the very political group Lesbik og Homofil Frigjoering. Her high media profile as leader of this group led to her being given the title of "national lesbian." She serves as the political advisor for the Socialist Left Party. She is married to her partner Bente Vinaes. *See also* Norway.

LIPSTICK LESBIAN. This term became popular in the 1980s to describe a feminine-dressed and made-up lesbian who previously might have been called a femme (q.v.).

LLANGOLLEN, LADIES OF. These two Irish women, Lady Eleanor Butler (1739–1829) and Sarah Ponsonby (1755–1831), had a fifty-year relationship that began in 1768. They eloped in 1778 and after first being caught by their families, they ran away together disguised as men. They bought a cottage called Plas Newydd in Llangollen Vale, Wales. There they lived happily, without husbands, and were called "Sisters in Love" by William Wordsworth. Their actual relationship has led to much speculation about their sexual involvement, but their romantic friendship (q.v.) is well recorded by them and others who visited their home.

LOG CABIN FEDERATION. The political organization of Republican gays founded in 1978. The Log Cabin Federation is not officially recognized by the Republican National Committee. Although the group makes contributions to Republican candidates (some of whom return the funds), the group usually backs fiscal conservatives who support gay rights.

LOOKISM. A bias or prejudice against people who are not conventionally pretty, who do not meet cultural standards of beauty, which for women includes standards of femininity. Lesbians who do not adopt the norms of beauty/femininity experience acts of prejudice or homophobia (qq.v.). Within the lesbian community as well as in the rest of society, lookism is connected with ageism (q.v.) and fatism (the bias against fat).

LORDE, AUDRE (1934–1992). Black lesbian-feminist and socialist. Lorde was an activist, writer, and professor of English literature at Hunter College, New York City. She wrote ten volumes of poetry and five works of prose, all of which challenge feminist theory. A prolific writer and poet, she was named the Poet Laureate of New York State in 1991. Her writings and speeches inhabit "the house of difference" and she advocated an alternative woman's culture working outside patriarchy's (q.v.) power positions. She believed that women must find their own voices and method to change patriarchal society. According to Lorde, "you cannot dismantle the master's house with his tools." Helping to make women, lesbians, and especially lesbians, of color visible were her goals "[b]ecause the misogynist world we live in wants us silent and dead, because our silence will not protect us." Her attempts to empower women were critiqued on its naive essentialism, which is also a critique of cultural feminism. She, in turn, critiqued the racism in the feminist movement and the sexism (qq.v.) in the African American community. *See also* Audre Lorde Project.

LOULAN, JOANN GARDNER (19??–). Therapist, writer, and sex activist. Loulan, as well as other sex therapists such as Betty Dodson and Susie Bright (q.v.), began to hold workshops and write books as lesbians began to take an interest in their bodies, sex, and sexual techniques partly as a result of the Sex Wars (q.v.). She is the author of many books on lesbian sexuality and practices. Currently, Loulan is living with a man, yet she still defines herself as lesbian. *See also* Hasbian.

LOVE, BARBARA J. (1937–). Writer, editor, and activist. Love describes her mission in life as making being a lesbian "ordinary." In 1971, she was part of a group of lesbians and gay men who helped persuade the American Psychiatric Association (APA) (q.v.) that homosexuality was not a mental illness. She coauthored *Sappho Was a Right-On Woman* in 1972 with her then lover Sidney Abbott (q.v.) Her mother marched with her in the 1973 Gay Pride Celebration carrying a sign that read "Mothers Support Your Lesbian Daughters." Mrs. Love then went on to cofound Parents and Friends of Lesbians and Gays (P-FLAG) (q.v.).

Love was a member of the Gay Liberation Front (GLF) and Radicalesbians (qq.v.). She returned to GLF when she felt that the Radicalesbians were becoming too strident to accomplish their goals. She founded the feminist group Matriarchists. She served on the board of the National Gay and Lesbian Task Force (NGLTP) (q.v). Love believes she was the first lesbian to dance with a woman at the White House in the 1970s. Most recently, she has won gold medals swimming in the Gay Games (q.v.) in Amsterdam in 1998 and in Melbourne, Austrialia (q.v.) in 2002 and in the Masters Championship 2002. She continues to swim and will continue to compete in the Gay Games. She began the project the Directory of Second-Wave Feminists, which is being compiled by the Veterans of Feminist America.

LUGONES, MARÍA (19??–). Philosopher, educator, and activist. Lugones currently teaches at Binghamton (New York) University where she is the director of the Latin American and Caribbean Area Studies program and teaches ethics, and social and political philosophy. She has published extensively in the area of philosophy of race, gender, and feminist (qq.v.) theory. She is a cofounder and director of the Escuela Popular Norteña, a grassroots center for popular education.

LUNDEN, BLUE (1937–1999). Activist. Active in the Antinuclear, Peace, Women's, and Lesbian movements, Blue Lunden was the matriarch and guardian of the woman's land, cofounded by Barbara Deming (q.v.) and called Sugar Loaf Women's Village, where women could live "gently on the earth." A film about her life, *Some Ground to Stand On*, tells of her coming of age as a working class butch (q.v.) lesbian in New Orleans in the 1950s. She was active in Older Lesbians Organizing for Change (q.v.).

LUPPIE. Lesbian Urban Professional (similar to Yuppie—Young Urban Professional). This term refers to the professionally employed, and thus monied and matieralistic lesbian who is part of the lesbian culture and community (qq.v.).

LYON, PHYLISS (1924–). Activist, writer, sex educator, and minister. With her life partner, Del Martin (q.v.), she has been a lesbian activist since 1955 when they and six other multiethnic lesbians founded the Daughters of Bilitis (DOB) (q.v.). She edited DOB's publication *The Ladder* (q.v.), at first using a pseudonym, then in the fourth issue using her real name—a courageous act during the McCarthy era (q.v.). When DOB dissolved in 1970, she and Martin became active in the National Organization for Women (NOW) (q.v.). She and Martin coauthored two books about lesbian life including *Lesbian/Woman* in 1972. Lyon earned her doctorate in human sexuality in 1976 and lectures on lesbianism and women's sexuality. She has been active in many groups concerning lesbians, health, and human rights (qq.v.) and is a member of most major lesbian and gay rights organizations.

– M –

MAGUIRE, ANN (1940–). Activist. A longtime community activist in Boston, Massachusetts, Maguire served as liaison to the gay and lesbian community to then Boston Mayor Raymond Flynn in 1974. She has worked in government in various health and human services capacities. She helped to found both the Massachusetts and the National Breast Cancer Coalitions, organizations which have promoted breast cancer (q.v.) research and education. Maguire is also a founding member of the Boston Lesbian and Gay Political Alliance and one of the activists who founded the Lesbian Avengers (q.v.).

MALE PRIVILEGE/MALE DOMINANCE. The assumption that being a male in a patriarchal (q.v.) society gives a boy/man greater access to resources—economic and political—including sexual access to women's bodies and labor.

MALE TO FEMALE (MTF). A transgendered (q.v.) person who is transitioning or has transitioned from male gender to female. MTFs are considered to be women, but since they are not woman-born women (q.v), they are usually excluded from women-only space since they still retain some vestiges of male privilege (q.v.). *See also* Female to Male; Michigan Womyn's Music Festival; Sex Reassignment.

MAN-HATING. Lesbians and feminists as independent women who successfully live or try to live without male dependency are painted by the media (q.v.) and society as man-haters. While Martha Shelley eloquently puts forward reasons why all women should hate men in her essay "Lesbianism and the Women's Liberation Movement" (1970)—from male contempt for women to actual violence against women—most lesbians and feminists do not hate men. They have to work with men, their fathers were men, they have sons, brothers, and so on. The myth of the man-hating feminist or lesbian is used to bring woman back into the patriarchal fold. *See also* Lesbian Baiting S.C.U.M. Manifesto.

MANNISH WOMAN. This term was used as a code for a butch (q.v.) lesbian.

MARCH, ARTEMIS (MARGE HOFFMAN) (1941–). Former member of Cell 16 (q.v.), March was the primary writer of "Woman-Identified Woman" (q.v) and founding member of Radicalesbians (q.v.). A transdisciplinary social theorist and former Bunting Fellow, she is developing a new, nondualistic social paradigm, "Quantum Social Theory." It enables us to demystify the origins and operation of western patriarchy (q.v.) and to see the structures which have enforced silence upon women and blocked the telling of any other story than the androcentric one.

MARCHES ON WASHINGTON. These marches on the nation's capitol for lesbian and gay rights started in 1979 with more than 100,000 marchers. The second march in 1987 drew 500,000 participants and featured a mass wedding and the AIDS/Names Project Quilt. About 250,000 people showed up for the 1992 march. The first International Dyke March organized by the Lesbian Avengers (q.v.) took place the evening before. The Millennium March in the year 2000 was very controversial since it was not a grassroots project and was seen as a commercial merchandising opportunity, although it was still attended by almost 600,000 people.

MARTIN, DEL (1921–). With her life partner Phyllis Lyon (q.v.) and six other multiethnic lesbians, she formed the first national lesbian organization, the Daughters of Bilitis (DOB) (q.v.) in 1955. She was its first president (1957–1960) and the first editor (1960–1962) of the organization's publication, *The Ladder* (q.v.). She also founded or cofounded many other lesbian, feminist, and political organizations ranging from the Council on Religion and the Homosexual in 1964, the Lesbian Mothers Union in 1971, the Alice B. Toklas Memorial Democratic Club in 1972, and the Coalition for Justice for Battered Women in 1975.

Martin cowrote with Lyons a letter to *The Advocate* about the sexism (q.v.) of gay men. When DOB disbanded in 1970 she turned her energies to the feminist movement and National Organization for Women (NOW) (q.v.) where she served on the Board of Directors

(1973–1974) and cochaired the National Task Force on Battered Women and Household Violence (1975–1977).

A social-justice activist involved in issues of human rights (q.v), abortion rights, and crime victims, Martin has been active in the domestic violence (q.v.) movement and authored *Battered Women.* With Lyon, she authored the lesbian political classic *Lesbian/Woman* (1972, 1991). Currently involved in issues related to aging women and lesbians and health (q.v) issues, Martin is also outspoken in insisting that lesbians do not get silenced and thus forgotten by the Queer (q.v.) movement.

MARXIST-FEMINISM. This is a form of feminism that applies Marx's theories to the study of gender (q.v.) and the means of production and reproduction. Marxist-feminists use Marxist economics, which are a critique of capitalism, as the primary analyses of women's oppression. They extend their analysis to the unpaid and unvalued role of women in the family and home. Marxist-feminists are at the forefront studying the impact of welfare reforms on women. *See also* Global Capitalism.

MASON, ANGELA (1944–). British activist. Mason has been involved in radical feminist and lesbian activism since the 1970s. She stood accused, along with eight others, of bombing right-wing targets. Mason was acquitted along with four others of the bombings. A former lecturer in sociology, she also practices law. In 1992, she was elected executive director of Stonewall Group (q.v.), which became even more political under her leadership, helping to change the United Kingdom's age of consent laws (qq.v.).

MATRIARCHISTS. A radical feminist group founded in New York City by Barbara Love (q.v.) and Liz Shankin. The Matriarchists published a self-titled newspaper during the early 1970s. The group also held weekly consciousness-raising (q.v.) sessions, wrote position papers, and hosted a series of conferences.

MATRIARCHY. Familial and political rule by women/mothers. Anthropologists have studied patriarchy (q.v.) in the different cultures and many feel that based on how male dominance is organized and justified, devaluing women's contributions, for instance, patriarchy (q.v.) is a cultural construction.

A primitive matriarchal culture is assumed by some feminists based on myths of ancient rule by women, including Amazons (q.v.) societies in which women make the major contribution to subsistence (this is true in agricultural societies), and the existence of matrilineal societies. Matrilineal societies, are those which trace lineage through the maternal (as opposed to through paternal) lines. Women have greater power in matrilineal cultures, such as that of the Iroquois, but they are not a matriarchy; instead they share power with males.

MATTACHINE SOCIETY (MS)/FOUNDATION. Founded by Harry Hay in Los Angeles, California, on November 11, 1950, the Mattachine Society is the oldest extant lesbian and gay rights organization in the United States (q.v.). MS is considered to be part of the Homophile movement (q.v.). The name Mattachine comes from a fifteenth-century all-male secret fraternity. Because of the McCarthy era, (q.v.) membership lists were not kept. The organization initially took on political issues such as police entrapment (q.v.), but the McCarthy-era witch hunts moderated the group so it became nonconfrontational. A 1953 membership convention led by the moderate conservative faction which included Marilyn Reiger and Pearl Hart (qq.v.) resulted in MS becoming "accomodationist" and the founders forced resignations, a separation from the communists, and an end to political actions.

In 1955, the group began publishing *The Mattachine Review*. Chapters were opened in Chicago, New York City, Philadelphia, and Washington, D.C. These chapters were more political than the national organization and remained active after the national Mattachine Society disbanded in 1961.

The Washington chapter held the first demonstration in front of the White House on May 29, 1965, to protest federal employment discrimination against lesbians and gays. Judy Grahn (q.v.) was one of the three women protesting; they were told to appear ladylike in their dress. This demonstration was followed in July by one at the Pentagon, and in August at the State Department. The Philadelphia chapter had picketed Independence Hall in support of gay rights in July 1965.

MAZER, JUNE (1929–1987). Mazer was an activist in the lesbian and gay movement as part of the American Civil Liberties Union (ACLU) (q.v.) South California's Lesbian and Gay Chapter, Connexxuss/ Centro de Mujeres and the San Francisco Lesbian Rights Project. Mazer was a board member of the Southern California Women for Understanding and the International Gay and Lesbian Archives. The West Coast Lesbian Collection, Oakland, California, was saved by Mazer (and her partner) and is named in her memory.

MCCARTHY ERA. The period between 1950 and 1954 when the House Un-American Activities Committee (HUAC), chaired by Senator Joseph McCarthy (R-Wisconsin) and assisted by (future president) Richard Nixon, hunted for enemies of the state—Communists, homosexuals, dissidents of all kinds—and persecuted alleged communists, communist sympathizers, sexual perverts, and alleged homosexuals. Many people who were investigated or named during the hearings lost their jobs or were blacklisted. In the military, thousands of women and men were dishonorably discharged, and 2,000 potential or actual federal employees lost their jobs because their sexual orientation was thought to open them up to the possibility of being blackmailed.

The McCarthy witch hunts helped to give rise to the 1950s sex panic (q.v.) about homosexuals and sexual perversion, which led to the surveillance of homosexual groups, intensified police raids of bars (q.v.), and loyalty oaths being required to ensure loyalty to the country and heterosexuality. Federal legislation was passed that prohibited gays and lesbians from immigrating to or even visiting the United States (q.v.).

MEAD, MARGARET (1901–1978). Anthropologist and writer. Mead and her mentor and lover Ruth Benedict (q.v.) are considered to be the founding mothers of American anthropology. Her work explores alternative sex and gender (q.v.) presentations in culture. She was one of the first proponents of bisexuality (q.v.).

MEDIA COVERAGE. One of the issues that lesbians and gays have been concerned with is receiving positive media coverage, or the lack thereof, in the popular press. Except for the "lesbian chic" (q.v.) period of 1992, lesbians have received little positive recognition in the press. The first political action taken by lesbians in postwar Germany (q.v.) was to combat negative lesbian stereotypes (q.v.) in a newspaper series. The Gay and Lesbian Alliance Against Discrimination (GLAAD) (q.v.) was founded to track media representation of gays and lesbians and to advocate for positive media coverage.

MEXICO. Mexico has had an underground political lesbian movement since the early 1970s. It went public in 1970 with the first Mexico City United Nations Conference on Women (q.v.) in 1970. The feminists groups who were trying to avoid the lesbian stigma were focusing on reproductive freedom. Lesbian groups were arguing that reproductive freedom could not exist without all sexual options. This split continues today within feminist groups, with lesbian activisits being marginalized.

Lesbian groups dispersed until the late 1980s when the movement was reenergized. In 1987, the First Regional Lesbian Encuentro was held. The National Coalition of Lesbian Feminists was organized in 1987. Lesbians were gaining visibility, networking with regional and international groups to advance lesbian rights in Mexico.

Patria Jimenez (q.v.), a lesbian-feminist activist (qq.v.), was elected to Mexico's Congress in July 1997. *See also* Latin America.

MEXICO CITY CONFERENCE, 1970 UNITED NATIONS CONFERENCE ON WOMEN. This first conference on women helped to legitimize both feminist and lesbian activism as women expanded networking and their political knowledge. While lesbians and the prospect of lesbianism created a scandal there, the homophobia (q.v.) allowed lesbians to visibly challenge compulsive heterosexuality (q.v.). Informal lesbian workshops helped provide a fora for Mexican lesbians and lesbians from other countries to network and organize. These were the only fora in which women could discuss their own sexuality—heterosexual, bisexual (q.v.), or lesbian. *See also* Beijing Conference; Human Rights; Nairobi Conference.

MICHIGAN WOMYN'S MUSIC FESTIVAL. The oldest continuing annual music and cultural event for women/lesbians celebrating women's music (q.v.). Referred to as "Michigan," this event has been held every August since 1975 on women-owned land. The weeklong festival is a bastion of lesbian separatism (q.v.). Male to Female (MTF) transsexuals (qq.v.) have been excluded for having had male privilege (q.v.) and not being "born women." The summer 2000 festival saw eight young lesbians from the ad-hoc Chicago group "Camp Trans" Planning Committee and the Boston and Chicago chapters of the Lesbian Avengers (q.v.) evicted after they took part in a protest where they self-identified as not being women-born women to protest the discriminatory women-only policy. *See also* Lesbian Land; Women's Music; Woman-Born Woman.

MIDDLE EAST. Muslim culture is highly gender-segregated and both Islamic religious texts and law condemn homosexuality. In Iran, lesbianism is punishable by one hundred lashes for the first offense, a death sentence is mandatory for the fourth offense. Due to the strict cultural and religious taboos of Islam, lesbians and gays are invisible in most of the Middle East, and there are few visible women's rights organizations except in major cities. These women's rights organizations do not mention lesbianism for fear it might derail the tenuous work they have done in securing women's rights and self-determination so far. Most women are forced to marry and women who do not exhibit sexual interest toward their husbands are subject to beatings and divorce. Lesbianism is extremely marginalized, though there may be social groups in some metropolitan areas, according to Middle Eastern lesbians who have emigrated to other countries. The Internet, though, is providing another means for women to network.

The only exception is Israel. Israeli lesbians and gays are accepted into military service, are not discriminated against in employment (since 1992), and most recently (2000), a lesbian couple has been granted coparenting rights. In Israel, there is the Community of Lesbian Feminists founded in 1987 to promote the legal, cultural, and political status of lesbians by challenging the social norms and asserting a lesbian-feminist presence. It publishes *CLAF Hazak* (*Strong Card*). There are also other lesbian groups such as Isha La'Isha (Woman to Woman), and lesbian and gay groups.

MILITARY/MILITARY ANTIGAY POLICY. *See* **DON'T ASK, DON'T TELL, DON'T PURSUE.**

MILLER, ISABEL. This is the pseudonym of Alma Routsong (q.v.).

MILLETT, KATE (1934–). Feminist theorist, author, sculptor, and artist. Millett (rhymes with "skillet") wrote the first radical feminist (q.v.) critique of sex and gender (q.v.) in *Sexual Politics* (1969, reissued in 2000). In this book, Millett theorizes that all male-female relationships are based on power, therefore, they are political. She advocates eliminating gender to improve women's lives in a patriarchal (q.v.) society. Her use of literary criticism to unearth the misogyny (q.v.) and patriarchal values in texts to support *Sexual Politics* changed academic literary studies.

Millett, an artist, academic, and activist during the early part of the Women's Liberation Movement (q.v.), was active in the National Organization for Women (NOW) (q.v.) where she headed the Task Force on Education.

In October 1970, she was outed (q.v.) as a lesbian in a meeting at Columbia University; although she was married to Fumio Yoshimura for ten years, she had relationships with women. *Time* magazine had her on the cover of its December 14, 1970, issue outing her nationally as a bisexual/lesbian in an attempt to discredit both feminism and Millett. Millett's book *Flying* (1974) documents this "personal is political" period.

Millett continued her activism in the feminist and lesbian movement as a member of Redstockings (q.v.). She later became a founding members of CR One and the Radicalesbians (qq.v.). In addition, she continues to advocate on issues of freedom of speech and sex liberation as a member of the Feminist AntiCensorship Task Force (q.v.).

Millett has published seven other books documenting her life, from exploring prostitution and feminism in *The Prostitution Papers* (1971) to the end of her relationship in *Sita* (1977). *The Basement* (1979) is about Sylvia Likens, a young teen who was tortured and sexually abused before being murdered by her foster mother and a gang of teenagers. *The Loony Bin Trip* (1990) documents Millett's experience with mental health institutions; she has become an antipsychiatric drug advocate. *The Politics of Cruelty* (1994) explores the control by the modern political state of citizen dissidents. She explores her relationship with her rich aunt who severed their relations over Millett's lesbianism in *A.D.* (1996). Her poignant autobiographical book about her mother and aging, *Mother Millett,* was published in 2001.

A lecturer, Millett has taught literary courses on an adjunct basis in the New York area. She has taken up the liveable wage and labor issues surrounding the use of adjunct professors.

Using the monies from her early books, Millett put a down payment on eighty-four acres of land in the mid-Hudson Valley, which she and a group of feminists have transformed into The Farm, a women's art colony and Christmas tree farm. At The Farm, Millett practices cultural feminism (q.v.) by teaching women to build and farm as well as giving them space to do their artwork and writing and a place to both practice and discuss feminist theories. Millett herself is a practicing artist and sculptor.

MISOGYNY. The hatred of women, their values, and beliefs. In a patriarchy (q.v.) this manifests itself through individual acts of violence against women, institutionalized public policies that discriminate against women, and cultural practices such as female genital mutilation (q.v.) that eliminate any pleasure a woman may feel during sexual intercourse. Lesbians may attract male wrath simply because they are unavailable sexually. Misogyny may be the origin of the dichotomy that finds women either evil or good, whores or madonnas. While predominately a characteristic of male sexism (q.v.), women may have misogynistic attitudes toward other women and toward themselves.

MONOGAMY. To have a sexual, loving relationship with only one person. Since society has viewed (male) homosexuals as nonmonogamous partly because same-sex marriage (q.v.) has not been a viable option, society tends to view all homosexuals—lesbians and gay men—as sexually nonmonogamous and engaging in serial sexual experiences without the bond of love. The ban against same-sex marriage institutionalizes this concept of nonmonogamous homosexual relationships. Couples who do want some social recognition of their relationship may opt for a commitment ceremony (q.v.), and in jurisdictions where they may garner some of the legal benefits of civil union or domestic partnership (qq.v.), they may so register. Many lesbians practice what is called "serial monogamy"—engaging in a series of long-term, committed relationships. Usually the couple remains friends after the break up, enlarging the lesbian's chosen family. There are polygamous and/or open relationships in some gay and lesbian partners, but these are negotiated between the partners, just as they are in the heterosexual population *See also* Families and Lesbians.

MORAGA, CHERRÍE (1952–). Writer, poet, professor, and activist. Moraga is the daughter of a Mexican woman and Anglo father who focuses on issues of race and (lesbian) sexuality. She coedited two landmark feminist collections, *This Bridge Called My Back: Writings of*

Radical Women of Color (1981) with Gloria Anzaldúa and *Cuentos: Stories by Latinas* (1983) with Ama Gomez and Mariana Romo-Carmona. She has written many books of prose and poetry including *Loving in the War Years: Lo Que Nunca Pasó por Sus Labios* (1983), which is considered to be the first openly lesbian Chicana poetry collection. Moraga is one of the cofounders of the (recently defunct) Kitchen Table Women of Color Press. She considers writing to be a political act. She writes about coming to terms with homophobia and racism as a lesbian of color (qq.v.). Moraga's current work includes plays that address Mexican cultural issues as well as political issues. She teaches Chicano studies and women's studies at Stanford University, Palo Alto, California.

MORAL MAJORITY. Founded by the fundamentalist Rev. Jerry Falwell in 1979, this conservative religious and political organization is the precursor to what is now called the Religious Right (q.v.). The Moral Majority was organized to combat feminism, the abortion rights movement, and the Equal Rights Amendment (qq.v.). The Moral Majority, which feminists, lesbians, and gays labeled on a bumper sticker as "neither Moral nor the Majority," disbanded in 1986.

MORAL PANIC. *See* **SEX PANIC.**

MORGAN, ROBIN (1941–). Radical and cultural feminist, poet, author, and former editor of *Ms. Magazine*. As a feminist and activist, she was a cofounder of New York Radical Women, Women Against Pornography (q.v.), and Women's International Terrorist Conspiracy from Hell (WITCH). Morgan documented the international women's movement in *Sisterhood Is Global* and continues her work in international feminism.

MUSIC. *See* **WOMEN'S MUSIC.**

– N –

NAIROBI CONFERENCE, 1985 UNITED NATIONS CONFERENCE ON WOMEN. Lesbians and their nongovernmental organizations (NGOs), after rumors they would not be given visas, successfully held workshops on lesbian rights and sexuality. Lesbians had a prominent informal conversation place on the lawn of the University of Nairobi's Great Court. There was a lesbian press conference where women from across the globe spoke. One Third World lesbian statement declared "If it seems that lesbianism is confined to white western women, it is often because Third World lesbians and lesbians of color (q.v.) come up against more obstacles to our visibility . . . the silence has to be seen as one more aspect of women's sexual repression. . . . The struggle for lesbian rights is indispensable to any struggle for basic human rights" (q.v.). This placed lesbian rights squarely as a part of human rights. A Dutch delegate made the first governmental statement defending lesbian rights in the United Nations at this conference. *See also* Beijing Conference; Mexico City Conference.

NATIONAL CENTER FOR LESBIAN RIGHTS (NCLR). This lesbian-feminist, multicultural, civil rights, legal resource center works to change discriminatory laws and generate new laws so that there may be a world were lesbians can live freely. The NCLR provides legal assistance and education on issues vital to the lesbian community from employment rights, partnerships, forms and legal documents, to health issues and adoption (q.v.).

Founded in 1977 in the United States (q.v.) as the Lesbian Rights Project, the NCLR is now a national organization. Its Public Policy Project conducts lesbian-centered policy analysis and advocates policies that represent lesbians' needs and concerns in national fora. The Lesbian of Color Project provides legal assistance to lesbians of color (q.v.) as well as conducting analyses on racism and homophobia (qq.v.), and forming coalitions with national and international lesbian and gay civil rights groups. The Youth Project provides legal representation, information, and advocacy for lesbian, gay, bisexual, and transgendered youth as they deal with governmental systems and institutions such as education, child welfare, and criminal justice.

NATIONAL GAY TASK FORCE/NATIONAL GAY AND LESBIAN TASK FORCE (NGLTF). The second oldest professional American lesbian and gay (and transgendered) civil rights advocacy group with a national perspective. It was the outgrowth of the defunct Gay Activists Alliance (GAA) (q.v.). Founded in 1973, the National

Gay Task Force added "Lesbian" to its name in 1986. The Board of the Task Force from its inception was 50 percent female.

From its first political action persuading advertisers to withdraw from a television program that portrayed gays negatively in 1974, to raising $1 million to fight the Dade County, Florida (q.v.), attack on homosexual rights in 1977, to the 1990s Workplace Initiative and the current series of Creating Change Conferences, the NGLTF has been in the forefront of lesbian and gay rights. It has also been occupied with fighting attacks by the Religious Right (q.v.). The Task Force has expanded its scope to include issues relevant to the transgendered community.

As the National Gay Task Force (NGTF), it was the first gay and lesbian activist (q.v.) organization to attend a meeting at the White House (1977). The task force now has a policy institute that researches and prepares white papers on issues relevant to the lesbian and gay community. The NGLTF provides grants to communities to combat antigay initiatives (q.v.).

NATIONAL LESBIAN CONFERENCE. The Daughters of Bilitis (DOB) (q.v.) sponsored the first public national lesbian convention in May 1960 held in San Francisco. The conference allowed the lesbians attending to network and discuss common issues and strategies. This conference has since served as the model for similar conferences throughout the world over the years; Sri Lanka's first lesbian conference in 2001 is just one example.

NATIONAL ORGANIZATION FOR WOMEN (NOW). Founded in 1966 by Betty Friedan (q.v.) and others to promote women's equality, NOW has become the largest feminist organization in the United States (q.v.).This is a far cry from the presidency of Betty Friedan, who called the lesbian rights issue a "lavender herring" that would delegitimate all feminists in the eyes of society, thus preventing them from achieving equality. Initially, NOW refused to address lesbian issues, which resulted in either lesbians leaving or being expelled from the organization. However, the events of 1970—the "Lavender Menace" (q.v.) takeover of the Second Congress to Unite Women (q.v.) in May 1970 and the October 1970 public outing of Kate Millett (qq.v.)—helped to get lesbian rights and issues acknowledged as legitimate concerns of all feminists by September 1971.

There was a lot of controversy between radical lesbian-feminists (q.v.) and heterosexual feminists which led to the gay/straight split (q.v.), since lesbian-feminists believed that heterosexual feminists were betraying the feminist cause if they slept with men. The National Sexuality and Lesbian Task Force of NOW was formed and in 1973 NOW publicly supported the lesbian and gay rights movement. Over the years, issues of freedom of sexual expression and practices have been incorporated into the NOW platform, the last such reform occurring in 1999. *See also* Atkinson, Ti-Grace; Brown, Rita Mae; Ireland, Patricia; Liberal Feminism; Radical Feminism.

NATURE OR NURTURE. This is the shorthand debate question of whether homosexuality is biological in nature or results from socialization (nurture). *See also* Constructionism v. Essentialism; Essentialist; Social Construction.

NAVRATILOVA, MARTINA (1956–). Czech-born American tennis star. She holds over 167 single and 164 double titles including multiple Wimbledon and U.S. Open championships. She was the first major athlete to come out (q.v.) while still an active tennis champion, which she did on national television in 1991. Her fans already knew about her lesbian relationships with Sandra Hayne, Nancy Lieberman, Rita Mae Brown (q.v.), and Judy Nelson—who brought a palimony (q.v.) suit against her. Although she lost a lot of product endorsements due to homophobia (q.v.) and had to endure homophobic coverage of her tennis matches, she understands the value of coming out and being a role model. She has been active in the lesbian and gay rights movement, especially in fighting Colorado (her home state) Amendment 2 (q.v.). *See also* King, Billie Jean.

NAZI PERSECUTION. During the early Nazi rule of Germany (q.v.) and ensuing World War II, the Nazis persecuted and perpetrated genocide that was not only limited to Jews but extended to all people that Adolf Hitler felt defiled Aryan racial purity. These groups included Gypsies, gay men, and lesbians. Claudia Schoppman, a German historian and expert on Nazi persecution of lesbians, claims that it is hard to get a true count of the number of lesbians who died at the hands of the Nazis because lesbianism was not against German law.

Lesbians were prosecuted for other offenses such as their leftist political activities or prostitution. Suspected lesbians were sexually abused in the Nazi death camps. *See also* Black Triangle; Pink Triangle.

NEAR, HOLLY (1949–). Singer-songwriter and activist. Near founded the all-woman Redwoods Records in 1972, releasing her first album the following year. She is considered a founding mother of women's music. *Imagine My Surprise!* (1978) is her coming out (q.v.) song, yet her 1990 autobiography reveals her bisexuality (q.v.). Near was one of the first performers who insisted on sharing a stage with a signer so that hearing-impaired lesbians could also enjoy her music and lyrics.

Near has been an activist in the antiwar movement of the 1960s, and now the 2000s, and the antinuclear and disabled rights movements. She still draws crowds of women when she performs on tour. *See also* Disabled Lesbians.

NESTLE, JOAN (1940–). Writer and activist on butch-femme (q.v.) relationships, working-class lesbians, and lesbian rights. Nestle is the founder of the Lesbian Herstory Archives (q.v.) and an English professor. Her writing stems from her involvement in the 1950s in a working-class lesbian bar (q.v.) as a young femme (q.v.). She also writes lesbian erotica (q.v.), which involved her in the feminist/lesbian Sex Wars (q.v.).

THE NETHERLANDS. In the Netherlands, lesbians had an active subculture in the bars (q.v.) before the world wars. Lesbians were active in the Resistance during World War II precisely because the occupying forces were prohibited from going to the bars, thus enabling the bars to become arms storehouses and meeting places for the Resistance. After World War II, the Cultuur-en-Ontspannings Centrum (COC), (q.v.) was founded on December 7, 1946, by a group which included three lesbians. The COC was established to promote integrated homosexual human rights (q.v.) during the postwar moral panic (q.v.) and to provide a safe social space for gays and lesbians. The COC was male-dominated; it was not until 1961 that the COC publication included lesbian writings.

In 1971 during the early women's movement, some lesbians split from the COC, forming groups such as Group 7152 and Lavender September to pursue lesbian political issues. Lavender September became a leader of the lesbian-feminist movement and tried to influence the feminist movement by claiming that "real" feminists were lesbians. In 1982 at the Pink Pride Demonstration, there was a riot which led the government to begin to listen to lesbian claims. In 1985, lesbian demands were included in the government's agenda for the Nairobi Conference (q.v.). In 1994, the Equal Rights Act formalized the equality of homosexuals and heterosexuals in the Netherlands. In 2001, the Netherlands' Parliament approved legislation allowing for same-sex marriages and adoptions (qq.v).

NEW LEFT. During the 1960s, this umbrella term covered the militant liberal, progressive, and Marxist political organizations that were attempting to change existing democracies by making them more inclusive and promoting individual freedom and expression. The membership in these groups overlapped and included those involved in antiwar, free speech, environmental, antinuclear, women's, black, and gay and lesbian groups since all these groups were targeting related oppressions. Some of these groups became quite militant.

NEW ZEALAND. In New Zealand, there has been an active lesbian and gay culture and movement since 1970 when the Dorian Society was founded. Following Stonewall (q.v.) in the United States, Gay Liberation Fronts (GLF) (q.v.) were organized. As with other GLFs, Alison Laurie and other lesbians felt disenfranchised and left to form Sisters for Homophile Equality (SHE) in 1973. Other radical gay feminist collectives followed, as did lesbian and feminist conferences. In the 1980s, lesbian separatism (q.v.) split some groups while others focused on issues of lesbian mothering and work on the Guardianship Amendment Bill.

An active lesbian liberation movement exists in New Zealand including the Maori and Pacific Island lesbian group Wahine Mo Nga Wahine. Lesbian activists promoted the first "Homosexual Law Reform Bill" which was proposed and withdrawn after a petition by the Coalition of Concerned Citizens (a religious coalition) gathered over 800,000 signatures. It was later proved that many signatures were either falsified or duplicated on this petition. Since most people in New Zealand are supportive of lesbian and gay civil rights, in 1993 New Zealand became one of the few countries with a national gay and lesbian civil rights statute, though the government is exempted. The lesbian movement has developed lesbian land and Lesbian Studies (qq.v.) and is actively seeking to pass a bill to prohibit discrimination against homosexuals which does not exempt the government, as well as a same-sex marriage (q.v.) bill.

NEWMAN, LESLEA (1955–). Writer and lecturer. Her children's book, *Heather Has Two Mommies* (q.v.), caused a controversy when it was included in the 1993 proposed Rainbow curriculum (q.v.) in New York City. Other topics in Newman's writings for adults include butch-femme relationships, AIDS (qq.v.), eating disorders, and sexual abuse.

NEWTON, ESTHER (19??–). Cultural anthropologist, academic, writer, and feminist. Newton's work has explored sexual politics and gender (q.v.). She authored one of the first academic studies of drag queens in *Mother Drag* (1972), a history of the lesbian and gay community of Cherry Grove (q.v.), Fire Island, and other works concerning feminism, lesbianism, and the academy, especially her evolving role as a butch (q.v.) lesbian in academia. *See also* Drag.

NOBLE, ELAINE (1942–). Politician, activist, and educator. Noble was the first openly lesbian (or gay) person elected (and reelected) to statewide political office as a Massachusetts state representative in November 1974 and 1976, respectively. She had previously taught at the university level and produced one of the first American gay and lesbian radio shows. She is a lesbian and gay rights activist and lobbyist. Currently, Noble is a prominent figure in the addiction (alcohol and drug abuse) movement promoting lesbian and gay treatment centers.

NORTH AMERICAN CONFERENCE OF HOMOPHILE ORGANIZATIONS (NACHO). Meeting for the first time in Kansas City, Kansas, in February 1966 and then in San Francisco in August, fifteen American homosexual rights organizations put together the first unified national homosexual rights federation of organizations. Although it was a looser federation than envisioned, it did produce two legal studies of the state of the homosexual in the United States (q.v.): *The Challenge and the Progress of Homosexual Law Reform* (1968) and *Homosexuals and Employment* (1970).

NACHO coordinated the first national political demonstrations in Washington, D.C., against the federal government's employment practices that discriminated against gays and lesbians, and against the military ban. NACHO also started a "Gay Is Good" campaign to destigmatize gayness as a mental illness as it strove to combat the American Psychiatric Association's (APA) (q.v.) medicalizing sexual orientation.

NACHO had three regional affiliates: in the east, the Eastern Regional Conference of Homophile Organizations (ERCHO) (q.v.); in the west and in the Midwest. NACHO's last convention was held in 1970 during which there were struggles between the Radical Caucus and the more mainstream members.

NORTHROP, ANN (1948–). Activist, journalist, and educator. Northrop has worked as a producer of CBS News, on ABC's *Good Morning America,* and as a commentator on DYKE-TV. She is an AIDS (q.v.) educator at the Harvey Milk School (q.v.) and an activist with the AIDS Coalition to Unleash Power (ACT-Up) and Lesbian Avengers (qq.v.). Northrop is vice president of the board of directors at the Institute for Gay and Lesbian Strategic Studies, a research think tank. In 1996, she unsuccessfully ran for vice president of the United States (q.v.) on the AIDS Cure Party ticket.

NORWAY. Norway is socially and legally tolerant of lesbians. Lesbians have been actively involved in holding Nordic Lesbian Conferences since 1974. Since 1981, antidiscrimination laws have included sexual orientation. There is also a law that prohibits public acts and language that incite hatred or contempt against a person based on their sexual orientation. In 1993, the Norwegian Parliament passed a domestic partnership (q.v.) law which gave lesbians and gays equal rights to marriage. Current issues that the lesbians and gay groups are working on include asylum and adoption (qq.v) rights, labor issues, and nondiscrimination in the church.

There are two national lesbian and gay political organizations, Det Norske Forbundet 1948 (DNF) (q.v.) and Fellesraadet for Homofile Organisasjoner I Norge (FHO). Another group, Lesbik og Homofil Frigjoering, was established in 1992. There are some smaller, more radical groups such as the Working Group for Gay Liberation (AHF). AHF began publishing the journal *Løvetann* in 1978; it became an independent journal in 1991. *See also* Eikvam, Turid; Europe; Lindstad, Gro.

– O –

OLD LESBIANS ORGANIZING FOR CHANGE (OLOC). Founded in 1989 by Shevy Healy and others, this San Francisco-based group "militantly embraces the word 'old." Its goal is to not segregate and isolate the aging lesbian, but to develop intergenerational and intercultural housing for all lesbians. *See also* Ageism; Gay and Lesbian Outreach to Elders; Health/Lesbian Health; Senior Action in a Gay Environment.

OLIVIA RECORDS. Founded in 1973 by a lesbian-feminist collective (q.v.), this is the premiere women's music (q.v.) recording label. Its first record in 1974 was a recording of Meg Christian with Cris Williamson on the flipside. Other Olivia artists include Linda Tillery, Teresa Trull, and Mary Watkins.

ON OUR BACKS. A play on the feminist publication *Off Our Backs*, *On Our Backs,* subtitled "entertainment for the Adventurous Lesbian," is a publication devoted to lesbian erotica (q.v.) and news. It was founded by Susie Bright (q.v.) in 1984.

ONE, INC./*ONE* MAGAZINE. The purpose of this homophile organization founded in 1952 was to publish its magazine, *One. One* was the first openly gay or lesbian publication in the United States (q.v.) whose purpose was to educate. In 1954, the Los Angeles Postmaster seized the publication calling an article about lesbians and another on gay marriage "obscene." The case went to the U.S. Supreme Court where, in a landmark decision, the Court allowed for the publication to freely discuss homosexuality in contexts other than religious, legal, or medical ones.

The February 1954 issue of *One,* entitled the "feminine viewpoint" issue, was completely written for and about lesbians. This was one of the only issues to ever sell out. Subsequent issues of *One* contained "The Feminine Viewpoint" as a regular feature. While *One* magazine ceased publication in 1968, One, Inc. continues to publish scholarly publications.

OPERATION RESCUE. Antiabortion group organized by Randall Terry. It is known for its violent disruption of abortion clinics by harassing and terrorizing women and health care providers. During the 1990s when the gays in the military issue came to the fore, this group added antigay and lesbian issues to its agenda. *See also* Abortions Rights Movement; Religious Right.

OPPRESSION(S). This is the unjust use of power and domination, which results in inferior treatment, inequality, and unfair privilege. Lesbians may be oppressed on at least two counts in a patriarchy (q.v.): because they are women (sexism [q.v.]) and because as lesbians they are not sexually available to men (heterosexism [q.v.]). Furthermore, lesbians may also be oppressed because they may be or may be perceived as non-white (racism [q.v.]), not rich (classism [q.v.]), or not physically able-bodied or not meeting the normal standards of beauty (lookism [q.v.]). The political act of lesbian resistance (q.v.) begins to challenge the oppressions and oppressors, male privilege (q.v.), and heterosexist privilege.

ORAL HISTORY PROJECTS. A means of capturing lesbian (and women's) history by interviewing members of the specific communities. The most famous lesbian oral history project is the Buffalo Oral History Project (q.v.).

OREGON CITIZENS ALLIANCE (OCA). A right-wing evangelically grounded conservative Christian group that supported Oregon's Ballot Measure 9, as well as local initiatives to prevent homosexuals from gaining "special rights" and prohibiting same-sex marriages, while supporting family values (qq.v.). Led by Lon Mabon, OCA based its grassroots strategies to stamp out homosexual threats on the 1992 Coloradans for Family Values campaign for Colorado's Amendment 2 (q.v). *See also* Dade County, Florida; Religious Right.

OSBORN, TORIE (1950–). Writer, women's music producer in the 1970s, and a lesbian activist. Osborn asked in 1990, "Are we the gay wing of the women's movement or the women's wing of the gay movement?" She served as executive director of both the National Gay and Lesbian Task Force (NGLTF) (q.v.) and the Los Angeles Gay and Lesbian Community Services Center. Previously, Osborn had been a member of the lesbian separatist world of women's music (qq.v.), organizing festivals, and was the business manager of Holly Near's (q.v.) record company.

OUT. To be out of the closet, being visible as a lesbian (or gay male). For many lesbians, being out is a political statement since it challenges male hegemony. *See also* Outing.

OUTING. The controversial political practice of publicly exposing a politician's or role model's homosexuality against their wishes. The person exposed is usually exposed as a hypocrite. The politician usually wields some power over decisions that negatively affect lesbians and gays or, if the person is a celebrity, should be a role model for lesbians and gays. Prior to 1989, when Michelangelo Signorile introduced the practice, the media considered a politician's or celebrity's homosexuality a private issue.

OUTRAGE! A British confrontational, media-savvy, direct action (q.v.) organization similar to the American group Queer Nation (q.v.), OutRage! was formed in 1990 to combat hate crimes (q.v.). Its mission has expanded to assert the human rights (q.v.) of all queer (q.v.) persons, and to promote sexual freedom including sexual determination. To date it is the longest surviving queer rights direct action group in the world. Its actions include many irreverent but nonviolent acts of civil disobedience, such as the Queer Valentine's Carnival, Exorcism of Homophobia, and "invasions" of the Vatican Embassy and Westminster Cathedral. When the Gay and Lesbian Centre closed in London, members of OutRage! began to meet in gay male bars (q.v.). Realizing that this excluded lesbians and other supportive women, they have both face-to-face meetings and virtual meetings on the Internet.

OWL. Older, wiser lesbian.

– P –

PACKING. In butch drag (qq.v.), the practice of stuffing one's underwear to simulate the bulge of a penis.

PACTE CIVIL DE SOLIDARITÉ (PAC). French "civil solidarity pact" that provides social and legal benefits for all cohabiting couples—same sex, heterosexual, sibling. *See also* France.

PAGLIA, CAMILLE (1947–). Writer and cultural critic. Paglia, an out (q.v.) lesbian, has outraged many women and lesbians by her provocative writings and media appearances where she glorifies gay men and their contributions to art and society as she denigrates women and lesbians.

PALIMONY. The concept that the "stay at home" partner in cohabiting same-sex relationships and unmarried heterosexual ones, deserves a form of alimony when the long-term relationship breaks up. *See also* King, Billie Jean; Navratilova, Martina.

PANCAKE. A butch (q.v.) who allowed herself to be "flipped" from a top (q.v.), the normal butch sexual position, to a passive bottom (q.v.). This phrase was common among the African American lesbian community in the 1950s.

PANZARINO, CONNIE (1947–2001). Writer, artist, and activist. Panzarino was a pioneer in the disability rights movement and within the lesbian and gay communities. She advocated accessibility, independence, antidiscrimination, privacy, self-image, and sexuality for disabled lesbians (q.v.). In the early 1970s, she founded Beechtree in Forestburgh, New York, as the first lesbian land for disabled lesbians (qq.v.). From 1986 to 1989, she was the director of the Boston (Massachusetts) Self Help Center. She authored the 1994 autobiographical book *The Me in the Mirror* as well as books explaining disability to children. She contributed regularly to the journal *New Mobility* and was on the editorial board of *Access Denied*. Panzarino served on the boards of the Disability Law Center, the Project for Women and Disability, and the Boston Center for Independent Living.

PARENTS AND FRIENDS OF LESBIANS AND GAYS (P-FLAG). An organization that serves as a support network for parents and friends of lesbians, gays, bisexuals, and transgendered (LGBTs) (qq.v.) persons. It is also a political advocacy group for LGBT rights, promoting the health and well-being of LGBT persons and their families in an adverse society. P-Flag helps to educate and enlighten the public and advocate to end discrimination and to ensure equal rights. P-FLAG was founded in 1981 in the United States (q.v.) after the parents of Morton Manford watched television footage of him being attacked at a gay rights protest. His parents marched in the 1972 Pride March (q.v.) with him. The support they received from other lesbian and gay people moved them to start a support group. At the 1973 Pride March, Barbara Love's (q.v.) mother was the only non-lesbian mother marching in the parade carrying a sign that read "Mothers Support Your Lesbian Daughters." Similar support groups emerged around the country and at a meeting of representatives of these groups after the 1979 March on Washington (q.v.). In 1981, the need for a national organization led to the formation of P-FLAG in Los Angeles with Adele Starr as founding president. Currently P-FLAG has its national office in Washington, D.C., with four hundred chapters in the United States and eleven other countries.

PARIS EXILES. American expatriates who settled in Paris between the world wars. Many of the women were artists and writers, and made up the lesbian salon of Natalie Barney (q.v.). Members included Barney's lover, painter Renée Vivian, modernist writer Djuna Barnes, publisher Sylvia Beach, and Gertrude Stein (qq.v.).

PARKER, PAT (1944–1989). Poet, educator, and activist. Parker was a black lesbian whose poetry challenged classism and deconstructed categories and identities. "Liberation Fronts" also highlighted the flaws she found in political movements. Her poetry chronicles unsung African American heroines. A former member of the Black Panther Party in the 1960s, she was a member of the Black Women's Revolutionary Council. She was active in the women's health care project of Oakland, California, working as a medical coordinator, expanding services to women throughout the area.

PARKHURST, CHARLIE (1812–1879). A passing (q.v.) woman, she drove a stagecoach. In Soquel Village, California, there is a memorial where she cast her vote in the presidential election of November 3, 1868. She is thought to have been the first woman to cast a presidential vote, but her sexual identity was only discovered after her death in 1879.

PARMAR, PRATIBHA (1967–). Activist, writer, and filmmaker. Born in Nairobi, Kenya, her family became refugees moving to the United Kingdom (q.v.) in 1967. Self-taught, her first video was made in 1986. Her work represents women of color (q.v.), lesbians, and gay men. Her films confront racism and sexual identity (*Sari Red* [1988] and *Memory Pictures* [1989]), the complexity of sexual identification (*Khush* [1991]), female genital mutilation (FGM) (q.v.) (*Warrior Marks: Female Genital Mutilation and the Sexual Blinding of Women* [1993]) and lesbian iconography (*Jodie, an Icon* [1996]). Parmar has made other films that deal with issues such as black feminism and AIDS (q.v.). She has coedited a book on queer (q.v.) identity and film, *Queer Looks: Perspectives on Lesbian and Gay Film and Video* (1993) and cowrote *Lesbians Talk* (1993) about safe sex and health issues.

PASSING. This is the act used to describe those who freely move in the culture or society in which they do not belong, passing as if they do. This term is usually applied to persons of color who pass in white society as white and homosexuals who pass as heterosexuals. In the lesbian and gay community, this includes acting or appearing as a male if one is female or vice versa, and/or as heterosexual if one is lesbian or gay. Passing as heterosexual can be attributed to being closeted (q.v.) or, for lesbians, having long hair, wearing dresses, being femme (q.v.).

Many women passed as males so that they might support themselves economically and some passed so that they could marry their female lovers. Some famous women who passed as males include Joan of Arc (1412–1431), Deborah Sampson (1760–1827) who fought in the American Revolution as a male soldier, the Big Band musician Billy Tipton (1915–1989), Charlie Parkhurst, politician Murray Hall, and more recently Leslie Feinberg (qq.v.).

PASTRE, GENEVIÈVE (1924–). French writer, publisher, and theorist. Prior to becoming involved in the 1970s French women's movement, Pastre was a teacher. She is a lesbian theorist and activist. She published the pioneering study *De l'Amour lesbien* in 1980 as well as the 1987 response to Michel Foucault (q.v.) *Athènes et le péril saphique.* She has served as president of Fréquence Gaie, the gay and lesbian radio station, founded the women's writing group Association des Octaviennes, and hosted European festivals for lesbian and gay writers. *See also* France.

PATIENCE AND SARAH. Written by Isabel Miller (penname of Alma Routsong [q.v.]), *Patience and Sarah* is considered to be the first lesbian novel with a happy ending. The story is based on Mary Ann Willson (q.v.) and Miss Brundage, two nineteenth-century women who settled in Greene County, New York. The book has been made into the first lesbian opera performed in New York City in the summer of 1998.

PATRIARCHY. Originally meaning the passage of one's lineage through the paternal line, patriarchy has come to mean the entire male-dominated sociopolitical and economic system of institutions, laws, and customs that privilege heterosexual males and oppress women, gay men, and lesbians. Patriarchal societies are inherently sexist since patriarchy involves the rule by men. They are also hierarchical, based on tradition, and exclude members of the underclasses from full citizenship (q.v.). Both feminist and lesbian political theory (qq.v.) consider patriarchy to be the cause of oppression (q.v.). *See also* Matriarchy.

PATTON, CINDY (19??–). Activist, writer, academic, and editor. She was the former editor of the *Gay Community News.* She cofounded the magazine *Bad Attitude.* She works as an activist and writes about AIDS (q.v.). Patton has written extensively on the politics of AIDS and lesbians as well as the development and impact of social movements. She was named the first Lesbian and Gay Studies faculty member at Emory University, Atlanta, Georgia, in 1997.

PENELOPE, JULIA (NÉE STANLEY) (1941–). Writer, scholar, freelance lexicographer, and copy editor. Her work on the nature of sexism (q.v.) in language is groundbreaking, especially *Speaking Freely: Unlearning the Lies of the Fathers' Tongue.* Her work also includes coediting with Sarah Lucia Hoagland *For Lesbians Only: A*

Separatist Anthology. This anthology is the definitive articulation of lesbianism as a theory of consciousness. She also coedited *Sinister Wisdom 15,* which is about violence against lesbians.

PERFORMANCE ART. A theatrical, artistic, live performance that is both experimental and political. Lesbian performance art problematizes and articulates identity and desire as it challenges the political and social norms. Many of these works are autobiographical as well as political such as the work of Holly Hughes (q.v.) and Carmelita Tropicana.

PÉTAIN–DE GAULLE LAW. This law reintroduced discriminatory criminal penalties for homosexual activity after 150 years of decriminalization. In 1942, Marshal Philippe Pétain instituted criminal penalties (three years in prison) for anyone under the age of twenty-one engaging in homosexual activity or anyone who engaged in homosexual activities with someone under the age of twenty-one. The age of consent (q.v.) had been sixteen for homosexual and heterosexual activity prior to 1942.

Charles de Gaulle's postwar French government reaffirmed this in 1945. In 1960, the French government under de Gaulle further criminalized indecent exposure with more severe penalties imposed on those committing homosexual acts than heterosexual ones. *See also* France.

PHARR, SUZANNE (c. 1945–). Writer, activist, and trainer. She was the organizer of the "No on Nine" (Oregon, 1990) and "Fight the Right" campaigns. Her writing on homophobia and the Religious Right (qq.v.) helps explain the inherent sexism (q.v.) of the modern socioeconomic patriarchy (q.v.).

PHELAN, SHANE (c. 1960–). Political scientist and writer. Phelan has written or edited several books on lesbian and gay politics and political theory. Her work advances lesbian-feminist theory by including the specificities of race on democratic identity politics. *Sexual Strangers* (2001) addresses the tension between exclusion and inclusion of lesbian and gay citizens as minority group members, in theory and in practice, in democracies. *Playing with Fire: Queer Pol-*

itics, Queer Theories (1997), which Phelan edited, is cutting-edge scholarship on queer (q.v.) law, politics, and policy. Phelan teaches Political Science at the University of New Mexico and she is chair of the American Political Science Association's Committee on the Status of Lesbians and Gays in the Profession.

PHELPS, JOHNNIE (1922–1997). A sergeant in the Women's Army Corps (WAC) during World War II who, when asked by General Dwight D. Eisenhower, her commanding officer, to provide him with a list of lesbians in her WAC battalion, said, " Sir, I'll be happy to do this investigation for you but you'll have to know that the first name on that list will be mine. . . . I think the General should be aware that among those women are the most highly decorated women in the war." Eisenhower told her to "Forget the order."

PHILIPPINES. Lesbians started to organize through their involvement in the women's movement. In 1993, a group of lesbian-feminists (q.v.) took part in the International Women's Day (q.v.) March in Manilla. Shortly thereafter, lesbian rights groups began to form around the country. Three groups, Womyn Supporting Womyn Committee (Centre), the Group, and LesBond, organized the 1996 First National Lesbian Rights Conference. This conference was attended by over two hundred Filipina lesbians.

PINK RIBBON (ROSAWINKEL). A loop of pink ribbon fastened to a lapel or shirt represents breast cancer (q.v.) awareness. Breast cancer is one of the health concerns facing lesbians. Lesbians, especially those who have not born children, are at risk for breast cancer. *See also* Health/Lesbian Health Issues.

PINK TRIANGLE. The symbol used by German Nazis (q.v.) before and during World War II to identify homosexuals. It was later adopted by the gay and lesbian community in remembrance. *See also* Black Triangle.

POLICE ENTRAPMENT. The semi-legal procedure in which plain-clothed police officers pretend to be gay men cruising in known pick-up areas such as parks, rest stops, etc. They arrest men who approach them allegedly for sexual favors. This procedure has been high on the gay male political agenda, sometimes to the detriment of issues relevant to lesbians.

POLITICAL DYKE. A lesbian who participates in political actions, an activist (q.v.). This term was used to distinguish oneself from the predominately nonsexual political lesbian (q.v.).

POLITICAL LESBIAN. A woman who becomes a lesbian because she feels loving (and identifying with) a male undermines her feminism. These women do not (initially) feel sexually attracted to other women and some political lesbians never engage in sexual relationships with other women. This lack of sexuality has been seen as problematic by sex-positive activists (q.v.), since it further downplays the role of sexual activity among lesbians and in the construction of the definition of lesbian. Some straight women became lesbians after being swayed by such political analysis as put forth by the Radicalesbians in *Woman-Identified Woman* or by writings of the Furies (qq.v.). *See also* Elective Lesbian; Primary Lesbian.

PORNOGRAPHY. The depiction in pictures and/or words of sexual activity to be viewed for sexual pleasure/arousal. Pornography has been defined as sexual, and thus, immoral and prurient. Pornography may be in the eyes of the beholder. What some people call pornography others call erotica (q.v.). Feminists moved the definition of pornography from the purely sexual to include those acts that normalize sexual violence against women. Andrea Dworkin (q.v.) defines pornography as anything that depicts the physical and mental oppression of women through sexual power relationships. What others consider erotica may just be an elitist version of the classist pornography.

Feminists and lesbians have been divided on whether pornography subjugates women by perpetuating the dominant male gaze. Women who are anticensorship feel that it may acknowledge women's sexuality and their right to express it. This has led to the feminist and lesbian Sex Wars (qq.v.).

Governments have taken action against the distribution of pornographic material, most notably the Canadian government's criminalization of any material that degrades a woman's self-esteem, equality, and safety. The Supreme Court of Canada (q.v.) has upheld this
law in *Regina v. Butler* (q.v), which sets forth guidelines which deem
violence, bondage, and child nudity as pornographic. Regrettably,
post-Butler the material that has been censored is feminist, lesbian,
and gay. Meanwhile, heterosexual (adult) "erotica" is widely circulated. *See also* Feminist Anticensorship Task Force.

PORTUGAL. In Portugal, lesbians are still largely invisible and isolated.
Closeted lesbians ran the feminist group Identificaçã-Documentaçã-
Mulheres (IDM) from 1977–1985. In the 1990s, lesbianism slowly began to emerge. The lesbian magazine *Organa* was published from
1990–1992, and since 1993, *Lilás* has been published. In 1996, the International Lesbian and Gay Association (q.v.) established a chapter in
Lisbon.

POST-OP. A person who has undergone sex reassignment (q.v.) surgery. *See also* Female to Male; Male to Female; Pre-Op; Transsexual.

POWER DYKE. A lesbian who is in a prominent and influential position.

PRATT, MINNIE BRUCE (1946–). Poet, essayist, and lecturer. She
was a founding member of the collective (q.v.) Feminary. The collective published a journal by the same name (1978–1983), which along
with a southern focus emphasized lesbian vision. The collective also
organized Woman Writes, the annual conference for lesbian writers.
   The idea of lesbian is evident in Pratt's work, such as her award-
winning poetry *Crimes against Nature* (1990). She has written stories
and essays on anti-Semitism and racism (q.v.) as well as on butch-
femme and transgender (qq.v.) relationships. Her life partner is the
transgender writer and activist Leslie Feinberg (q.v.).

PREJUDICE. Preconceived ideas, without any basis, about a specific
group or groups of people, which influence one's attitudes and behaviors toward those people. Most prejudices result in negative,

derogatory behavior. A person's prejudices may be legitimized by cultural or political traditions and institutions.

Prejudice against lesbians and gay men is called "homophobia" (q.v.); when directed just at lesbians it is called "lesbiphobia" (q.v.). This prejudice can manifest itself as violence against the lesbian or gay person, or can be more subtle, but still destructive, and result in social, economic, or political discrimination. For example, the opinion that lesbians are morally flawed and should not be teaching children can result in political prohibitions against out (q.v.) lesbians teaching, or more subtly based, one's opinion that the teacher up for tenure or promotion is lesbian can cause the denial of tenure or promotion.

PRE-OP. Pre-sex reassignment surgery (q.v.). A person who is living as a person of the other sex and is undergoing hormonal and cosmetic treatment to change outward, visible gender characteristics (such as facial hair and muscle tone). Pre-op persons may or may not undergo surgery on their genitals to reassign their sex from their birth sex due to the cost of the procedure or for other reasons. *See also* Female to Male; Male to Female; Post-Op; Transsexual.

PRIDE CELEBRATIONS. Marches, festivals, and dances, usually around the anniversary of the Stonewall Riots (q.v.) that proclaim solidarity of the lesbian, gay, bisexual, and transgendered community. *See also* Pride March.

PRIDE MARCH. Public marches held to proclaim solidarity and pride of gays and lesbians. The first Pride March took place in New York City in July 1969 just after Stonewall (q.v.). Subsequent marches have taken place in cities around the globe, not only to mark the anniversary of Stonewall each June, but throughout the year to mark the birth of gay and lesbian pride.

PRIMARY LESBIAN. A lesbian who feels her lesbianism is innate or biological. *See also* Elective Lesbian; Political Lesbian.

PRISONS. While lesbians have not been arrested as much as gay males have for their sexuality or sexual actions, there have been arrests, convictions, and prison terms for women since the seventeenth century in the United States (q.v.). Lesbians in prison have been themes in films (q.v.) and pop culture in the 1940s and 1950s with butch (q.v.) prison matrons or prisoners preying on the innocent femmes (q.v.). This is counter to reality where it is the butch prisoner who is the victim of violence in prisons.

Activists (q.v.) have taken up prisoners' rights, especially discrimination based on sexual orientation such as the denial of probation and parole, visitation rights, and the right to receive lesbian material.

Women prisoners incarcerated at the Women's House of Detention in New York City supposedly took part in the Stonewall Riots (q.v.). The prison, near the Stonewall Inn, housed mainly women of color (q.v.) who communicated with their women friends through the windows of the prison and, during the riots, threw out burning bedding and other objects.

PRIVACY, RIGHT TO. The right to privacy is seen as a necessary right in sexual relations between consenting adults without government intervention in the bedroom. This includes the constitutionally constructed right to be private in one's sexual practices, though this may only be construed for heterosexual sexual practices in the light of *Bowers v. Hardwick* (q.v.).

PROVINCETOWN/P-TOWN. Lesbian and gay resort tourist town and artist haven at the end of Cape Cod, Massachusetts.

PUBLIC DISPLAY(S) OF AFFECTION (PDA). Kissing, hugging, or hand holding in a public space or in view of others. PDA between heterosexual (q.v.) couples is seen as appropriate behavior, but between same-gender couples may instigate homophobic (q.v.) reactions.

PURITAN(ISM). The American culture of sexual prudishness, especially when it comes to explicit sexual behavior, even though sex in the form of the heterosexual female is used to sell most objects.

– Q –

QUEER. A derogatory term for homosexual, reclaimed by the radical lesbian, gay, bisexual, and transgendered (qq.v) activists and queer theorists in the 1980s as a more inclusive term. Queer activists and theorists believe that gender (q.v.) and sexual identity are fluid. Some female queer theorists do not refer to themselves as either lesbian or women, but as queer(s). Or they may refer to themselves as boyz, andros, trannie boys, FTM, girlz, boychick, femme, stone butch (qq.v), or queer. Each name refers to a gender identification that is not mainstream. The term "queer" and its variants are problematic for some lesbians, especially for lesbian-feminists (q.v.) since woman/lesbian is erased when the more male-identified term is used. *See also* Queer Theory.

QUEER NATION. A direct action (q.v.) group founded in 1990 to combat homophobia and hate crimes (qq.v.). This group is anti-assimilationist as demonstrated by its slogan "We're Here. We're Queer. Get Used to It." Their take-no-prisoners attitude quickly spread from New York City to other cities as Queer Nation groups held actions about a broad array of issues, some of which had nothing directly to do with lesbian and gay rights such as protests against the 1991 Persian Gulf War. Other groups started having internal disputes similar to the ones that earlier gay and lesbian groups had over issues such as racism and gender/sexism (q.v.).

QUEER STUDIES. An emerging theoretical academic field of study that questions accepted ideas of sexual and sociopolitical identity and community. Queer Studies is an outgrowth of Gay Studies, Gender Studies, and Women's Studies. Some lesbians feel that Queer Studies glorifies the male homosexual to the exclusion of women/lesbians.

QUEER THEORY. Based on the works of Michel Foucault and Judith Butler (qq.v.), queer theory is the questioning of sexual identities and practices that attempts to denaturalize subjective heterosexual norms and practices. While queer theory also draws heavily from lesbian-feminist (q.v.) analysis of heterosexism (q.v.), lesbian-feminists (q.v.) such as Del Martin, Artemis March, and Sheila Jeffreys (qq.v.) to name a few, find this problematic since it submerges and subordinates lesbian issues to the male-identified category (queer) and its agenda. Some female queer theorists further disappear lesbians by referring to themselves as "queer" rather than as women or lesbians. This may be a result of Butler's work based on Monique Wittig's (q.v.) statement that lesbians are not women since they are not relational to men: "*women,* even in the plural a troublesome term, [is] a site of contest." Thus, the gender catergory "woman" is problematic as a site of identity. Other criticisms of queer theory are that not only does it focus primarily on masculinity and gay male sexuality, it also tends to overlook issues of race and class.

– R –

RACAULT, FRANÇOISE LA (1756–1815). The stage name of French actress Françoise Marie Antoinette Joseph Saucerotte. She was the president of the Sapphic Sect of Anandrynes founded in 1770 by Thérèse de Fluery.

RACISM. Racism is the assumption that one race is superior to others. In practice, in Western Europe and North America, it is the assumption that the white or Caucasian race is superior to all other races and involves privileging that "whiteness" legally and socially. But similar manifestations exist for other races in other regions. In the United States (q.v.), black lesbian-feminists (q.v.) identified this form of oppression and devaluation that along with classism (q.v.), allows the dominant group of people to exploit the other. Racism is also a problem for latinas/latinos in the United States and for other minority groups vis-à-vis the majority in countries around the world. Some people consider race to be a social construction (q.v.).

RADICAL FEMINISM. Radical feminism goes beyond the liberal feminist (q.v.) fight against sexism (q.v.) in society. Radical feminists claim that women have historically been oppressed in nearly every known society. This oppression (q.v.) is usually unrecognized by both the victims and the oppressors and cannot be alleviated just by other social changes (such as the elimination of classism [q.v.]). Women's oppression is a template for all other types and forms of oppression.

This is a form of feminism that holds that women need to be in control of their bodies and their sexuality. Radical feminism's analyses of women's oppression in a patriarchy (q.v.) is directly tied to women's lack of bodily autonomy. Their goal is to end male domination and control of women's bodies and sexuality. Many radical feminists (q.v.), but not all, are lesbians; others are cultural feminists (q.v.)

RADICAL FEMINISTS. One of the groups whose goal was to end male domination and control of women's bodies and sexuality as a means for radical societal change. *See also* Radical Feminism.

RADICALESBIANS. Formed by women who left the National Organization for Women (NOW) (q.v.). during the lesbian purges and others who because of the sexism in the Gay Liberation Front (GLF) and the Gay Activists Alliance (GAA) (qq.v.) felt these bodies were not meeting their needs or considering their issues as lesbians.

Rita Mae Brown, Sidney Abbott, Artemis March (née March Hoffman), Barbara Love, Martha Shelley (qq.v.), Ellen Bedoz (Shumsky), Suzanne Bevier, Michela Griffo, Lois Hart, and Arlene Kisner were the original members and authors of the Radicalesbian's manifesto "Woman-Identified Woman" (q.v.). March was the primary writer and the opening line "Lesbian is the rage of all women" is attributed to Sidney Abbott. This manifesto provides one of the most cogent critiques of heterosexism (q.v.) then and today. Woman-identified woman is a less loaded term than lesbian and may be applied to any feminist who feels solidarity with other women. This concept was the driving force behind their analyses of lesbianism as a political choice for women.

The Radicalesbians first called themselves the "Lavender Menace" (q.v.) and took over the second Congress to Unite Women (q.v.) in New York City on May 1, 1970. Other women joined them at this point. The Radicalesbians dissolved by 1971, after some of the original members went back to the GLF and formed the GLF's Women's Caucus, and the remaining members tried to form an unsuccessful collective (q.v.).

RAINBOW CURRICULUM. The inclusive multicultural curriculum that the New York City School Board developed in 1989. This caused an uproar with the conservative Queens School Board 24 because the curriculum included lesbian and gay culture and history. Mary Cummins, the president of Queens Board 24, thought that including lesbians and gays as if they were minorities would demean the "true" minorities and refused to have the curriculum taught. This quickly spread through other conservative and religious leaders to other school boards, which were afraid that the Manhattan liberals and gays were going to recruit their children. The Rainbow curriculum failed to be accepted, but the targeted populations—working poor and minorities—turned out in record numbers at the next school board election and voted in more progressive school board members. *See also Heather Has Two Mommies;* Newman, Leslea; Religious Right.

RAINBOW FLAG. Designed by Gilbert Baker in 1978 to represent lesbian and gay pride, the multicolored flag originally was pink, red, orange, yellow, green, turquoise, indigo, and violet. It was soon modified to red, orange, yellow, green, blue, and purple because these colors were available for mass production.

RAPE. Rape is an act of sexual aggression and power; it is used to control women (primarily) and their actions and choices. Thus, rape is considered to be a feminist (q.v.) issue. Rape has been defined by the heterosexist (q.v.) culture and legal system as vaginal penetration by a penis.

Lesbians who are raped by men are invisible since their rape, if reported, falls under the rubric of women being raped, unless the crime can be considered a hate crime (q.v.). As an act of antilesbian violence, lesbians who are raped by men face homophobic reactions by medical and police personnel. Some lesbians feel even more vulnerable having had their bodies and their lesbianism violated by a male. In some cases of antilesbian violence, the rape may take place in front of lovers and family. Lesbian rape victims also need to be counseled about birth control.

There are lesbians who are raped by other lesbians. Some sources state that one in every three lesbians has experienced sexual assault and/or rape by another lesbian; disabled lesbians are more likely to be victims of sexual assault/rape. The sexual agressor may be either butch or femme (qq.v.). These assaults/rapes are also invisible since the victims, though suffering the same trauma as women raped by men, do not think that same-sex assault is "as bad" as that by men, are in denial that women can hurt one another, or do not want to betray the lesbian community and further feed into society's homophobia (q.v.).

Groups are forming to help lesbian rape victims and to educate the community such as San Francisco Women Against Rape.

RED RIBBONS. A loop of red ribbon fastened to one's lapel represents AIDS (q.v.) awareness. Lesbians were very influential in AIDS awareness and caregiving to persons with AIDS (PWAs). Pink ribbons (q.v.) signify breast cancer awareness. *See also* AIDS Coalition to Unleash Power (ACT-Up).

REDSTOCKINGS. A radical feminist group founded in 1969 by Shulamith Firestone and Ellen Willis. It developed the "Redstocking Manifesto" and the concept of consciousness-raising (q.v.), the speakouts, and the pro-woman line. Redstockings was responsible for the Miss America Pageant demonstration in which undergarments and cosmetics were burned, which the media called "bra burning."

REDWING, DONNA (OLSON) (19??–). Social justice activist and organizer. A Native American and feminist, Redwing has been active in the Gay and Lesbian Rights movement of the late 1980s. From 1989 to 1993, Redwing was the executive director of the largest lesbian organization in the Pacific Northwest, the Lesbian Community Project located in Portland, Oregon. During her time there, she helped to lead the fight against Measure 9, the antigay initiative (q.v.). Redwing was named *Advocate Magazine's* Woman of the Year for 1992. She has started grassroots networks; monitored media representations of lesbians, gays, bisexuals, and transgendered/transsexual (qq.v.) people (LGBTs); and served as field and community affairs director for the Gay and Lesbian Alliance Against Antidefamation (GLAAD) (q.v.).

From 1996 until 2001, Redwing was a field director for the Human Rights Campaign (HRC) (q.v.). Redwing was the 2001 recipient of the Interfaith Alliances' Walter Cronkite Faith and Freedom Award for her work in bringing the LGBT activists (q.v.) and faith communities together. Currently, she has joined the Gill Foundation as director of its Outgiving Project, a technical assistance and training program for LGBT persons to expand both the amount of donations and the number of donors.

REGINA v. BUTLER. A 1992 ruling of the Supreme Court of Canada (q.v.), which criminalized pornography (q.v.) since it is harmful to women's physical safety, equality, and self-esteem. Heterosexual pornographic works still circulate; it is lesbian and feminist writings and erotica (q.v.) that are suppressed. In an ironic twist, the antipornographer Andrea Dworkin's (q.v.) books have been seized at the border.

REIGER, MARILYN "BOOPSIE" (19??–). Reiger was the head of the Oakland, California, chapter of the Mattachine Society (MS) (q.v.) in the early 1950s. She was part of the moderate group, along with Pearl Hart (q.v.), which played a pivotal role at the 1953 convention and led to MS becoming accomodationist.

RELIGION. Most major religions, except for Buddhism, have condemned same-sex relationships at one point or another in their history, even though they may foster same-sex communities such as convents and monastic communities. While most modern religious groups still condemn same-sex relations, a few accept them. An example is the Central Conference of American Rabbis, the American Reform Jewish leaders, which voted on March 30, 2000, to celebrate same-sex unions, saying that it is not a sin to be lesbian or gay; it is a sin to have prejudices and strike out against lesbians and gays. The Anglican Communion—the Church of England and the Episcopal Church—and the Lutheran Church were the first western religions to call for legal tolerance of lesbians and gays. The United Church of Christ, an ecumenical Protestant denomination, has been one of the most progressive churches when dealing with same-sex issues, congregants and church leaders, having ordained a gay male as early as in 1972.

Buddhist attitudes toward sexuality vary by country, but for the most part it does not distinguish between same-sex or heterosexual erotic acts. Buddhism is considered to be the only sex-positive (q.v.) world religion.

Christianity, on the other hand, is considered to be one of the major sex-negative (q.v.) world religions. Christian opposition to extramarital sexuality as well as homosexuality can be traced to interpretations of sections of the Bible especially Leviticus (q.v.). There is a split between fundamentalist Christian groups and mainstream Christian denominations. Fundamentalists view all nonprocreational sex or even the promotion of homosexuality as a sin, which promotes homophobia (q.v.). Because many fundamentalists believe that homosexuality is a choice, homosexuals may be cured. Roman Catholics also condemn homosexuality, but do call for compassion. The Roman Catholic Church's stand on issues such as abortion, AIDS, and same-sex marriages (qq.v.) has made it a target of many direct actions groups such as the AIDS Coalition to Unleash Power (ACT-Up) (q.v.). There are support groups within the Catholic Church that are advocating change, such as Dignity. Orthodox Eastern churches, which include the Greek and Russian Orthodox Churches, may have historically tolerated same-sex relations according to John Boswell, though there have been some politically motivated persecutions of homosexuals. For the most part, although the Orthodox Eastern churches consider homosexuality a perversion and a failing, they advocate medical and psychiatric treatment for homosexuals to restore their procreational sexual identities. Other religions, such as Scientology, also purport to cure homosexual members. Mormons, members of the Church of Jesus Christ of Latter Day Saints, although (originally) sexual nonconformists themselves with the practice of polygamy, excommunicate homosexuals.

In the contemporary lesbian community, many women are former nuns, since as nuns they did not have to marry and found like-minded companions. John Boswell and Judith Brown have documented western religions' attitudes toward homosexuality.

One of the most controversial issues, even among those religions and denominations that choose to welcome lesbian and gay congregants, concerns the ordination of homosexual religious leaders, deacons, and priests—whether they are practicing homosexuals or celibate. In 1994, OutRage! (q.v.) began to out (q.v.) homosexual bishops within the Anglican Church; this direct action (q.v.) eventually led the Anglican bishops to publicly renounce homophobia. Baptists, Episcopalians, Presbyterians, Quakers, and the United Church of Canada are among the Christian denominations that tolerate homosexuality, but have not accepted homosexual religious leaders.

Islam, another major world religion, views homosexuality as it does adultery or extramarital sex: as endangering the social order, especially if it is made public. There are some differences in interpretation of Islam; for instance, Swahili Muslim women encourage same-sex relationships, which are not necessarily sexual, between independent older women and younger women.

Judaism's several branches each have their own policies toward homosexuality. Reform Judaism, as mentioned above, is the most accepting. The Conservative branch of Judaism stresses the spirit of the Torah and Bible, and depending on congregation, may be more tolerant of homosexuality. Orthodox Judaism, which tends to take a more literal reading of both the Bible and Torah, is intolerant of homosexuality. It views all nonprocreational sex negatively and sex between women as obscene. There are over forty gay and lesbian outreach synagogues. The first, Beth Chayim Chadahism, was founded in Los Angeles in 1973, followed by New York City's Congregation Beth Simchat Torah the following year. There are lesbian Jewish groups worldwide connected by the World Congress of Gay and Lesbian Jewish Organizations. These groups have helped the Lesbian and Gay Rights movement in the Jewish state of Israel (*see* Middle East) to flourish. The year 1979 saw the ordination of the first gay (male) rabbi. The first lesbian rabbi, Janet Ross Mander, was hired by Congregation Beth Simchat Torah in 1983.

Wicca (Wicce) or witchcraft, a religion that predates Christianity, is one that is commonly practiced among lesbians, since it celebrates the Great Goddess Diana (Artemis) and the goddess within each woman and her connection with nature.

The Metropolitan Community Church (MCC), established in 1968, is a gay and lesbian nondenominational Christian church which accepts gays and lesbians of all faiths. In fact, American Jewish lesbians and gays first held their meetings and services at MCC. See *also* Ex-Gay Ministry; Religious Right.

RELIGIOUS RIGHT. This is an American coalition of predominantly Christian conservative fundamentalist religions (q.v.), leaders, and ministries. It is also referred to as the Christian Right or Christian Coalition that includes Protestant Christians and Baptists. Other conservative religions also have their fundamentalist sects (Islamic, Orthodox Judaism, and Catholic), which when appropriate have mobilized with the Christian Coalition. The leaders of the Religious Right see the push for lesbian and gay rights, and for women's rights more generally, as challenges to the existing traditional civil order and leading the United States (q.v.) and the world into "an age of godlessness."

The Religious Right has been fighting gay and lesbian rights and any other challenges to the traditional family and family values (q.v.) such as feminism (q.v.), through media (q.v.) campaigns, ballot initiatives repealing existing laws, and state and federal legislation such as the Defense of Marriage Act (q.v.) in the United States and in other countries around the globe. They have joined forces with the ex-gay movement (q.v.) and with conservative politicians to push their agendas nationally and internationally. For instance, Senator Jesse Helms (R-North Carolina) has helped to pass legislation limiting U.S. funding of United Nation programs that support, advocate, or fund any groups that work on issues such as family planning (reproductive rights) and/or lesbian and gay issues such as age of consent laws (q.v.) or gay rights.

The Religious Right has used videos such as *The Gay Agenda* and *Gay Rights, Special Rights* to vilify lesbians and gays and to rally financial and political support for its initiatives among conservative working poor and people of color and their communities. The Religious Right also uses these tools and other homophobic rhetoric to rally its own followers and to raise money.

Some of the dominant secular and nonsecular groups that are associated with the Religious Right are the American Family Association, Christian Coalition, Concerned Women of America, Eagle Forum, Family Research Council, Focus on the Family, Free Congress Foundation, Operation Rescue, Oregon Citizens Alliance (qq.v.), Traditional Values Coalition, and earlier the Moral Majority (q.v.). *See also* Equal Rights; Leviticus; Special Rights.

RENT PARTIES. Also known as "house parties," rent parties originated in Harlem in the 1920s. Guests of these house parties paid entrance fees to help their hosts pay the rent. These parties were usually attended by a mix of lesbians, gays, and straights. Rent parties were also held during the 1960s and 1970s to help pay the rent and costs for many lesbian, gay, and feminist organizations and newspapers. *See also* Harlem Renaissance.

RESISTANCE. Merely being lesbian in a patriarchal society is seen as a political act, an act of resistance, since lesbians are not sexually available to men. Being an out (q.v.) lesbian is to publicly announce by one's presence and actions that one does not fit into the patriarchy (q.v.), thus challenging that male hegemonic to change. *See also* Lesbian Resistance.

REVOLUTION. An event, an invention, or a political action that completely changes civil and political society. For lesbians, gays, and feminists, the concept of "Come the revolution" means things will be different for them, they will no longer be oppressed.

RICH, ADRIENNE (1929–). Activist, poet, and writer. She coined the term "compulsory heterosexuality" (q.v.) to describe the social conditioning of women to believe that relationship with a male (marriage and then mothering) was the only course available to them.

RIOT GRRRLS. The punk rock music phenomenon that is in-your-face, profemale, and prosexuality—lesbian, heterosexual, or bisexual.

ROBERTS, SHELLY (1943–). Writer and activist. Roberts was one of the first popular lesbian humorists. She is a frequent lecturer at pride celebrations (q.v.), on television, and at universities. She is on the board of the Human Rights Campaign (HRC) (q.v.). Most recently, she was involved with the Millennium celebration in Atlanta, Georgia.

ROMANTIC FRIENDSHIP. In the late nineteenth and early twentieth centuries, the socially accepted intimate friendship of two unmarried women, described in words of love, unbroken until one of the women married. Many times the women lived their lives together. *See also* Boston Marriage.

ROMO-CARMONA, MARIANA (1952–). Chilean-born writer, editor, and activist whose focus is on working-class lesbians of color (q.v.). She won the Astraea Foundation (q.v.) Lesbian Fiction prize in 1991. Her poetry and fiction have been widely anthologized. *Living at Night,* her lesbian novel set in the 1970s, was published in 1998. She currently teaches creative writing at Goddard College, New Hampshire, where she helps marginalized writers cross the intersection of culture, gender, and class.

ROOSEVELT, ELEANOR (1884–1962). First Lady of the United States and human rights activist (qq.v.). She had a wide circle of social activist lesbian friends. She situated her lover, Lorena Hickok (q.v.), in the White House with her and authored numerous letters to Hickok when they were apart. In 1948, she was involved in writing and promoting the United Nations (q.v.) Declaration of Human Rights and continued to be a human rights activist until her death.

ROUTSONG, ALMA (1924–1996). Novelist, editor, and activist. She was an officer in the Daughters of Bilitis (DOB) (q.v.) and active in the Gay Liberation movement. Writing under the penname of Isabel Miller (which is an anagram for "lesbian"), she wrote historical lesbian novels with positive role models and happy endings (as opposed to lesbian pulp fiction which had the lesbians paying for the sin of being lesbian by dying or going to prison). Her most famous and now classic novel was *Patience and Sarah* (1972) (q.v.), which she originally self-published in 1969 as *A Place for Us*. This story was based on the painter Mary Ann Willson (q.v.) and her partner Miss Brundage who lived in upstate New York during the 1820s. Routsong was a mentor for other lesbian writers.

RUBIN, GAYLE (c. 1940–). Academic and sex activist. Rubin was founder of the west coast Samois (q.v.), a lesbian sadomasochism (S/M) (q.v.) group. Rubin's writing, especially the 1984 "Thinking Sex: Notes for a Radical Theory of the Politics of Sexuality" (reprinted in most lesbian and gay readers), provides a context for understanding sex panics (q.v.) and the resulting oppression of sexual expression.

RULE, JANE (1931–). Canadian American writer. Rule is the author of such classic lesbian books as *Desert of the Heart,* which was made into the classic lesbian film *Desert Hearts.* She has been committed to changing the climate for lesbians and gays first through her writings, and since the early 1990s, through her activism in literary and gay rights issues.

RUSS, JOANNA (1937–). Radical feminist, essayist, science fiction writer, and children's fiction author. Russ's early short story "Scenes from Domestic Life" (1968) explored lesbian sexuality. She continued to incorporate feminist and lesbian issues into her fiction as she also became an academic activist in the Civil Rights, Feminist, and Lesbian and Gay Rights movements (qq.v.). Russ's best-known book is the lesbian separatist (q.v.) utopian classic *The Female Man* (1975).

RUSSIAN RIVER. North of San Francisco, California, this area has become a haven for lesbians and gays. *See also* Streicher, Rikki.

– S –

SADOMASOCHISM (S/M). Consensual sexual practice that explores power and pain in scenes (or fantasies) of domination and submission. S/M practices involve at minimum two partners, the dominant sadist and the seemingly passive masochist. S/M practioners claim that the masochist is the one in control since she may at anytime end the sex play. S/M practioners may publicly wear leather clothing and chains advertising their penchant for S/M. These women are referred to as leather dykes (q.v.). *See also* Pornography; Sex Positive; Sex Radicals; Sex Wars.

SALSA SOUL SISTERS. *See* **AFRICAN ANCESTRAL LESBIANS UNITED FOR SOCIAL CHANGE.**

SAME-SEX MARRIAGE. Same-sex couples in the United States (q.v.) have been discriminated against because they need over three hundred separate legal documents to replicate the same legal standing that heterosexual couples have in the state of matrimony. Some of these issues include inheritance (non-married couples are taxed up to 50 percent on their inheritance from their partners), hospital visitation rights, automatic health care proxy, child custody (q.v.), and power of attorney.

Same-sex marriage has not been legal in the United States. When the state of Hawaii court found the ban on same-sex marriages against the state constitution, the federal government quickly passed the Defense of Marriage Act (q.v.), which allows other states not to honor any same-sex marriage. Thirty-two other states also passed legislation that bans same-sex marriage. The Hawaii state legislature subsequently followed suit, banning same-sex marriages. The voters in California passed the Knight Initiative (q.v.), which defines marriage as an act between a man and a woman. Vermont has come the closest to allowing same-sex marriage by calling it civil union (q.v.).

Outside of the United States, same-sex domestic partnerships (q.v.)—same-sex recognized partnerships—or civil marriages exist in Finland, Greenland, Iceland, Hungary, the Netherlands (q.v.), Germany (q.v.), and France (q.v.). These unions are almost, but not quite equal to their heterosexual counterpart, since they do not recognize gay adoptions (q.v.). Same-sex marriages are fully recognized in Norway and Denmark (qq.v.). In January 2001, some Canadian ministers began to announce in church the banns for gay and lesbian couples thinking this may allow for civil recognition of same-sex marriage in Canada (q.v.). The two couples—one lesbian, the other gay men—in Toronto believe they have used the Ontario Marriage Act to legally marry. The act says that if a couples' banns are announced in church three Sundays in a row, it carries the same legal weight as a marriage license from City Hall. In this way, the Metropolitan Community Church issued legal marriage certificates to the couples, but the Ontario provincial government has not recorded the marriage.

The Vatican, in response to the number of countries recognizing same-sex marriages and adoptions, issued the seventy-six-page "Family, Marriage, and 'de facto' Union" document. It calls such legal recognition of same-sex unions and families "a serious sign of the contemporary breakdown in the social and moral conscience," deriding unions and adoptions as such putting children in "a great danger."

There is some criticism by lesbian-feminists (q.v.) of the right-to-marry agenda being promoted by the major gay rights organizations. Their critique of the agenda is that there has been no feminist analysis of marriage applied to the right for gays and lesbians to marry. *See also* Domestic Partnerships; Full Faith and Credit Clause; Kowalski, Sharon; Pacte Civil de Solidarité.

SAMOIS. This is considered to be the first lesbian-feminist sadomasochistic (S/M) (qq.v.) and leather organization in the United States (q.v.). It was founded in San Francisco in 1978. Members of the group were pro-sex activists during the lesbian Sex Wars (qq.v.). The book *Coming to Power* (1981) is a collection of writings by various members including Gayle Rubin and Pat Caflia (qq.v.). These writings include erotica (q.v.) as well as information on S/M. Samois disbanded in 1983–1984, but other lesbian S/M groups still exist.

SAMTÖKIN 78. Founded in 1978, this is Iceland's national gay and lesbian rights organization. Recognized by the government, this organization fights homophobia (q.v.), and any distinctions between homosexuals and heterosexuals. To this end, the group has helped pass the most progressive domestic partnership (q.v.) registration act, which recognizes joint child custody (q.v.). Samtökin 78 is working toward eliminating all discrimination based on sexual orientation.

SAPPHIC/SAPPHISTRY. Derived from Sappho (q.v.), meaning "having to do with lesbians and their love."

SAPPHIRE (ROMONA LOFTON) (1950–). Performer, writer, and educator. An African American lesbian-feminist (qq.v.), Sapphire examines issues of racism, sexism, heterosexism, and violence against women (qq.v.) in both her writings and performances. She began NAPS which is considered to be the first black lesbian performance group in 1977.

SAPPHO (c. 620–560 BC). Greek poet. Called the tenth muse by Plato, Sappho ran a school for girls to study music, dance, and the arts on the island of Lesbos. She wrote over eight volumes of poetry, much of which was intentionally destroyed during medieval times. The surviving fragments of her work are love poems addressed to women.

SAPPHO AWARD OF DISTINCTION. An award given annually by Astraea National Lesbian Foundation (q.v.).

SCHULMAN, SARAH (1958–). Author, playwright, and activist. Schulman has written nine books including *My American History: Lesbian and Gay Life during the Reagan/Bush Years* (1994). Schulman cofounded the Lesbian Avengers (q.v.) because she realized the invisibility of lesbians (and women) after her activist work in the AIDS Coalition to Unleash Power (ACT-Up) (q.v.) which focused mainly on gay men with AIDS/HIV (q.v.) and disregarded women with AIDS/HIV until the late 1980s. Her work has received numerous awards including the 1997 Stonewall Award for "improving the lives of gays and lesbians in the U.S."

SCOTTISH MINORITIES GROUP. This was the Scottish gay rights group founded in 1969 that originally focused only on gay issues. After the Scottish criminal statutes were amended, it continued its work on both lesbian and gay rights as the Scottish Homosexual Rights Group (1978) and is currently known as OUTRIGHT Scotland. *See also* United Kingdom.

S.C.U.M. MANIFESTO. This manifesto, produced by Valerie Solanas (q.v.), was mimeographed and sold on the street. It was supposed to be from the radical lesbian (q.v.) Society for Cutting Up Men (S.C.U.M.), but only Solanas was a member. The manifesto was a call for women to overthrow government, eliminate the monetary system, automate, and destroy the male sex.

SECOND-PARENT ADOPTION/COADOPTION. The legal adoption (q.v.) of a child by the other, same-sex parent. For instance, in a lesbian couple, while one woman may bear the child and be the child's biological mother, her partner will, where possible, adopt the child so that the child has legal protections if something should happen to the biological parent. Or in the case of a lesbian couple adopting a child, both women become the child's mothers. There are still many states and countries that prohibit lesbians and gays from adopting or foster parenting a child and this has become a key issue.

SECOND WAVE OF FEMINISM. This is the rejuvenation of the women's movement in the United States and Europe (qq.v.) during the early 1960s. The second wave of feminism picked up from the first wave of feminism (q.v.), which had secured voting rights for most women. The second wave dealt with issues of employment, reproductive rights, and sexuality such as lesbianism. The movement split between the liberal feminists and the more radical feminists (qq.v.). *See also* The Feminists; Friedan, Betty; The Furies; Lavender Menace; National Organization for Women; Radicalesbians.

SENECA FALLS. The town in upstate New York where, in 1848, the "Declaration of Sentiments" was written and read, triggering the first wave of feminism (q.v.). The "Declaration of Sentiments" articulated the need for women to control their bodies, own property, be educated, and be fully franchised citizens (having voting rights).

SENIOR ACTION IN A GAY ENVIRONMENT (SAGE). SAGE was founded on November 2, 1977, in New York City. It is a support organization for aging lesbians and gay men, providing educational, recreational, and social outlets and services as well as services for the homebound. SAGE advocates for the visibility and rights of the aging lesbian and gay person in a community that is youth oriented. It is the model for other organizations for the aging lesbian and gay population such as the San Francisco Gay and Lesbian Outreach to Elders (GLOE) (q.v.). SAGE begat SAGENET, the nationwide network of local community-based programs serving lesbian, gay, bisexual, and transgendered (LGBT) seniors. *See also* Ageism; Lesbian Health; Old Lesbians Organizing for Change.

SEPARATISM. *See* **LESBIAN SEPARATISM**.

SERGEANT. A butch (q.v.) lesbian in the 1930–1950s.

SEX NEGATIVE. Deriving from the 1980s Sex Wars (q.v.), a person who is closed to all types of sexual expression and practice. Sex-negative lesbians have also given rise to the archetypal sexless lesbian. *See also* Sex Positive/Sex-Positive Radical.

SEX PANIC. Periods when public policy and laws are implemented to curtail deviant sexual activity. The most recent sex panic occurred with the advent of AIDS (q.v) when municipalities passed ordinances closing (gay) bath houses, raided gay bars (q.v.), and identified gay prisoners.

SEX POSITIVE/SEX-POSITIVE RADICAL. A person who is open to all forms of sexual expression and sexual practices including sadomasochism (S/M), pornography, and erotica (qq.v.); in short, someone whose expression of sexuality is outside the norm of acceptable or vanilla sex (q.v.). The opposite of someone who is sex positive (q.v.) is a person who is sex negative (q.v). A sex-negative person is usually antipornography and an assimilationist (qq.v.); a sex-negative person feels that those expressions of sexuality outside the norm hurt the acceptability of the mainstream lesbians and gays. These terms came to be as a result of the sex panics and the lesbian Sex Wars (qq.v.).

SEX RADICALS. These are persons who are sex positive (q.v.) and whose sexual expression is outside the accepted norm. *See also* Rubin, Gayle; Sadomasochism; Sex Wars.

SEX REASSIGNMENT. The surgical change of a person's birth genitals to those of the opposite sex. This is the final stage in the transition from one sex to another and usually requires having lived and passed (q.v.) as a member of the intended opposite sex with attendant hormonal treatments for two years prior to surgery. *See also* Female to Male; Gender; Male to Female; Post-Op; Pre-Op; Transsexual.

SEX-ROLE STEREOTYPES. These are the dichotomous and traditional masculine/feminine roles for both the heterosexual and lesbian and gay populations. These gender (q.v) stereotypes are learned behavior according to one's culture.

SEX VARIANT. Someone whose sexuality and/or sexual expression is out of the norm of heterosexual expression. This was one of the terms used to describe homosexuals prior to 1969.

SEX WARS. The heated debate in the 1980s and early 1990s that was publicly initiated at the conference "The Scholar and the Feminist IX— Toward a Politics of Sexuality" held at Barnard College in New York City on April 24, 1982. It was engaged among feminists and lesbians about sexuality and sexual practices. Some cultural historians trace the roots of the wars back to the radicalization of the women's movement and the politicalization of "lesbian" by lesbian-feminists (q.v.) in the early 1970s.

The key issues were pornography (q.v.), sadomasochistic sexual practices, and violence against women. Some women wanted to eliminate all pornography because it oppressed women and believed that some sexual practices, such as sadomasochism (S/M) (q.v.), demeaned women and were acts of violence against women. Public sexual presentation such as butch, femme, and wearing leather (qq.v.), was also questioned as replicating heterosexual practices.

Others believed that the full range of women's desires and sexual practices and presentations should be acceptable to all. The pro-sex camp felt that issues of freedom of expression as well as sexual education and autonomy of women's bodies were at stake.

While the sex wars split both the feminist and lesbian communities, the proliferation of lesbian erotica (q.v.) and the acceptance of butch and femme sexual presentation in the mid- to late 1990s indicate that there is now a diversity of sexual expression accepted by both feminists and lesbians.

SEX WORKERS. People who earn their living in the sex trades such as prostitutes and strippers. Some sex workers have chosen their work and claim autonomy (q.v.) of their body and its use; others are coerced into the sex trade, especially young Asian girls and women used in sexual tourism.

SEXISM. In a patriarchy (q.v.), this is discrimination based on the belief that males are superior to females, having privileges and power. This discrimination may be both culturally and legally institutionalized. Liberal feminism's (q.v.) primary critique of patriarchy was its sexism, which caused discrimination against women. If there was adequate similarity (equality) between the sexes then no differences could justify discrimination. The most basic form of sexist analysis is to change the sex of the individual being discriminated against and see if that discrimination still would hold. *See also* Male Privilege.

SEXUAALINEN/SEKSUAALINEN TASAVERTAISUUS (SETA). This is the Finnish national gay and lesbian rights (q.v.) umbrella organization that was founded in 1971. SETA is composed of sixteen local and national autonomous organizations working for gender and sexual equality. Governed by a board from each of the sixteen member organizations, SETA's goals include influencing politics to end discrimination against gender differences, educational and social work, working to combat AIDS (q.v.), and providing social events and meetings. The organization publishes *Magazine Z* six times a year as well as prominent books and theses. SETA organizes film festivals and pride marches (q.v.) as well as meeting places for groups such as the TransHelsinki, serving the transgendered (q.v.) community and events for the leather and fetish group, MSC Finland. SETA also has a foundation that supports research and projects. *See also* Finland.

SEXUAL AUTONOMY. *See* **AUTONOMY (SEXUAL).**

SEXUAL CASTE SYSTEM. The radical feminist (q.v.) theory that societies not only have an economic class system that needs to be overturned, but one based on gender and sexual identity. The sexual caste system privileges male heterosexuals over all and male homosexuals over lesbians.

SEXUAL HARASSMENT. The act of coercing sexual favors from an individual by offering or withholding job benefits or making the work environment hostile and intolerable by the use of sexual talk, pictures, and ennui. Harassment relies on the sexism, racism, and classism (qq.v.) of society to force those weaker to give in to those who hold the power.

Lesbians are very susceptible to being sexually harassed, especially if they are not out (q.v.) and therefore have to maintain a heterosexual posture to be rewarded. In the military, many women were called lesbians and discharged because they would not give in to the sexual advances of male officers or others. The women's choice is to either give in to the heterosexual pressure or to be labeled a lesbian regardless of their sexual orientation.

While sexual harassment has been predominately heterosexual and male to female, there are some cases of females harassing subordinate males. The 1998 U.S. Supreme Court found in *Oncale v. Sundowner Offshore Services, Inc.* that same-sex harassment may exist.

SEXUAL LAW REFORM SOCIETY. *See* **HOMOSEXUAL LAW REFORM SOCIETY.**

SEXUAL LIBERTIES. Sexual freedom from government regulation. In the United States (q.v.), such protection falls under the right to privacy (q.v.). The Supreme Court has, since *Griswold v. Connecticut* (1968), limited the State's regulation of sexual practice. But the *Bowers v. Hardwick* (q.v.) decision implies that only heterosexual domestic (vs. public) and matrimonial sexual practices fall under the right to privacy.

SEXUAL MCCARTHYISM. Based on the anticommunist and anti-homosexual McCarthy hearings of the 1950s, the term "sexual McCarthyism" was coined to indicate the cultural distaste for public non-normative (nonmonogamous, nonmarital) sexuality during the presidential sex scandal of 1998 involving Bill Clinton and Monica Lewinsky. It has come to include the actions of those who squelch sexuality and/or sexual practices in current sex panics (q.v.) such as rezoning initiatives and health codes. *See also* McCarthy Era; Zoning.

SEXUAL MINORITIES ASSOCIATION. *See* **UNION OF LESBIANS AND HOMOSEXUALS.**

SEXUAL OUTLAW. Lesbians (and homosexuals) may be called this because they do not perform heterosexual or normative sex, there are laws against homosexual practices, and also just for being perceived as lesbian or homosexual a person may be discriminated against. Lesbians often feel outside the law and some relish that desperado feeling. *See also* Lesberado; Rubin, Gayle.

SHELLEY, MARTHA (19??–). Radical lesbian and cofounder of the Gay Liberation Front (GLF) and Radicalesbians (qq.v.). She is a sexual liberationist; she wrote that "the worst part of being homosexual was keeping it secret." Her analyses in "Lesbianism and the Women's Liberation Movement" of the lesbian as a sexual orientation and a woman who is independent of men, explains why lesbians and all women may be man-haters. Her "Notes of a Radical Lesbian" are also of interest here.

SIGNIFICANT OTHER. One's chosen partner in life.

SILENCING. By overt or covert omission, ignoring the needs, concerns, and wants of a group of people in public discourse and presentation. Women's sexuality has been silenced by overt practices and laws; lesbians have been silenced by the conflation of all homosexuality to be "read" as gay male needs and concerns. *See also* Lesbian Invisibility; Woman-Identified Woman.

SIMO, ANA (1946–). Writer, playwright, and activist. Simo is a cofounder of the Lesbian Avengers (q.v.), Dyke TV, and Medusa's Revenge, the first lesbian theater in New York City. A television, print and on-line activist journalist, and news producer, she is also cofounder and editor of the on-line magazine *The Gully* and teaches writing workshops.

SISTERHOOD. The community of lesbians, feminists, and/or women. This is the idea that all women or all members of a specific category of women share a common connection regardless of any cultural differences, a concept fundamental to moral relativism as well as lesbian ethics. *See also* Cross-Cultural Perspectives.

SMASH. Coined at women's colleges at the end of the nineteenth century and in the early twentieth century, this term means a young woman's crush or intense emotional infatuation on another woman. Smashes were usually seen as passing phases and were accepted, though some smashes developed into long-term Boston marriages (q.v.). It was not until the publication of Havelock Ellis's *Sexual Inversion* in 1897, coupled with Sigmund Freud's (q.v.) writings of the 1920s, that smashes were seen as abnormal and perversions and strongly discouraged.

SMITH, ANN (1944–). South African activist and scholar. Smith was a founding member of South Africa's (q.v.) first gay and lesbian group, Gay Association of South Africa (GASA). She successfully helped GASA become affiliated with the International Lesbian and Gay Association (ILGA) (q.v.) and was a cofounder of the lesbian support group Womanspace. Smith offered the first course on lesbian literature at the University of Witwatersrand in 1995. She coorganized the first academic lesbian and gay studies conference held in South Africa at the University of Cape Town, also in 1995.

SMITH, BARBARA (1946–). Black feminist theorist, activist, and writer. Smith cofounded the Combahee River Collective (q.v.) in the early 1970s. With a group of women that included Audre Lorde and Cherríe Moraga (qq.v.), she founded Kitchen Table Women of Color Press in 1981. She has edited many works including black women's studies anthologies and a history of African American lesbians and gays.

SMITH, LILLIAN (1897–1966). Southern writer and editor. She focused on works that explored both race relations and gender (q.v.) roles, though she was private about her own lesbian sexuality. Her books *Strange Fruit* (1944) and *One Hour* (1959) explored both race and lesbian issues in the context of cultural sexual repression.

SOCIAL CONSTRUCTION OF GENDER. The postmodern theory that gender (q.v.) is learned rather than a biological fact. Gender is a result of the environment, specific cultural mores, and circumstances. Most social constructionists oppose the rigid binary construction of gender as being either male or female. For lesbians, this means that "lesbian" as it was understood at the end of the twentieth century, did not exist for women who lived in the late nineteenth century in Boston marriages (q.v.), although today we may ascribe "lesbian" characteristics to them. We now understand "lesbianism" as the current social and political sexual identity construct. *See also* Faderman, Lillian; Social Constructionism.

SOCIAL CONSTRUCTIONISM. The postmodern theory that relates all facets of life—politics, history, and the arts—to the social conditions, culture, and context of the specific circumstance and time. All interactions are encoded and must be read in context. Perspective is then based upon deliberately constructed social reality, which is changing as it is created. Reality is based on a system of societal relationships. Identities, such as lesbian, are self-described, multiple, and fragmented depending on who is "reading" and who is "presenting" the identity. *See also* Butler, Judith; Constructionism v. Essentialism; Essentialism; Foucault, Michel; Identity Politics; Social Construction of Gender.

SOCIETY FOR HUMAN RIGHTS. This was the very first and short-lived gay and lesbian organization in the United States (q.v.). It was founded in Chicago, Illinois, in 1924 and published the first homosexual magazine, *Friendship and Freedom,* which appeared for two issues.

SODOMY. Nongenital to genital sexual practices (between same-sex couples or heterosexual couples). These sexual practices are seen as nonreproductive and at various times have been outlawed. Currently, six states in the United States (q.v.) outlaw only same-sex sodomy. The question of criminalizing only same-sex sodomy versus all acts of sodomy has been challenged in Minnesota and Arkansas. The number of states outlawing both homosexual and heterosexual sodomy decreased to eleven when Arizona repealed its sodomy laws in 2001. In many other countries, only male-to-male sodomy is outlawed since women are considered not to engage in any sexual activity except that with a man. *See also Bowers v. Hardwick* (1986).

SOLANAS, VALERIE (1936–1988). Artist and radical lesbian. Solanas is best known for shooting and wounding the pop artist Andy Warhol in 1968 when he would not produce her play, *Up Your Ass*. She is also known for the radical "S.C.U.M. Manifesto" (q.v.). She played a tough dyke (q.v.) in Warhol's film *I, a Man*.

SOUTH AFRICA. It was because of the activism of a small group of lesbians and gays that the African National Congress adopted a gay rights platform plank. With the overthrow of apartheid in South Africa and the emergence of a democratic government with a new Constitution written under the leadership of Nelson Mandela in 1994 and adopted in 1996, lesbian and gay civil rights are protected.

Gay rights groups such as the Gay Association of South Africa (GASA) (q.v.), Lesbians, Gays against Oppression, and the National Coalition for Gay and Lesbian Equality are active in promoting and securing gay rights. GASA was formed in 1982; apolitical, it was dominated by white males. Gay and Lesbian Organization of the Witwatersrand (GLOW) (q.v.), formed in 1988, was founded as a multiracial group to end discrimination. GLOW organized the first Lesbian and Gay Pride March (q.v.) in 1990. *See also* Ditsie, Palesa; Lapinsky, Sheila.

SOVIET UNION, FORMER. After the dissolution of the Soviet Union, many of the former states, now countries in their own right, decriminalized homosexuality—Armenia, Estonia, Latvia, Moldova, Russia, and Ukraine. There are now many publications that have replaced *Tema* (1990–1993), the first gay and lesbian publication that was harassed by the KGB. There is a federation that links the many gay and lesbian associations throughout the former Soviet Union, *Treugolnik*. *See also* Union of Lesbians and Homosexuals.

SPAHR, JANE ADAMS (1946–). Presbyterian minister. Ordained in 1974, Reverend Spahr has been an activist for lesbians, gays, bisexuals, transgendered (qq.v), and intersexed inclusion within the Presbyterian Church, USA, and in society. A victim of the Presbyterian Church's homophobia, she is personally involved in public battle over homophobia (q.v.) in the church. Since 1978, the church's policy is that homosexuality is incompatible with ministry. Spahr's life as a lesbian wife and mother is documented in the 1996 video *Your Mom's a Lesbian, Here's Your Lunch. Have a Good Day at School.* *See also* Religion.

SPAIN. Lesbians in Spain were also active in the feminist movement, although because of Spanish law and culture, they were closeted. Since the death of Francisco Franco in 1975, lesbians have become more visible. Lesbians felt that the feminist movement was too heterosexist. During the 1980s, several political pressure groups were formed to fight for lesbians' legal recognition. In 1990, lesbians joined with gay men in the Coordinadora Gai-Lesbiana working on a myriad of issues from fighting AIDS (q.v.) to social and legal changes. The prominent lesbian political group is Group Lesbos (formerly Grup Lesbia), which originated in Barcelona, Catalonia.

SPECIAL RIGHTS. The Religious Right (q.v.) in the United States (q.v.) claims that lesbians, gays, and transgendered persons who benefit from antibias laws (q.v.) are receiving special rights. They claim that such initiatives extend special rights or allow lesbians and gays more rights than ordinary people have when, in fact, these initiatives just allow equal civil rights to lesbians and gays. To the contrary, it is still legal in many places to discriminate against lesbians, gays, and transgendered persons in employment, housing, health, and other civil activities. *See also* Equal Rights.

SPINSTER. An unmarried woman of a certain age, sometimes used as code for lesbian.

STEIN, GERTRUDE (1874–1946). Expatriate writer. Stein grew up in California and left for France (q.v.) in 1903 with her brother Leo. It was in Paris that she met her lifelong companion Alice B. Toklas (1877–1967). They remained in France until their deaths and are buried in a joint plot in Père Lachaise Cemetery, Paris. Stein and Toklas created one of the renowned intellectual and artistic salons of the time, frequented by composers, writers, and artists such as Virgil Thomson, Ernest Hemingway, and Pablo Picasso as well as other expatriate lesbians such as Sylvia Beach (q.v.). Her writing style included the use of repetition, unconventional narratives and association, a genre she called "verbal portraits," and encoding words, especially those concerning lesbianism. Her best-known work, *The Autobiography of Alice B. Toklas,* was published in 1933. Her last work was the libretto *The Mother of Us All* (1946) for Virgil Thomson's opera about feminist Susan B. Anthony (q.v.). Toklas and Stein lived together for forty years in what some have derided as a mimicry of a heterosexual couple with Toklas playing the part of the wife. Both Jewish, Stein and Toklas fled Nazi-occupied Paris during World War II to live in their country home in the Rhône Valley. *See also* Paris Exiles.

STEREOTYPES. Culturally perpetuated stereotypes of lesbians during the twentieth century have been that of sinister seductresses (who in films died for their sins), sexually preying on innocent heterosexual women, menaces to society, man-hating, mannish spinsters (q.v.) who wear comfortable shoes. Many times, the lesbian is depicted as sexless since she is not, nor can be socially, sexually partnered. In short, culturally negative personal and physical attributes are assigned to the lesbian, and the lesbian is discredited as "other" and outside normal society. Many lesbians who do not want to be stigmatized, discredited, or discriminated against opt to affect a heterosexual woman's feminine appearance and dress, thus passing (q.v.) as heterosexual and receiving heterosexual privileges (q.v.). Other lesbians adopt an "in-your-face" behavior and appearance that underscores their lesbian identity (q.v.). Prior to the late twentieth century, lesbians might have opted to pass as men. *See also* Prejudice.

STIMPSON, CATHERINE R. (1936–). Feminist writer, educator, and editor. Stimpson served as a director of the MacArthur Foundation that hands out the so-called "genius" awards. She is Dean of the Graduate School of Arts and Sciences at New York University.

STONE BUTCH. A butch (q.v.) lesbian who derives sexual pleasure from pleasuring her partner, but does not want to be touched herself.

STONEWALL/STONEWALL RIOTS. The three days of riot that erupted after police raided the Stonewall Inn, a Greenwich Village, New York, gay bar (q.v.) on the night of June 27, 1969. This raid has come to mark the birth of the contemporary Lesbian and Gay Rights movement in the United States (q.v.) and abroad.

Stonewall has also become a euphemism for critical turning points in gay/lesbian history. For instance, Australia's (q.v.) Stonewall took place in July 1978 after police arrested lesbian and gay merrymakers at the first Mardi Gras held in Sydney. This touched off protests around Australia, rejuvenating the country's Lesbian and Gay Rights movement.

STONEWALL GROUP. Founded in May 1989 by Sir Ian McKellen, Pam St. Clement, and other prominent British activists. These lesbians and gay men became United Kingdoms' (q.v.) first gay and lesbian lobbying organization. Issues that it lobbied for included AIDS funding, age of consent laws, and equal rights (qq.v.). It joined with the International Lesbian and Gay Association (ILGA) (q.v.) to ensure that lesbian and gay rights were incorporated into the then European Community's documents.

STRAIGHT/STRAIGHT WOMEN. Socially normative; heterosexual; heterosexual women.

STRAIGHT GAY ACTIVISTS (SGA). This is a new category of gay and lesbian activists, people who are heterosexual but who are working for lesbain and gay issues. SGAs, members of Parents and Friends of Lesbians and Gays (P-Flag) (q.v.), volunteers, and board members and staff members of lesbian and gay rights organizations such as the Human Rights Campaign (HRC) (q.v.), have begun to work in the movement. They believe in equal rights and want to fight discrimination and injustices and consider lesbian and gay civil rights to be the cutting edge of the social justice movement. *See also* Activism.

STREICHER, RIKKI (1926–1994). Activist and business woman. She owned Maud's in San Francisco with Gloria Grant, the oldest lesbian bar in continuous operation from 1966 until it closed in 1989. The bar was one of the mainstays of lesbian culture (q.v.) at a time when lesbians were still closeted (q.v.). Maud's was the center of lesbian life, supporting softball teams and fund raisers for lesbian activists (q.v.), besides socializing and dancing. *Last Call at Maud's,* a film by Paris Poirier, documents the bar, the lesbian patrons of this internationally renowned meeting place, and Streicher herself. She also owned the bars Vieux Carré and Amelia's, both located in the Russian River (q.v.), north of San Francisco.

As an activist, Streicher took on leadership roles in the Society for Individual Rights (SIR) and the Federation of Gay Games. She was an organizer of the Gay Games (q.v.) and received the Community Service Award from the Gay and Lesbian Historical Society. Mary Sanger, her lover of eighteen years, survived her. *See also* Bar Culture.

STUD. An alternative term for butch (q.v.) among the African American lesbian community of the 1940s and 1950s.

STUDENT HOMOPHILE LEAGUE (SHL). The first organization of lesbians and gays on American university campuses. It was founded at Columbia University and soon after at New York University, New York City, in 1966. Subsequently, other chapters were organized on campuses on the east coast, and after Stonewall (q.v.), throughout the country. In the 1970s and 1980s, many of the early SHL groups evolved into other gay and lesbian student organizations such as the Bisexual Gay and Lesbian Association (BiGALA) (q.v.).

STYLE WARS. The lesbian-feminist (q.v.) debate in the 1980s about lesbian's and women's clothing and presentation. Some felt that androgenous (q.v.) clothing—jeans, flat shoes, shirt—was the proper attire since it did not play into socially correct feminine attire; others felt that women should be free to choose their clothing. *See also* Lesbian Thought Police.

SUBCULTURE. A minority group's community and culture as opposed to the dominant (heterosexual) culture. Lesbians have developed their own communities and subculture with language, customs, symbols, (q.v.) and mores unique to each lesbian community (q.v.).

SUFFRAGE MOVEMENT. One of the main goals of the first wave of feminists (q.v.) was for women to have the right to vote—to be fully franchised citizens of the state. Women obtained the vote in 1921 in the United States (q.v.), but as late as 1970 in Switzerland. Suffrage movements still exist, for instance, women in Kuwait still do not have the vote and their legislature failed to pass a law granting women voting rights in the fall of 2000. *See also* Anthony, Susan B.

SWEDEN. In 1864, "fornication against nature" was criminalized, and although the law included both men and women, only men were targeted in its enforcement. Lesbians were regarded as less of a danger to society. This law remained in force until 1944 when consensual same-sex relationships were made legal.

Lesbians have long recognized Queen Christina (1626–1689) (q.v.) as a lesbian. In 1925, at the "female citizens' school" organized by the women's rights movement in Sweden, lesbians took part as students and teachers. The first homosexual organization, a chapter of the Danish Federation, was formed in 1950, but few women participated. The first lesbian group was Diana, organized in the mid-1950s to give lesbians a social space. Swedish lesbians participated in the first Nordic lesbian conference in 1974 which was followed by subsequent ones. Lesbian-feminists left the Swedish Federation for Gay and Lesbian Rights (RFSL) and formed separate lesbian political organizations such as the Lesbian Front (LF) in 1976 and Lesbian Nation (LN) in 1988. LF was a socialist women's organization and LN a lesbian separatist (q.v.) one. Lesbians also continue to be involved in women-only education groups.

Sweden recognized cohabitation between couples of the same sex "as a fully acceptable form of relationship" in 1973. Laws governing the age of consent (q.v.) were changed in 1978 to 15 years of age for both homosexual and heterosexual sex. In 1987 laws were passed, prohibiting discrimination based on sexual orientation and against derogatory speech made about homosexuality. The year 1988 saw same-sex cohabiting couples granted the same status and rights as heterosexual unmarried, but cohabiting couples. In 1995, same-sex couples were granted registered domestic partnership (q.v.) status with a secular ceremony. This partnership has the same rights as heterosexual marriage except that the couple may not adopt children or be artificially inseminated (q.v.).

SYMBOLS. Symbols have the power to identify and bring together communities; the lesbian community (q.v.) is no exception. In the beginning of the twenty-first century, the predominant lesbian symbols are the labrys; the colors violet, lavender, or purple; vulva hands; the pink triangle; the rainbow flag (qq.v.); and two interlocking female symbols.

SZIVARVANY. *See* **HOMEROS LAMBDA.**

– T –

TAKE BACK THE NIGHT. An annual nighttime candlelit rally held in many cities around the globe. The first Women Take Back the Night event happened when women attending the 1976 International Tribunal on Crimes Against Women in Belgium walked with lighted candles to protest violence in the lives of women around the world. This women's rally symbolizes the inability of women to move as freely and without the threat of violence as males. It usually involves survivors speaking out against violence by men. Take Back the Night marches are a means to increase community awareness and educate women and others about the extent of violence against women, to raise the collective voice to act politically, and empower individuals to take direct action (q.v.) against violence. A related action is the Clothesline Project. This is a clothesline hung with tee-shirts drawn by survivors of domestic violence (q.v.) to air society's "dirty laundry," to give voice to a crime that is usually hidden, while educating others.

TAYLOR, VALERIE (née Velma Nacella Young) (1913–1997). Activist and author. In 1965, she was a founding member of Mattachine Midwest in Chicago, Illinois. A poet and short-story writer, she also wrote lesbian-theme novels. Her writing was published in *The Ladder* (q.v.) in the early 1960s. Taylor founded the Lesbian Writers Conference in 1974. She was involved in many issues: lesbian and gay rights, antiwar, and the rights of the poor, disabled, and elderly.

THIRD SEX. Karl Heinrich Ulrichs used the term to represent homosexuals in his work from 1862–1879. His theory was that men who loved men and women who loved women were thought to be the third sex—neither men nor women. Heterosexual men were the first sex; heterosexual women were the second sex.

THIRD WAVE OF FEMINISM. The feminist movement of the 1990s and beyond, which includes issues of race, class, age, and sexual orientation in its definition of oppression (q.v.). It wages its fight to transform society by being inclusive and adroitly using the media (q.v.) and modern technology to connect and communicate. Third wave feminist actions include a bus ride across the United States (q.v.) to register voters for the 1996 elections as well as direct actions (q.v.) targeting specific issues such as reproductive and sexual freedoms, women's health, the environment, poverty, and social justice, and also the grassroots National Young Women's Day of Action. *See also* First Wave of Feminism; Second Wave of Feminism.

THOMAS, MARTHA CAREY (1857–1935). Feminist, social activist, and educator. She was the first woman president of Bryn Mawr College, Bryn Mawr, Pennsylvania, in 1894, and lived (sequentially) in the president's house with the two women she called her "wives" —Mary Gwinn and Mary Elizabeth Garrett.

THOMPSON, KAREN. *See* **KOWALSKI, SHARON and KAREN THOMPSON.**

TIAS, LAS. "The aunts" in Spanish, used to describe two women who lived together.

TOBIN, KAY (1930–). Activist, photographer, and writer. Tobin was an early activist with the Daughters of Bilitis (DOB) (q.v.). It was at a 1961 DOB picnic that she met her life partner Barbara Gittings (q.v.). Her photography documented the early lesbian and gay rights pickets in Washington, D.C., other historic lesbian and gay events, and lesbian life and activism. Tobin was one of the founders of the Gay Activist Alliance (GAA) (q.v.) and the still active Gay Women's Alternative (1973) in New York City. She also helped to found the Gay People in Christian Science. Her book *The Gay Crusaders* (1972) written with Randy Wicker, documented the new gay militancy. She is still active with the Homophile Action League. She runs a gay realtors organization.

TOMBOY. Young girls who act and/or dress as young boys. Tomboys might or might not grow up to be lesbians.

TOP. The active sexual participant. *See also* Bottom.

TORTILLA. Spanish slang for "lesbian" or "dyke."

TRANSGENDER. A person whose gender (q.v.) presentation or expression blurs normative gender categories. The transgendered person transgresses the traditional representation of the sex he/she was born with, for example, cross-dressers, drag kings, or transvestites (qq.v.). They are sometimes self-referred to as trannie boys, boychicks (q.v.), or boyz if they identify as male. *See also* Queer.

TRANSSEXUAL (TS). Persons who are preparing to or have had sexual reassignment (q.v.) surgery. They may be male to female (MTF) or female to male (FTM) (qq.v.), heterosexual, homosexual, or bisexual (q.v.). In lesbian separatist (q.v.) space, MTF are excluded because they have had male privilege (q.v.) and there may still be vestiges of such privilege in their actions. Sometimes they are self-referred to as trannie boys.

TRANSVESTITE (TV). A person, usually male, who dresses and acts as a member of the opposite sex. A TV may or may not be homosexual.

TRATNIK, SUZANA (1963–). Slovenian lesbian activist and editor. Tratnik founded the first lesbian organization, Lesbian Licit (LL), in Slovenia in 1988. LL evolved from the feminist group Licit. She coedits the gay and lesbian magazine *Revolver,* as well as editing the lesbian bulletin *Pandora.* Tratnik has compiled *L,* an anthology of the Slovenian lesbian movement. She is actively working to increase lesbian visibility with her work in the media (q.v.). She organizes an international lesbian camp and a lesbian film week. *See also* Eastern Europe.

TRIBADISM. The mutual rhythmic rubbing of genitals against the thigh or genitals of one's partner to achieve orgasm. Young girls and young lesbians practice this form of sex play.

TRUJILLO, CARLA (19??–). Academic, Latina activist, artist, and writer. Trujillo has written extensively on Chicana lesbians. A Chicana lesbian-feminist (q.v.), she has been developing Chicana lesbian theory. She proposes that "Chicana lesbians pose a threat to [the] Chicano community" (1990) not because they are adopting a white position, but that they are challenging the community to be for women in the community, sex positive (q.v.), and egalitarian.

TSUI, KITTY (KIT FAN TSUI) (1952–). Hong Kong-born activist and writer. Tsui came out (q.v.) in the early 1970s. As an activist, she advocated for Asian lesbian visibility. To this end, she coauthored *Coming Out: We Are Here in the Asian Community: A Dialogue with Three Asian Women* (1979) with Barbara Noda and Z. Wong. She was also a founding member of the collectives (q.v.) Unbound Feet and Unbound Feet Three and edited their poetry anthologies. Her own poetry is a construction of her identity as a Chinese American lesbian. She has competed in the Gay Games (q.v.) as a body builder.

TWO-SPIRITED. This is a term used by contemporary Native Americans for lesbian and gay people; it refers to having both feminine and masculine spirits inside. The two-spirited tradition has influenced the

Homophile movement (q.v.) as well as the gay and lesbian movements. The ideas of humanity's relationship to the environment, as well as its antipatriarchal goddess worship, is credited with the rebirth of spiritualization in the Gay and Lesbian Rights (q.v.) movement.

TYRANNY OF STRUCTURELESSNESS. Jo Freeman's analysis of nonhierarchical egalitarian organizations that are limited in their effectiveness because every member performed all tasks and decision making was based on consensus. This was the reason given for the failure of most such groups. *See also* Collective; The Furies.

– U –

UNION OF LESBIANS AND HOMOSEXUALS. Originally named the Sexual Minorities Association when it was founded in Moscow in 1989, this was the first public lesbian and gay rights organization in the then Soviet Union (q.v.). The purpose of this organization was both social and political—to change the legal code which criminalized (male) homosexuality, to educate about AIDS (q.v.), and to dispel myths about homosexuality. It was replaced by the Moscow Union of Lesbians and Homosexuals cofounded by Yevgenia Debryanski. This group was short-lived, only to be replaced by Liberation cofounded by the same people in 1991.

UNITED KINGDOM. The United Kingdom has been home to many lesbian literary, theater, and arts groups. Politically, lesbians began organizing in 1963 with the lesbian social group Kenric (q.v.) and with the publication of *Arena 3* (1963–1971) and *Sappho* (1972–1981). Lesbians were active both in the women's movement and the Gay Liberation Front (GLF) (q.v.). Women in the GLF embraced feminism and its politics and tried to encourage feminism throughout the GLF. The GLF took part, for instance, in International Women's Day in 1971 and 1973. Still perceived to be male-dominated, women focused their attention on feminist organizations and withdrew from the GLF.

In 1983 and 1984, lesbians held two successful conferences—Lesbian Sex and Sexual Practice, and Lesbian Studies—in London. These conferences led to the formation of the Lesbian Archive (now located in Glasgow, Scotland) and the Lesbian History Group (which ended in 1994). In 1988, the antigay Clause 28 (q.v.), which prohibited the promotion of homosexuality, was passed. Radical lesbian groups emerged to protest Clause 28, which is still in force. Groups such as the Lesbian Avengers (q.v.), Older Lesbian Network, and RADS are still active as is the queer OutRage! (q.v.).

While the Lesbian and Gay Centre has closed, and lesbians and gays are being incorporated into the social fabric of the United Kingdom, this does not mean that all issues have been satisfactorily resolved. Issues such as gay parenting rights, especially in Northern Ireland, and homophobia (q.v.) are still at the forefront. Most recently in 2001, when homophobic remarks appeared on the government's on-line citizen space, quick action was taken to institute antihomophobic guidelines.

UNITED LESBIANS OF AFRICAN HERITAGE (ULOAH). This organization was formed in August 1990 in Los Angeles, California. Its purpose is to provide education and services especially for economic security, history, pride, and inclusivity; it also serves as a networking source for black lesbians. ULOAH sponsors the three-day retreat SISTAHFest 3, held annually.

UNITED NATIONS (UN). The international organization formed in 1945 to deal with global political issues and human rights (q.v.). The UN has, through its Commission on the Status of Women, promoted women's rights on all fronts political, social, economical, medical, social, and civil. The UN adopted the Convention of Political Rights of Women in 1953 and the Convention on the Elimination of All Forms of Discrimination Against Women in 1979. The UN has also sponsored global conferences on the status of women held in Mexico City, Nairobi, and Beijing (qq.v.). It is at these conferences that sexual autonomy (q.v.), including lesbian rights, have been broached in a global setting.

UNITED STATES. The United States Gay and Lesbian Rights movement started in the 1950s with the Homophile (q.v.) movement and the founding of the Mattachine Society (MS) and the Daughters of Bilitis (DOB) (qq.v.) These were groups that worked as social organizations for lesbians and gays, and strove to educate the public to accept lesbians and gays as members of society. The Stonewall Riots (q.v.) that took place in Greenwich Village, New York City, in June 1969 birthed the contemporary and more politically radical Gay and Lesbian Rights movement.

Lesbians who were at that time active in the Women's Liberation movement (q.v.) were experiencing what they labeled as heterosexism (q.v.). Across the country in women's groups, lesbians were either in the closet (q.v.), silenced when they brought up issues concerning sexual orientation, or in some cases even shunned when their lesbianism was made public. This almost universal experience for lesbians led to the formation of lesbian-only groups such as the Chicago Lesbian Liberation and Los Angeles's Lesbian-Feminists. Lesbians who became active members of the gay rights movements experienced sexism (q.v.), as their agendas were predominantly male and the gay males did not want to give up their male privilege (q.v.).

These women joined together and formed lesbian-feminist (q.v.) organizations, which produced some of the most cogent analyses of the sociopolitical and economic patriarchal (q.v.) state. Many of these groups dissolved under the stridency of their members, but the theory and cultural practices still exist, as do some groups of lesbian separatists (q.v.) and lesbian-feminists. Other lesbians formed ethnic-based groups to deal with their own specific race-complicated oppressions (q.v.) such as Lesbianas Latinamericanas. And yet others challenged the inherent racism of the "normative" groups and added their analysis and theory of the patriarchal state: the Combahee River Collective (q.v.), for instance. Some women rejoined the women's movement and the gay rights movement in order to procure their rights.

The visibility of lesbians and gays and their political movements to achieve equality led to a conservative and religious backlash (q.v.) and resulting political battles. The major national gay and lesbian rights organizations—the National Gay and Lesbian Task Force (NGLTF) and the Human Rights Campaign (HRC) (qq.v.)— have focused on the passage of laws prohibiting discrimination based on sexual orientation. However, more recently the focus of these mainstream rights organizations have shifted to what some call an assimilationist (q.v.) agenda. For instance, there has been a lot of focus on what some call the "bourgeois issue of same-sex marriage" (q.v.) without a feminist analysis of marriage as an institution. This agenda item overlooks the more radical needs and issues of the grassroots communities and groups.

The advent of AIDS/HIV (q.v.) found many lesbians caring for their ill gay friends and joining in activist groups that focused on AIDS and health-related political issues. During this period, queer theory (q.v.) and activism were also coming to the fore. When some lesbians realized that lesbian health and other issues were being ignored, they formed the Lesbian Avengers (q.v.) and other feminist and lesbian activist groups such as Women's Action Coalition (WAC). *See also* Lesbian Culture; Religious Right.

– V –

VAID, URVASHI (1959–). Lawyer, activist, and writer. She is a former executive director of both the National Gay and Lesbian Task Force (NGLTF) (q.v.) and its Policy Institute.

VANILLA SEX. Sex that is consider conventional, boring, without sadomasochistic (S/M) (q.v.) sexual play.

VICE VERSA. The first lesbian magazine founded and edited by Lisa Ben (q.v.) from 1947 to 1948. The subtitle on this hand-typed, twelve-copy per issue journal was "America's Gayest Magazine." The issues then were circulated among friends. All the articles—news, editorial, cultural reviews, and creative stories—were written by Edith Eyde (a.k.a Lisa Ben). Many articles were later reprinted in *The Ladder* (q.v.).

VICINUS, MARTHA (1939–). Writer and scholar. Vicinus has pioneered Lesbian Studies (q.v.). She coedited *Hidden from History: Reclaiming the Gay and Lesbian Past* (1989). She also edited *Lesbian Subjects: Feminist Studies Reader* (1996). She is a distinguished professor of English and Women's Studies at the University of Michigan, Ann Arbor.

VILLAROSA, LINDA (1959–). Journalist and editor of *Essence* magazine.

VINCENZ, LILLI (1937–). Activist. Vincenz was a member of the Mattachine Society (q.v.) of Washington, D.C. She was the only self-identifying and out (q.v.) lesbian (out of three women) to picket the White House on April 17, 1965. Although she had been in Germany, she served in the U.S. Army until she was accused of being a lesbian and discharged. She was the editor of *The Homosexual Citizen*, a radical, militant, civil rights publication. She is a practicing pyschotherapist. With her partner, Nancy Ruth Davis, she founded the Community for Creative Self-Development in Washington, D.C.

VIOLET or LAVENDER. The flowers and colors associated with Sappho (q.v.) who allegedly wore garlands of violets; these are now also associated with lesbians. Violets were worn in England during the sixteenth century by men and women to indicate they were not to marry. Bourdet's play, *The Captive* (1926), one of the first plays on Broadway with a lesbian theme, also used violets to symbolize lesbian love.

VIVIEN, RENÉE (PAULINE TARN) (1877–1909). Poet and writer. She was part of the Paris exiles (q.v.) where her first lover, Natalie Barney (q.v.), was the inspiration for many of her poems. Vivien translated Sappho's (q.v.) poetry from Greek into French.

VULVA HANDS. A gesture—placing the two forefingers and thumbs together to form a triangle and held over the head—used in lesbian gatherings and rituals beginning in the 1980s. This lesbian symbol (q.v.) is prevalent in lesbian jewelry.

– W –

WALD, LILLIAN (1867–1940). Peace activist, social worker, and nurse. Wald founded the Henry Street Settlement House, New York City, in 1893.

WARING, MARILYN (1952–). New Zealand politician and scholar. Waring became the first woman and youngest member of the New Zealand (q.v.) Parliament in 1975. A political economist, she authored

If Women Counted: A New Feminist Economics in 1988. Waring, an out (q.v.) lesbian, is politically active working for lesbian and gay rights. She currently is an associate professor at Massey University, Auckland.

WILLS, SUE (1944–). Australian writer and activist. Wills was an early leader of the lesbian and gay movement in Australia (q.v.) as part of Campaign Against Moral Persecution (CAMP) (q.v.). Her work focused on the abuse of homosexuals by the psychiatric profession. She also helped to develop an understanding between women's liberation and lesbian rights through her involvement in CAMP's Women's Association. Her writings document the history and issues of the Lesbian and Gay Rights movement in Australia. Wills has also worked on the government's Royal Commission into Human Relationships, developing an understanding of the publics views concerning homosexuals.

WILLSON, MARYANN (WILSON) (c1800–1850). Artist. Around the 1820s, Wilson moved from Connecticut to upstate New York's Greene County with Miss Brundage, her wife. Willson was a primitive watercolor painter who lived with Miss Brundage, a farmer. They were the characters on which the first lesbian novel with a happy ending was based—*Patience and Sarah* (q.v.), written by Alma Routsong (q.v.).

WITTIG, MONIQUE (1935–2003). French philosopher, writer, and educator. She was active in the French feminist and gay movements in Paris in 1968. In 1970 she coauthored a manifesto for the French feminist movement. She was a founding member of the radical lesbian group Goiunes Rouge (Red Dykes) and the radical feminist (q.v.) group Féministes Révolutionaires. One of the first political actions she took part in was placing a wreath inscribed to the "unknown wife of a soldier" at the tomb of the unknown soldier in Paris circa 1968. In 1970, Wittig became the spokeswoman for the Féministe Révolutionaires. She ended her commitment to specific groups in 1973.

A materialist feminist who believes in social constructionism (q.v.), Wittig is best known for her critique that " a lesbian is not a woman" since "woman" is a social construction related to "man" and lesbian is not defined by any relationship to man. Her work also rejects the dichotomy masculine/feminine. Her best-known works include the novel *Les Guérillères* (1969) and *The Straight Mind* (1992). Wittig also coauthored a lesbian (re)vision of the history of the world titled *Brouillon pour un dictionnaire des amantes* (1975). She emigrated to the United States (q.v.) in 1976. Wittig taught Women's Studies and French Literature at the University of Arizona. She remained involved in French lesbian politics until her death. *See also* France.

WOLFE, MAXINE (19??–). Lesbian-feminist activist who cofounded the Lesbian Avengers (q.v.).

WOLFENDEN REPORT, AKA REPORT OF THE COMMITTEE ON HOMOSEXUAL OFFENSES AND PROSITIUTION. A 1951 purge of the British foreign service and military of homosexuals and subsequent labeling of homosexuals as security risks, patterned after a similar policy in the United States (q.v.). The United Kingdom (q.v.) then had a number of highly publicized cases involving public (political and cultural) figures being persecuted for their homosexual identity. The tactics of the police also came into question. Named after its chair, Sir John Wolfenden, this committee was established in 1954 by the British Home Secretary in response to public pressure to reevaluate British law pertaining to sexual offenses, especially homosexual ones.

After hearing much testimony, the report was issued in 1957. Part one dealt with prostitution, and the second part dealt with homosexuality. In short, it stated that the law criminalizing homosexuality should not be used to regulate sexual morals between consenting adults acting in private. The law could be used to strengthen prohibitions against public displays of homosexuality and sex with minors. It recommended raising the age of consent (q.v.) from sixteen to twenty-one, with a twelve-month statute of limitations on consensual homosexual infractions and a reduction of the crime of buggery to misdemeanor. This report set in motion the liberalization of British laws pertaining to homosexuals.

WOLFF, CHARLOTTE (1897–1986). German-born Jewish writer and medical doctor. In 1933, shortly after being arrested in Berlin for wearing men's clothing and for espionage, Wolff emigrated to Paris. She specialized in the study of hands (cheirology), and her hand-reading led her to a theory of diagnosis. In 1936 she moved to London. Her book, *The Hand in Psychological Diagnosis*, was published in 1952. Her research expanded to include lesbianism and bisexuality. Her books, *Love between Women* (1972) and *Bisexuality: A Study* (1977), influenced Germany's (q.v.) lesbian movement. In 1974 she accepted an invitation from Lesbos 74 (also known as L.74) to address Berlin's lesbian community. Her autobiographical books, *On the Way to Myself* (1969) and *Hindsight* (1980), also developed her theory that lesbianism was the ideal twinship.

WOMAN-BORN WOMAN/WOMYN-BORN WOMYN. The term used to identify women who were born woman as opposed to male to female transgendered persons who may have had, and retain, male privilege (q.v.). Identifying or declaring oneself a woman-born woman helps to keep "women only" or lesbian-separatist (q.v.) space pure. This version of the women's/lesbian's community's "Don't Ask, Don't Tell" policy has been challenged at the Michigan Womyn's Music Festival (q.v.) by transgendered, transsexual persons, and lesbian and queer activists identifying as boyz, andros, trannie boys, lesbian, bi, FTM, girls, boychick, femme, stone-butch, or simply queer (qq.v.).

WOMAN-IDENTIFIED WOMAN. Coined by the Radicalesbians (q.v.) in 1970 in their treatise by the same name. The term was used as a euphemism for lesbian, though the writers of the treatise claim it could be used for any feminist who identified first with women. The paper was written in part because of the lesbian-baiting (q.v.) tactic used to split the women's movement. Women who were male-identified or who sought male approval were made aware of their male identification. The treatise called for all women to be women-identified rather than male-identified. The treatise was a sophisticated analysis of patriarchy, oppression (qq.v), sexual orientation, heterosexism, and feminism (qq.v.).

WOMEN OF COLOR. This term refers to any non-Caucasian female—African American, Asian, black, Hispanic, Latina or Native American. *See also* Black Lesbians; Lesbians of Color.

WOMEN'S LIBERATION MOVEMENT. The name given to the second wave of feminism (q.v.) since its goal was to liberate women from the political, social, cultural, and economic oppression of sexist patriarchal (qq.v.) society. The Women's Liberation movement was made up of grassroots local groups of women. Many of the women who joined this movement had experience organizing political actions in the Civil Rights movement or the New Left (q.v.) but left these movements when they realized that the movements privileged males and oppressed the women activists. One male movement leader actually said that the women in the movement were there for making coffee and bedding.

The women's groups utilized political analysis based on consciousness-raising (CR) (q.v.). Realizing that the "personal is political," the women organized political direct actions (q.v.) as well as educational self-help projects around issues such as rape and battering (qq.v.). The more radical groups tried to be nonhierarchical. Other groups were more mainstream, such as the National Organization of Women (NOW) (q.v.).

Lesbians were active in many women's groups from the outset, as they had been in the first wave of feminism (q.v.). For many lesbians, their sexuality was kept closeted (q.v.) since early feminist analysis centered on sexism not heterosexism (qq.v.). The specter of lesbianism or the questioning of heterosexism was seen as a tactic that would keep all women marginalized. It was not until after the Lavender Menace (q.v.) took over the Second Congress to Unite Women (q.v.) that sexual orientation began to be included in feminist analyses.

For some, heterosexual women who still engaged in sexual relations with men were seen as "sleeping with the enemy" and not true feminists. This attitude led to the development of political lesbians (q.v.), women who choose the adoption of a lesbian sexual orientation to be truly consistent in their political feminism. This led to the gay/straight split (q.v.) and to the feminist and lesbian movements.

The right for women to control not only their reproductive health and their bodies, but also their sexual orientation has been a major focus of the second wave (q.v.) of the Women's Liberation movement, as it continues to be a focus of the contemporary third wave, human rights, and lesbian rights (qq.v.) movements.

WOMEN'S MUSIC. One major element in the American folk tradition is music performed for women, by women, produced by women, and usually with a feminist and/or lesbian voice. Excluded from mainstream music, women began their own labels. Olivia Records was the first. Margie Adams, Cris Williamson, Alix Dobkin (q.v.), Meg Christian, and Holly Near (q.v.) are women's music legends. There are music festivals that celebrate women's music, for instance, the Michigan Womyn's Music Festival (q.v.), the Women's Music festival in Bloomington, Indiana, and the New England Women's Music (NEWMAR).

In rock music there have been a few out (q.v.) lesbian performers who have national followings such as k.d. lang and Melissa Etheridge (q.v.). The punk rock music scene has given birth to what is called Queercore that features lesbian, gay, bisexual, and transgendered musicians. Tribe 8, 7 Year Bitch, and L7 are some of the dyke (q.v.) bands. Tribe 8's music is not only dyke music but also feminist. The lesbian-feminist (q.v.) record label Mr. Lady is one of the promoters of new women's and lesbian music.

On a more traditional musical note, while there have always been trouser roles (male roles sung by female performers), there is only one lesbian opera to date, *Patience and Sarah* (q.v.), which is based on Alma Routsong's (q.v) book of the same title.

There are also gay and lesbian choruses and bands (q.v.) that perform for the community and at pride marches (q.v.).

WOMMIN/WOMYN/WIMMIN. Alternative spellings of woman /women to avoid the patriarchal root "man."

WOOLEY, MARY (1863–1947). Educator and writer. A president of Mount Holyoke College, Holyoke, Massachusetts, she was the only female participant in the Geneva Arms Conference of 1932.

WOOLF, VIRGINIA (1882–1941). Probably the most famous of the writers who made up the Bloomsbury Group. Woolf wrote many novels and essays including *A Room of One's Own* (1928), which is considered to be a primary feminist text. Her fiction includes *Orlando: A Biography* (1928), which explores issues of gender (q.v.) identification and nonconformity.

WORKING-CLASS LESBIAN CULTURE. During the mid-twentieth century, working-class lesbians did not have the mobility or the resources that their middle- and upper-class sisters had. Working-class lesbian life centered around bars. *See also* Bar Culture; Buffalo Lesbian Oral History Project.

– X –

XING, JIN (19??–) Chinese choreographer. A former Army colonel and founder of China's first independent modern dance troupe, Jin Xing is the first out transsexual (qq.v) in China.

– Y –

YOURCENAR, MARGUERITE (1903–1987). Belgian-born French writer. She became the first woman inducted into the prestigious Académie Française (in 1980). Her writings often include male homosexuals. When the press speculated about her sexuality she said, "Because I lived with a woman for forty years, people assume I'm a lesbian." While she did live with Grace Frick from 1939 until Frick's death in 1979, she believed that her private life belonged in "the shadows" (1984).

Yourcenar did expound on her same-sex attractions and sexuality in the third volume of her autobiography *Quoi? L'Éternité* (1988). While disdaining modern sexual categories, she advocated sexual liberation. She understood the political connection between homosexuality and acts of intolerance, having what she called "minority tastes" herself.

– Z –

ZAP. A political direct action (q.v.) meant to catch the media's (q.v.) attention and attract the public.

ZAREMBA, EVE (1930–). Canadian writer and activist. Zaremba authored *Privilege of Sex: A Century of Canadian Women* in 1972. She is also credited with creating the first lesbian detective, Helen Karemos, who appeared in a series of books. The first of these, *A Reason to Kill,* was written in 1978.

As a feminist activist, Zaremba worked in the Toronto women's movement. She helped to cofound the first women's center in Canada (q.v.) in 1972, Women's Place, the Women's Credit Union in 1974, and the feminist newspaper *Broadside* in 1978. As a lesbian activist, Zaremba wanted a separate and autonomous lesbian movement and to that end, in 1976, she helped to found the Lesbian Organization of Toronto (LOOT). *See also* Detective Fiction.

ZIMBABWE. The Gays and Lesbians of Zimbabwe (GALZ) (q.v.) was founded in 1989 as a social venue for isolated gays and lesbians. When an ad describing their counseling service was rejected by the national daily newspaper, GALZ galvanized into a political organization. It has withstood attacks from the virulent antigay Zimbabwe government. President Robert Mugabe has stated that "homosexuals have no rights" and were "worse than pigs and dogs." GALZ is globally recognized for its gay and lesbian rights and human rights (q.v.) work. *See also* Africa.

'ZINE. A low-budget magazine on a specific issue or topic. Celebrity 'zines are called fanzines. Many 'zines are quite political.

ZONING. The use of zoning regulations as well as public health laws is a means of controlling sexual expression and activity, especially in times of sex panics (q.v.). In New York City under Mayor Rudolph Guiliani, zoning amendments to preserve the quality of life have impacted the sex workers (q.v.), booksellers, and both the heterosexual and gay and lesbian sex industry.

ZUNA INSTITUTE. This is the first national black lesbian (q.v.) organization whose purpose is to improve the quality of life for black lesbians, advocate for their rights and issues—health, education, economic development, equality, and other public policies—and most importantly to make black lesbians visible. Zuna is an offshoot of the National Black Lesbian and Gay Leadership Forums, and was introduced at the thirteenth forum in 2001. *See also* Black Lesbians.

Bibliography

Contents

Introduction

The following bibliography is meant to be an overview of the writings and resources currently available on lesbian politics and issues at the beginning of this millennium. Because there is overlap, some resources on gay males as well as feminism are included. This bibliography is not inclusive, since research and writing about lesbian politics, issues, and culture is still in its infancy, especially when compared to writings about homosexual males. Writing about lesbian politics and culture is a growing academic and popular field; histories, narratives, and new theoretical writings are being published at an increasing pace. This bibliography highlights those works considered to be among the key writings that help form the political and cultural basis for the Lesbian Liberation movement (LLM), and an attempt has been made to identify the most current books on each topic from which a reader can plumb other readings.

The overarching purpose of this bibliography is to assist those interested in pursuing further research by providing a starting point. Included are only a few journal article and specific anthology selection citations, but the bibliographies in most of the books will act as a reference for further readings. In order to help researchers begin, the readings which will lay a foundation for one's own research have been identified. The following pages also set forth those foundational readings based on the categories in this bibliography. It should be noted that some of the books are mentioned more than once; this is because the categories are inevitably artificial and overlap.

To understand the complexity of the politics and history of the Lesbian Liberation movement, a good starting place for research would be to utilize an annotated bibliography in conjunction with a more encyclopedic work and a general historic reference to provide an overview. Dolores Maggiore's *Lesbianism: An Annotated Bibliography and Guide to the Literature* gives an overview of the sociocultural issues. Robert Ridinger's *The Gay and Lesbian Movement: References and Resources* and Linda Garber's *Lesbian Sources: A Bibliography of Periodical Articles, 1970-1990* include the basic bibliography for readings about political and historic issues. *Encyclopedia of Lesbian Histories and Cultures* edited by Bonnie Zimmerman used in conjunction with Steve Hogan and Lee Hudson's *Completely Queer: The Gay and Lesbian Encyclopedia* provide an objective overview and guide to the political issues and history of the Lesbian Liberation movement and the intersection of the LLM with the theories and practices of the Women's Liberation, Gay Liberation, and Queer movements. *For Lesbians Only: A Separatist Anthology* edited by Sarah Lucia Hoagland and Julia Penelope and *We Are Everywhere: A Historical Sourcebook of Gay and Lesbian Politics* edited by Mark Blasius and Shane Phelan are excellent collections of primary source documents that help elucidate both the context, theories, and issues surrounding the politics of the Lesbian Liberation movement.

Lillian Faderman's *Surpassing the Love of Men: Romantic Friendship and Love between Women, from the Renaissance to the Present, Odd Girls and Twilight Lovers: A History of Lesbian Life in Twentieth-Century America*, and *To Believe in Women: What Lesbians Have Done for America: A History* along with Audre Lorde's *Zami, a New Spelling of My Name* all have narratives that provide an understanding of the intersection of lesbianism, culture, and politics.

For an overview of lesbians' impact on popular culture, Kathleen Martindale's *Un/Popular Culture: Lesbian Writing after the Sex Wars* and *Lesbian Texts and Contexts: Radical Revisions* edited by Karla Jay and Joanne Glasgow are quite sufficient. Of course, one should read Kate Millett's *Sexual Politics* to fully understand the politics of the misogynistic canon.

For social, political, and philosophical writings, particularly useful would be an anthology such as Henry Abelove et al.'s *The Lesbian and Gay Reader,* along with Monika Reinfelder's *Amazon to Zami: Toward a Global Lesbian Feminism* and Urvashi Vaid's *Virtual Equality* to provide an overview of lesbian politics, theories, and issues, historical and current, local and global. One would be remiss not to read the classic theoretical essays "Women-Identified Women" by the Radicalesbians and Adrienne Rich's "Compulsory Heterosexuality and Lesbian Existence." Some other readings that broaden one's understandings of lesbian liberation include Judy Grahn's *Another Mother Tongue: Gay Words, Gay Worlds,* Cherríe Moraga and Gloria Anzaldúa's *This Bridge Called My Back: Writings of Radical Women of Color,* and Julia Penelope and Sarah Lucia Hoagland's *For Lesbians Only.* Judith Butler's *Gender Trouble: Feminism and the Subversion of Identity,* which is considered a foundational work in queer theory, should be read in conjunction with Annamarie Jagose's *Introduction to Queer Theory* and tempered with Sheila Jeffreys's *The Lesbian Heresy.*

For an overview of lesbian history and politics, Mark Blasius and Shane Phelan's *We Are Everywhere* provides primary source documents from the 1700s onward. Margaret Cruikshank's *The Gay and Lesbian Liberation Movement* provides a view of the movement as a sociopolitical change agent, and unlike most books of its kind, gives women their due. Both Sidney Abbot and Barbara Love's *Sappho Was a Right-On Woman* and Del Martin and Phyllis Lyon's *Lesbian/Woman* are classics that should not be overlooked. For a more global perspective of lesbian politics, Frédéric Martel's *The Pink and the Black: Homosexuals in France since 1968* and Sharon Lim-Hing's *The Very Inside: An Anthology of Writings by Asian and Pacific Islander Lesbian and Bisexual Women* along with Aart Hendriks, Rob Tielman, and Evert van der Veen's *The Third Pink Book* are good starting points. Arlene Stein's *The*

Stranger Next Door clearly articulates the triangulation of the Religious Right, gay civil rights, and economics in small-town communities.

For premodern histories, one should start with Judith Brown's *Immodest Acts: The Life of a Lesbian Nun in Renaissance Italy*. Carroll Smith-Rosenberg's *Disorderly Conduct: Visions of Gender in Victorian America* is another classic. To gain an understanding of the lesbian community pre-Stonewall, the following two books are suggested: Elizabeth Lapoovsky Kennedy and Madeline Davis's *Boots of Leather, Slippers of Gold: The History of a Lesbian Community* and Andrea Weiss and Greta Schiller's *Before Stonewall: The Making of a Gay and Lesbian Community*.

While there are many books that chronicle the contemporary Lesbian and Gay Liberation movements, the following provide a good foundation for further research: Nancy Myron and Charlotte Bunch's *Lesbianism and the Women's Movement*, Lynne Hart and Elaine Miller's *All the Rage: Reasserting Radical Lesbian Feminism*, and Barry D. Adam, Jan Willem Duyvendak, and Andre Krouwel's *The Global Emergence of Gay and Lesbian Politics: National Imprints of a Worldwide Movement*. Sarah Schulman's *The Lesbian Avenger Handbook: A Handy Guide to Homemade Revolution* offers a methodology to achieve change.

For those interested in Lesbian Studies, Bonnie Zimmerman and Toni McNaron's *The New Lesbian Studies: Into the Twenty-First Century* and Esther Rothblum's *Classics in Lesbian Studies* both have overviews of this interdisciplinary academic subject.

There are many books that explore lesbian culture, from Liz Gibbs's *Daring to Dissent: Lesbian Culture from Margin to Mainstream* to Cathy Dunsford and Susan Hawthorne's *The Exploding Frangipangi*.

Joan Nestle's *The Persistent Desire: A Femme-Butch Reader* explores butch-femme relationships. Julia Penelope and Susan Wolfe's *The Original Coming Out Stories* documents the process of revealing to oneself and to others one's sexual identity. Susan Fox Rogers's *Sportsdyke* explores the lesbian's relationship to athletics.

Beth Mintz and Esther Rothblum's *Lesbians in Academia: Degrees of Freedom* is a good book to begin with to look at issues facing lesbians in academia. Amy Gluckman and Betsey Reed's *Homo Economics* and Rosalyn Baxandeall and Linda Gordon's *America's Working Women* provide a firm understanding of economic and employment issues facing lesbians today.

Jocelyn White and Marissa Martinez's *The Lesbian Health Book* and the Boston Women's Health Book Collective's *The New Our Bodies, Ourselves* lay out the health issues and care for lesbians.

Rachel Rosenbloom's *Unspoken Rules: Sexual Orientation and Women's Human Rights* sets forth the issues clearly. For research on law and politics, Shelan Phane's *Sexual Stranger: Gays, Lesbians and Dilemmas of Citizenship* and Angelina Wilson's *A Simple Matter of Justice* discuss the overarching issues, and Wallace Swan's *Gay/Lesbian/Bisexual Public Policy Issues* looks at specific policy issues.

Alan Bérubé's *Coming Out Under Fire* and Randy Shilts's *Conduct Unbecoming: Lesbians and Gays in the U.S. Military* cover the issues raised by lesbians serving in the military. Michelangelo Signorile's *Queer in America* sets forth the reasoning for outing gays and lesbians, especially those who are imposing homophobic policies on others.

For books on lesbians and religion, Rebecca Alpert's *Like Bread on the Seder Plate*, Stephen Murray and Will Roscoe's *Islamic Sexualities,* and Nancy Wilson's *Our Tribe* explore how lesbians transform (or not) three basic religions, Judaism, Islam, and Christianity. Didi Herman's *The Anti-Gay Agenda* covers the Religious Right's work against lesbians and gays in the United States and beyond. Anna Marie Smith's *New Right Discourse on Race and Sexuality* focuses on the United Kingdom.

The Sex Wars are succinctly set forth in Lisa Duggan and Nan Hunter's *Sex Wars*. The Sex Wars began at the conference documented in Carole Vance's *Pleasure and Danger.* Amber Hollibaugh's *My Dangerous Desires: A Queer Girl Dreaming Her Way Home* helps to put into context sex-positive lesbian-feminists. These books should be read with Sheila Jeffrie's *The Lesbian Heresy* and Catherine MacKinnon's *Only Words,* which set out the other side of the Sex War debate over pornography and sadomasochistic sex.

Violence and Social Injustice against Lesbians, Gays and Bisexuals edited by Lacey Sloan and Nora Gustavsson set forth the impact of hate crimes and homophobia. Kerry Lobel's *Naming the Violence* uncovers how internalized homophobia leads to lesbian battering.

With the lesbian baby boom and teenagers discovering their sexuality, many books have been written on lesbian parenting and gay youth. Merilee Clunis and G. Dorsey Green introduce family issues in *The Lesbian Parenting Book,* while the National Center for Lesbian Rights'

Lesbian Mother Litigation Manual outlines the legal matters. Rita Reed's *Growing Up Gay* provides a touchstone for lesbian adolescents. While Michel Foucault's *The History of Sexuality, volume 1* is the foundation for queer theory, Annamarie Jagose's *Introduction to Queer Theory* clearly explains the impact of lesbian-feminist thought on queer theory.

Of the numerous periodicals and journals published over the years, the ones that reflect or reflected (some journals have ceased publication) the current state of lesbian thought and politics include *GLQ: A Journal of Lesbian and Gay Studies, The Journal of Lesbian Studies, The Lesbian Review of Books, Off Our Backs, Seattle Gay News,* and *Sojourner.*

Lesbian history is being saved in archives and libraries from the Lesbian Herstory Archive in New York to academic archives, which incorporate lesbian history with their women's history such as Duke University or the Sophia Smith Collection at Smith College, many of which may be accessed at least partially on-line. Scholars are urged to check their local lesbian historical collections usually found at the local lesbian and gay center, and to talk with gay and lesbian elders for their oral histories.

The Internet also provides some good resources on the World Wide Web (WWW), but due to the transitory nature of web servers and providers, these sites are constantly changing, migrating, or no longer supported. Using a search engine such as google.com (www.google.com) with the terms "lesbian politics" or "lesbian history" will provide the researcher with the most current Websites available. Many of the lesbian and gay organizations also maintain Websites; these sites provide good links to other issue-specific sites. The sites listed here are portals to other sites.

1. Bibliographies

Allen, Jane, et. al. comps. *Out on the Shelves: Lesbian Books in Libraries.* Newcastle-under-Lyme, U.K.: Association of Assistant Librarians, 1989.

Brantenberg, Gerd, et al. "Annotert bibliografi over lesbisk litteratur I Skandinavia 1900–1984." In *Pa sporet av den tapte lyst: kjaelighet mellom kvinner som litteraert motiv.* Oslo, Norway: Aschenhoug, 1986.

Bullough, Vern, et al., eds. *An Annotated Bibliography of Homosexuality.* New York: Garland, 1976.

Clardy, Andrea. *A Word to the Wise: A Writer's Guide to Feminist and Lesbian Periodicals and Publishers.* Ithaca, N.Y.: Firebrand Books, 1993.

College Art Association of America, Gay and Lesbian Caucus. *Bibliography of Gay and Lesbian Art.* New York: Gay and Lesbian Caucus, College Art Association of America, 1994.

Courouve, Claude. *Bibliographie des Homosexualités.* Paris: C. Courouve, 1978.

Crawford, William, comp. *Homosexuality in Canada: A Bibliography.* Toronto: Canadian Gay Archives Publications, 1984.

Dall'Orto, Giovanni. *Leggare Omosessuale: Bibliografia.* Turin, Italy: Gruppo Abele, 1984.

Day, Frances Ann. *Lesbian and Gay Voices: An Annotated Bibliography and Guide to Literature for Children and Young Adults.* Westport, Conn.: Greenwood Press, 2000.

Dempsey, Brian. *Pink Papers: An Annotated Bibliography of Lesbian and Gay Journals.* Edinburgh, Scotland: USG, 1995.

Dynes, Wayne R. *Homosexuality: A Research Guide.* New York: Garland, 1987.

Fout, John. *A Select Bibliography on the History of Sexuality.* Annandale-on-Hudson, N.Y.: Committee on Lesbian and Gay History, Bard College, 1989.

Garber, Linda. *Lesbian Sources: A Bibliography of Periodical Articles, 1970–1990.* New York: Garland Press, 1993.

Garza, Luis Alberto de la. *Preliminary Chicano and Latino Lesbian and Gay Bibliography.* Berkeley, Calif.: Archivos Rodrigo Reyes, 1994.

Gillon, Margaret. *Lesbians in Print: A Bibliography of 1500 Books with Synopses.* Irvine, Calif.: Bluestocking Books, 1995.

Gittings, Barbara. *A Gay Bibliography.* Philadelphia: Task Force on Gay Liberation, American Library Association, 1974.

Harris, Paul, ed. *The Queer Press Guide 2000.* New York: Painted Leaf Press, 1999.

Herzer, Manfred. *Bibliographie zur Homosexualität: Verzeichnis des deutschsprachigen nichtbellestristischen Schriftums zur weiblichen und männlichen Homosexualität: Aus den Jahren 1466 bis 1975 in chronologischer Reihenfolge.* Berlin: Winkel, 1982.

Hurley, Michael. *A Guide to Gay and Lesbian Writing in Australia.* St. Leonards, Australia: Allen and Unwin, 1996.

Iwata, Junichi. *Nanshoku bunken shoshi.* Tokyo: Koten Bunko, Showa 31, 1956.

Maggiore, Dolores J. *Lesbianism: An Annotated Bibliography and Guide to the Literature, 1976–1991.* 2nd ed. Metuchen, N.J.: Scarecrow Press, 1992.

Malinowsky, Robert. *International Directory of Gay and Lesbian Periodicals.* Phoenix, Ariz.: Oryx Press, 1987.

Miller, Alan, comp. *Our Own Voices: A Directory of Lesbian and Gay Periodicals, 1890–1990.* Toronto: Canadian Gay Archives, 1991.

Nordquist, Joan. *Queer Theory: A Bibliography.* Santa Cruz, Calif.: Reference and Research Services, 1997.

Potter, Clare. *The Lesbian Periodicals Index.* Tallahassee, Fla.: Naiad Press, 1986.

Ridinger, Robert B. *The Gay and Lesbian Movement: References and Resources.* New York: G. K. Hall, 1996.

Robert, J. R. *Black Lesbians: An Annotated Bibliography.* Tallahassee, Fla.: Naiad Press, 1981.

Silva, Rosemary, comp. *Lesbian Quotations.* Boston: Alyson, 1993.

Task Force on Lesbian and Gay Issues, Council on Social Work Education. *An Annotated Bibliography of Lesbian and Gay Readings.* New York: Council on Social Work Education, 1983.

2. Almanacs/Encyclopedias/Dictionaries/Indices

Alyson Almanac. A Treasury of Information for the Gay and Lesbian Community. Boston: Alyson, 1989.

Boles, Janet K., and Diane Long Hoeveler. *Historical Dictionary of Feminism.* Lanham, Md.: Scarecrow Press, 1996.

Brandhorst, Henny, ed. *Queer Thesaurus: An International Thesaurus of Gay and Lesbian Index Terms.* Amsterdam: Homodok, 1997.

Brelin, Christa, ed. *Strength in Numbers: A Lesbian. Gay, and Bisexual Resource.* Detroit: Visible Ink Press, 1996.

Clardy, Andrea. *Words to the Wise: A Writer's Guide to Feminist and Lesbian Periodicals and Publishers.* 3rd ed. Ithaca, N.Y.: Firebrand Books, 1990.

Connor, Randy, et al., eds. *Cassell's Encyclopedia of Queer Myth, Symbol and Spirit: Gay, Lesbians, Bisexual and Transgender Lore.* London: Cassell Academic, 1998.

Dotson, Edisol. *Putting Out: The Essential Publishing Resource for Lesbian and Gay Writers.* Pittsburgh: Cleis Press, 1994.

Dynes, Wayne R., ed. *Encyclopedia of Homosexuality.* 2 vols. New York: Garland Press, 1990.

Fletcher, Lynne Yamaguchi. *Lavender Lists: New Lists about Lesbian and Gay Culture, History, and Personalities.* Boston: Alyson, 1990.

———. *The First Gay Pope and Other Records.* Boston: Alyson, 1992.

GLB Information Network. *Gay Guide Canada.* Toronto: Gay Guide Canada, 1997.

Hammond, Harmony. *Lesbian Art in America: A Contemporary History.* New York: Rizzoli, 2000.

Harris, Paul, ed. *The Queer Press Guide 2000.* New York: Painted Leaf Press, 1999.

Hogan, Steve, and Lee Hudson. *Completely Queer.* New York: Henry Holt, 1998.

Hunt, Ronald J. *Historical Dictionary of the Gay Liberation Movement: Gay Men and the Quest for Social Justice.* Lanham, Md.: Scarecrow Press, 1999.

Katz, Jonathan. *Gay/Lesbian Almanac.* New York: Harper and Row, 1983.

Malinowski, Sharon. *Gay and Lesbian Literature.* Detroit: St. James Press, 1994.

Malinowsky, H. Robert, comp. *International Directory of Gay and Lesbian Periodicals.* Phoenix, Ariz.: Oryx Press, 1987.

Mankiller, Wilma, et al. eds. *The Reader's Companion to U.S. Women's History.* Boston: Houghton Mifflin, 1998.

Marcus, Eric. *Is it a Choice?: Answers to 300 of the Most Frequently Asked Questions about Gays and Lesbians.* San Francisco: Harper, 1993.

Mewton, David. *Gay and Lesbian Rights: A Reference Handbook.* Santa Barbara, Calif.: ABC-Clio, 1994.

Miller, Alan V., comp. *Directory of the International Association of Lesbian and Gay Archives and Libraries.* Toronto: Canadian Gay Archives, 1987.

———. *Our Own Voices: A Directory of Lesbian and Gay Periodicals, 1890–1990: Including the Complete Holdings of the Canadian Gay Archives.* Toronto: Canadian Gay Archives, 1991.

National Museum and Archive of Lesbian and Gay History, comp. *The Lesbian Almanac.* New York: Berkeley Books, 1996.

Out Magazine, ed. *The Gay and Lesbian Address Book.* New York: Berkely Publishing, 1995.

Potter, Clare, ed. *Lesbian Periodicals Index.* Tallahassee, Fla.: Naiad Press, 1986.

Richards, Dell. *Lesbian Lists: A Look at Lesbian Culture, History, and Personalities.* Boston: Alyson, 1990.

Ridinger, Robert B., comp. *An Index to The Advocate: The National Gay Newsmagazine, 1967–1982.* Los Angeles: Liberation, 1987.

———. *The Gay and Lesbian Movement: References and Resources.* London: G.K. Hall, 1996.

Rutledge, Leigh. *The Gay Decades: From Stonewall to the Present: The People and Events That Shaped Gay Lives.* New York: Plume, 1992.

Salmonson, Jessica Amanda. *The Encyclopedia of Amazons: Women Warriors from Antiquity to the Modern Era.* New York: Paragon House, 1991.

Schlager, Neil, ed. *The St. James Press Gay and Lesbian Almanac.* Detroit: St. James Press, 1998.

Sherrill, Jan-Mitchell. *The Gay, Lesbian, and Bisexual Students' Guide to Colleges, Universities, and Graduate Schools*. New York: New York University Press, 1994.

Singer, Bennett L., and David Deschamps, eds. *Gay and Lesbian Stats: A Pocket Guide of Facts and Figures*. New York: New Press, 1994.

Sorrells, James. *The Directory of Gay, Lesbian and Bisexual Community Publications in the United States and Canada*. Guerneville, Calif.: James Sorrells, 1993.

Stewart, William. *Cassell's Queer Companion: A Dictionary of Lesbian and Gay Life and Culture*. London: Cassell, 1995.

Summers, Claude. *The Gay and Lesbian Literary Heritage*. New York: Henry Holt, 1995.

Tyrkus, Michael. *Gay and Lesbian Biography*. Detroit: St. James Press, 1997.

Witt, Lynn. *Out in All Directions: The Almanac of Gay and Lesbian America*. New York: Warner Books, 1995.

Zimmerman, Bonnie, ed. *Encyclopedia of Lesbian Histories and Cultures*. New York: Garland Press, 1999.

3. General Reference

Arnup, Katherine, et al., eds. "Être Lesbienne." *Documentation sur la Recherche Féministe* 12, 1 (1983).

Blackwood, Evelyn, and Saskia Wieringa, eds. *Female Desires: Same-Sex Relations and Transgender Practices across Cultures*. New York: Columbia University Press, 1999.

Blasius, Mark, and Shane Phelan. *We Are Everywhere*. New York: Routledge, 1997.

Freedman, Estelle B., et al., eds. "The Lesbian Issue." *Signs: Journal of Women in Culture and Society* 9, 4 (1984).

Gross, Larry, and James D. Woods, eds. *The Columbia Reader on Lesbians and Gay Men in Media, Society and Politics*. New York: Columbia University Press, 1999.

Hoagland, Sarah Lucia, and Julia Penelope, eds. *For Lesbians Only: A Separatist Anthology*. London: Onlywomen Press, 1991.

Jay, Karla, and Allen Young. *Out of the Closets*. New York: New York University Press, 1992.

"The Lesbian History Issue." *Frontiers: A Journal of Women's Studies* 4, 3 (1979).

Witt, Lynn, Sherry Thomas, and Eric Marcus, eds. *Out in All Directions*. New York: Warner Books, 1995.

4. Biographies/Correspondence/Memoirs

Aldrich, Robert, and Garry Wotherspoon, eds. *Who's Who in Gay and Lesbian History: From Antiquity to World War II*. New York: Routledge, 2000.

——. *Who's Who in Gay and Lesbian History: From World War II to the Present Day*. New York: Routledge, 2001.

Anzaldúa, Gloria, and Analouise Keating, eds. *Interviews/Entrevistas*. New York: Routledge, 2002.

Baker, Michael. *Our Three Selves: The Life of Radclyffe Hall*. London: H. Hamilton, 1985.

Benstock, Sheri. *Women of the Left Bank: Paris 1900–1940*. Austin: University of Texas Press, 1986.

Broe, Mary Lynn, ed. *Silence and Power: A Reevaluation of Djuna Barnes*. Carbondale: Southern Illinois University Press, 1991.

Brown, Judith C. *Immodest Acts: The Life of a Lesbian Nun in Renaissance Italy*. New York: Oxford University Press, 1986.

Cook, Blanche Wiesen. *Eleanor Roosevelt*. 2 vols. New York: Viking, 1994 and 1998.

——. "Outing History: A Biographical Review Essay." *Out Magazine* February/March 1994.

Cowan, Thomas Dale. *Gay Men and Women Who Enriched the World*. Boston: Alyson, 1992.

Davis, Natalie Zemon. *Women on the Margins: Three Seventeenth-Century Lives*. Cambridge, Mass.: Harvard University Press, 1995.

Faderman, Lillian. *Surpassing the Love of Men: Romantic Friendship and Love between Women, from the Renaissance to the Present*. New York: Morrow, 1981.

——. *Odd Girls and Twilight Lovers: A History of Lesbian Life in Twentieth-Century America*. New York: Columbia University Press, 1991.

——. *To Believe in Women: What Lesbians Have Done for America: A History*. New York: Houghton Mifflin, 1999.

Gingrich, Candace. *Accidental Activist: A Personal and Political Memoir*. New York: Scribner, 1996.

Grier, Barbara, and Coletta Reid, eds. *Lesbian Lives: Biographies of Women from* The Ladder. Oakland, Calif.: Diana Press, 1976.

Hansen, Karen V. "'No Kisses is like Youres': An Erotic Friendship between Two African-American Women during the Mid-Nineteenth Century." In Martha Vicinus, ed. *Lesbian Subjects*. Bloomington: Indiana University Press, 1996.

Hernando, Sil, and Alejandra Sarda. *Better: Oral Life Stories by Argentine Lesbians 1930–1976*. Toronto: Women's Press, 1977.

Jay, Karla. *The Amazon and the Page: Natalie Clifford Barney and Renée Vivien.* Bloomington: Indiana University Press, 1988.
———. *Tales of the Lavender Menace: A Memoir of Liberation.* New York: Basic Books, 1999.

Likosky, Stephen, ed. *Coming Out: An Anthology of International Gay and Lesbian Writings.* New York: Pantheon, 1992.

Lindemann, Marilee. *Willa Cather, Queering America.* New York: Columbia University Press, 1999.

Lorde, Audre. *Zami, a New Spelling of My Name.* Trumansburg, N.Y.: Crossing Press, 1982.

MacKay, Anne, ed. *Wolf Girls at Vassar: Lesbian and Gay Experiences 1930-1990.* New York: St. Martin's Press, 1993.

Mavor, Elizabeth. *The Ladies of Llangollen: A Study in Romantic Friendship.* London: Joseph, 1971.

Navratilova, Martina. *Martina.* New York: Knopf, 1985.

Nestle, Joan. *A Fragile Union: New and Selected Writings.* San Francisco: Cleis Press, 1998.

Richards, Dell. *Superstars: Twelve Lesbians Who Changed the World.* New York: Carroll and Graf, 1993.

Rothblum, Esther D., and Kathleen A. Brehony, eds. *Boston Marriages: Romantic but Asexual Relationships among Contemporary Lesbians.* Amherst: University of Massachusetts Press, 1993.

Russell, Paul Elliott. *The Gay 100: A Ranking of the Most Influential Gay Men and Lesbians, Past and Present.* New York: Carol, 1995.

Sarton, May. *May Sarton: A Self-Portrait.* Edited by Marita Simpson and Martha Wheelock. New York: W.W. Norton, 1986.

Scanlon, Jennifer, ed. *Significant Contemporary Feminists.* Westport, Conn.: Greenwood Press, 1999.

Souhami, Diane. *Gertrude and Alice.* New York: Pandora, 1991.

Stein, Arlene. *Sex and Sensibility: Stories of a Lesbian Generation.* Berkeley: University of California Press, 1997.

Sweetman, David. *Mary Renault: A Biography.* London: Chatto and Windus, 1993.

Tyrkus, Michael, ed. *Gay and Lesbian Biography.* Detroit: St. James Press, 1997.

Wells, Anna Mary. *Miss Marks and Miss Woolley.* Boston: Houghton Mifflin, 1978.

Wickes, George. *The Amazon of Letters: The Life and Loves of Natalie Barney.* New York: Putnam, 1976.

Yeager, Kenneth E. *Trailblazers: Profiles of America's Gay and Lesbian Elected Officials.* New York: Harrington Park Press, 2000.

Zimmerman, Bonnie. " The Politics of Transliteration: Lesbian Personal Narratives." *Signs: Journal of Women in Culture and Society* 9, 4 (1984): 663–682.

5. Literature/Film and Video/Performance

Arrizon, Alicia. *Latina Performance: Traversing the Stage.* Bloomington: Indiana University Press, 1999.

Bad Object Choices. *How Do I Look? Queer Film and Video.* San Francisco: Bay Press, 1991.

Barnard, Ian. "Queer Fictions: Gay Men with/and/in/near/or Lesbian Feminisms." *LIT: Literature Interpretation Theory* 4, 4 (1993): 261–274.

Boffin, T., and J. Fraser. *Stolen Glances: Lesbians Take Photographs.* New York: Pandora/HarperCollins, 1991.

Capsuto, Steven. *Alternate Channels: The Uncensored Story of Gay and Lesbian Images on Radio and Television 1930s to the Present.* New York: Ballantine, 2000.

Case, Sue-Ellen. *The Domain-Matrix: Performing Lesbian at the End of the Print Culture.* Bloomington: Indiana University Press, 1997.

———. *Split Britches: Lesbian Practice/Feminist Performance.* New York: Routledge, 1996.

Castle, Terry. *The Apparitional Lesbian.* New York: Columbia University Press, 1993.

Darren, Alison. *Lesbian Film Guide.* New York: Cassell, 2000.

Donoghue, Emma, ed. *Poems between Women: Four Centuries of Love, Romantic Friendship, and Desire.* New York: Columbia University Press, 1997.

Dyer, Richard. *Now You See It: Studies on Lesbian and Gay Film.* New York: Routledge, 1990.

Fleming, Lee. *Hot Licks: Lesbian Musicians of Note.* Charlottetown, Canada: Gynergy Books, 1996.

Foster, David William. *Gay and Lesbian Themes in Latin American Writing.* Austin: University of Texas Press, 1991.

Gever, Martha, John Greyson, and Pratibha Parmar, eds. *Queer Looks: Perspectives on Lesbian and Gay Film and Video.* New York: Routledge, 1993.

Grier, Barbara. *Lesbiana: Book Reviews from* The Ladder, *1966–1972.* Reno, Nev.: Naiad Press, 1976.

Gross, Larry, et al., eds. *Sexual Minorities in the Mass Media.* New York: Oxford University Press, 1988.

Hadleigh, Boze. *The Lavender Screen: The Gay and Lesbian Films: Their Stars, Makers, Characters, and Critics.* Secaucus, N.J.: Carol, 1992.

———. *Hollywood Lesbians: Conversations with Sandy Dennis, Barbara Stanwyck, Majorie Main, Nancy Kulp, Patsy Kelly, Agnes Moorehead, Edith*

Head, Dorothy Azner, Capucine, Judith Anderson. New York: Barricade Books, 1994.

Hammer, Barbara. "Lesbian Filmmaking: Self-Birthing." *Film Reader* 5 (1982) 60–66.

Hammond, Harmony. *Lesbian Art in America: A Contemporary History.* New York: Rizzoli, 2000.

Hanson, Ellis. *Out Takes: Queer Theory and Film.* Durham, N.C.: Duke University Press, 1999.

Heathcote, Owen, Alex Hughes, and James Williams, eds. *Gay Signatures: Gay and Lesbian Theory, Fiction and Film in France, 1945–1999.* London: Berg, 1999.

Holmlund, Chris, and Cynthia Fuchs. *Between the Sheets, In the Streets: Queer, Lesbian and Gay Documentary (Visible Evidence).* Minneapolis: University of Minnesota Press, 1997.

Holoch, Naomi, and Joan Nestle, eds. *The Vintage Book of International Lesbian Fiction: An Anthology.* New York: Vintage, 1999.

Jackson, Claire, and Peter Tapp. *The Bent Lens: A World Guide to Gay and Lesbian Film.* St. Kilda, Australia: Australian Catalogue Company, 1997.

Jay, Karla, and Joanne Glasgow, eds. *Lesbian Texts and Contexts: Radical Revisions.* New York: New York University Press, 1990.

Kabir, Shameem. *Daughters of Desire: Lesbian Representations in Film.* London: Cassell Academic, 1997.

Kahn, Douglas, and Diane Neumaier, eds. *Cultures in Contention.* Seattle, Wash.: Real Comet, 1985.

Keesey, Pam, ed. *Daughter of Darkness: Lesbian Vampire Stories.* Pittsburgh: Cleis, 1993.

Kotz, Liz. "Anything but Idyllic: Lesbian Filmmaking in the 1980s and 1990s." In Arlene Stein, ed. *Sisters, Sexperts, Queers: Beyond the Lesbian Nation.* New York: Penguin, 1993.

Krouse, Matthew, ed. *The Invisible Ghetto: Lesbian and Gay Writing from South Africa.* East Haven, Conn.: Inbook, 1993.

Lebow, Alisa. "Lesbians Make Movies." *Cinéaste* 20, 2 (1983): 18–23.

Lilly, Mark, ed. *Lesbian and Gay Writing: An Anthology of Critical Essays.* London: Macmillan, 1990.

Maddison, Stephen. *Fags, Hags and Queer Sisters.* Houndmills, U.K.: Palgrave, 2000.

Malinowski, Sharon, et al., eds. *The Gay and Lesbian Literary Companion.* Detroit: Visible Ink Press, 1995.

Mann, William J. *Behind the Screen: How Lesbians and Gays Shaped Hollywood, 1910–1969.* New York: Viking Press, 2001.

Martindale, Kathleen. *Un/Popular Culture: Lesbian Writing after the Sex Wars.* Albany: State University of New York Press, 1997.

Mayne, Judith. *Framed: Lesbians, Feminists and Media Culture.* Minneapolis: University of Minnesota Press, 2000.

McLaren, Jay. *An Encyclopedia of Gay and Lesbian Recordings.* Amsterdam: J. McLaren, 1992.

McLellan, Diana. *The Girls: Sappho Goes to Hollywood.* New York: St. Martin's Press, 2000.

Millett, Kate. *Sexual Politics.* New York: Simon and Schuster, 1969.

Muñoz, Josòe Esteban, and Amanda Barrett, eds. "Queer Acts." *Women and Performance: A Journal of Feminist Theory* 16 (1996).

Munt, Sally, ed. *New Lesbian Criticism: Literary and Cultural Readings.* New York: Columbia University Press, 1992.

Murray, Raymond. *Images in the Dark: An Encyclopedia of Gay and Lesbian Film and Video.* Rev. ed. New York: Plume, 1996.

Nelson, Emmanuel. *Critical Essays: Gay and Lesbian Writers of Color.* Binghamton, N.Y.: Harrington Park Press, 1993.

———, ed. *Critical Essays: Gay and Lesbian Writers of Color.* Binghamton, N.Y.: Harrington Park Press, 1994.

Newton, Esther. "The Mythic Mannish Lesbian: Radclyffe Hall and the New Woman." *Signs: Journal of Women in Culture and Society* 9, 4 (Summer 1984): 557–575.

Olson, Jenni, ed. *The Ultimate Guide to Lesbian and Gay Film and Video.* New York: Serpent's Tale, 1996.

Parish, James Robert. *Gays and Lesbians in Mainstream CineMass: Plots, Critiques, Casts and Credits for 272 Theatrical and Made-for-Television Hollywood Releases.* Jefferson, N.C.: McFarland, 1993.

Peterson, Jane T., and Suzanne Bennett. *Women Playwrights of Diversity: A Bio-Bibliographical Sourcebook.* Westport, Conn.: Greenwood Press, 1997.

Pollack, Sandra, and Denise Knight, eds. *Contemporary Lesbian Writers of the United States: A Bio-Bibliographical Critical Sourcebook.* Westport, Conn.: Greenwood Press, 1993.

Ringer, R.J., ed. *Queer Words, Queer Images: Communication and the Construction of Homosexuality.* New York: New York University Press, 1994.

Robinson, Christopher. *The Scandal in Ink: Male and Female Homosexuality in Twentieth-Century French Literature.* New York: Cassell, 1995.

Rohy, Valerie. *Impossible Women: Lesbian Figures and American Literature.* Ithaca, N.Y.: Cornell University Press, 2000.

Rule, Jane. *Lesbian Images.* New York: Pocket Books, 1976.

Russo, Vito. *The Celluloid Closet.* New York: Harper and Row, 1981.

Schuster, Marilyn R. *Passionate Communities: Reading Lesbian Resistance in Jane Rule's Fiction.* New York: New York University Press, 1999.

Sedgewick, Eve Kosofsky. *Epistemology of the Closet.* Berkeley: University of California Press, 1990.

Smith, Patricia J. *Lesbian Panic,* New York: Columbia University Press, 1997.

Stewart, Stephen. *Gay Hollywood Film and Video Guide: 75 Years of Gay and Lesbian Images in the Movies.* 2nd ed. Laguna Hills, Calif.: Companion, 1994.

Summers, Claude J., ed. *The Gay and Lesbian Literary Heritage: A Reader's Companion to the Writers and Their Works from Antiquity to the Present.* New York: Henry Holt, 1995.

Weiss Andrea. *Vampires and Violets: Lesbians in the Cinema.* London: Jonathan Cape, 1992.

Wolverton, Terry, ed. *Hers 3: Brilliant New Fiction by Lesbian Writers.* New York: Faber and Faber, 1999.

Zimet, Jaye. *Strange Sisters: The Art of Lesbian Pulp Fiction, 1949–1969.* New York: Viking, 1999.

Zimmerman, Bonnie. *The Safe Sea of Women: Lesbian Fiction, 1969–1989.* Boston: Beacon, 1990.

6. Philosophy, Social and Political Theory (including Feminism)

Abelove, Henry, M. A. Barale, and D. Halperin, eds. *The Lesbian and Gay Reader.* New York: Routledge, 1993.

Allen, Jeffner. *Lesbian Philosophy.* Palo Alto, Calif.: Institute of Lesbian Studies, 1986.

———, ed. *Lesbian Philosophies and Cultures.* Albany: State University of New York Press, 1990.

Altman, Dennis, et al., eds. *Homosexuality, Which Homosexuality?* Amsterdam: Uitgeverij An Dekker/Schorer, 1988.

Atkinson, Ti-Grace. "Lesbianism and Feminism." In Phyllis Birkby, et al., *Amazon Expedition: A Lesbian-Feminist Anthology.* Washington, D.C.: Times Change Press, 1973.

———. *Amazon Odyssey.* New York: Links, 1974.

———. "Radical Feminism: A Declaration of War." In Marilyn Pearsall, ed. *Women and Values: Readings in Recent Feminist Philosophy.* Belmont, Calif.: Wadsworth, 1986.

Beck, Evelyn Torton, ed. *Nice Jewish Girls: A Lesbian Anthology.* Watertown, Mass.: Persephone Press, 1982.

Birkby, Phyllis, et al. *Amazon Expedition: A Lesbian-Feminist Anthology.* Washington, D.C.: Times Change Press, 1973.

Blasius, Mark. *Gay and Lesbian Politics: Sexuality and the Emergence of a New Ethic.* Philadelphia: Temple University Press, 1994.

Bristow, Joseph, and Angelia Wilson, eds. *Activating Theory: Lesbian, Gay, Bisexual Politics.* London: Lawrence and Wishart, 1993.

Brodribb, Somer. *Nothing Mat(t)ers: A Feminist Critique of Postmodernism.* Melbourne, Australia: Spinifex Press, 1992.

Brown, Lester B., ed. *Two Spirit People: American Indian, Lesbian Women and Gay Men.* New York: Haworth, 1997.

Butler, Judith. *Gender Trouble: Feminism and the Subversion of Identity.* New York: Routledge, 1990.

———. *Bodies That Matter: On the Discursive Limits of "Sex."* New York: Routledge, 1993.

———. *Excitable Speech: Contemporary Scenes of Politics.* New York: Routledge, 1997.

Calhoun, Chesire. "Separating Lesbian Theory from Feminist Theory." *Ethics* 104, 3 (April 1994): 558–581.

Card, Claudia. *Lesbian Choices.* New York: Columbia University Press, 1995.

———, ed. *Adventures in Lesbian Philosophy.* Bloomington: Indiana University Press, 1994.

Cocks, Joan. "Wordless Emotions: Some Critical Reflections on Radical Feminism." *Politics and Society* 13, 1 (1984): 1–26.

Cook, Blanche Wiesen. "Women Alone Stir My Imagination: Lesbianism in the Cultural Tradition." *Signs* vol. 4. (Summer 1979).

Daly, Mary. *Gyn/Ecology: The Metaethics of Radical Feminism.* Boston: Beacon Press, 1979.

———. *Pure Lust: Elemental Feminist Philosophy.* Boston: Beacon, 1984

De Cecco, John P., and John Elia, eds. *If You Seduce a Straight Person, Can You Make Them Gay? Issues in Biological Essentialism versus Social Constructionism in Gay and Lesbian Identities.* Binghamton, N.Y.: Harrington Park Press, 1993.

Deitcher, David, ed. *The Question of Equality.* New York: Scribner, 1995.

de Lauretis, Teresa, ed. *Queer Theory: Lesbian and Gay Sexualities.* Bloomington: Indiana University Press, 1991.

Ditzinger, Celia, and Rachel Perkins. *Changing Our Minds: Lesbian Feminism and Psychology.* New York: New York University Press, 1993.

Doan, Laura, ed. *The Lesbian Postmodern.* New York: Columbia University Press, 1994.

Dorenkeam, Monica, and Richard Henke, eds. *Negotiating Lesbian and Gay Subjects.* New York: Routledge, 1994.

Douglas, Carol Anne. *Love and Politics: Radical Feminist Lesbian Theories.* San Francisco: Ism Press, 1990.

Duberman, Martin, ed. *Queer Representations.* New York: New York University Press, 1997.

Duggan, Lisa. "Making It Perfectly Queer." *Socialist Review* 22, 1 (1992): 11–31.

Edge, Simon. *With Friends Like These . . . : Marxism and Gay Politics (Listen Up!).* London: Cassell Academic, 1995.

Eng, David, and Alice Hom, eds. *Q & A: Queer in Asian America.* Philadelphia: Temple University Press, 1998.

Epstein, Julia, and Kristina Straub. *Body Guards: The Culture and Politics of Gender Ambiguity.* London: Routledge, 1991.

Ferree, Myra Marx, and Beth Hess. *Controversy and Coalition: The Feminist Movement.* Boston: Twayne, 1985. Rev. ed. New York: Maxwell Macmillan, 1994.

Freeman, Jo. *The Politics of Women's Liberation: A Case Study of an Emerging Social Movement and Its Relation to the Policy Process.* New York: David McKay, 1975.

Frye, Marilyn. *The Politics of Reality: Essays in Feminist Theory.* Trumansburg, N.Y.: Crossing Press, 1983.

———. *Willful Virgin: Essays in Feminism 1992.* New York: Crossing Press, 1992.

Fuss, Diana. *Essentially Speaking: Feminism, Nature and Difference.* New York: Routledge, 1989.

Fuss, Diana, ed. *Inside/Out: Lesbian Theories, Gay Theories.* New York: Routledge, 1991.

Gluckman, Amy, and Betsey Reed. *Homo Economics: Capitalism, Community, and Lesbian and Gay Life.* New York: Routledge, 1997.

Gornick, Vivian, and Barbara Moran, eds. *Woman in Sexist Society.* New York: Basic, 1971.

Grahn, Judy. *Another Mother Tongue: Gay Words, Gay Worlds.* Boston: Beacon Press, 1990.

Harne, Lynne, and Elaine Miller. *All the Rage: Reassertion of Radical Lesbian Feminism.* New York: Teacher's College Press, 1997.

Hart, John, and Diane Richardson, eds. *The Theory and Practice of Homosexuality.* London: Routledge, 1981.

Hart, Lynda. *Fatal Women: Lesbian Sexuality and the Mark of Aggression.* Princeton, N.J.: Princetown University Press, 1994.

Heller, Dana, ed. *Cross-Purposes: Lesbians, Feminists, and the Limits of Alliance.* Bloomington: Indiana University Press, 1997.

Hendriks, Aart, Rob Tielman, and Evert van der Veen, eds. *The Third Pink Book.* Buffalo, N.Y.: Prometheus, 1993.

Herve, Florance. *Namibia: Frauen machen sich ein.* Berlin: Orlanda Frauenverlag, 1993.

Hoagland, Sarah Lucia. *Lesbian Ethics: Toward New Values.* Palo Alto, Calif: Institute of Lesbian Studies, 1988.

Hoogland, Renée C. *Lesbian Configurations.* New York: Columbia University Press, 1997.

Inness, Sherrie. *The Lesbian Menace: Ideology, Identity and Representation of Lesbian Life.* Amherst: University of Massachusetts Press, 1997.

Jacobs, Sue-Ellen, Wesley Thomas, and Sabine Land, eds. *Two-Spirit People: Native American Gender Identity, Sexuality, and Spirituality.* Urbana: University of Illinois Press, 1997.

Jagose, Annamarie. *Queer Theory.* New York: New York University Press, 1996.

Jakobson, Janet. *Working Alliances and the Politics of Difference.* Bloomington: Indiana University Press, 1998.

Jay, Karla, and Allen Young, eds. *Lavender Culture.* New York: Harcourt Brace Jovanovitch, 1978.

Jay, Karla, and Joanne Glasgow, eds. *Lesbian Texts and Contexts: Radical Revisions.* New York: New York University Press, 1990.

Jung, Patricia, and Ralph Smith. *Heterosexism.* Albany: State University of New York Press, 1993.

Kanter, Hannah et al., eds. *Sweeping Statements: Writings from the Women's Liberation Movement (1981–1983).* London: Women's Press, 1984.

Kaplan, Morris B. *Sexual Justice.* New York: Routledge, 1997.

Katz, Jonathan Ned. *The Invention of Heterosexuality.* New York: Plume, 1995.

Kitzinger, Celia. *The Social Construction of Lesbianism.* London: Sage, 1987.

Marotta, Toby. *The Politics of Homosexuality.* Boston: Houghton Mifflin, 1981.

McIntosh, Mary. "The Homosexual Role." *Social Problems* 16 (1968): 182–192.

Merck, Mandy. *Coming Out of Feminism?* Malden, Mass.: Blackwell, 1998.

Miller, Diane H. *Freedom to Differ: The Shaping of the Gay and Lesbian Struggle for Civil Rights.* New York: New York University Press, 1998.

Millett, Kate. *Sexual Politics.* New York: Simon and Schuster, 1969.

Mohin, Lillian. *An Intimacy of Equals: Lesbian Feminist Ethics.* New York: Haworth, 1996.

Moraga, Cherríe, and Gloria Anzaldua, eds. *This Bridge Called My Back: Writings of Radical Women of Color.* Watertown, Mass.: Persephone, 1981.

Morgan, Robin, ed. *Sisterhood Is Powerful: An Anthology of Writings from the Women's Liberation Movement.* New York: Vintage, 1970.

Morton, Donald. "The Politics of Queer Theory in the (Post) Modern Moment." *Genders* 17 (Fall 1993): 121ff.

——, ed. *The Material Queer: A LesBiGay Cultural Studies Reader.* Boulder, Colo.: Westview Press, 1996.

Munt, Sally. *Heroic Desire: Lesbian Desire and Cultural Space.* New York: New York University Press, 1998.

Nava, Michael, and Robert Dawidoff. *Created Equal: Why Gay Rights Matter to America.* New York: St. Martin's Press, 1994.

O'Sullivan, Sue. *I Used to Be Nice: Reflections on Feminist and Lesbian Politics*. London: Cassell Academic, 1996.

Penelope, Julia. *Call Me Lesbian: Lesbian Lives, Lesbian Theory*. Trumansburg, N.Y.: Crossing Press, 1992.

Penelope, Julia, and Sarah Hoagland, eds. *For Lesbians Only*. London: Onlywomen, 1988.

Peters, Julie, and Andrea Wolper, eds. *Women's Rights, Human Rights: International Feminist Perspectives*. New York: Routledge, 1995.

Pharr, Suzanne. *Homophobia: A Weapon of Sexism*. Little Rock, Ark.: Chardon Press, 1988.

Phelan, Shane. *Identity Politics. Lesbian Feminism and the Limits of Community*. Philadelphia: Temple University Press, 1989.

———, ed. *Playing with Fire*. New York: Routledge, 1997.

Queen, Carol, and Lawrence Schimel, eds. *PoMoSexuals: Challenging Assumptions about Gender and Sexuality*. San Francisco: Cleis Press, 1997.

Raffo, Susan, ed. *Queerly Classed: Gay Men and Lesbians Write about Class*. Boston: Southend Press, 1997.

Reinfelder, Monika, ed. *Amazon to Zami: Towards a Global Lesbian Feminism*. London: Cassell, 1996.

Rich, Adreinne. "Compulsory Heterosexuality and Lesbian Existence." *Signs* 5 (1980): 631–690.

Roscoe, Will. *Changing Ones: Third and Fourth Genders in Native North America*. New York: St. Martin's Press, 1998.

Rosenbloom, Rachel, ed. *Unspoken Rules: Sexual Orientation and Women's Human Rights*. New York: Cassell, 1996.

Roy, Carolle. *Les Lesbiennes et le Féminisme*. Montreal: Éditions Saint-Martin, 1985.

Rule, Jane. *Lesbian Images*. Trumansburg, N.Y.: Crossing Press, 1982.

Rust, Paula. *Bisexuality and the Challenge to Lesbian Politics: Sex, Loyalty, and the Revolution*. New York: New York University Press, 1995.

Schwartz, Adria. *Sexual Subjects: Lesbians, Gender and Psychoanalysis*. New York: Routledge, 1997.

Sedgwick, Eve Kosofsky. *Epistemology of the Closet*. Berkeley: University of California Press, 1990.

Silver, Diane. *The New Civil War*. New York: Franklin Watts, 1997.

Smith, Barbara. *The Truth That Never Hurts: Writings on Race, Gender, and Freedom*. New Brunswick, N.J.: Rutgers University Press, 1998.

Smyth, Cheryl. *Lesbians Talk Queer Notions*. London: Scarlet Press, 1992.

Somerville, Soibhan. *Queering the Color Line: Race and the Invention of Homosexuality in American Culture*. Durham, N.C.: Duke University Press, 2000.

Stambler, Sookie, comp. *Women's Liberation: Blueprint for the Future*. New York: Ace, 1970.

Stein, Arlene. "Sisters and Queers: The Decentering of Lesbian Feminism." *Socialist Review* 22, 1 (January 1992): 33–55.

———, ed. *Sisters, Sexperts, Queers.* New York: Plume, 1993.

Taylor, Verta, and Leila Rupp. "Women's Culture and Lesbian Feminist Activism: A Reconsideration of Cultural Feminism." *Signs: Journal of Women in Culture and Society* 19 (1993): 32–61.

Trebilcot, Joyce. *Dyke Ideas.* Albany: State University of New York Press, 1994.

Trujillo, Carla, ed. *Living Chicana Theory.* San Francisco: Third Women Press, 1997. Berkeley, Calif.: Third Woman Press, 1998.

Tucker, Naomi, ed. *Bisexual Politics: Theories, Queries and Visions.* New York: Haworth, 1995.

Vaid, Urvashi. *Virtual Equality.* New York: Anchor, 1995.

Warner, Michael, ed. *Fear of a Queer Planet.* Minneapolis: University of Minnesota Press, 1993.

Weed, Elizabeth, and Naomi Schor, eds. *Feminism Meets Queer Theory.* Bloomington: Indiana University Press, 1997.

Weeks, Jeffrey. *Sexuality and Its Discontents: Meanings, Myths, and Modern Sexualities.* Boston: Kegan Paul, 1985.

Weston, Kath. *Long Slow Burn: Sexuality and Social Science.* New York: Routledge, 1998.

Whisman, Vera. *Queer By Choice.* New York: Routledge, 1996.

Wilson, Angelia, ed. *A Simple Matter of Justice?* London: Cassell, 1995.

Wittig, Monique. *Les Guérillères.* New York: Viking, 1971.

———. *The Straight Mind and Other Essays.* Boston: Beacon, 1992.

7. History (and Politics)

General References

Adam, Barry. *The Rise of a Gay and Lesbian Liberation Movement.* New York: Twayne, 1995.

Beemyn, Brett. *Creating a Place for Ourselves: Lesbian, Gay and BiSexual Community Histories.* New York: Routledge, 1997.

Blasius, Mark, and Shane Phelan, eds. *We Are Everywhere: A Historical Sourcebook in Gay and Lesbian Politics.* New York: Routledge, 1997.

Bonnet, Marie-Jo. *Un Choix sans Équivoque.* Paris: Denoël-Gonthier, 1981.

Cant, Bob, and Susan Hemmings, eds. *Radical Records.* London: Routledge, 1988.

Chou, Wah-Shan. *Tongzhi: Politics of Same-Sex Eroticism in Chinese Societies.* New York: Haworth, 2000.

Clendinenn, Dudley, and Adam Nagourney. *Out for Good: The Struggle to Build a Gay Rights Movement in America.* New York: Simon and Schuster, 1999.

Cook, Blanche Wiesen. "The Historical Denial of Lesbianism: A Review Essay." *Radical History Review* 20 (Spring/Summer 1979).

Cornwell, A. *Black Lesbian in White America.* Tallahassee, Fla.: Naiad Press, 1983.

Cruikshank, Margaret. *The Gay and Lesbian Liberation Movement.* New York: Routledge, 1992.

Deaderick, Sam, and Tamara Turner. *Gay Resistance: The Hidden History.* Scattle, Wash.: Red Letter Press, 1997.

D'Emilio, John. *Making Trouble: Essays on Gay History, Politics, and the University.* New York: Routledge, 1992.

D'Emilio, John, and Estelle Freedman. *Intimate Matters: A History of Sexuality in America.* New York: Perennial Library, 1988.

Duberman, Martin. *About Time: Exploring the Gay Past.* Rev. ed. New York: Meridian, 1991.

Duberman, Martin, Martha Vicinus, and George Chauncey Jr., eds. *Hidden From History: Reclaiming the Gay and Lesbian Past.* New York: NAL and Meridian, 1989.

Ehrenreich, Barbara, and Deirdre English. *Witches, Midwives and Nurses: A History of Women Healers.* 2nd ed. Old Westbury, N.Y.: Feminist Press, 1973.

Faderman, Lillian. *To Believe in Women: What Lesbians Have Done for America.* Boston: Houghton Mifflin, 1999.

Gay American Indians, and W. Roscoe. *Living the Spirit.* New York: St. Martin's Press, 1988.

Gibbs, J., and S. Bennett, eds. *Top Ranking: A Collection of Articles on Racism and Classism in the Lesbian Community.* Brooklyn, N.Y.: February 3rd Press, 1980.

Gibbs, Liz, ed. *Daring to Dissent: Lesbian Culture from Margin to Mainstream.* London: Cassell, 1994.

Grier, Barbara, and Colette Reid, eds. *The Lavender Herring: Lesbian Essays from The Ladder.* Baltimore: Diana Press, 1976.

Hamer, Emily. *Britannias Glory: A History of Twentieth-Century Lesbians.* London: Casswell, 1995.

History Project, The, comp. *Improper Bostonians: Lesbian and Gay History from the Puritans to Playland.* Boston: Beacon, 1998.

Katz, Jonathan Ned. *Gay American History: Lesbians and Gay Men in the U.S.A.: A Documentary History.* Rev. ed. New York: Meridian, 1992.

Kepner, Jim. *Becoming a People: A 4,000 Year Chronology of Gay and Lesbian History.* Los Angeles: J. Kepner, 1995.

Lesbian History Group. *Not a Passing Phase: Reclaiming Lesbians in History, 1840–1985.* London: Women's Press, 1993.

Lim-Hing, Sharon, ed. *The Very Inside: An Anthology of Writings by Asian and Pacific Islander Lesbian and Bisexual Women.* Toronto: Sister Vision, 1994.

Lorde, Audre. *Sister Outsider.* Trumansburg, N.Y.: Crossing Press, 1984.

Marcus, Eric. *Making History: The Struggle for Gay and Lesbian Equal Rights, 1945–1990: An Oral History.* New York: HarperCollins, 1992.

Marotta, Toby. *The Politics of Homosexuality: How Lesbians and Gay Men Have Made Themselves a Political and Social Force in Modern America.* Boston: Houghton Mifflin, 1981.

Martel, Frédéric. *The Pink and the Black: Homosexuals in France since 1968.* Translated by Jane Marie Todd. Standford, Calif.: Stanford University Press, 1999.

Martin, Del, and Phyllis Lyon. *Lesbian/Woman.* San Francisco: Glide, 1972.

McGarry, Molly, and Fred Wasserman. *Becoming Visible: An Illustrated History of Lesbian and Gay Life in the Twentieth Century.* New York: Viking Penguin, 1998.

McLeod, Donald W. *Lesbian and Gay Liberation in Canada: A Selected Chronology, 1964–1975.* Toronto: ECW Press/Homewood Books, 1996.

Nickels, Thom. *Gay and Lesbian Philadelphia.* Dover, N.H.: Arcadia, 2002.

Offen, Karen. *European Feminisms, 1700–1950: A Political History.* Stanford, Calif.: Stanford University Press, 2000.

Onge, Jack. *The Gay Liberation Movement.* New York: Alliance Press, 1971.

Peiss, Kathy, and Christina Simmons, eds. *Passion and Power: Sexuality and History.* Philadelphia: Temple University Press, 1989.

Phelan, Shane. *Identity Politics: Lesbian Feminism and the Limits of Community.* Philadelphia: Temple University Press, 1989.

———. *Getting Specific: Postmodern Lesbian Politics.* Minneapolis: University of Minnesota Press, 1994.

Ramos, Juanita, ed. *Compañeras: Latina Lesbians.* New York: Latina Lesbian History Project, 1987.

Richmond, Len, and Gary Nogura. *The Gay Liberation Book.* New York: Ramparts, 1973.

Stein, Arlene. *The Stranger Next Door.* Boston: Beacon, 2001.

Stryker, Susan, and Jim Van Buskirk. *Gay by the Bay: A History of Queer Culture in San Francisco.* San Francisco: Chronicle, 1996.

Thadani, Giti. *Sakhiyani: Lesbian Desire in Ancient and Modern India.* London: Cassell, 1996.

Thompson, Mark, ed. *Long Road to Freedom:* The Advocate *History of the Gay and Lesbian Movement.* New York: St. Martin's Press, 1994.

Trujillo, Carla, ed. *Chicana Lesbians.* Berkeley, Calif.: Third World Press, 1991.

Vicinus, Martha. "Lesbian History: All Theory and No Facts or All Facts and No Theory." *Radical History Review* 60 (Fall 1994): 52ff.

Walters, Suzanna. *All the Rage: The Story of Gay Visibility in America.* Chicago: University of Chicago Press, 2001.

Weeks, Jeffrey. *Coming Out: Homosexual Politics in Britain, from the Nineteenth Century to the Present.* London: Quartet Books, 1977.

———. *Sex, Politics and Society: The Regulation of Sexuality since 1800.* London: Longman, 1981.

Wheelwright, Julie. *Amazons and Military Maids: Women Who Dressed As Men in the Pursuit of Life, Liberty and Happiness.* Boston: Pandora, 1989.

Young, Allen. *Gays under the Cuban Revolution.* San Francisco: Grey Fox, 1981.

Ancient/Medieval/Early Modern

Bailey, Derrick Sherwin. *Homosexuality and the Western Christian Tradition.* Hamden, Conn.: Archon Books, 1975.

Boswell, John. *Christianity, Social Tolerance, and Homosexuality: Gay People in Western Europe from the Beginning of the Christian Era to the Fourteenth Century.* Chicago: University of Chicago Press, 1980.

Bray, Alan. *Homosexuality in Renaissance England.* 2nd ed. London: Gay Men's Press, 1988.

Brooten, Bernadette. *Love between Women: Early Christian Responses to Female Homoeroticism.* Chicago: University of Chicago Press, 1998.

Brown, Judith C. *Immodest Acts: The Life of a Lesbian Nun in Renaissance Italy.* New York: Oxford University Press, 1986.

Cantarella, Eva. *Bisexuality in the Ancient World.* New Haven, Conn.: Yale University Press, 1992.

Cavin, S. *Lesbian Origins.* San Francisco: Ism, 1985.

Crompton, Louis. "The Myth of Lesbian Impunity: Capital Laws from 1270–1791." *Journal of Homosexuality* 6 (1980–81): 11–25.

Donahue, Emma. *Passions between Women: British Lesbian Culture, 1668–1801.* London: Scarlet, 1993.

Dover, Kenneth James. *Greek Homosexuality.* Updated ed. Cambridge, Mass.: Harvard University Press, 1989.

Goodich, Michael. *The Unmentionable Vice: Homosexuality in the Middle Ages.* Santa Barbara, Calif.: ABC-Clio, 1979.

Halperin, David M. *One Hundred Years of Homosexuality: And Other Essays on Greek Love.* New York: Routledge, 1990.

Rabinowitz, Nancy Sorkin, and Lisa Suanger, eds. *Among Women: From the Homosocial to the Homoerotic in the Ancient World.* Austin: University of Texas, 2002.

Sautman, Francesca Canadé, and Pamela Sheingorn, eds. *Same Sex Love and Desire among Women in the Middle Ages.* Houndmills, U.K.: Palgrave, 2001.

Traub, Valerie. *The Renaissance of Lesbianism in Early Modern England.* London: Cambridge University Press, 2002.

Winkler, John J. *The Constraints of Desire: The Anthropology of Sex and Gender in Ancient Greece.* New York: Routledge, 1990.

The Early Homosexual Rights Movement (1864–1945)

Chauncey, George. *Gay New York: Gender, Urban Culture, and the Making of the Gay Male World, 1890–1940.* New York: Basic, 1994.

Cory, Donald Webster. *The Lesbian in America.* New York: Citadel Press, 1964.

D'Emilio, John. *Sexual Politics, Sexual Communities: The Making of a Homosexual Minority in the United States, 1940–1970.* Chicago: University of Chicago Press, 1983.

Everard, Myriam. *Ziel en Zinnen. Over liefde en lust tussen vrouwen in de tweede helft vad de achttiende eeuw.* Groningen, Netherlands: Historische Uitgeverij, 1994.

Faderman, Lillian, and Brigitte Eriksson, eds., *Lesbians in Germany, 1890's–1920's.* 2nd ed. Tallahassee, Fla.: Naiad Press, 1990.

Freedman, Estelle. "Separatism as Strategy: Female Institution Building and American Feminism." *Feminist Studies* 5, 3 (Fall 1979): 512–529.

Grau, Gunter, ed. *Hidden Holocaust? Gay and Lesbian Persecution in Germany, 1933–45.* Translated by Patrick Camiller. New York: Cassell, 1995.

Hall, Lesley A. *Sex, Gender and Social Change in Britain since 1880.* Houndmills, U.K.: Palgrave, 2000.

Hirschfeld, Magnus. *The Restoration of the Good Name of Homosexual Men and Women and Other Writings.* Translated by Michael Lombardi-Nash. Jacksonville, Fla.: Urania Manuscripts, 1992.

Lauritson, John, and David Thorstad. *The Early Homosexual Rights Movement (1864–1935).* New York: Times Change, 1974.

Kaiser, Charles. *The Gay Metropolis (1940–1996).* Boston: Houghton Mifflin, 1997.

Kokula, Ilse. *Weibliche Homosexualität um 1900 in zeitgenossischen Dokumenten.* Munich: Women's Offensive, 1981.

Rothblum, Esther, and Kathleen Brehony. *Boston Marriages.* Amherst: University of Massachusetts Press, 1993.

Sautman, Francesca Canadé. "Invisibile Women: Lesbian Working Class Culture in France, 1880–1930." In Jeffrey Merrick and Bryan Ragan, Jr., eds. *Homosexuality in Modern France.* Oxford: Oxford University Press, 1996.

Smith-Rosenberg, Carroll. "The Female World of Love and Ritual: Relations between Women in Nineteenth Century America." In Nancy Cott and E. Pleck, eds. *A Heritage of Her Own*. New York: Touchstone Press, 1979.

——. *Disorderly Conduct.: Visions of Gender in Victorian America*. New York: Knopf, 1986.

——. "Discourses of Subjectivity: The New Woman 1870–1936." In Martin Duberman, et al., eds. *Hidden from History*. London: Penguin, 1991.

Souhami, Diana. *The Trials of Radclyffe Hall*. New York: Doubleday, 1999.

Vicinus, Martha. *Independent Women: Work and Community for Single Women, 1850–1890*. Chicago: University of Chicago Press, 1985.

White, Chris, ed. *Nineteenth-Century Writings on Homosexuality: A Sourcebook*. London: Routledge, 1999.

The Modern Homosexual and Lesbian Movement (1945–1969)

Bérubé, Alan. *Coming Out Under Fire: The History of Gay Men and Women in World War Two*. New York: Free Press, 1990.

Cory, Donald Webster. *The Lesbian in America*. New York: Citadel Press, 1964.

D'Emilio, John. *Sexual Politics, Sexual Communities: The Making of a Homosexual Minority in the United States, 1940–1970*. Chicago: University of Chicago Press, 1983.

Esterberg, Kristin. "From Accommodation to Liberation: A Social Movement Analysis of Lesbians in the Homophile Movement." *Gender and Society* 8 (1994): 424–443.

Glamuzina, Julie. *Outfront: Lesbian Political Activity in Aotearoa, 1962–1985*. Hamilton, New Zealand: Lesbian Press, 1993.

Kennedy, Elizabeth Lapovsky. "Telling Tales: Oral History and the Construction of Pre-Stonewall Lesbian History." *Radical History Review* 62 (1995): 58–79.

Kennedy, Elizabeth Lapovsky, and Madeline D. Davis. *Boots of Leather, Slippers of Gold: The History of a Lesbian Community*. New York: Routledge, 1993.

Kuda, Marie J. "Chicago Gay and Lesbian History: From Prairie Settlement to WWII." *Outlines* 8, 1 (1964): 25–32.

Newton, Esther. *Cherry Grove, Fire Island: Sixty Years in America's First Gay and Lesbian Town*. Boston: Beacon, 1993.

Power, Lisa. *No Bath but Plenty of Bubbles: An Oral History of the Gay Liberation Front, 1970–1973*. London: Cassell, 1996.

Schiller, Greta, and Andrea Weiss. *Before Stonewall: The Making of the Gay and Lesbian Community*. Tallahassee, Fla.: Naiad Press, 1989.

Smith, Patricia Juliana. *Queer Sixties*. New York: Routledge, 1999.

Teal, Don. *The Gay Militants*. New York: Stein and Day, 1971.

Tobin, Kay, and Randy Wicker. *The Gay Crusaders*. New York: Arno Press, 1975.

Weiss, Andrea, and Greta Schiller. *Before Stonewall: The Making of a Gay and Lesbian Community*. Tallahassee, Fla.: Naiad Press, 1988.

Wolfenden, Sir John, et al. *Report of the Committee on Homosexual Offenses and Prostitution*. Westport, Conn.: Greenwood Press, 1976.

The Contemporary Lesbian and Gay Liberation Movement (1969–)

Abbott, Sidney, and Barbara Love. *Sappho Was a Right-On Woman*. New York: Stein and Day, 1972.

Adam, Barry D. *The Rise of a Gay and Lesbian Movement*. New York: Twayne, 1995.

Adam, Barry D., Jan Willem Duyvendak, and Andre Krouwel, eds. *The Global Emergence of Gay and Lesbian Politics: National Imprints of a Worldwide Movement*. Philadelphia: Temple University Press, 1999.

Aliaga, Juan Vicente. *Identidad y Diferencia: Sobre la Cultura Gay en España*. Barcelona: Editorial Gay y Lesbiana, 1997.

Arguelles, Lourdes, and B. Ruby Rich. "Homosexuality, Homophobia, and Revolution: Notes toward an Understanding of the Cuban Lesbian and Gay Male Experience." *Signs: Journal of Women in Culture and Society* 9 (1984): 683–699.

Auchmuty, Rosemary, Sheila Jeffries, and Elaine Miller. "Lesbian History and Gay Studies: Keeping a Feminist Perspective." *Women's History Review* 1, 1 (1992).

Bannerji, Kaushalya, eds. "Lesbians and Politics." *Canadian Women's Studies* 16, 2 (Spring 1996).

Bastista, Adriana, and Gina Fratti. *Liberación Homosexual*. Mexico: Posada, 1984.

Bawer, Bruce. *A Place at the Table: The Gay Individual in American Society*. New York: Poseiden Press, 1993.

Bell, Laurie. *On Our Own Terms*. Toronto: Coalition for Lesbian and Gay Rights in Ontario, 1991.

Birkby, Phyllis, et al. *Amazon Expedition: A Lesbian-Feminist Anthology*. Washington, D.C.: Times Change Press, 1973.

Botero, Ebel. "Our Sisters and Brothers in Colombia." *Gay Community News* 8, 25 (1981): 12.

Brody, Michel, ed. *Are We There Yet? A Continuing History of Lavender Women, a Chicago Lesbian Newspaper, 1971–1976*. Iowa City, Iowa: Aunt Lute, 1985.

Bunch, Charlotte. *Passionate Politics: Feminist Theory in Action*. New York: St. Martin's Press, 1987.

Bunch, Charlotte, and Nancy Myron, eds. *Lesbianism and the Women's Movement*. Baltimore: Diana Press, 1975.

Button, James W., Barbara Rienzo, and Kenneth Wald. *Private Lives, Public Conflicts*. Washington, D.C.: CQ Press, 1997.

Catalano, Donald, and Richard Steinman. "Eastern European Gay Groups Meet." *Gay Community News* 15, 42 (1988): 4.

Chauvin, Lucien. "Organizing Gay Men and Lesbians in Peru." *Gay Community News* 8, 18 (1980): 7.

Chesser, Lucy. "Australasian Lesbian Movement, 'Claudia's Group', and Lynx: 'Non-Political' Lesbian Organisation in Melbourne, 1969–1980." *Hecate* 22, 1 (1996): 69–91.

Clapham, A., and C. Waadijk, eds. *Homosexuality—A European Community Issue*. Dordrecht, Netherlands: Nijhoff, 1993.

Combahee River Collective. *The Combahee River Collective Statement: Black Feminist Organizing in the Seventies and Eighties*. New York: Kitchen Table Women of Color Press, 1986.

Deichter, David, ed. *Over the Rainbow: Lesbian and Gay Politics in America since Stonewall*. London: Boxtree, 1995.

——. *The Question of Equality: Lesbian and Gay Politics in America since Stonewall*. New York: Simon and Schuster, 1995.

D'Emilio, John. *Sexual Politics, Sexual Communities*. Chicago: University of Chicago Press, 1983.

Duberman, Martin. *About Time*. New York: Meridian, 1991.

——. *Stonewall*. New York: Dutton, 1993.

Echols, Alice. *Daring to Be Bad*. Minneapolis: University of Minnesota Press, 1989.

Elshtain, Jean Bethke. "Homosexual Politics." *Salmagundi* 58–59 (1982–83): 252.

Essig, Laurie. *Queer in Russia: A Story of Sex, Self, and the Other.* Durham, N.C.: Duke University Press, 1999.

Fernandes, Marisa. *Lésbicas no Brasil: contribuição para avaliação da década da mulher 1985/1995*. São Paolo, Brazil: Coletivo de Feministas Lésbicas, 1994.

Fernbach, David. *The Rise and Fall of the GLF.* London: LSE Gay Culture Society, 1973.

Freeman, Mark, and Michael Ward. "Defending Gay Rights." *Radical America* 13, 4 (1979): 11.

Front Homosexuel d'Action Révolutionnaire. *Rapport contre la Norm alité*. Paris: Éditions Champs Libre, 1971.

Fuskova, Ilse, and Claudina Marek. *Mujeres que se Aman*. Buenos Aires: Sudamericana, 1995.

Galloway, Bruce, ed. *Prejudice and Pride: Discrimination against Gay People in Modern Britain*. Boston: Kegan Paul, 1984.

Gevisser, Mark, and Edwin Cameron, eds. *Defiant Desire: Gay and Lesbian Lives in South Africa.* Johannesburg: Ravan Press, 1994.

Goodman, Gerre, et al. *No Turning Back: Lesbian and Gay Liberation for the '80s.* Philadelphia: New Society, 1983.

Harne, Lynne, and Elaine Miller, eds. *All the Rage: Reasserting Radical Lesbian Feminism.* London: Women's Press, 1996.

Hawthorne, Susan. "The History of the Contemporary Australian Women's Movement." *Journal of Australian Lesbian Feminist Studies* 2, 1 (1992): 71–79.

Healey, Emma, and Angela Mason, eds. *Stonewall Twenty-Five: The Making of the Lesbian and Gay in Britain.* London: Virago Press, 1994.

Hendriks, Aart, Rob Tielmand, and Evert van der Veen, eds. *The Third Pink Book: A Global View of Lesbian and Gay Liberation and Oppression.* Buffalo, N.Y.: Prometheus, 1993.

Herman, Didi. *Rights of Passage: Struggles for Lesbian and Gay Legal Equality.* Toronto: University of Toronto Press, 1994.

Herman, Didi, and Carl Stychin, eds. *Legal Inversions: Lesbians, Gay Men, and the Politics of Law.* Philadelphia: Temple University Press, 1996.

Herzog, Mark. *The Lavender Vote: Lesbians, Gay Men, and Bisexuals in American Politics.* New York: New York University Press, 1996.

Hollibaugh, Amber L. *My Dangerous Desires: A Queer Girl Dreaming Her Way Home.* Durham, N.C.: Duke University Press, 2000.

International Lesbian and Gay Association. *ILGA Pink Book.* Utrecht: Interfacultaire Werkgroep Homostudies, Rijksuniversiteit Utrecht, 1988– .

Irish Council for Civil Liberties. *Equality Now for Lesbians and Gay Men.* Dublin: Irish Council for Civil Liberties, 1990.

Johnston, Jill. *The Lesbian Nation.* New York: Touchstone, 1973.

Kennedy, Elizabeth, and Madeline D. Davis. *Boots of Leather, Slippers of Gold: The History of a Lesbian Community.* New York: Routledge, 1993.

Kirk, Marshall, and Hunter Madsen. *After the Ball: How America Will Conquer Its Fear and Hatred of Gays in the 1990s.* New York: Doubleday, 1989.

Kitzinger, Celia. *The Social Construction of Lesbianism.* London: Sage, 1987.

Koedt, Anne, Ellen Levine, and Anita Rapone, eds. *Radical Feminism.* New York: Quadrangle, 1973.

Kohn Loncarica, Alfredo, Argentino J. Landaburu, and Elena Pennini. "Cecilia Grierson y el Primer Congreso Femenino Internacional." *Revista Todo es Historia* 64 (1986): 62–67.

Kyper, John. "Organizing in Mexico." *Gay Community News* 7, 8 (1979): 10.

Las Entendidas. *Memoria de un Encuentro Inolvidable: Segundo Encuentro Lesbico-Feminista de America Latina y el Caribe.* San Jose, Costa Rica: Imprenta Carcemo, 1991.

Lemke, Jurgen. *Gay Voices from East Germany.* Translated by Steven Stoltenberg, et al. Bloomington: Indiana University Press, 1991.

Leong, Russell, ed. *Asian American Sexualities: Dimensions of the Gay and Lesbian Experience.* New York: Routledge, 1996.

Lesbian and Gay Media Advocates. *Talk Back: The Gay Person's Guide to the Media Action.* Boston: Alyson, 1982.

Lesbian History Group. *Not a Passing Phase.* London: Women's Press, 1996.

Lorde, Audre. *Sister Outsider: Essays and Speeches by Audre Lorde.* Freedom, Calif.: Crossing Press, 1984.

Marotta, Toby. *The Politics of Homosexuality.* Boston: Houghton Mifflin, 1981.

Martel, Frédéric. *Le Rose et le Noir: Les Homosexuels en France depuis 1968.* Paris: Seuil, 1996.

Martin, Del, and Phyllis Lyon. *Lesbian/Woman.* San Francisco: Glide, 1972.

Mitchell, Pam, ed. *Pink Triangles: Radical Perspectives on Gay Liberation.* Boston: Alyson, 1980.

Myron, Nancy, and Charlotte Bunch. *Lesbianism and the Women's Movement.* Baltimore: Diana Press, 1975.

Neemyn, Brett, ed. *Creating a Place for Ourselves: Lesbian, Gay, and Bisexual Community Histories.* New York: Routledge, 1997.

Neild, Suzanne, and Rosalind Pearson. *Women Like Us.* London: Women's Press. 1992.

Nestle, Joan. *A Restricted Country.* Ithaca, N.Y.: Firebrand, 1987.

Phelan, Shane. "(Be) Coming Out: Lesbian Identity and Politics." *Signs: Journal of Women in Culture and Society* 18, 4 (1993): 764–790.

Prada, Danda, ed. *Women of South America.* Munich: Frauenoffensive, 1993.

Ramos, Juanita, ed. *Compañeras: Latina Lesbians (An Anthology).* New York: Latina Lesbian History Project, 1987.

Ratti, Rakesh, ed. *A Lotus of Another Color: An Unfolding of the South Asian Gay and Lesbian Experience.* Boston: Alyson, 1993.

Rayside, David. *On the Fringe: Gays and Lesbians in Politics.* Ithaca, N.Y.: Cornell University Press, 1998.

Reinfelder, Monika. *Amazon to Zami: Towards a Global Lesbian Feminism.* London: Cassell, 1997.

Rich, Adrienne. "Compulsory Heterosexuality and Lesbian Existence." *Signs: Journal of Women in Culture and Society* 5, 4 (1980): 631–660.

Rose, Kieran. *Diverse Communities: The Evolution of Lesbian and Gay Politics in Ireland.* Cork, Ireland: Cork University Press, 1994.

Ross, Becki. *The House That Jill Built: A Lesbian Nation in Formation.* Toronto: University of Toronto Press, 1995.

Rutledge, Leigh W. *The Gay Decades: From Stonewall to the Present: The People and Events That Shaped Gay Lives.* New York: Penguin-Plume, 1992.

Schulman, Sarah. *The Lesbian Avenger Handbook: A Handy Guide to Homemade Revolution.* New York: S. Schulman, 1993.

———. *My American History: Lesbian and Gay Life during the Reagan/Bush Years*. New York: Routledge, 1994.

Stein, Edward, ed. *Forms of Desire: Sexual Orientation and the Social Constructionist Controversy*. New York: Garland Press, 1990.

Stone, Sharon Dale, ed. *Lesbians in Canada*. Toronto: Between the Lines, 1990.

Streitmatter, Rodger. *Unspeakable: The Rise of the Gay and Lesbian Press in America*. Boston: Faber and Faber, 1995.

Taylor, Verta, and Leila Rupp. "Women's Culture and Lesbian Feminist Activism: A Reconsideration of Cultural Feminism." *Signs: Journal of Women in Culture and Society* 19, 1 (1988): 32–61.

Teal, Donn. *The Gay Militants*. New York: Stein and Day, 1971.

Thompson, Denise. *Flaws in the Social Fabric: Homosexuals and Society in Sydney*. Sydney, Australia: Allen and Unwin, 1985.

Thompson, Martha. "Comments on Rich's 'Compulsory Heterosexuality and Lesbian Existence.'" *Signs: Journal of Women in Culture and Society* 6, 4 (1981): 790–794.

Tratnik, Suzana, and Nataša S. Segan. *Zbornik o Lezbičnem Gibanju na Slovenskem 1984–5*. Ljubljana, Slovenia: ŠKUC-Lambda, 1995.

Trujillo, Carla, ed. *Chicana Lesbians: The Girls Our Mothers Warned Us About*. Berkeley, Calif.: Third Woman Press, 1991.

Whisman, Vera. *Queer by Choice*. New York: Routledge, 1996.

Williams, Susan. *Lesbianism: A Socialist Feminist Perspective*. Seattle, Wash.: Radical Women, 1973.

Wolf, Deborah G. *The Lesbian Community*. Berkeley: University of California Press, 1980.

Woo, Merle. *Yellow Woman Speaks*. Seattle, Wash.: Radical Women Publications, 1986.

8. Lesbian Studies

Abelove, Henry, Michele Barale, and David M. Halperin, eds. *Lesbian and Gay Studies Reader*. New York: Routledge, 1993.

Cruikshank, Margaret, ed. *Lesbian Studies: Present and Future*. Old Westbury, N.Y.: Feminist Press, 1982.

De Lauretis, Teresa. "Queer Theory: Lesbian and Gay Studies: An Introduction." *Differences: A Journal of Feminist Cultural Studies* 3 (Summer 1991): iii–xviii.

Duberman, Martin, ed. *Queer World: The Center for Lesbian and Gay Studies Reader*. New York: New York University Press, 1997.

Medhurst, Andy, and Sally R. Mint. *Lesbian and Gay Studies: A Critical Introduction.* London: Cassell Academic, 1997.

Moran, Leslie J. *Legal Queeries: Lesbian, Gay and Transgender Legal Studies.* London: Cassell Academic, 1998.

Nardi, Peter M., and Beth E. Schneider. *Social Perspectives in Lesbian and Gay Studies: A Reader.* New York: Routledge, 1998.

Ristock, Janice, and Catherine G. Taylor. *Inside the Academy and Out: Lesbian/Gay/Queer Studies and Social Action.* Toronto: University of Toronto Press, 1998.

Robeson, Ruthann. *Sappho Goes to Law School: Fragments in Lesbian Legal Theory.* New York: Columbia University Press, 1998.

Rothblum, Esther D., ed. *Classics in Lesbian Studies.* New York: Harrington Park Press, 1997.

Vicinus, Martha, ed. *Lesbian Subjects: A Feminist Studies Reader.* Bloomington: Indiana University Press, 1996.

Wilton, Tamsin. *Lesbian Studies: Setting an Agenda.* New York: Routledge, 1995.

Zimmerman, Bonnie, and Toni A. H. McNaron, eds. *The New Lesbian Studies: Into the Twenty-First Century.* New York: Feminist Press at the City University of New York, 1996.

9. Lesbian Culture

General

Allen, P. G. *The Sacred Hoop: Recovering the Feminine in American Indian Traditions.* Boston: Beacon, 1986.

Cheney, Joyce, ed. *Lesbian Land.* Minneapolis: Word Weavers, 1985.

Chou, Wah-Shan. *Tongzhi: Politics of Same-Sex Erotocism in Chinese Societies.* New York: Harrington Park Press, 2000.

Comas-Díaz, Lillian, and Beverly Greene, eds. *Women of Color.* New York: Guilford, 1994.

Cornwell, A. *Black Lesbian in White America.* Tallahassee, Fla.: Naiad Press, 1983.

Cottingham, Laura. *Lesbians Are So Chic . . . : . . . That We Are Not Really Lesbians at All.* London: Cassell Academic, 1996.

Creekmur, Corey, and Alexander Doty, eds. *Out in Culture: Gay, Lesbian, and Queer Essays on Popular Culture.* Durham, N.C.: Duke University Press, 1995.

Dunsford, Cathie, and Susan Hawthorne, eds. *Exploding Frangipani.* Auckland, New Zealand: New Women's Press, 1991.

Eng, David L., and Alice Y. Hom. *Q & A: Queer in Asian America*. Philadelphia: Temple University Press, 1998.

Essig, Laurie. *Queer in Russia: A Story of Sex, Self, and the Other*. Durham, N.C.: Duke University Press, 1999.

Felner, Julie. "Lipstick and Lesbians" *Ms. Magazine* 6, 3 (November/December 1995): 85.

Gevisser, Mark, and Edwin Cameron. *Defiant Desire: Gay and Lesbian Lives in South Africa*. New York: Routledge, 1995.

Giallombardo, Rose. *Society of Women: A Study of a Woman's Prison*. New York: Wiley, 1966.

Gibbs, J., and S. Bennett, eds. *Top Ranking: A Collection of Articles on Racism and Classism in the Lesbian Community*. Brooklyn, N.Y.: February 3rd Press, 1980.

Gibbs, Liz, ed. *Daring to Dissent: Lesbian Culture from Margin to Mainstream*. New York: Cassell, 1994.

Hoagland, Sarah Lucia, and Julia Penelope, eds. *For Lesbians Only: A Separatist Anthology*. London: Onlywomen, 1988.

Hark, Sabine, ed. *Grenzen Lesbischer Identitäeten*. Berlin: Querverlag, 1996.

Inness, Sherrie. *The Lesbian Menace: Ideology, Identity and the Representation of Lesbian Life*. Amherst: University of Massachusetts Press, 1997.

Jay, Karla, ed. *Dyke Lives: From Growing Up to Growing Old, A Celebration of the Lesbian Experience*. New York: Basic, 1995.

Lewin, Ellen. *Inventing Lesbian Cultures in America*. Boston: Beacon, 1996.

Manahan, Nancy. *On My Honor: Lesbians Reflect on their Scouting Experience*. Northboro, Mass.: Madwoman, 1997.

Marcus, Eric. *Is It a Choice?: Answers to 300 of the Most Frequently Asked Questions about Gays and Lesbians*. San Francisco: Harper, 1993.

Mollenkott, Virginia R. *Sensuous Spirituality: Out from Fundamentalism*. New York: Crossroad Press, 1992.

Munoz, Jose Esteban. *Disidentifications: Queers of Color and the Performance of Politics*. Minneapolis: University of Minnesota Press, 1999.

Parikas, Dodo. Öppenhetens Betydelse: *Homo-och bisexuella I Sverige mellan perversitet och dygdemönster*. Stockholm: Carlsson Bok förlag, 1995.

Patton, Cindy, and Benigno Sanchez-Eppler, eds. *Queer Diasporas*. Durham, N.C.: Duke University Press, 2000.

Ramos, Juanita, ed. *Compañeras: Latina Lesbians, an Anthology*. Albany, N.Y.: Kitchen Table Women of Color Press, 1983.

——, ed. *Compañeros: Latina Lesbians*. New York: Latina Lesbian History Project, 1987.

Ratti, Rakesh, ed. *A Lotus of Another Color: An Unfolding of the South Asian Gay and Lesbian Experience*. Boston: Alyson, 1993.

Somerville, Siobhan B. *Queering the Color Line: Race and the Invention of Homosexuality in American Culture.* Durham, N.C.: Duke University Press, 2000.

Schaefer, Claudia. *Danger Zones: Homosexuality, National Identity, and Mexican Culture.* Tucson: University of Arizona Press, 1996.

Shugar, Dana R. *Separatism and Women's Community.* Lincoln: University of Nebraska Press, 1995.

Stevens, Robin, ed. *Girlfriend Number One: Lesbian Life in the 90s.* San Francisco: Cleis, 1994.

Stone, S., ed. *Lesbians in Canada.* Toronto: Between the Lines, 1990.

Thadani, Giti. *Sakhiyani: Lesbian Desire in Ancient and Modern India.* London: Cassell Academic, 1996.

Tremain, Shelley, ed. *Pushing the Limits: Disabled Dykes Produce Culture.* London: Women's Press, 1996.

Trujillo, Carla, ed. *Chicana Lesbians: The Girls Our Mothers Warned Us About.* Berkeley, Calif.: Third World Press, 1991.

Walser, Lee. *Between Sodom and Eden.* New York: Columbia University Press, 2000.

Ward, David A., and Gene Kassebaum. *Women's Prison: Sex and Social Structure.* Chicago: Aldine, 1965.

Weinstock, Jacqueline, and Esther Rothblum, eds. *Lesbians and Friendships: Ourselves and Each Other.* New York: New York University Press, 1996.

Aging

Adelman, M., ed. *Longtime Passing: Lives of Older Lesbians.* Boston: Alyson, 1986.

Almvig, C. *The Invisible Minority: Aging and Lesbianism.* Utica, N.Y.: Institute of Gerontology, Urical College of Syracuse, 1982.

Kehoe, M. *Lesbians over 60 Speak for Themselves.* New York: Harrington Park Press, 1989.

MacDonald, B., and C. Rich, *Look Me in the Eye.* San Francisco: Spinsters Ink, 1983.

Martin, Del, and Phyllis Lyon. "The Older Lesbian." In Betty Berzon and Robert Leighton, eds. *Positively Gay.* Millbrae, Calif.: Celestrial Arts.

Poor, M. "Older Lesbians." In M. Cruikshank, ed. *Lesbian Studies: Present and Future.* Old Westbury, N.Y.: Feminist Press, 1982.

Sang, B., A. Smith, and J. Warshow, eds. *Lesbians at Midlife: The Creative Transition.* San Francisco: Spinsters Ink, 1991.

Schoenberg, R., R. Goldberg, and D. A. Shore, eds. *With Compassion toward Some.* New York: Harrington Park Press, 1984.

Butch-Femme

Faderman, Lillian. *Odd Girls and Twilight Lovers: A History of Lesbian Life in Twentieth-Century America.* New York: Columbia University Press, 1991.

Halberstam, Judith. *Female Masculinity.* Durham, N.C.: Duke University Press, 1998.

Harris, Laura, and Elizabeth Crocker. *Femme: Feminists, Lesbians and Bad Girls.* New York: Routledge, 1997.

Koertge, Noretta. "Butch Images 1956–86." *Lesbian Ethics* 2 (1986).

Martin, Biddy. *Femininity Played Straight: Gender, Sexuality, Subjectivity.* New York: Routledge, 1997.

Nestle, Joan, ed. *The Persistent Desire: A Femme-Butch Reader.* Boston: Alyson, 1992.

Murray, Sarah. "Dragon Ladies, Draggin' Men: Some Reflections on Gender, Drag, and Homosexual Communities." *Public Culture* 6, 2 (Winter 1994): 343–363.

Coming Out

Darty, T., and S. Potter, eds. *Women-Identified Women.* Palo Alto, Calif.: Mayfield Press, 1984.

Jenseen, Karol L. *Lesbian Epiphanies: Women Coming Out Later in Life.* New York: Harrington Park Press, 1999.

Moore, Lisa C., ed. *Does Your Mama Know? An Anthology of Black Lesbian Coming Out Stories.* Decatur, Ga.: Redbone Press, 1997.

Penelope, Julia, and Susan J. Wolfe, eds. *The Original Coming Out Stories.* Expanded ed. Freedom, Calif.: Crossing Press, 1989.

Drag Kings

Burana, Lily, Roxxie, and Linnea Due, eds. *Dagger: On Butch Women.* Pittsburgh: Cleis Press, 1994.

Chinn, Sarah, and Kris Franklin. "King of the Hill: Changing the Face of Drag—Interview with Dred." In Sally Munt, ed. *Butch-Femme: Inside Lesbian Gender.* London: Cassell, 1998.

Halberstam, Judith. *Female Masculinity.* Durham, N.C.: Duke University Press, 1998.

Halberstam, Judith. "Mackdaddy, Superfly, Rapper: Gender, Race and Masculinity in the Drag King Scene." *Social Text* (Fall 1997): 104–131.

Halberstam, Judith, and Del LaGrace Volcano. *The Drag King Book.* London: Serpent's Tail, 1999.

Kroker, Arthur, and Marilouise Kroker. "Finding the Male within and Taking Him Cruising: Drag King for a Day." In A. Kroker and M. Kroker, eds. *The Last Sex: Feminism and Outlaw Bodies.* New York: St. Martin's Press, 1993.

Sports

Cahn, Susan K. *Coming on Strong: Gender and Sexuality in Twentieth-Century Women's Sport.* New York: Free Press, 1994.

Griffin, Pat. *Strong Women, Deep Closets: Lesbians and Homophobia in Sport.* Champaign, Ill.: Human Kinetics, 1998.

Rogers, Susan Fox. *Sportsdykes: Stories from On and Off the Field.* New York: St. Martin's Press, 1994.

Young, P. D. *Lesbians and Gays and Sports.* New York: Chelsea House, 1995.

10. Contemporary Issues

Academics/Education

Garber, Linda, ed. *Tilting the Tower: Lesbians Teaching Queer Subjects.* New York: Routledge, 1994.

Griffin, Gabriele, and Sonya Andermahr, eds. *Straight Studies Modified: Lesbian Interventions in the Academy.* London: Cassell Academic, 1997.

Gross, Larry, and James D. Woods, eds. *The Columbia Reader on Lesbians and Gay Men in Media, Society, and Politics.* New York: Columbia University Press, 1999.

Herbeck, Karen. *Gay and Lesbian Educators: Personal Freedoms, Public Constraints.* Malden, Mass.: Amethyst, 1997.

Jeffries, Sheila. "The Queer Disappearance of Lesbian Sexuality in the Academy." *Women's Studies International Forum* 17, 5 (1994): 459–472.

Jennings, Kevin, ed. *One Teacher in 10: Gay and Lesbian Educators Tell Their Stories.* Boston: Alyson, 1994.

Khayatt, Madida. *Lesbian Teachers: An Invisible Presence.* Albany: State University of New York Press, 1992.

Kissen, Rita. *The Last Closet: The Real Lives of Lesbian and Gay Teachers.* Portsmouth, N.H.: Heinemann, 1996.

Kitzinger, Celia. "Beyond Boundaries: Lesbians in Academe." In Susanne S. Lie and Virginia O'Leary, eds. *Storming the Tower: Women in the Academic World.* New York: Kogan Page, 1990.

McNaron, Toni A. H. *Poisoned Ivy: Lesbian and Gay Academics Confronting Homophobia.* Philadelphia: Temple University Press, 1997.

Mintz, Beth, and Esther Rothblum, eds. *Lesbians in Academia: Degrees of Freedom.* New York: Routledge, 1997.

National Gay and Lesbian Task Force. *LGBT Campus Organizing.* New York: National Gay and Lesbian Task Force, 1995.

Parmeter, Sarah-Hope, and Irene Reti, eds. *The Lesbian in Front of the Classroom: Writings by Lesbian Teachers.* Santa Cruz, Calif.: Herbooks, 1988.

Spurlin, William, ed. *Lesbian and Gay Studies and the Teaching of English: Positions, Pedagogies, and Cultural Politics.* Urbana, Ill.: National Council of Teachers of English, 2000.

Woog, Dan. *School's Out: The Impact of Gay and Lesbian Issues on America's Schools.* Boston: Alyson, 1995.

Employment

Badgett, Lee. "The Wage Effects of Sexual Orientation Discrimination." *Industrial and Labor Relations Review* 48, 4 (1992): 726–739.

Baxandall, Rosalyn, and Linda Gordon, eds. *America's Working Women: A Documentary History.* New York: Norton, 1995.

Dunne, Gillian. *Lesbian Lifestyles: Women's Work and the Politics of Sexuality.* Toronto: University of Toronto Press, 1996.

Frank, Miriam, and Desma Holcomb. *Pride at Work: Organizing for Lesbian and Gay Rights in Unions.* New York: Lesbian and Gay Labor Network, 1990.

Gluckman, Amy, and Betsey Reed, eds. *Homo Economics: Capitalism, Community, and Lesbian and Gay Life.* New York: Routledge, 1997.

Hunt, Gerald, ed. *Laboring for Rights: Unions and Sexual Diversity across Nations.* Philadelphia: Temple University Press, 1999.

Kohn, Sally. *The Domestic Partnership Organizing Manual for Employee Benefits.* New York: Policy Institute of the National Gay and Lesbian Task Force, 1999.

Krupat, Kitty, and Patrick McCreery, eds. *Out at Work: Building a Gay-Labor Alliance.* Minneapolis: University of Minnesota Press, 2000.

Matthaei, Julie. "The Sexual Division of Labour, Sexuality, and Lesbian/Gay Liberation: Towards a Marxist-Feminist Analysis of Sexuality in U.S. Capitalism." *Review of Radical Political Economics* 27, 2 (1995): 1–37.

Morgan, Kris S., and Laura S. Brown. "Lesbian Career Development, Work Behavior, and Vocational Counseling." *Counseling Psychologist* 19, 2 (1991): 273–291.

Schneider, Beth. "Peril and Promise: Lesbian Workplace Participation." In Laurel Richardson and Verta Taylor, eds. *Feminist Frontiers.* 3d ed. New York: Random House, 1993.

Taylor, Verta and Nicole Rayburn. "Identity Politics as High Risk Activism: Career Consequences for Lesbian, Gay and Bisexual Sociologists." *Social Problems* 42, 2 (1995): 252–273.

Young, Carole. "LESY-Adelaide: An Example of a Lesbian Economy." *Lesbian Ethics* 4, 2 (1991): 62–66.

Health

Black, C. *Double Duty-Gay-Lesbian.* Denver, Colo.: MAC, 1990.

Boston Women's Health Collective. *The New Our Body, Ourselves.* New York: Simon and Schuster, 1992.

Brown, S., D. Connors, and N. Stern, eds. *With the Power of Each Breath: A Disabled Woman's Anthology.* Pittsburgh: Cleis Press, 1985.

Brownworth, Victoria, and Susan Raffo. *Restricted Access: Lesbians on Disability.* Seattle, Wash.: Seal Press, 1999.

Brunner, C. *For Concerned Others of Chemically Dependent Gays and Lesbians.* Minneapolis, Minn.: Hazelden, 1987.

Burch, Beverly. *Other Women.* New York: Columbia University Press, 1997.

Falco, K. *Psychotherapy with Lesbian Clients—Theory into Practice.* New York: Brunner/Mazel, 1990.

Hepburn, C., and B. Gutierrez. *Alive and Well.* Freedom, Calif.: Crossing Press, 1988.

Kominaro, S. *Accepting Ourselves.* San Francisco: Harper, 1989.

Loulan, Joann. *The Lesbian Erotic Dance.* San Francisco: Spinsters Ink, 1990.

Luczak, Raymond, ed. *Eyes of Desire: A Deaf Gay and Lesbian Reader.* Boston: Alyson, 1993.

McDonald, H., and Audrey Steinhorn. *Homosexuality.* New York: Continuum, 1990.

O'Donnell, M., et al. *Lesbian Health Matters!: A Resource Book about Lesbian Health Matters.* Santa Cruz, Calif.: Santa Cruz Women's Health Collective, 1979.

Patty, C., and J. Kelly. *Making It—A Woman's Guide to Sex in the Age of AIDS.* Ithaca, N.Y.: Firebrand, 1990.

Rieder, I., and P. Ruppelt, eds. *AIDS: The Women.* San Francisco: Cleis Press, 1988.

Rosser, Sue V. "Ignored, Overlooked, or Subsumed: Research on Lesbian Health and Health Care." *NWSA Journal* 5, 2 (1993): 183–203.

Rothblum, E., and E. Cole, eds. *Loving Boldly: Issues Facing Lesbians.* New York: Harrington Park Press, 1989.

Saxton, M., and Florence Howe, eds. *With Wings.* New York: Feminist Press, 1987.

Silverstein, C. *Gays, Lesbians, and Their Therapists.* New York: Norton, 1991.
Thompson, Karen, and Julie Andrzejewski. *Why Can't Sharon Kowalsi Come Home?* Duluth, Minn.: Spinsters Ink, 1989.
White, Jocelyn, and Marissa C. Martinez. *The Lesbian Health Book: Caring for Ourselves.* Seattle, Wash.: Seal Press, 1997.
Ziebold, T., and J. Mongeon, eds. "Alcoholism and Homosexuality." *Journal of Homosexuality* 7, 4 (1982).

Human Rights

Dunton, Chris, and Mai Palmberg. *Human Rights and Homosexuality in Southern Africa.* London: Coronet, 1996.
Thomas, Lawrence, and Michael Levin. *Sexual Orientation and Human Rights.* Lanham, Md.: Rowman & Littlefield, 1999.
Rosenbloom, Rachel. *Unspoken Rules: Sexual Orientation and Women's Human Rights.* London: Cassell Academic, 1996.
Wintemut, Robert. *Sexual Orientation and Human Rights: The United States Constitution, the European Convention and the Canadian Charter.* London: Oxford University Press, 1997.

Law and Politics

Achtenbeg, Roberta. *Lesbian and Gay Parenting: A Psychological and Legal Perspective.* San Francisco: National Center for Lesbian Rights, 1987.
———. *Preserving and Protecting the Families of Lesbians and Gay Men.* San Francisco: National Center for Lesbian Rights, 1991.
Adam, Barry, Jan Willem Duyvendak, and Andre Krouwel. *The Global Emergence of Gay and Lesbian Politics: National Imprints of a Worldwide Movement.* Philadelphia: Temple University Press, 1998.
Anderson, Shelley. *Out in the World: International Lesbian Organizing.* Ithaca, N.Y.: Firebrand, 1991.
Arriola, Elvia. "Gendered Inequality: Lesbians, Gays, and Feminist Legal Theory." *Berkeley Women's Law Journal* 9 (1994): 103–143.
Baily, Robert W. *Gay Politics, Urban Politics: Power, Conflict, and Democracy: American Politics into the 21st Century.* New York: Columbia University Press, 1998.
Baird, Robert M., and Stuart Rosenbaum, eds. *Same-Sex Marriage: The Moral and Legal Debate.* Amherst, N.Y.: Prometheus, 1997.
Bamforth, Nicholas. *Sexuality, Morals and Justice: A Theory of Lesbian and Gay Rights and the Law.* London: Cassell Academic, 1996.

Bell, David, and Jon Binnie. *The Sexual Citizen: Queer Politics and Beyond.* London: Polity Press, 2000.

Blasius, Mark. *Gay and Lesbian Politics: Sexuality and the Emergence of a New Ethic.* Philadelphia: Temple University Press, 1995.

———. *Sexual Identities, Queer Politics.* Princeton, N.J.: Princeton University Press, 2001.

Brandt, Eric. *Dangerous Liasons: Blacks, Gays and the Struggle for Equality.* New York: New Press, 1999.

Butler, Judith. *Excitable Speech: A Politics of the Performative.* New York: Routledge, 1997.

Cahill, Sean, and Eric Ludwig. *Courting the Vote: The 2000 Presidential Candidates' Positions on Gay, Lesbian, Bisexual and Transgender Issues.* New York: Policy Institute of the National Gay and Lesbian Task Force, 1999.

Cain, Patrica. "Lesbian Perspective, Lesbian Experience, and the Risk of Essentialism." *Virginia Journal of Social Policy and Law* 2 (1994): 43–73.

———. *Rainbow Rights: The Role of Lawyers and Courts in the Lesbian and Gay Civil Rights Movement.* Boulder, Colo.: Westview, 2000.

Coles, Matthew. *Try This at Home! A Do It Yourself Guide to Winning Lesbian and Gay Civil Rights Policy.* Dexter, Mich.: New Press, 1996.

D'Emilio, John, William B. Turner, and Urvashi Vaid, eds. *Creating Change: Sexuality, Public Policy and Civil Rights.* New York: St. Martin's Press, 2000.

Duffy, D. "Battered Lesbians: Are They Entitled to a Battered Woman Defense?" *Journal of Family Law* 29 (1991): 879–899.

Eaton, Mary. "At the Intersection of Gender and Sexual Orientation: Toward a Lesbian Jurisprudence." *Southern California Review of Law and Women's Studies* 3 (1994): 183–218.

Fuller, Janine, and Stuart Blackley. *Restricted Entry: Censorship on Trial.* Vancouver: Press Gang, 1995.

Gerstmann, Evan. *The Constitutional Underclass: Gays, Lesbians and the Failure of Class-Based Equal Protection.* Chicago: University of Chicago Press, 1999.

Gil de la Madrid, M., ed. *Lesbians Choosing Motherhood: Legal Implications of Donor Insemination.* San Francisco: National Center for Lesbian Rights, 1991.

Grey, Antony. *Speaking Out: Writings on Sex, Law, Politics and Society, 1954–1995.* London: Cassell Academic, 1997.

Groocock, Veronica. *Changing Our Lives: Lesbian Passions, Politics, Priorities.* London: Cassell Academic, 1996.

Harne, Lynne, and Elaine Miller, eds. *All the Rage: Reasserting Radical Lesbian Feminism.* New York: Teachers College Press, 1996.

Harvard Law Review Editors, eds. *Sexual Orientation and the Law.* Cambridge, Mass.: Harvard University Press, 1990.

Herman, Didi. *Rights of Passage: Struggles for Lesbian and Gay Legal Equality.* Toronto: University of Toronto Press, 1994.

——. "A Jurisprudence of One's Own? Ruthann Robson's Lesbian Legal Theory." *Canadian Journal of Women and Law* (1994): 509–522.

Herman, Didi, and Carl Stychin, eds. *Legal Inversions: Lesbians, Gay Men, and the Politics of Law.* Philadelphia: Temple University Press, 1995.

Herzog, Mark. *The Lavender Vote: Lesbians, Gay Men, and Bisexuals in American Electoral Politics.* New York: New York University Press, 1996.

Hitchens, D. *Lesbian Rights Handbook: A Legal Guide to Lesbians.* San Francisco: Lesbian Rights Project, 1982.

——. *Lesbian Mother Litigation Manual.* San Francisco: National Center for Lesbian Rights, 1990.

Kaplan, Morris. *Sexual Justice: Democratic Citizenship and the Politics of Desire.* New York: Routledge, 1997.

Keen, Lisa, and Suzanne Goldberg. *Strangers and the Law: Gay People on Trial.* Ann Arbor: University of Michigan Press, 1998.

Leonard, Arthur S., ed. *Homosexuality and the Constitution.* New York: Garland, 1997.

Maggiore, D., ed. *Lesbians and Child Custody.* New York: Garland, 1992.

Majury, Diana. "Refashioning the Unfashionable: Claiming Lesbian Identities in the Legal Context." *Canadian Journal of Women and the Law* 7 (1994): 286–311.

Mohr, Richard. *Gays/Justice.* New York: Columbia University Press, 1988.

——. *A More Perfect Union: Why Straight America Must Stand Up for Gay Rights.* Boston: Beacon, 1995.

Murphy, Timothy, ed. *Gay Ethics: Controversies in Outing, Civil Rights and Sexual Science.* New York: Haworth Press, 1995.

National Organization for Women (NOW). *Lesbian Rights: A Woman's Issue, A Feminist Issue.* New York: National Organization for Women, 1980.

Nava, Michael, and Robert Davidoff. *Created Equal: Why Gay Rights Matter to America.* New York: St. Martin's Press, 1997.

O'Carroll, Ide, and Eoin Collins, eds. *Lesbian and Gay Visions of Ireland: Towards the Twenty-First Century.* London: Cassell Academic, 1996.

Oliver, Marilyn Tower. *Gay and Lesbian Rights: A Struggle.* Berkeley Heights, N.J.: Enslow, 1998.

People for the American Way. *Hostile Climate: A State-by-State Report on Anti-Gay Activity.* Washington, D.C.: People for the American Way. 1993.

Phelan, Shane. *Identity Politics: Lesbian Feminism and the Limits of Community.* Philadelphia: Temple University Press, 1991.

——. *Getting Specific: Postmodern Lesbian Politics.* Minneapolis: University of Minnesota Press, 1994.

——. *Sexual Stranger: Gays, Lesbians and Dilemmas of Citizenship.* Philadelphia: Temple University Press, 2001.

Policy Institute of the National Gay and Lesbian Task Force. *Capital Gains and Losses 1999.* New York: Policy Institute of the National Gay and Lesbian Task Force, 1999.

Rayside, David. *On the Fringe: Gays and Lesbians in Politics.* Ithaca, N.Y.: Cornell University Press, 1998.

Richards, David. *Women, Gays and the Constitution: The Grounds for Feminism and Gay Rights in Culture and Law.* Chicago: University of Chicago Press, 1998.

——. *Identity and the Case for Gay Rights: Race, Gender, Religion as Analogies.* Chicago: University of Chicago Press, 1999.

Riggle, Ellen, and Barry Tadlock, eds. *Gays and Lesbians in the Democratic Process.* New York: Columbia University Press, 1999.

Rights of Women Lesbian Custody Group. *Lesbian Mothers' Legal Handbook.* London: Women's Press, 1986.

Rimmerman, Craig. *The Politics of Gay Rights.* Chicago: University of Chicago Press, 2000.

Robson, Ruthann. *Lesbian (Out)Law: Survival under the Rule of Law.* Ithaca, N.Y.: Firebrand, 1992.

——. *Sappho Goes to Law School: Fragments in Lesbian Legal Theory.* New York: Columbia University, 1998.

Roliff, Tamara. *Gay Rights.* New York: Greenhaven Press, 1997.

Rubenstein, William B. *Cases and Materials on Sexual Orientation and the Law.* St. Paul, Minn.: West, 1997.

Samar, Vincent. *The Right to Privacy: Gays, Lesbians and the Constitution.* Philadelphia: Temple University Press, 1992.

Silver, Diane. *The New Civil War: The Lesbian and Gay Struggle for Civil Rights.* New York: Franklin Watts, 1997.

Smith, Barbara. *The Truth That Never Hurts: Writings on Race, Gender and Freedom.* New Brunswick, N.J.: Rutgers University Press, 1998.

Smith, Raymond, and Donald Haider-Markel. *Gay and Lesbian Americans and Political Participation: A Reference Handbook.* Santa Barbara, Cal.: ABC-Clio, 2002.

Stychin, Carl, and Shane Phelan, eds. *A Nation by Rights: National Cultures, Sexual Identites and the Discourse of Rights.* Philadelphia: Temple University Press, 1998.

Swan, Wallace. *Gay/Lesbian/Bisexual/Transgender Public Policy Issues: A Citizen's and Administrator's Guide to the New Cultural Struggle.* New York: Haworth Press, 1997.

Tucker, Scott. *Fighting Words: An Open Letter to Queers and Radicals.* London: Cassell Academic, 1996.

van der Meide, Wayne. *Legislating Equality: A Review of Laws Affecting Gay, Lesbian, Bisexual and Transgendered People in the United States.* New York: Policy Institute of the National Gay and Lesbian Task Force, 1999.

Yang, Alan. *From Wrongs to Rights: Public Opinion on Gay and Lesbian Americans Moves Toward Equality.* 1973–1999. New York: Policy Institute of the National Gay and Lesbian Task Force, 1999.

Wilson, Angelina, ed. *A Simple Matter of Justice? Theorising Lesbian and Gay Politics.* London: Cassell, 1995.

Wyland, F. *Motherhood, Lesbianism, and Child Custody.* London: Falling Wall Press, 1977.

Military

Able v. U.S. U.S. Court of Appeals 2nd Circuit 1995 1/3/95 Docket No. 94–6181, 1995.

Bérubé, Alan. *Coming Out under Fire: The History of Gay Men and Women in World War Two.* New York: Free Press, 1990.

Cammermeyer, Margarethe. *Serving in Silence.* New York: Viking, 1994.

Dyer, Kate, ed. *Gays in Uniform: The Pentagon's Secret Reports.* Boston: Alyson, 1990.

Humphrey, Mary Ann. *My Country, My Right to Serve.* New York: HarperCollins, 1990.

Margarethe Cammermeyer v. Les Aspin. No. C92-9422 U.S. District Court, Western District of Washington, Seattle Div. 850 F. Supp. 910 (QRD).

Meinhold v. U.S. DoD No 93-56354 U.S. Court of Appeals, Ninth Circuit, 1994 U.S. App. Lexis 23705 (QRD).

National Defense Research Institute (RAND), *Sexual Orientation and U.S. Military Policy.* (MR-323-OSD) (1993).

Rimmerman, Craig, ed. *Gay Rights, Military Wrongs: Political Perspectives on Lesbians and Gays in the Military.* New York: Garland, 1996.

Shilts, Randy. *Conduct Unbecoming: Lesbians and Gays in the U.S. Military: Vietnam to the Persian Gulf.* New York: St. Martin's Press, 1993.

Steffan v. Aspin. No. 91-5409 U.S. Court of Appeals, Nov 16, 1993 (QRD).

Steffan v. Perry. U.S. Court of Appeals, Dec 1994 U.S. App Lexis 33045 (QRD).

Wolinsky, Marc, and Kenneth Sherrill, eds. *Gays and the Military.* Princeton, N.J.: Princeton University Press, 1993.

Outing

Gross, Larry. *Contested Closets: The Politics and Ethics of Outing.* Minneapolis: University of Minnesota Press, 1993.

Johansson, Warren, and William Percy. *Outing: Shattering the Conspiracy of Silence.* New York: Haworth Press, 1994.

Signorile, Michelangelo. *Queer in America: Sex, the Media, and the Closets of Power.* New York: Random House, 1993.

Religion

Alpert, Rebecca. *Like Bread on the Seder Plate: Jewish Lesbians and the Transformations of Tradition.* New York: Columbia University Press, 1997.

Beck, Evelyn T., ed. *Nice Jewish Girls: A Lesbian Anthology.* Boston: Beacon, 1989.

Brooten, Bernadette. *Love between Women: Early Christian Responses to Female Homoeroticism.* Chicago: University of Chicago Press, 1996.

Bull, Chris, and John Gallagher. *Perfect Enemies.* Madison, Ala.: Madison Books, 2001.

Connor, Randy, David H. Sparks, and Mariya Sparks. *Cassell's Encyclopedia of Queer Myth, Symbol, and Spirit: Gay, Lesbian, Bisexual, and Transgender Lore.* London: Cassell, 1997.

Curb, Rosemary, and Nancy Manahan, eds. *Lesbian Nuns: Breaking Silence.* Tallahassee, Fla.: Naiad Press, 1985.

Moore, Tracy, ed. *Lesbiot: Israeli Lesbians Talk about Sexuality, Feminism, Judaism, and Their Lives.* London: Cassell, 1995.

Murray, Stephen O., and Will Roscoe, eds. *Islamic Sexualities: Culture, History, and Literature.* New York: New York University Press, 1997.

Nugent, Robert, ed. *A Challenge to Love: Gay and Lesbian Catholics in the Church.* New York: Crossroad, 1987.

Wilson, Nancy. *Our Tribe: Queer Folks, God, Jesus, and the Bible.* San Francisco: Harper San Francisco, 1995.

Zanotti, Barbara, ed. *A Faith of One's Own: Explorations by Catholic Lesbians.* Trumansburg, N.Y.: Crossing Press, 1986.

Sex Wars and Practices

Atkins, Dawn. *Lesbian Sex Scandals: Sexual Practices, Identities and Politics.* New York: Harrington Park Press, 1998.

Brittain, Vera. *Radclyffe Hall: A Case of Obscenity?* South Brunswick, N.J.: A. S. Barnes, 1969.

Calfia, Pat. "Feminism and Sadomasochism." *Heresies* 12 (1981).

——. *Sapphristy: The Book of Lesbian Sexuality.* Tallahassee, Fla.: Naiad Press, 1988.

——. *Macho Sluts.* Boston: Alyson, 1989.

Creet, Julia. "Daughters of the Movement: The Psychodynamics of Lesbian S/M Fantasy." *Differences: A Journal of Feminist Cultural Studies* 3, 2 (Summer 1991): 135–159.

Daly, Meg. *Surface Tensions: Love, Sex, and Politics between Lesbians and Straight Women.* New York: Touchstone, 1996.

Dugan, Lisa, and Nan Hunter. *Sex Wars.* New York: Routledge, 1995.

Foster, Thomas, Carol Siegel, and Ellen Berry, eds. *Sex Positives?: The Cultural Politics of Dissident Sexualities.* New York: New York University Press, 1997.

Foucault, Michel. *The History of Sexuality.* London: Allen Lane, 1978.

Healy, Emma. *Lesbian Sex Wars.* London: Virago, 1996.

Hollibaugh, Amber L. *My Dangerous Desires: A Queer Girl Dreaming Her Way Home.* Durham, N.C.: Duke University Press, 2000.

Jay, Karla. *Lesbian Erotics.* New York: New York University Press, 1995.

Jeffries, Sheila. *The Spinster and Her Enemies: Feminism and Sexuality 1880–1930.* London: Pandora, 1985.

———. *Anticlimax: A Feminist Perspective on the Sexual Revolution.* London: Women's Press, 1990.

———. *The Lesbian Heresy: A Feminist Perspective on the Lesbian Sexual Revolution.* North Melbourne, Australia: Spinifex Press, 1993.

Linden, Robin, et al., eds. *Against Sadomasochism.* Palo Alto, Calif.: Frog In the Well Press, 1982.

Loulan, JoAnn. *Lesbian Sex.* San Francisco: Spinsters Ink, 1984.

———. *The Lesbian Erotic Dance.* San Francisco: Spinsters Ink, 1990.

MacKinnon, Catherine A. *Only Words.* Cambridge, Mass.: Harvard University Press, 1993.

Martindale, Kathleen. *Un/Popular Culture: Lesbian Writing after the Sex Wars.* Albany: State University of New York Press, 1997.

Merck, Mandy. *Perversions: Deviant Readings.* New York: Routledge, 1993.

Roof, Judith, Larry Gross, and Lillian Faderman, eds. *A Lure of Knowledge: Lesbian Sexuality and Theory.* New York: Columbia University Press, 1993.

Samois. *Coming to Power: Writings and Graphics on Lesbian S/M.* 3d ed. Boston: Alyson, 1987.

Snitow, Ann, Christine Stansell, and Sharon Thompson. *Powers of Desire: The Politics of Sexuality.* New York: Monthly Review Press, 1983.

Stewart, Susan. *Drawing the Line: Lesbian Sexual Politics on the Wall.* Vancouver: Press Gang, 1991.

Vance, Carole S., ed. *Pleasure and Danger.* New York: Pandora, 1992.

Violence/Homophobia

Black, Allida M. "Perverting the Diagnosis: The Lesbian and the Scientific Basis of Stigma." *Historical Reflections* 20 (1994): 201–216.

Brenner, Claudia, and Hanna Ashley. *Eight Bullets: One Woman's Story of Surviving Anti-Gay Violence.* New York: Firebrand, 1995.

Comstock, Gary. *Violence against Lesbians and Gay Men.* New York: Columbia University Press, 1991.

Fone, Bryon. *Homophobia: A History.* New York: Metropolitian, 1999.

Herek, Gregory M., and Kevin Berrill. *Hate Crimes: Confronting Violence against Lesbians and Gay Men.* Newbury Park, Calif.: Sage, 1992.

Hilton, Bruce. *Can Homophobia Be Cured? Wrestling with Questions That Challenge the Church.* Nashville: Abington Press: 1992.

Jenness, Valerie, and Kendal Broad. *Hate Crimes: New Social Movements and the Politics of Violence.* New York: Aldine de Gruyter, 1997.

Kirk, M., and H. Madsen *After the Ball—How America Will Conquer Its Fear and Hatred of Gays in the 90s.* New York: Plume, 1989.

Russell, Glenda. *Voted Out: The Psychological Consequences of Anti-Gay Politics.* New York: New York University Press, 2000.

Simpson, R. *From the Closets to the Courts.* London: Penguin, 1976.

Sloan, Lacey, and Nora Gustavsson, eds. *Violence and Social Injustice against Lesbians Gays and Bisexuals.* Binghamton, N.Y.: Haworth Press, 1998.

Tigert, Leanne McCall. *Coming Out through Fire: Surviving the Trauma of Homophobia.* Cleveland: United Church Press, 1999.

Violence/Lesbian Battering

Comstock, Gary. *Violence against Lesbians and Gay Men.* New York: Columbia University Press, 1991.

Duffy, D. "Battered Lesbians: Are They Entitled to a Battered Woman Defense?" *Journal of Family Law* 29 (1991): 879–899.

Hunter, J. "Violence against Lesbian and Gay Youth." *Journal of Interpersonal Violence* 5, 3 (1990): 295–300.

The Lesbian Caucus. *Voices of Battered Lesbians.* Boston: Massachusetts Coalition of Battered Women, 1990.

Lie, G., and S. Gentlewarrier. "Intimate Violence in Lesbian Relationships: Discussions of Survey Findings and Pratice Implications." *Journal of Social Service Research* 15, 1–2, (1991): 41–59.

Lobel, Kerry. *Naming the Violence: Speaking Out about Lesbian Battering.* New York: Seal Press, 1986.

Youth/Families

Ali, Turan, et al., eds. *We Are Family: Testimonies of Lesbian and Gay Parents.* London: Cassell Academic, 1996.

Alyson, Sasha, ed., *Young, Gay and Proud!* 3d ed. Boston: Alyson, 1991.

Arnup, Katherine. *Lesbian Parenting.* New York: Firebrand, 1987.

Benkov, Laura. *Reinventing the Family: The Emerging Story of Lesbian and Gay Parents.* New York: Crown, 1994.

Bernstein, Mary, and Renate Reimann, eds. *Queer Families, Queer Politics.* New York: Columbia University Press, 2001.

Bozett, Frederick W., and Marvin Sussman, eds. *Homosexuality and Family Relations.* New York: Harrington Park Press, 1990.

Calhoun, Chesire. *Feminism, the Family, and the Poitics of the Closet: Lesbian and Gay Displacement.* London: Oxford University Press, 2000.

Carrington, Christopher. *No Place Like Home: Relationships and Family Life among Lesbians and Gay Men.* Chicago: University of Chicago Press, 1999.

Clunis, D. Merilee, and G. Dorsey Green. *The Lesbian Parenting Book: A Guide to Creating Families and Raising Children.* Seattle, Wash.: Seal Press, 1995.

Corley, Rip. *The Final Closet: The Gay Parents' Guide for Coming Out to Their Children.* Miami, Fla.: Editech Press, 1990.

Ettelbrick, Paula L. "Wedlock Alert: A Comment on Lesbian and Gay Family Recognition." *Journal of Law and Policy* 5, 1 (1996): 107.

Griffin, Kate, and Lisa Mulholland, eds. *Lesbian Motherhood in Europe.* London: Cassell Academic, 1997.

Heron, Ann, ed., *One Teenager in Ten: Writings by Gay and Lesbian Youth.* Boston: Alyson, 1983.

Jagger, Gill, and Caroline Wright. *Changing Family Values: Feminist Perspectives.* New York: Harrington Park Press, 1999.

Kendell, Kate, ed. *Lesbians Choosing Motherhood: Legal Implications of Alternative Insemination and Reproductive Technologies.* San Francisco: National Center for Lesbian Rights, 1996.

Lehr, Valerie. *Queer Family Values: Debunking the Myth of the Nuclear Family.* Philadelphia: Temple University Press, 1999.

Lesbian Mother Litigation Manual. 3d ed. San Francisco: National Center for Lesbian Rights, 1996.

Lewin, Ellen. *Recognizing Ourselves: Ceremonies of Lesbian and Gay Commitment.* New York: Columbia University Press, 1999.

Maggiore, D., ed. *Lesbians and Child Custody.* New York: Garland, 1992.

Mallon, Gerald P. *We Don't Exactly Get the Welcome Wagon: The Experiences of Gay and Lesbian Adolescents in Child Welfare Systems.* New York: Columbia University Press, 1998.

Moraga, Cherie. *Waiting in the Wings: Portrait of a Queer Motherhood.* Ithaca, N.Y.: Firebrand, 1997.

Patterson, Charlotte, ed. *Lesbian, Gay and Bisexual Identities in Families: Psychological Perspectives.* New York: Oxford University Press, 1998.

Pies, C. *Considering Parenthood: A Workbook for Lesbians.* San Francisco: Spinsters Ink, 1985.

Pollack, Sandra, and J. Vaughn, eds. *Politics of the Heart: A Lesbian Parenting Anthology.* Ithaca, N.Y.: Firebrand, 1987.

Rafkin, Louise. *Gay and Lesbian Couples and Parenting.* New York: Chelsea House, 1999.

——, ed. *Different Daughters: A Book by Mothers of Lesbians.* San Francisco: Cleis Press, 1987.

Reed, Rita. *Growing Up Gay: The Sorrows and Joys of Gay and Lesbian Adolescence.* New York: W.W. Norton, 1997.

Saphira, M. *Amazon Mothers.* Ponsonby, New Zealand: Papers and Books, 1984.

Shapiro, Julie. "Custody and ConduConn.: How the Law Fails Lesbian and Gay Parents and their Children." *Indiana Law Journal* 71 (1996): 623.

Sinclair, Andrew. "A Conservative Case for Gay Marriage." *The New Republic,* 28 August 1989.

Singer, Bennett, ed. *Growing Up Gay/Lesbian.* New York: Norton, 1994.

Thompson, Julie. *Mommy Queerest: Contemporary Rhetoric of Lesbian Maternal Identity.* Amherst: University of Massachusetts Press, 2002.

Weston, Kath. *Families We Choose: Lesbians, Gays, Kinship.* New York: Columbia University Press, 1991.

Whitlock, K. *Bridges of Respect: Creating Support for Lesbian and Gay Youth.* Philadelphia: American Friends Service Committee, 1988.

11. The Religous Right

Bransford, Stephen. *Gay Politics vs. Colorado and America: The Inside Story of Amendment 2.* Cascade, Calif.: Sardus Press, 1994.

Bull, Chris, and John Gallagher. *Perfect Enemies: The Religious Right, the Gay Movement, and the Politics of the 1990s.* New York: Crown, 1996.

Goldstein, Richard. *The Attack Queers: Liberal Society and the Gay Right.* London: Verso, 2002.

Herman, Didi. *The Anti-Gay Agenda: Orthodox Visions and the Christian Right.* Chicago: University of Chicago Press, 1997.

National Gay and Lesbian Task Force, Political Research Associates, and Equal Partners in Faith. *Calculated Compassion: How the Ex-Gay Movement Serves the Right's Attack on Democracy.* New York: National Gay and Lesbian Task Force, 1998.

Pharr, Suzanne. *In the Time of the Right: Reflections on Liberation.* Little Rock, Ark.: Women's Project, 1996.

Smith, Anna Marie. *New Right Discourse on Race and Sexuality: Britain 1968–1990.* Cambridge: Cambridge University Press, 1994.

Stein, Arlene. *The Stranger Next Door.* Boston: Beacon, 2001.

12. Queer Theory and Politics

Butler, Judith. *Gender Trouble: Feminism and the Subversion of Identity.* New York: Routledge, 1990.

Foucault, Michel. *The History of Sexuality, vol. 1: An Introduction.* Translated by Robert Hurley. New York: Vintage, 1980.

Jagose, Annamarie. *Queer Theory: An Introduction.* New York: New York University Press, 1996.

Haperin, David. *Saint Foucault; Towards a Gay Hagiography.* New York: Oxford University Press, 1995.

Ingram, Gordon Brent, Anne-Marie Bouthillette, and Yolanda Retter, eds. *Queers in Space: Communities/Public Places/Sites of Resistance.* Seattle, Wash.: Bay Press, 1997.

Kirsch, Max. *Queer Theory and Social Change.* New York: Routledge, 2001.

Phelan, Shane. *Playing with Fire: Queer Politics, Queer Theories.* New York: Routledge, 1997.

Raffo, Susan, ed. *Queerly Classed: Gay Men and Lesbians Write about Class.* Boston: Southend Press, 1997.

Rubin, Gayle. "Thinking Sex: Notes for a Radical Theory of the Politics of Sexuality." In Carole Vance, ed. *Pleasure and Danger: Exploring Female Sexuality.* London: Routledge, 1984.

Sedgewick, Eve Kosofky. *Epistemology of the Closet.* Berkeley: University of California Press, 1990.

Wittig, Monique. *The Straight Mind and Other Essays.* Boston: Beacon, 1992.

13. Periodicals/Journals

The Advocate. Los Angeles: Liberal Publications, September 1967.

Amazon Quarterly. Oakland, Calif. and Somerville, Mass.: Publisher Fall 1972–March 1975 (9 issues).

Australasian Gay and Lesbian Law Journal. Annandale, Australia: The Federation Press, 1993– .

Black Forum. Los Angeles. 1988– .

Black Lesbian Newsletter. San Francisco. 1982– .

Clit 007. Geneva, Switzerland. 1981– .

Color Life: The Lesbian, Gay, Twospirit & Bisexual People of Color Magazine. New York. 1992– .

Coming Out Rage. New York, May 1973 (1).

Cowrie. New York, June 1973–August/September/October 1974 (7).

Critical InQueeries. Australia. 1998– .

Curves (Formerly *Deneuve*). San Francisco. 1996– .

Desperate Living. Baltimore. May/June 1973–Winter 1977 (7).

Diversity: The Lesbian Rag. Vancouver. 1988– .

Dyke: A Quarterly. New York, Winter 1975–1976–Summer 1978 (6).

Dykes and Gorgons. Berkeley, Calif., May/June 1973 (1).

Echo of Sappho. Brooklyn, N.Y., May/June 1973 (1).

Feminary. Chapel Hill, N.C., Spring 1978–vol. 12, no. 1, 1982 (8).

Focus. Boston and Cambridge, Mass., March 1971–November/December 1982 (112).

Furies. Washington, D.C., January 1972–May/June 1973 (10).

The Gay and Lesbian Review Worldwide. (Formerly *The Harvard Gay and Lesbian Review.* Cambridge, Mass., 1994–1999). Cambridge, Mass. 2000.

Gay Community News. Boston. 1973–1992; 1994–1999.

Gay Perspectives. Sydney, Australia. 1992– .

Girlfriends. Halfmoon Bay, Calif. 1994– .

GLAADnotes. Los Angeles. 1999– .

GLQ: A Journal of Lesbian and Gay Studies. Yverden, Switzerland. 1993– .

GLQ. Durham, N.C. 1994– .

Handbuch zu Lesbischen und Schwulen Studien in der Schweiz. Zurich, Switzerland. 1996– .

Homophile Action League Newsletter. Philadelphia. November 1968–April 1971 (20).

Journal of Australian Lesbian Feminist Studies. Haymarket, Australia, 1991–1995.

The Journal of Gay, Lesbian, and Bisexual Identity. New York, Haworth Press, 1974–1999.

The Journal of Homosexuality. New York: Haworth Press, 1974– .

The Journal of Lesbian Studies. Binghamton, N.Y.: Haworth Press, 1997– .

Index des Révues Lesbiennes Canadiennes. Montreal. 1994– .

The Ladder (16 Vols.). San Francisco: Daughters of Bilitis, 1956–1972.

Lambda Book Report. Washington, D.C. 1989– .

Lavender Woman. Chicago. November 1971–July 1976 (26).

Law and Sexuality: A Review of Lesbian, Gay, Bisexual, and Transgender Legal Issues. New Orleans. 1998– .

The Leaping Lesbian. Ann Arbor, Mich. January 1977–March 1981 (22).

The Lesbian Connection. East Lansing, Mich. 1974– .

Lesbian Connections. Seattle, Wash. Spring 1979 (1).

Lesbian Contradiction: A Journal of Irreverent Feminism. 1982–1983.

Lesbian Ethics. Venice, Calif. 1984– .

The Lesbian Feminist. New York. August 1973–Fall 1979 (27).

Lesbian/Gay Law Notes. New York. June 1984– .

Lesbian Health Issues Newsletter. San Francisco. 1994– .

Lesbian Herstory Archives Newsletter. New York. 1975–1999.

The Lesbian Lipservice. Ann Arbor, Mich. July 1975–February 1976 (6).
Lesbian Network. Rozelle, Australia. 1985– .
The Lesbian Newsletter. Ann Arbor, Mich. March 1975–May 1975 (4).
The Lesbian Review of Books. Altadena, Calif. 1994–2002.
The Lesbian Tide. Los Angeles August 1971–May/June,1980 (69).
Lesbian Voices. San Jose, Calif. Winter 1974–October 1981 (12).
Lesbians Fight Back. Philadelphia. July 1972–September/October 1972 (3).
Lesbians of Color Caucus Quarterly. Seattle, Wash. Spring 1979 (1).
Maiden Voyage. Boston. December 1969–February 1971 (13).
The Mattachine Review (12 Vols.). New York: Arno Press, 1975.
Mother. Stanford, Calif. June–December 1971 (7).
Mother Jones Gazette. Knoxville, Tenn. January 1973–September 1974 (3).
National Lesbian Information Service News. San Francisco. May 1972 (1).
The New York Native. New York. 1984– .
Off Our Backs. Washington, D.C. 1970– .
The OLOC Reporter. Houston. 1989– .
On Our Backs. San Francisco. 1984– .
One Magazine: The Homosexual Viewpoint. Los Angeles: One, Inc. 1953–1968.
One to One. New York. Winter 1973 (1).
Out. New York. 1992– .
Out. Dublin, Ireland. 1984–1986.
Out. Auckland, New Zealand. 1977– .
Out and About. Seattle, Wash. May 1976–December 1982 (79).
Outweek. New York. 1989–1991.
Outwords. Toronto. 1999– .
Portcullis. Los Angeles. January–February 1972 (2).
Proud Woman. Stanford, Calif. March/April 1972 (1).
Purple Rage. New York. 1972 (1).
Purple Star. Ann Arbor, Mich. Spring 1971 (1).
QW. New York. 1991–1992.
Radical Chick: The Lesbian Feminist Bimonthly. New York. 1992–1994.
Rites Magazine for Lesbian and Gay Liberation. Toronto. 1983–1991
Sapphire. San Francisco. February–March 1973 (2).
Satin for Gay Women. San Jose, Calif. September–November 1974 (3).
Seattle Gay News. Seattle, Wash. 1975– .
Sojourner. Jamaica Plain, Mass. 1975– .
So's Your Old Lady. Minneapolis. February, 1973–September, 1979 (22).
Spectre. Ann Arbor, Mich. March/April 1971– January/February 1972 (6).
The Tide. Los Angeles. 1971–1974.
Très Femmes. San Diego. June and October 1972 (2).

Tribad: A Lesbian Separatist Newsjournal. New York. 1977–1994.
The Udder Side. New York. April 1973 (1).
Vice Versa. Los Angeles. June 1946–February 1948 (9).
Visabilities: The On-Line Lesbian Lesbian Magazine. www.wowwomen.com/
   visabilities/2000– .
We Got It. Madison, Wis. January 1975–June 1976 (12).
Wicce. Philadelphia. Fall 1973–Summer 1974 (4).
Womenews. University of Northern Illinois, Chicago. 1978– .
Womenews. Iowa State University, Ames. 1976–1984, 1984– .

14. Archives/Libraries

Archives Gaies du Québec. 4067 St Laurent, Suite 202, Montreal, Quebec,
   Canada.
Archives, Recherches et Cultures Lesbienness. BP 622 75531, Paris, Cedex 11,
   France.
Archivi Lesbici Italiana. Centro Femminista Sepatista, Via San Francesco di
   Sales, 1A I-oo165, Rome, Italy.
Australian Gay Archives. Box 124, Parkville, 3052 Australia.
Black Gay Archives. Box 30004, Philadelphia, PA 19103.
Blanche Baker Memorial Library and Archives/ONE, Inc. 3340 Country Club
   Drive, Los Angeles, CA 90019.
Canadian Gay and Lesbian Archives. P.O. Box 636, Station A, Toronto, On-
   tario, Canada M5W 1G2.
Center for Research and Education in Sexuality. San Francisco State University,
   Psychology Building 502, 1600 Holloway Ave., San Francisco, CA 94132.
Connecticut Lesbian Archives. c/o The Hill Center, 350 Farmington Ave., Hart-
   ford, CT 06105.
Contemporary Culture Collection. Temple University. Philadelphia, PA 19122.
Dallas Gay and Lesbian Historic Archives. 270 Reagan, Dallas, TX 75201.
Douglas County Gay Archives. P.O. Box 942, Dillard, OR 97432.
Forbundent af 1948. Landsforeningen for bosser og lesiske. Bibliotek og arkiv.
   Postbox 1023 DK-1007 Lobenhaven K, Denmark.
Gay and Lesbian Archives of Philadelphia. c/o T. Avicolli, 1329 Pine St.,
   Philadelphia, PA 19107.
Gay and Lesbian Archives of Texas. P.O. Box 16041, c/o IH, Houston, TX 77222.
Gay and Lesbian Archives of Washington, D.C. P.O. Box 4218, Falls Church,
   VA 22044.
Gay and Lesbian Historical Society of Northern California. P.O. Box 424280,
   San Francisco, CA 94142.

Gay Community Archives. c/o Hirschfeld Centre, 10 Fownes St., Dublin 2, Ireland.

Hall-Carpenter Archives. BM Archives, London WC1N 3XX, England.

Harvey Milk Archives. P.O. Box 14405, San Francisco, CA 94114.

Henry Gerber–Pearl M. Hart Library and Archives. Midwest Lesbian and Gay Resource Center, 3352 N. Paulina St., Chicago, IL 60657-1038.

Homodok Homo/Lesbisch Documentatiecentrum. Oudesijds Achterburgwal 185, NL-1012 DK, Amsterdam, Netherlands.

Homophile Research Library. c/o The Church of the Beloved Disciple, 348 W. 14th St., New York, NY 10014.

Homosexual Information Center. P.O. Box 8252, Universal City, CA 91618.

International Gay and Lesbian Archives. P.O. Box 38100, Los Angeles, CA 90028.

International Woman Artist Archives. P.O. Box 1033, Hadley, MA 01035.

Irish Gay Rights Movement Library. P.O. Box 739, Dublin 4, Ireland.

Jewish GLBT Archives. 1407-50 Alexander St., Toronto, ONT M4Y 1B6, Canada.

June Mazer Lesbian Collection. 626 N. Robertson Blvd., West Hollywood, CA 90069.

Kentucky Collection of Her-Story. P.O. Box 1701, Louisville, KY 40201.

Kinsey Institute for Social Research. 416 Morrison Hall, Bloomington, IN, 45401.

Lavender Archives. P.O. Box 2337, Philadelphia, PA 19103.

Labadie Collection. University of Michigan, 711 Harlem Hatcher Library. Ann Arbor, MI 48109-1205.

Les Lesbianaires. Centre de Documentation et de Recherches sur le Lesbianisme Radicals BP 2024 Bruxelles 1, 1000 Bruxelles.

LesbenArchiv. AM Zwinger 16, 4800 Bielefeld 1, Germany.

Lesbian and Gay Archives of Naiad Press. P.O. Box 10543, Tallahassee, FL 32302.

Lesbian and Gay Archives of New Zealand. Box 11-695 Manners St. P.A., Wellington, New Zealand.

Lesbian Archive and Information Centre. c/o Glasgow Women's Library, 109 Trongate Glasgow, Scotland G1 5hd.

Lesbian Archives. P.O. Box 27008, Wellington, New Zealand.

Lesbian Heritage/DC. Washington Area Women's Center, 1519 P St. NW, Washington, DC 20005.

Lesbian Heritage Group. c/o Pacific Women's Resource, 4253 Roosevelt Ave. NE, Seattle, WA 98105.

Lesbian Herstory Archives. P.O. Box 1258, New York, NY 10116.

Lesbian and Gay Historical Society of San Diego. P.O. Box 40389, San Diego, CA 92164.

Lesbianissme Radicals. BP 2024 Brussels 1, 1000 Brussels, Belgium.

Lesbisch Archief Amsterdam. Eerste Helmersstr. I7I 1054 CX Amsterdam, Netherlands.

Lesbisch Archief Leeuwarden. Anna Blaman Huis, Postbus 4062, 8901 EB Leewarden Friesland, Netherlands.

Lesbisch Archief Leiden. c/o Myriam Everard Plantage 6, 2311 JC Leiden, Netherlands.

Lesbisch Archief Utrecht. Postbus 24037, 3502 MA Ultrecht, Netherlands.

Librarie Lesbienne, Feministe, Gaie. 3636 Boul. St. Laurent, Montreal, Quebec, Canada H2G 3C9.

Lovetann. Boks 3392, Sagene 0405, Oslo, Norway.

Metropolitan Community Church Library. 1919 Decatur, Houston, TX 77007.

Midwest Gay and Lesbian Archive. c/o GAU, P.O. Box 60046, Chicago, IL 60660.

Nancy Cardenas Lesbian Documentation Center and Historical Archive for Mexico, Latin America, and the Caribbean. Norma Mogrovejo A.P.M.-7459 C.P. Mexico D.F.

National Archives of Black Women's History. National Council of Negro Women, 1318 Vermont Ave. NW, Washington, DC 20005.

National Coalition of Black Archives. P.O. Box 57236, Washington, DC 20037.

National Gay Archives. P.O. Box 38100, Los Angeles, CA 90038.

National Lesbian Archives-Poland. c/o Olga Stefaniuk u.Sukiennicza 7m 70 PL-91851 Lodz, Poland.

National Museum and Archive of Lesbian and Gay History. Lesbian and Gay Community Services Center, 208 West 13th St., New York, NY 10011.

New York Public Library, Division of Humanities, Social Sciences and Special Collections. Fifth Avenue and 42nd St., New York, NY 10018.

New Zealand Lesbian Archives. c/o Windeler Talyor R., R.D. 1 Hamilton, New Zealand.

Pat Parker/Vito Russo Center Library. Lesbian and Gay Community Services Center, 208 West 13th St., New York, NY 10011.

Pilar Lopez Diez. La Mujer Feminista Calle Almagro 28 Madrid 28010, Spain.

Queensland Gay Archives. GPO 2030, Brisbane 4001 Australia.

Regumi Studio. c/o Joki Nakazawa Building 3F, 32 Araki-cho Shinjuku-ku, Tokyo, Japan 161.

Schlessinger Library. Radcliffe College, 10 Garden St., Cambridge, MA 02138.

Sophia Smith Archives. Amazonian Activity, N. Phyliss Birkby Collection, Smith College, Northampton, MA 01063.

Southeastern Lesbian Archives. ALFA, Duke University Library, Duke University, Durham, NC 27706.

Southern Gay Archives. P.O. Box 2118, Boca Raton, FL 33432.

Spinnboden-Lesbenarchiv. Burgsdorfstr. 1 1000 Berlin 65, Germany.

State Historical Society of Wisconsin. Women's Periodicals Collection, 816 State St., Madison, WI 53706.

Stonewall Library and Archives. 330 SW 2 St., Fort Lauderdale, FL 33315.
Tennessee Lesbian Archives. c/o Catherine Risingflame Moirai, P.O. Box 252, Okra Ridge Farm, Luttrell, TN 37779.
Third World Women's Archive. P.O. Box 159, Bush Terminal Station, Brooklyn, NY 11232.
Traces/Archives Lesbiennes. CP 244 succ Beaubien, Montreal, Quebec H2G 3C9, Canada.
West Coast Lesbian Collections. P.O. Box 23753, Oakland, CA 94623.
Women's Collection, Special Collections Department, Northwestern University Library, 1937 Sheridan Road, Evanston, IL 60201.
Women's Music Archives. 208 Wildflower Lane, Fairfield, CT 06430.

15. Internet Websites

Archives and History

Canadian Lesbian and Gay Archives. www.clga.ca
Duke Library—Includes lesbian-feminist and lesbian pulp fiction resources. www.scriptorium.lib.duke.edu/women
Hall-Carpenter Archives, London. www.lse.ac.uk/library/archive/gutoho/hall_carpenter_archives.htm
Homodok and Lesbian Archives, Amsterdam. www.homodok-laa.nl
Lesbian Herstory Archives. www.lesbianherstoryarchives.org
Lesbian History Project. www-lib.usc.edu/retter/main.html

Culture

Amazon Bookstore, Minnestoa. www.amazonfembks.com
Center for Lesbian and Gay Studies. Web.gsuc.cuny.edu/clags
Children of Lesbians and Gays Everywhere. www.colage.org
Dred Kings. www.dredking.com
Family Pride Coalition. www.familypride.org
International Drag King Extravaganza. www.idke.com

General

Lesbian Visibility. www.lesbian.org
Planetout. www.planetout.com
Gay.com. www.gay.com
Gay Today News. www.gaytoday.com

Organizations

American Civil Liberties Union. www.aclu.org
Asian/Pacific Lesbians and Gays, Inc. www.apgf.com
Black Gay and Lesbian Leadership Forums. www.nblglf.org
Gay and Lesbian Alliance Against Defamation. www.glaad.org
Gay and Lesbian Anti-Violence Project. www.avp.org
Gay and Lesbian Arabic Society. heb.net/glas
Gay, Lesbian and Straight Education Network. www.glsen.org
Human Rights Campaign. www.hrc.org
International Gay and Lesbian Human Rights Commission. www.iglhrc.org
Lambda. www.lambda.org
Lesben im Bibliothekswen. www.inetservice.de/frauenpower/navbibi
National Association of Lesbians, Gay, Bisexual and Transgendered Community Centers. www.lgbt.org
National Gay and Lesbian Task Force. www.ngltf.org
National Latino/Latina Lesbian and Gay Oganization. www.llego.org
National Lesbian and Gay Journalist Association. www.nlgja.org
Parents and Friends of Lesbians and Gays. www.pflag.org
Trikone. www.trikone.org

Search Engines

www.ask.com
www.google.com
www.yahoo.com

About the Author

JoAnne Myers (B.A. Skidmore College, M.S., Ph.D. Rensselaer Polytechnic Institute) is an assistant professor of Political Science at Marist College in Poughkeepsie, New York. There, she is codirector of the Women's Studies program and coordinator of the annual Women and Society Conference. She has served on the executive Board of Directors of Grace Smith House, providing services and housing for victims of domestic violence, and the Hudson River Sloop *Clearwater*, an environmental education and advocacy organization. She is a founding advisory board member of the Lorena Hickok Memorial and Scholarship Fund. An out lesbian, feminist, and activist, she teaches and has written about feminist political theory, public policy and women, and environmental policy.